HOLDING TOGETHER

HOLDING TOGETHER

THE HIJACKING OF RIGHTS IN AMERICA AND
HOW TO RECLAIM THEM FOR EVERYONE

JOHN SHATTUCK, SUSHMA RAMAN, AND MATHIAS RISSE

THE
NEW
PRESS

NEW YORK
LONDON

Requests for permission to reproduce selections from this book should be made through our website: https://thenewpress.com/contact.

Published in the United States by The New Press, New York, 2022
Distributed by Two Rivers Distribution

ISBN 978-1-62097-714-9 (hc)
ISBN 978-1-62097-724-8 (ebook)
CIP data is available

The New Press publishes books that promote and enrich public discussion and understanding of the issues vital to our democracy and to a more equitable world. These books are made possible by the enthusiasm of our readers; the support of a committed group of donors, large and small; the collaboration of our many partners in the independent media and the not-for-profit sector; booksellers, who often hand-sell New Press books; librarians; and above all by our authors.

www.thenewpress.com

Book design and composition by Bookbright Media
This book was set in Minion and DIN Condensed

Printed in the United States of America

10 9 8 7 6 5 4 3 2 1

*Dedicated to the legacies of John Lewis
and Ruth Bader Ginsburg*

CONTENTS

FOREWORD

MARTHA MINOW*

Rights are both ideals and measures of the shortfall of human societies. The distance between rights declared and realized in the United States has inspired struggles for change through politics, education, and law even before the nation started. Setbacks in the realization of rights motivate the thoroughgoing and vigorous chapters of this timely book. Integrating history, politics, public opinion data, and law, *Holding Together* shines a blazing light on both the promise of rights and the paths needed to realize that promise.

Bridging the distance between promise and reality of rights requires facts, norms, agitation, and above all, the motivation to pursue the challenge. Justice Thurgood Marshall once explained, "A child born to a Black mother in a state like Mississippi . . . has exactly the same rights as a White baby born to the wealthiest person in the United States. It's not true, but I challenge anyone to say it is not a goal worth working for." Providing an unflinching view of the distance between stated ideals and actual practices, this book makes the case for connecting the ideal and the real in treatments of voting rights, money in politics, civic education, racial justice, women's rights, and rights for people with diverse sexual and gender identities. Political polarization and technological changes challenge the realization of rights and compound the tensions perhaps unavoidably present if rights are to reach everyone. There are tensions between rights and also between rights and other social goods. Consider free speech versus freedom from violent hatreds, religious liberty versus women's rights and LGBTQ rights, gun rights versus public safety, and personal privacy versus security afforded by digital and surveilling technologies. Similarly,

---

*300th Anniversary University Professor, Harvard University; former dean, Harvard Law School; most recent book: *Saving the News: Why the Constitution Calls for Government Action to Preserve Freedom of Expression.*

the practices of police, courts, and prisons and the treatment of immigrants and asylum-seekers reflect the tensions between ideals of individual dignity and equality and claims of community safety and security. Lessons from historical struggles and attention to current contexts are essential starting points for strategies to bridge the distance between the ideals and the reality. The discipline to craft concrete policy recommendations is the challenge powerfully accepted by this book as it tackles the often-cavernous gap between what is and what should be.

The United States did not invent rights. But the nation's identity is bound up with the legal, political, and moral commitment to freedom and equality for each individual. Indeed, it is rights that hold Americans who lack common ethnicity, religion, and ancestry together. Yet the realities are riven by failures, struggles, conflicts, and contradiction. The stirring words of the Declaration of Independence hold as "self-evident" that "all men are created equal; that they are endowed by their Creator with certain unalienable rights; that among these are life, liberty, and the pursuit of happiness." Its author Thomas Jefferson enslaved more than six hundred human beings over the course of his lifetime. Along with other founders of the nation, Jefferson endorsed a constitution significantly departing from the Declaration's announced vision.

When celebratory narratives of social movements and courageous leaders depict ever-expanding circles of inclusion for American rights, they must be met with sober study of set-back and backlash. This contrast is echoed in debates over the nation's narrative and even over the facts. The *New York Times* marked the 400th anniversary of slavery in America with the 1619 historical report of America's original sin and its living legacies. This initiative in turn triggered varied controversies and also prompted President Donald Trump to launch the 1776 Commission and its contrary, triumphant report. Beyond the experts' views about factual details and theories of causation, the dispute reflects sharp disagreements over America's future prospects.

The stories of the past are mobilized as part of ongoing conflicts over both the vision and reality of rights in America. Antislavery social reformer Frederick Douglass taught, "Without a struggle, there will be no progress." So it is with any effort to redeem the promise of rights. Even what counts as progress elicits debate and struggle. Admirably clear about what counts as progress, this book embraces a distinctive and ambitious view of rights affirming the identities, equal chances, and security for all persons.

Most striking in this clear-eyed and engaged work of scholarship is the repeated demonstration that current overt policies in the United States block and impair rights in ways directly opposed by significant majorities of Americans. As the book demonstrates, opinion polls show large bipartisan majorities of Americans want to protect voting rights with legislated improvements to facilitate early voting and reduce voting restrictions. Supermajorities of both parties want independent commissions to determine the map of legislative districts rather than partisan gerrymandering. Americans overwhelmingly want sharp reductions of unregulated money in election campaigns, with federal enforcement of rules and disclosure of all donors to campaigns. Nonetheless, the Supreme Court has issued decisions making any such reforms difficult to adopt and enforce.

Similarly, a substantial majority of Americans believe abortion should be legal in at least most cases if not always. They are more concerned about policies making abortion too difficult to obtain than policies making it too easily available, despite Supreme Court decisions proceeding in the opposite direction. A supermajority of people from both major political parties who responded to a survey endorse limits on gun sales through gun shows without private background check. Accountability by police for violent or unlawful behavior, and independent review of complaints of police misconduct, garner overwhelming public support. Yet such policies are ensnared in political and union opposition. Laws against hate crimes, environmental protection for members of marginalized communities, protections against workplace barriers for persons with disabilities, access to quality education for all children, health care insurance coverage for everyone, and economic investment in African American, Native American, and Latinx American communities living with the results of discriminatory public policies—all of these elicit vibrant and powerful endorsement by substantial majorities. Political and court-made barriers stand in the way. The demand to guard personal privacy and ensure security of personal data echoes in responses of Republican and Democratic majorities who share desires to halt the spreading of disinformation by social media platform companies and reverse the jeopardy to democracy.

Nearly as many people of both parties also assert that Americans have more in common than many think. Although the protection of individual rights cannot be left to majorities, the endorsement of deep majorities for fundamental rights should propel action. And the gaps between Americans' reported views and the laws, policies, and circulating narratives expose unacceptable defects in institutional practices and maybe even in their design in a nation ostensibly organized as a representative democracy. This means the legislatures are not in fact representative of the people. Instead, they show systematic deformities due to the self-interest of incumbents, the manipulation by dominant political parties, the influence of tiny numbers of large donors, and the structures established long ago to protect slaveholders. They also demonstrate the oddities and manipulations in federal judicial selection processes, and the failures of government agencies entrusted with public duties (such as the Federal Election Commission, effectively inoperable for several years).

The vision and recommendations advanced in *Holding Together* gain support from the very contrast between public opinion and current practices that it reports. So too, the book's steady attention to responsibilities connected with rights fortifies the authors' vision. Responsibilities of government to recognize and enforce rights are crucial, but equally vital are responsibilities of individuals and communities to become and stay engaged, even if that means struggling for big changes in governing practices, rules, and politics. Essential responsibilities also involve sustained work on the predicates for democratic governance: education, social trust, and viable news media. These predicates, presumed by the Constitution, do not have constitutional guarantees and yet few of their commitments will be possible without fulfilling and bolstering the predicates of meaningful education for all children and ongoing instruction for adults, sufficient social trust within and across communities, and effective gathering and reporting of news.

Public and private investments and policies are needed to tackle what impairs or erodes education, trust, and news. Investments of time, money, and attention are vital because without these elements, there cannot be a vigilant populace, and without a vigilant populace, rights will not be realized. The project of rights fundamentally requires people to reclaim human control and accountability as digital technologies and artificial intelligence reshape society—challenges that could not have been imagined by those who first articulated human rights. Rights against manipulation by social media, rights to engage in productive work, and other contemporary rights will require imagination and effort in the wake of changing technologies and forces underway and yet to be unleashed. *Holding Together* explicitly addresses the United States, even as existing and yet-unrealized rights are imperiled across the globe.

Redeeming the rights Americans expect and need requires attention to history, politics, law, practice, and above all, imagination. "Reality can be beaten with enough imagination," wrote Samuel Clemens, more commonly known as Mark Twain, the American writer celebrated for wit, social criticism, and inventiveness. He also said, "The secret of getting ahead is getting started." That must be true too if we are to traverse the real and ideal, fueled with the insights and arguments of this valuable book.

INTRODUCTION: THE STRUGGLE FOR RIGHTS

As citizens of a democracy built on unprecedented diversity, Americans are bound together not by common ancestry and blood ties but by the promise of equal rights and responsibilities. Without this promise as its lodestar, there can be no democracy, only factions competing for dominance and groups struggling for survival.

The United States is a nation with a long history of internal conflict and an imperfect Constitution promising but not yet delivering rights equally to all its citizens. This book is about the ongoing struggle to realize these rights and the responsibilities that go with them. It is about the effort to unite a majority of Americans around a shared vision of equality and liberty, despite a disruptive minority that seeks to hijack and deny rights to others, as it has done throughout American history. It is about the actions that are needed to overcome the denial of rights and to reclaim them for everyone.

This is a tall order, but not beyond reach. In a July 2020 national poll taken four months into the COVID pandemic, a bipartisan 71 percent of Americans expressed the view that "Americans have more in common than many people think."[1] In a second poll taken after fifteen months of deadly pandemic, economic hardship, racial reckoning, political insurrection, and an attack on the U.S. Capitol, the "more in common" view had risen to 88 percent.[2] A supermajority of 84 percent reported in May 2021 that "events in recent months have made me think differently about the role and responsibility of government to protect the rights of all Americans," and 85 percent said that recent events made them "think differently about the responsibility Americans have to our fellow citizens." In a time of crisis Americans are searching for a renewal of the values that hold them together as a nation.

These values have a complicated origin in American history. The drafters of the Declaration of Independence expressed their commitment to the principle that all people "are created equal [and] are endowed with certain unalienable rights." A decade later in the Constitution the founders announced their intent "to secure the Blessings of Liberty to ourselves and our Posterity." The Declaration was a document of dissent, justifying resistance when rules and institutions had become tyrannical. The Constitution was a document of consent, establishing rules and institutions to safeguard liberty.

The promise of equal rights and responsibilities was sharply limited by the founders, most of whom were wealthy, White, slaveholding men. The Constitution was intentionally oblique on the subject of race, but it legitimized enslavement and restricted rights to White males. All women and many categories of men were excluded. Subsequent generations have labored with limited success to realize the promise of equal rights. There has been progress, but with constant setbacks, especially for those not included in the original promise.

The westward expansion of the United States during the nineteenth century was marked by exclusion and inequality. The government intensified its persecution of indigenous people through the Indian Removal Act of 1830, which forced Native American tribes to move under military gunpoint to inferior territory. Enslaved people and Black freemen were systematically denied rights. The Fugitive Slave Law of 1850 and the *Dred Scott* decision of 1857 proclaimed that the rights and privileges conferred upon American citizens did not apply to Black people. Starting in the 1850s, the Know-Nothing Movement, a far-right, intensely anti-Catholic, nativist party, violently discriminated against new immigrants from Italy and Germany. The Chinese Exclusion Act of 1882 banned all Chinese immigration, and the Dawes Act of 1887 destroyed traditional Native American communities by imposing private property law.

In the face of racism and bigotry, oppressed groups in the nineteenth century nevertheless persevered to achieve progress in expanding rights. Many enslaved people risked and lost their lives during a century of struggle to achieve freedom. Women met at the 1848 Seneca Falls Convention to launch a demand for women's equality, progressively achieving over the next seventy years the rights to work, to hold public office, and eventually to vote. Following the 1863 Emancipation Proclamation granting freedom to enslaved people, America underwent a "Second Founding"[3] through a series of constitutional amendments that recognized citizenship for all persons born in the United States, and granted all men, including those formerly enslaved, the right to vote and hold property. Despite these post–Civil War "Reconstruction Amendments" expanding legal rights, the Electoral College, an institution originally designed to enhance the political power of slaveholding states, was left unchanged and remains in the Constitution to this day, a symbol of the racism and White supremacy on which the nation was founded.

In reaction to the expansion of rights, a long post-Reconstruction era was marked by severe repression of Black Americans by White supremacists who used systemic violence and enactment of state "Jim Crow" laws forcibly to impose racial segregation. Segregation was upheld by the Supreme Court in 1896 in *Plessy v. Ferguson*, legalizing the notorious "separate but equal" doctrine. The systemic violence enforcing segregation was symbolized by more than four thousand documented lynchings of Black Americans between 1882 and 1968. The courageous work in the 1890s of Black investigative journalist Ida B. Wells demonstrated that lynchings—as the key component of racial oppression—spread fear through the Black population and led to massive internal migration. In 1921, the massacre of an estimated three hundred Black Americans in Tulsa, Oklahoma, was the largest single example of this systemic oppression and violence perpetrated by state officials and ordinary citizens.

Race-based nationalism continued throughout the first half of the twentieth century with the rise of the Ku Klux Klan, which fomented violence not only against African Americans, but also against newly arrived immigrants. The government enacted repressive immigration laws targeting Chinese, Arab, and Eastern and Southern European immigrants. Meanwhile, enactment of the Espionage and Sedition Acts during World War I chilled free speech by repressing protests and criticism of the government.

Following the economic and social disruption of the Great Depression, the presidency of Franklin Delano Roosevelt developed a series of programs and regulations, financial reforms, and public works projects collectively known as the New Deal. Designed to restore the economy, these reforms included the creation of an insurance system for unemployed Americans, as well as government support for dependent children and the disabled. Even as these economic rights were being recognized, however, congressional segregationists succeeded in excluding domestic and agricultural laborers from Social Security benefits, disproportionately impacting Black Americans working in these sectors.

In his 1941 State of the Union, Roosevelt outlined new interpretations of rights and freedoms, emphasizing the interrelationship of economic, social, political, and civil rights, including "freedom from want," "freedom of speech," "freedom of worship," and "freedom from fear." While the federal government was pursuing these programs to increase freedom and opportunity for citizens, however, Roosevelt issued an executive order interning more than one hundred thousand Japanese Americans, and his administration was reluctant to protect refugees during World War II. The government was slow to respond to the Holocaust, denying refugee status and visas to Jews and other persecuted people during World War II. After the war, an international human rights movement grew out of the urgency of opening borders to refugees. Following Roosevelt's death, Eleanor Roosevelt helped lead this movement by chairing the United Nations committee that wrote the Universal Declaration of Human Rights.

Political freedom and freedom of speech came under attack in the early postwar period. In the late 1940s and 1950s, hysteria over politically exaggerated threats of communists and anarchists led to the investigation and repression of citizens accused by Senator Joseph McCarthy and other nativist politicians of being "subversive elements." During the 1950s, White nationalists and White supremacists directed violent attacks against Black Americans, Jews, and people they considered threats to national security.

Meanwhile, progress was made toward the promise of equal rights. In the 1950s and 1960s, the U.S. Supreme Court recognized rights through constitutional interpretation. *Brown v. Board of Education* ended the notorious "separate but equal" doctrine of segregation, and *Loving v. Virginia* struck down laws banning interracial marriage. This period also ushered in a Supreme Court-driven expansion of the rights of the accused and extended the Bill of Rights to states and municipalities, when it had previously applied only to the federal government.

In the 1960s, decades of oppression of African Americans and other people of color exploded into a new protest movement for civil rights. Using mass mobilization and civil disobedience, civil rights leaders like Martin Luther

King Jr. and John Lewis sparked the movement to end the Jim Crow laws that enforced segregation. The movement achieved major policy victories in the Civil Rights Act of 1964, the Voting Rights Act of 1965, and other federal legislation outlawing discrimination on the basis of race, color, sex, religion, or national origin.

During the 1970s, women organized to demand an Equal Rights Amendment to the Constitution. That effort has not yet succeeded, but the women's movement spotlighted issues of gender inequality, leading to increased employment opportunities for women, laws against sexual violence, and the passage of federal legislation to promote gender equality in education. At the same time, gay rights advocates protested throughout the 1970s and 1980s for the repeal of discriminatory laws and for medical treatment for the burgeoning AIDS crisis.

The rights movements were pushed back in the 1980s. Attacks were made against the new legislative remedies for racial discrimination and against the Supreme Court's 1973 decision upholding reproductive rights. Judges appointed during the Reagan administration began to close off access to the courts for rights violations. The deterioration of rights continued after the turn of the century, despite gains in disability and LGBTQ rights and new protections against employment discrimination. The 2001 Patriot Act expanded surveillance and eroded privacy rights in the name of fighting terrorism, and the use of torture and indefinite detention was instituted as part of the George W. Bush administration's "war on terror." The Supreme Court's decision in 2013 striking down core provisions of the Voting Rights Act led to a return of discriminatory voting practices in many states.

Rights and responsibilities in the United States were under siege during the presidency of Donald Trump. A violent insurrection at the Capitol Building and elsewhere in January 2021 was perpetrated against the electoral process, the Congress, and other democratic institutions. In an attempt to overturn the results of the 2020 election, Trump promoted vast lies and disinformation about alleged and totally unsubstantiated voter fraud. State legislative efforts were undertaken to restrict and suppress voting rights. Racial discrimination in law enforcement remained pervasive, illustrated by the stark fact that Black men are two-and-a-half times more likely to be killed by police than White men.[4] Cruelty against refugees and asylum-seekers was carried out in violation of international and domestic law. Judicial independence came under intense political pressure. Patterns of authoritarian rule emerged, characterized by official disregard of scientific evidence and the rule of law. The quality of public discourse was degraded by a polarizing political atmosphere exemplified by the endless barrage of vindictive presidential tweets. New forms of digital surveillance and personal data collection further weakened the right to privacy, and other violations of rights were magnified by technological changes in which many actors seemed beyond the reach of accountability to citizens and the government.

Amid all these threats, the COVID public health crisis put additional strain on rights and responsibilities. The pandemic laid bare the structural racism affecting Black Americans and other people of color, whose health and livelihoods were at far greater risk than those of non-minorities because of the socioeconomic effects of deeply rooted racial discrimination. The pandemic impacted overcrowded prisons and demonstrated the vulnerability of elderly Americans with limited means in nursing homes ravaged by COVID. The pressure that rising COVID cases and deaths put on the health care system, the collapse of the economy, the increase in home evictions, and the unprecedented levels of unemployment all wreaked havoc on the principles of liberty and equality.

The electoral process was in grave danger in the 2020 presidential election year. Voting in person was risky to health and voting by mail came under attack by President Trump, who in August 2020 raised the prospect of postponing the election on the basis of unsubstantiated claims of fraud. In September, Trump called mail-in voting "a whole big scam" and refused to commit to accepting the results of the election and allowing a peaceful transition of power.

The deepening threat to rights and freedoms sparked new activism by political movements working to advance rights and reconstruct democratic institutions. Nationwide protests against racism stimulated by Black Lives Matter, as well as demonstrations against sexual violence led by the #MeToo movement, were powerful examples of this activism and the possibilities of transformation. On the other hand, fear of change produced a backlash against rights, including demands for "law and order" in response to calls to end institutional racism in law enforcement. Fear was manipulated by President Trump and other politicians seeking to polarize citizens and provoke attacks on the rights of "others." Divisive leadership stirred up factions in a widely diverse nation whose identity should be defined by the equal rights and responsibilities of all its citizens.

The election of Joe Biden to the presidency brought the possibility of change. In the wake of the violent attack on the Capitol and the outgoing president's failed attempt to thwart the democratic process, the Biden administration announced a series of initiatives to provide relief from the pandemic, begin to redress racial and economic inequality, strengthen voting rights, revitalize the economy, and rebuild the nation's infrastructure. The country remained politically polarized, but the new president seemed to count on a bold agenda to capture the hopes of a new majority for a democratic transformation and the reimagining of rights and responsibilities. This agenda was challenged by a new state legislative campaign to roll back rights, including voting rights and reproductive rights, launched in Republican-controlled states led by Texas and reflected in broad Republican congressional opposition to the Biden administration's rights agenda.

In the run-up to the 2020 presidential election people were well aware that their rights were under attack. A nationwide poll conducted in July 2020 by the Harvard Kennedy School Carr Center for Human Rights Policy with support from the Institute of Politics revealed that 75 percent of Americans across the political and demographic spectrum believed that rights are "very important" but are "not very secure." Despite partisan divides over the election, more than two-thirds of respondents (71 percent) said they believed that people in the United States "have more in common with each other than many people think," including 74 percent of Democrats, 78 percent of Republicans, and 66 percent of Independents. Central to their perspective was the U.S. system of rights and responsibilities, with 81 percent—a supermajority across all demographic and political subgroups—believing that "without our freedoms America is nothing."

In May 2020, the police murder of George Floyd, yet another unarmed Black man, cast a new spotlight on racism and reignited the movement for racial justice in the United States. An outpouring of public anger by millions of Americans of all races, generations, and socioeconomic backgrounds in

George Floyd mural on 38th and Chicago in Minneapolis, Minnesota. Photo by Jeremy Bishop via Unsplash.

the midst of the pandemic conveyed the urgency of taking action to protect human rights in the United States.[5]

Demands for rights come in many forms. During the pandemic a minority of Americans have claimed their liberty is stifled when they are required by public health authorities to wear masks to prevent the spread of the COVID virus. But one person's claim of liberty does not justify trampling on the rights of others, and no single claim can be allowed to cancel out other rights.

Americans are inspired by the promise of rights and have an expansive view of their rights. More than three-quarters—and more than 60 percent from both political parties—believe that the following rights are "very important," but only a small minority believe that these rights are "very secure":

Voting (86% very important–34% very secure)
Equal opportunity (86%–14%)
Racial equality (85%–17%)
Equal protection (85%–12%)

Protests in Philadelphia, Pennsylvania, June 2020. Photo by Chris Henry via Unsplash.

Quality education (85%–17%)

Clean air and water (85%–17%)

Personal safety (85%–16%)

Affordable health care (83%–10%)

Free speech (83%–22%)

Privacy (82%–13%)

Protection of personal data (79%–11%)

The right of a woman to choose (76%–16%)

Rights carry responsibilities. The government has a responsibility to protect rights and the people have a responsibility to respect them. The May 2020 poll showed a majority of Americans believing that neither the government nor the people were exercising their responsibilities to protect and respect rights. Sixty percent believed that the government was "not doing a good job protecting and enforcing the rights of citizens and others lawfully in the United States," and 63 percent believed that Americans "are not doing a good job protecting the rights of other Americans." The Trump administration's ineffective response to the pandemic as well as the economic and racial crises caused people to think differently about the government's responsibility to protect rights, and the responsibility of Americans to their fellow citizens.

The shared belief of a broad majority of Americans in the promise of rights and the responsibility of government and citizens to protect them shows there may now be an opportunity to bridge some polarizing divisions, connect people with differing conceptions of their rights, and redefine what it is to be a citizen in a nation of ever-expanding diversity. Our polls found strong majorities supporting rights in areas embroiled in political controversy, including immigration, policing, and women's autonomy. The constitutional system of rights and responsibilities is a work in progress that must always be improved. That is what the Constitution's goal of creating "a more perfect union" is all about.

Americans have struggled for nearly two-and-a-half centuries to realize the promise of rights and overcome threats to democracy. The promise and threats are interrelated and demand a transformative response. There have been major transformations at other pivotal moments in our nation's history—at its founding during the American Revolution, second founding after the Civil War, recovery from the Great Depression, and reimagining by the Civil Rights Movement. Can today be a similar moment of transformation, turning threats into opportunities through the power of civic activism, voting, and government intervention? Can we reimagine the promise of rights to hold us together as a nation of diverse histories, identities, and lived experiences?

These questions come from many sources across the political and demographic spectrum. They were in the air in a series of town hall meetings of broadly representative groups of citizens that we convened in March and April 2020 in Phoenix, Arizona; Detroit, Michigan; and Atlanta, Georgia. They emerged from the results of the July 2020 and May 2021 national polls that we commissioned of nationwide samples of two thousand Americans from all demographic groups and political perspectives. The questions were asked by experts and practitioners who participated in a series of seminars and consultations in 2020 and 2021 that prepared the way for this book. Research was conducted by a team organized by the Carr Center for Human Rights Policy. The town hall meetings were hosted by the Carr Center with support from the Harvard Kennedy School Institute of Politics, and the two national polls were conducted by the National Opinion Research Center at the University of Chicago.

Holding Together offers a panoramic view of the current rights landscape in the United States. It shows how rights have been hijacked by a destructive minority and how they can be reclaimed by a determined majority. It is written not for experts but for a general audience and for policymakers. It aims for breadth rather than depth of analysis. It makes recommendations to policymakers at national, state, and local levels for reimagining the rights and responsibilities that are at the core of American national identity. The recommendations vary from broad and structural to detailed and instrumental depending on context and circumstances. The book covers major categories of rights defined by the Constitution, laws, and customs of the United States. It is not comprehensive—for example, it does not cover the rights of children, environmental rights, or rights established by international law—but offers an overview of the U.S. democratic process (voting rights, money in politics, civic education); equal protection and equality of opportunity (racial justice, women's rights, LGBTQ rights, rights of individuals with disability, economic inequality); freedoms of speech and religion (speech and media, religious liberty and civil rights, hate crimes); due process of law (criminal justice, immigration, gun rights and public safety); and rights of privacy (personal data and surveillance).

Holding Together depicts a nation wrestling with its values at a moment of urgency in which a transformation like the one brought about by the Civil Rights Movements might again be achieved through advocacy, determination, and struggle.

HOLDING TOGETHER

Part I

The Democratic Process

Part I

The Democratic Process

1

Voting Rights Battleground

As Congress debated a $2 trillion economic relief bill for coronavirus in March 2020, President Donald Trump made a stunning announcement: "The things they had in there were crazy," he told Fox News. "They had levels of voting, that if you ever agreed to it, you'd never have a Republican elected in this country again."[1] His comments, referring to new proposals for voting by mail and same-day registration, made explicit a strategy he had been pursuing throughout his presidency: to reduce voter participation in the United States.

Eight months later, Trump attempted to overturn the 2020 presidential election by mounting a campaign of disinformation with claims that the election was "stolen" from him by "massive voter fraud." These claims were unanimously rejected as baseless by eighty federal and state judges across the country, including some appointed by Republican presidents or elected as Republicans. Trump's attack on the election was a direct assault on the voting rights of the electoral majority that had defeated him. It stimulated a violent attack on the U.S. Capitol in which seven people died and which resulted in Trump's second impeachment by the House of Representatives.

The right to vote is the right by which all other rights are created and maintained in a democracy. While the founders only entrusted that right to a narrow group of people—property-owning White men—suffrage has been expanded throughout the past two centuries to include virtually all Americans, allowing citizens a say in who will govern them and what policies they will pursue. Political campaigns to suppress or dilute votes corrode democracy, frustrate the popular will, and stimulate polarization.

Suppression of an inclusive electoral system is not new. Throughout the nineteenth and much of the twentieth century, dominant political forces prevented

Led by Hosea Williams and John Lewis, six hundred civil rights protesters crossed the Edmund Pettus Bridge and encountered Alabama state troopers on what is known today as "Bloody Sunday," March 7, 1965. Photo by Spider Martin via National Archives.

voting by African Americans and other people of color, women, immigrants, and young people.[2] Manipulation of voting in the twentieth century included racist suppression of African American votes, first by Democrats and later by Republicans.[3] These practices are blatant examples of the vulnerability of the electoral process to partisan manipulation and the necessity of reform to safeguard voting rights, especially among these vulnerable groups.

The 2020 presidential election produced a record-breaking voter turnout. A total of 159.2 million ballots were cast by 67 percent of eligible voters, the highest turnout in 120 years. For the first time, more people voted early or by mail than in person on Election Day. All fifty states increased their turnout over the previous presidential election in 2016, although there were wide variations between the state with the highest turnout rate (Minnesota at 80 percent) and the one with the lowest (Oklahoma at 55 percent). Two demographic aspects of the 2020 voting levels stood out. One was the high turnout among young people and people of color favoring Democrats, and the other was the rise in turnout among White non-college-educated voters favoring Republicans.

Prior to the 2020 presidential election, voting expansion had peaked in 2008. Barack Obama was elected president that year by a coalition that included 15 million first-time voters, 11.5 percent of the total, including a large proportion of people of color and young people. That year, African American voting participation increased by 5 percent and youth participation by 2 percent over 2004 election numbers, resulting in the highest participation by African American and eighteen- to twenty-four-year-old voters in thirty years.[4] The African American turnout rate continued to increase to a high of 67 percent in 2012, exceeding the White turnout rate for the first time since the U.S. Census Bureau began reporting voting participation by race.[5] By 2016, however, turnout had fallen by seven percentage points for African Americans from their participation peak in 2012 and six points for eighteen-to-twenty-four-year-old voters from their peak in 2008.[6] From 2008 to 2016 the turnout of all people of color combined dropped by four points.[7]

Many factors contributed to the 2016 falloff in voting participation by minorities and youth voters and people of color, including the identities of the candidates themselves. According to the Brookings Institution, political efforts to halt the expansion of voting rights through voting regulations played a significant role,[8] as did a 2013 Supreme Court decision invalidating core provisions of the Voting Rights Act of 1965.[9]

Since 2008, as this chapter will recount, a systematic campaign to curtail voting rights has been carried out by Republicans. This campaign has included onerous new identification requirements, reduced voting hours, restricted access to early voting and voting by mail, purging of voter rolls, and a wide variety of other state-level regulatory measures to make voting more difficult and exert partisan control over the election process. As of December 2021, nineteen states with Republican-controlled legislatures had enacted thirty-three new laws that restrict access to the vote. Proponents of the new restrictions have sought to justify these measures by making unsupported claims of widespread voter fraud, despite multiple studies finding no evidence to justify such claims. In response to the suppression campaign, a major countermovement has emerged that seeks to reclaim and protect voting rights at both federal and state levels.

EXPANDING THE RIGHT TO VOTE

There was no explicit right to vote in the original Constitution of 1789. The Constitution gave states the authority to administer and regulate voting, and each state determined who was eligible, leading to inconsistent voting participation rates among the states that continues today. The Constitution, however, also gives Congress and the federal courts the authority to review state voting regulations and to impose national standards through legislation or judicial review. The Voting Rights Act of 1965, a major achievement of the Civil Rights Movement, is a prime example of the power of Congress to impose national voting standards to uphold the constitutional protection of the right to vote.

Originally, each state limited the electorate to male property owners. Property ownership as a condition of voting was progressively abolished by the states. Subsequent political struggles for voting rights produced a series of constitutional amendments further expanding suffrage.

Adopted in 1870 following the Civil War, the Fifteenth Amendment formally guaranteed the right to vote regardless of "race, color, or previous condition of servitude." For nearly a century after its adoption, however, African Americans and other people of color were barred from voting in many states through racially targeted measures such as poll taxes, literacy tests, "good moral character" requirements, and "grandfather clauses."[10] Attempts to break or protest this racist system of Jim Crow laws were constantly met with violence or retribution throughout the nineteenth and early twentieth centuries. By 1912, African American voting in the South had been suppressed to just 2 percent from earlier participation rates of over 60 percent in the years immediately following ratification of the Fifteenth Amendment.[11] It took nearly a century and the enactment of the Voting Rights Act for African American voting participation again to reach the immediate post–Civil War levels. Passed with a bipartisan majority in 1965, the Voting Rights Act prohibited any kind of tests to vote, and set up a system of federal monitoring in areas where racial discrimination was judged to have occurred, including the states of Alabama, Alaska, Georgia, Louisiana, Mississippi, South Carolina, and Virginia.[12]

Voting rights were further expanded by a long campaign for suffrage by women, who used marches, civil disobedience, and lobbying to achieve the right to vote first at the state level—starting with Wyoming in 1890—and then nationally with the passage of the Nineteenth Amendment in 1920. As a result of voting rights expansion, the number of eligible voters in the United States is now close to the total population of adult U.S. citizens, excluding persons with felony convictions and citizens of U.S. territories who are not eligible to vote.[13] Nevertheless, actual *voting participation* by citizens eligible to vote remains below participation levels in many other democratic countries.[14]

Woman suffrage banner carried by suffragettes in their Golden Lane spectacle, approximately 1910 to 1919. Photo via the Irma and Paul Milstein Division of United States History, Local History and Genealogy, New York Public Library.

CAMPAIGN TO RESTRICT VOTING

Fear of demographic change, intensified by the surge in voting by people of color and younger voters in 2008 and again in 2020, has motivated the political campaign by the Republican Party to reverse the long-term trend of expanding voting rights by using the tools of regulatory suppression. The non-Latinx White population in the United States is aging, and younger generations are increasingly more diverse, representing a threat to Republicans, since voters of color are more likely to vote Democratic.[15]

According to U.S. Census Bureau statistics, non-Latinx Whites are the only population group projected to decline as a percentage of the voting population from 2016 to 2060, by a predicted 9.5 percent, while mixed-race groups are projected to increase by 197.8 percent, Asians by 101.0 percent, Latinx American by 93.5 percent, and African Americans by 41.1 percent.[16] The White population will no longer be a majority by 2044, when the United States will be a nation without any one racial or ethnic group constituting a majority.[17] These demographic trends have fueled fears among some White voting blocs that their status and privilege are under threat, making the preservation of White identity a potent political issue.[18]

Most modern voting suppression laws in recent decades have originated from the Republican Party. That is not to say one party has been historically more virtuous than the other; after all, the Republican Party is also "the party of Lincoln" that more than a century ago expanded the right to vote through the emancipation and enfranchisement of Black men. In the early twentieth century, it was the Democratic Party that suppressed the vote of Black citizens through Jim Crow laws, demonstrating that parties will push for voter expansion or voter suppression if it is in their interest. As African Americans shifted to the Democratic Party, and the two parties diverged in their demographic makeup, demographic factors increasingly favored the Democratic Party. Since 1964, when President Lyndon Johnson signed the Civil Rights Act into law, on average 88 percent of African American voters have voted for Democratic candidates.[19] By 2017, White adults made up 83 percent of Republican voters, while only 59 percent of Democratic and Democratic-leaning registered voters were White adults.[20]

Demographic fears and increased turnout by people of color and youth have fueled voter suppression efforts. Since 2010, new regulations to restrict voting have been imposed in twenty-five states: Alabama, Arizona, Arkansas, Florida, Georgia, Illinois, Indiana, Iowa, Kansas, Mississippi, Missouri, Montana, Nebraska, New Hampshire, North Carolina, North Dakota, Ohio, Rhode Island, South Carolina, South Dakota, Tennessee, Texas, Virginia, West Virginia, and Wisconsin.[21] Twenty-one of these states were won by the Republican candidate, Donald Trump, in the 2016 election.[22] In only three states, Illinois, Rhode Island, and West Virginia, have Democratic-controlled legislatures imposed new voting restrictions in the last decade.[23]

Voting restrictions have disproportionately impacted voting participation by people of color, the poor, and foreign-born citizens. For example, stricter identification requirements have made it harder for people without acceptable photo identification or stable addresses to vote.[24] Closing polling places means that people have to travel longer distances to vote, a barrier for voters with limited access to transportation. Other recent state policies, such as Georgia's blocking of voting by those whose registration information is not an "exact match" to the information on their state-issued ID, have been found to have a disproportionate impact on voters in communities of color.[25]

Fifteen states that enacted new voting regulations after 2010 showed drops in voter turnout between 2012 and 2016.[26] In Wisconsin, a study estimated that 16,800 people in two counties may not have voted in the 2016 election because they believed that they did not have the photo ID newly required or because they were actually turned away following a voter ID law enacted by the Republican-majority state legislature in 2011. A survey of registered non-voters in those two counties showed that Black and lower-income non-voters were more likely than White and higher-income non-voters to state that the reason they did not vote was the new law.[27]

The disproportionate impact of new voting regulations on people of color has been exacerbated by the withdrawal of federal safeguards of voting rights. In a 2013 decision in *Shelby County v. Holder*, the Supreme Court struck down the formula of the 1965 Voting Rights Act used by the federal government to determine whether state voting restrictions have a racially discriminatory impact. And in a 2021 ruling in *Arizona v. Democratic National Committee*, the Court further weakened the Act by upholding state restrictions that had been challenged as racially discriminatory. In the majority opinion in *Shelby*, the Court held that "the Voting Rights Act employed extraordinary measures to address an extraordinary problem. . . . The conditions that originally justified these measures no longer characterize voting in the covered jurisdictions."[28] Despite the Court's conclusion, a decrease in voting by people of color following the *Shelby* decision proved to be greatest in areas with a history of racial discrimination that were previously required to submit proposed voting law changes to the Justice Department for review.

The impact of *Shelby* has made voting by people of color more difficult in areas previously covered by the Voting Rights Act, for example, through wide-sweeping voter roll purges and the closure of polling locations.[29] Previously, state and local jurisdictions under the Voting Rights Act were required to ask permission from the federal government before enacting changes to voting laws—a process known as "pre-clearance." Following the *Shelby* decision, these jurisdictions have purged their voter rolls at a 40 percent higher rate than jurisdictions that were not covered by the Act.[30] The Leadership

Conference on Civil and Human Rights found that the jurisdictions formerly subject to pre-clearance closed at least 1,688 polling places between 2012
and 2018. A total of 1,173 polling places were closed after the Supreme Court
struck down the pre-clearance requirement. As a result, some areas now have
a critical lack of polling locations, with more than one in five polling locations
closed in Arizona and seven counties in Georgia with only one polling place.[31]

RED HERRING—VOTER FRAUD

Republican proponents of stricter voting laws claim restrictions are necessary to prevent voter fraud. There is little evidence to support this assertion.
Former President Trump has repeatedly claimed, without evidence, that widespread voter fraud was committed by his opponents in both the 2020 and 2016
presidential elections, asserting that there were 3 to 5 million illegal votes cast
in the 2016 election.[32] On November 27, 2016, he tweeted, "In addition to winning the Electoral College in a landslide, I won the popular vote if you deduct
the millions of people who voted illegally."[33] On January 25, 2017, Trump
tweeted, "I will be asking for a major investigation into VOTER FRAUD,
including those registered to vote in two states, those who are illegal and . . .
even, those registered to vote who are dead (and many for a long time)."[34]
The White House produced no evidence to support these claims, which were
intended to encourage regulation to suppress voting, not combat fraud.

Long before Donald Trump's baseless claims of fraud were repeated before
and after the 2016 and 2020 presidential elections, similar claims were made
without evidence by other Republican officials. In 2005, for example, the U.S.
Senate Republican Policy Committee stated in a report that "voter fraud continues to plague our nation's federal elections, diluting and canceling out the
lawful votes of the vast majority of Americans."[35] The report contained no
credible evidence to back up the claim. In the 2018 elections, allegations of
fraud in Florida and Arizona were made by Republican politicians. In Florida's
senate race, Republican Rick Scott filed a lawsuit alleging "rampant fraud" in
the counties that heavily favor Democrats because those counties took longer
to tally the votes. However, records released in response to the lawsuit did not
include any evidence to support the accusations of fraud,[36] and the Florida

Department of State, which oversees elections, did not receive or observe any credible evidence of fraud or criminal activity.[37] In Arizona's 2018 Senate race, the Arizona Republican Party accused the Maricopa County Recorder of "premeditated destruction of evidence" after "voting irregularities" in the election.[38] Again, however, no evidence of voter fraud was produced, and Republican Martha McSally conceded the race to Democrat Kyrsten Sinema.[39] In Kentucky, Governor Matt Bevin claimed that there were a "number of significant irregularities" and "thousands of absentee ballots that were illegally counted" in the November 2019 gubernatorial election.[40] No evidence was produced to back up this claim, and Bevin eventually conceded the race after losing a recount.[41]

Bipartisan studies have concluded that there has been little evidence of widespread voter fraud in modern American elections. The Heritage Foundation, a conservative think tank, has compiled a nationwide database of charges of voter fraud over the past thirty-nine years (from 1982 to 2021). As of May 2021, 1,143 charges have resulted in criminal convictions, an average of just thirty convictions nationally per year.[42] A 2017 national voting study by the Brennan Center for Justice, an academic policy center and think tank, concluded very few noncitizens voted in the 2016 election. Across the forty-two jurisdictions studied, "election officials who oversaw the tabulation of 23.5 million votes . . . referred only an estimated thirty incidents of suspected noncitizen voting for further investigation or prosecution. In other words, improper noncitizen votes accounted for 0.0001 percent of the 2016 votes in those jurisdictions." Forty of the forty-two jurisdictions reported no incidents of noncitizen voting in 2016. In the ten counties with the largest noncitizen populations, only one reported any instances of noncitizen voting; this instance comprised fewer than ten votes. In states where claims of noncitizen voting were made, no official surveyed in the study identified an incident of noncitizen voting in 2016.[43]

In February 2017, President Trump established the Presidential Advisory Commission on Election Integrity to investigate voter fraud in the 2016 election. The Commission produced no significant evidence of voter fraud and was disbanded in January 2018 after it became the target of at least seven lawsuits accusing it of violating federal laws ranging from transparency to discrimination.[44] Documents released from the lawsuits, including emails and PowerPoint presentations from the two meetings held by the panel, contained no evidence of widespread voter fraud.[45] A 2017 study published in the journal *Electoral Studies* also examined President Trump's accusations of voter fraud by looking closely at three states where Trump claimed such fraud took place—New Hampshire, Virginia, and California—and found "little evidence consistent with widespread and systematic fraud."[46] The study's results were "consistent with various state-level investigations conducted in the initial months of 2017, all of which have failed to find any evidence of widespread voter fraud in the 2016 General Election."[47]

Despite the consistent lack of evidence, the prevention of voter fraud has been used for decades to justify voter suppression. For example, in Alabama in 1981, a "re-identification" bill was passed, with the claimed justification of preventing fraud, which purged voting rolls in three counties with sizeable African American populations and required purged voters to go to the courthouse to "re-identify" themselves to reregister. This resulted in a 43 percent decline in African American registration in these counties.[48] In 1986 a "ballot integrity" program was launched by the Republican National Committee (RNC) in Louisiana, Indiana, and Missouri without legislative authority under a claim that dead or fictional people were casting ballots. State party officials sent mail to registered voters in heavily Democratic areas in the three states with the instruction to "return to sender" if undeliverable and a return address of the Ballot Integrity Group Inc., a Chicago company hired by the RNC. The Ballot Integrity Group turned over the returned letters to election officials to encourage them to purge voters from election rolls. Democrats filed a lawsuit, which made public a memo that described the program's goal: "I would guess that this program will eliminate at least 60–80,000 folks from the rolls," one GOP operative wrote. "If it's a close race, which I'm assuming it is, this could keep the [B]lack vote down considerably."[49]

Republicans challenged efforts to expand voting by mail in response to the coronavirus pandemic, citing fraud and partisan concerns.[50] President Trump repeatedly attacked universal mail-in voting, saying, for example, "It's much easier for them to forge ballots and send them in, it's much easier for them to cheat with universal mail-in ballots." At the same time, however, he has supported absentee voting, which is essentially the same as mail-in voting and follows the same processes. The states that conduct mail-in voting have implemented extensive verification systems to prevent fraud, and there has been no evidence that mail-in voting has led to fraud any more than in-person voting.[51]

TOOLBOX OF VOTING RESTRICTIONS

Voting restriction efforts by Republicans since 2010 have employed a wide range of tools. The regulatory toolbox includes stricter identification requirements, restrictions on voter registration and voter registration drives, bans on voting by people with felony convictions, purges of voter rolls, limitations on early and absentee voting, and consolidation of polling places. The following examples are illustrative:

Identification laws, which request or require some form of identification to vote, are currently used by thirty-six states as a reasonable safeguard against voter fraud. The requirement generally allows a range of acceptable documents such as a driver's license or another state-issued ID card, a military or Veterans Affairs card, or a tribal ID. In some cases, voters without an acceptable ID can sign an affidavit of identity.[52] However, several states have enacted new stricter ID requirements since 2010 that eliminate the affidavit-of-identity option and further restrict the types of IDs accepted at polling places, limiting voting by minorities and young people. States with new stricter ID requirements enacted since 2010 include Alabama, Arizona, Arkansas, Iowa, Kansas, Mississippi, Missouri, New Hampshire, North Carolina, North Dakota, Rhode Island, South Carolina, Tennessee, Texas, Virginia, and Wisconsin.[53] These laws require voters to show a specified form of identification. In Tennessee, for example, student IDs and photo IDs not issued by the federal or state government are not accepted.[54] North Dakota's 2017 identification law requires a form of ID that includes a residential address. This requirement has depressed the vote of the twenty thousand Native Americans who live on reservations in North Dakota, since many do not have conventional addresses.

Restrictions on voter registration drives have been enacted by several states since 2010. Between 2011 and 2012 alone, at least eight states introduced or passed legislation to restrict voter registration drives, with Colorado, Florida, New Mexico, and Texas implementing the most severe restrictions.[55]

Registration drives by civic organizations aim to increase voter participation by helping voters register to vote. While restriction advocates have stressed the need for training to ensure that forms are filled out correctly, voter registration organizations have seen the enactment of such laws by Republican lawmakers as an effort to decrease participation by minorities.[56]

In 2019, a new Tennessee law threatened civil and criminal charges against third-party voter registration organizations. Under the law, the state is authorized to fine groups that submit one hundred or more voter registration forms that lack a complete name, address, date of birth, declaration of eligibility, and signature.[57] In response, the Equity Alliance, a group registering African American voters in Tennessee, said the law "is blatantly racist and mirrors the Jim Crow-era intimidation used to stifle decades of progress our nation and our state has made to ensure voting rights for people of color."[58] A U.S. district judge enjoined enforcement of the law in September 2019, calling it a "punitive regulatory scheme."[59]

Florida passed a law in 2011 that required groups registering voters to turn in registration forms within forty-eight hours; the previous deadline was ten days. After the law was put into place, organizations such as the League of Women Voters and Rock the Vote stopped voter registration drives in Florida and voter registration declined significantly. In 2012, a federal judge blocked the provisions of the law requiring the forty-eight-hour turnaround, calling them "harsh and impractical."[60] In legislation passed in 2021, Florida law was amended to provide third-party voter registration organizations fourteen days to submit a voter registration form after the applicant has completed it.[61]

Prohibition of voting by persons with felony convictions is a longstanding limitation on the right to vote, notwithstanding the Fifteenth Amendment's prohibition against denying or abridging the right to vote "on account of . . . previous condition of servitude," which some legal scholars argue should make denial of the right to vote for people with felony convictions unconstitutional.[62] Under the Fourteenth Amendment, however, the right to vote can be abridged for "participation in rebellion, or other crime," a provision that the Supreme Court ruled in a 1974 case could be used to support felony disenfranchisement.[63]

After 2010, three states adopted new restrictions on voting by persons with felony convictions: Florida, Iowa, and South Dakota. Florida's law prohibiting people with felony convictions from voting has been challenged since 2018. Until 2018, Florida had the highest number of people barred from voting due to a felony conviction (approximately 1.4 million). In 2011, Republican Governor Rick Scott had implemented a multi-year waiting period before people with felony convictions could be considered on a case-by-case basis for clemency and reinstatement of voting rights.[64] In November 2018, however, Florida adopted a ballot initiative restoring voting rights to people with felony convictions, except for those convicted of murder and sex offenses.[65] The Florida legislature weakened the constitutional amendment by passing a law that required people with felony convictions to pay all court fines and fees associated with their sentence first before being able to register to vote. A U.S. district court ruled that this requirement would amount to a poll tax and discriminate against people with felony convictions who cannot afford to pay.[66] The Eleventh Circuit Court of Appeals, however, reversed the district court decision invalidating the new law, and the appellate decision was upheld by the U.S. Supreme Court, allowing the law to go into effect.[67]

In Iowa, a 2005 gubernatorial executive order allowed voting rights for people with felony convictions to be reinstated after completion of probation or parole. In 2011, this was reversed, and restoration of voting rights for these individuals was determined on a case-by-case basis that required fulfillment of certain prerequisites such as paying back court costs.[68] In 2020, a new gubernatorial executive order restored voting rights to people with felony convictions, except felony homicide offenses, upon completion of prison, probation, parole, or special sentence.[69]

Prior to 2012, people with felony convictions in South Dakota lost their right to vote only while incarcerated, but since 2012 they have also lost their right to vote until they have completed not only incarceration but also probation, parole, and restitution, including all fines and fees.[70]

As of April 2021, eleven states have laws in place that permanently disenfranchise people with certain felony convictions or require a pardon, an additional waiting period following completion of sentence, and/or additional action for voting rights to be restored. In seventeen states, people with felony convictions lose their right to vote during and after incarceration; voting rights are restored after parole and/or probation, and in some states after the payment of all outstanding legal financial obligations. In twenty states, people with felony convictions lose their right to vote while incarcerated, receiving automatic restoration upon release.[71]

Voter roll purges are removals of registered voters from voting rolls. The stated goal of purges is to keep rolls up to date by removing voters who have died or moved away. However, voter roll purges can be used to shrink the voter base, and therefore must be conducted with clear criteria under strict due process standards.[72] Federal standards for purges were established in the 1993 National Voter Registration Act (NVRA). The Act requires voter-list maintenance programs to be uniform, nondiscriminatory, and in compliance with the Voting Rights Act of 1965. It also mandates that people may not be removed from voter rolls because they failed to vote, and voter purges cannot be undertaken within ninety days of a federal election.[73]

Since 2013, several states have conducted purges not in accordance with the NVRA. As of 2018, Alabama and Maine had policies in effect to use data from the Interstate Voter Registration Crosscheck Program to immediately remove voters from the rolls without providing the notice and waiting period required by federal law. Arizona regulations permit Crosscheck purges during the ninety-day period leading up to an election.

The Crosscheck Program was created by the Kansas Secretary of State and by 2017 was in use in twenty-eight states, mainly with Republican administrations.[74] It was designed to identify individuals who had voted in multiple states in order to find voters who had moved or committed fraud. It has been found, however, to be notoriously prone to error. A Stanford study found that it "would eliminate about two hundred registrations used to cast legitimate votes for every one registration used to cast a double vote"—a 99.5 percent rate of error.[75] After numerous legal challenges, the Crosscheck Program was shut down in December 2019.[76] A reliable alternative form of interstate cooperation is the Electronic Registration Information Center now in use in most states.

As of 2019, failing to vote and not replying to a postcard confirming one's address or updating voter registration information triggered automatic removal from the rolls in seven states.[77] In these states, people who have not voted in recent elections are put at risk of being purged. At least 17 million voters were purged nationwide between 2016 and 2018. This rate is similar to the number of voters purged between 2014 and 2016, but considerably higher than between 2006 and 2008.[78]

Voter roll purges can have a disproportionate effect on voters of color, as illustrated by Georgia's "exact match" registration law, requiring voters' personal information on their registration form to match exactly the information on file with the state. In October 2018, an Associated Press investigation found that 53,000 registrations were listed as "pending purge" by the office of the Secretary of State, 70 percent of whom were African American voters.[79] Researchers at Princeton University found that voters of color were disproportionately affected by exact match—"match rates using exact matching are nine and six percentage points lower for Black and Hispanic voters, respectively, than for White voters."[80]

New restrictions on early voting were successfully imposed by ten states between 2010 and 2019: Arizona, Florida, Georgia, Iowa, Nebraska, North Carolina, Ohio, Tennessee, Texas, and West Virginia. The restrictions included shortening the period allowed to vote early and cutting back the use of mobile sites for early voting. In Georgia, for example, the state legislature reduced the early voting period from forty-five to twenty-one days. Some states have also placed new restrictions on mail-in and absentee voting, including Arizona, Iowa, and Ohio. Arizona made it illegal to collect and turn in another voter's completed mail-in ballot even with the voter's permission, and Ohio passed a law prohibiting individual county election boards from sending unsolicited absentee ballot applications.[81]

The closing of polling places has been carried out by several states since 2010. Voters whose precinct polling place has been closed are reassigned to another precinct, often farther from where they live. This discourages voter turnout. A study concluded that between 2013 and 2016, counties in areas that had previously required federal pre-clearance because of a record of racial discrimination drastically reduced the numbers of polling places. In 165 of 381 counties examined, a total of 868 polling places were removed. Arizona closed 212 polling places between 2013 and 2016, more than any other state, including a 63 percent reduction in Cochise County, 50 percent in Graham County, and 48 percent in Gila County—counties with substantial minority populations.[82] A new voting law in Georgia enacted in March 2021 greatly reduces the number of "drop boxes" for voting and effectively bans mobile voting centers.[83]

Restrictions on student voting are implicitly imposed by domicile requirements. New Hampshire requires voters to show that they are "domiciled" in the state in order to register, a requirement that impacts college students and deters them from voting.[84] Polling place laws and ID requirement laws have also affected student voting. In 2019, Texas outlawed polling places that did not stay open during the entire early-voting period, which affected temporary early-voting sites on college campuses.[85] Florida significantly limited early-voting sites at state universities by requiring certain early-voting locations to offer "sufficient non-permitted parking."[86] In 2011, Wisconsin passed a law to allow for student IDs to serve as valid identification for voting, but only if the identification includes a signature and an expiration date not more than two years after the date it was issued, even if issued by a four-year institution. Student voter registration and turnout in Wisconsin fell sharply in 2016, when the state's voter ID law first applied to students.[87]

Legislative gerrymandering represents the most effective way to dilute votes. This technique involves the drawing of boundaries of electoral districts in a way that aims to maximize the chances of election for members of a given party. Partisan gerrymandering makes it possible for the party that controls the drawing of district boundaries to receive a minority of votes in a future election but still gain a majority of legislative seats, turning redistricting into a partisan weapon to use against political opponents.[88]

A wave of partisan gerrymandering after 2010 enabled Republicans, who by then controlled fifty-nine state legislative chambers, to capture 53 percent of U.S. congressional seats in 2012 while winning only 47 percent of the national congressional vote.[89] Democrats also engaged in gerrymandering in Maryland, but since 2010 the practice has been carried out extensively, systematically, and almost exclusively by Republicans.[90] Anti-gerrymandering reforms require the appointment of independent commissions responsible for approving maps for legislative districts based on rational geographic and municipal boundaries.

The Electoral College presents a major impediment to free and fair elections. Created as a means of protecting the interests of less populous states in presidential elections, the Electoral College boosted the political power of Southern slaveholding states where the Constitution's notorious three-fifths compromise counted three out of five slaves as "people." After the Thirteenth Amendment abolished slavery and the Fifteenth Amendment expanded the right to vote, the Electoral College continued the possibility that the will of the majority might be discounted in presidential elections. As a result it has "encourage[ed] presidential campaigns to concentrate their efforts in a few states that are not representative of the country at large," and "hand[ed] victory to the loser of the popular vote twice in the past two decades."[91]

RESTORING THE RIGHT TO VOTE

In response to voter restrictions and voter suppression since 2010, a sustained counter-campaign to restore the right to vote helped produce record-breaking turnouts in the 2018 midterm elections and the 2020 presidential election. More than 122 million people voted in 2018, the highest participation rate in a midterm election in forty years.[92] In 2020, 159.2 million cast their ballots, the highest turnout ever.[93]

Although a wide variety of voting restrictions have been implemented since 2010, grassroots legislative efforts and federal court challenges have pushed back against voter suppression and succeeded in enacting new state-level voting laws to implement automatic voter registration, same-day voter registration, pre-registration, online registration, vote-at-home, no-excuse absentee voting, voting rights restoration for people with past felony convictions, and early voting. In January 2019 and again in 2021, legislation was introduced in Congress seeking to incorporate many of these reforms at the federal level. The bill, the For the People Act, passed the House in March 2019 and again in March 2021, but has been blocked by filibuster from being taken up in the Senate.[94] Meanwhile, several Republican-controlled state legislatures, led by Texas and Georgia in early 2021, have renewed the Republican campaign to curtail minority and youth voting by enacting highly restrictive new state voting laws.

At the state level, multiple reforms and restrictions have been enacted. State laws passed in recent years to expand voting include the following.

Automatic voter registration (AVR) is one of the most effective ways that states can increase voter participation. By automatically registering eligible voters when they interact with government agencies, AVR streamlines the voter registration process and removes barriers to registration. This makes voter registration "opt-out" instead of "opt-in"; eligible citizens who interact with government agencies for any reason are automatically registered to vote or have their existing registration information updated unless they affirmatively decline.[95] As of 2020, twenty states and Washington, DC, have implemented Automatic Voter Registration (AVR). These states include Alaska, California, Colorado, Connecticut, Georgia, Illinois, Maine, Maryland, Massachusetts, Michigan, New Mexico, Nevada, New Jersey, New York, Oregon, Rhode Island, Vermont, Virginia, Washington, and West Virginia.[96]

Transparency in voter roll purges. In September 2019, Ohio publicly released a list of 235,000 names that were proposed to be purged from the voter rolls. Voters could check their registration status online, and voting rights organizations were able to cross-check the list with their own records. It was found that 20 percent of the people on the list should not have been at risk of purging. Making these records transparent allowed people the chance to check their registration and prevent themselves from being wrongly removed from the rolls.[97]

Restoration of voting rights for people with past felony convictions. Between 1997 and 2018, nearly half of all U.S. states (twenty-three) took steps to restore the voting rights of these individuals.[98]

Online voter registration. Over the last decade, the registration process has been simplified in many states through legislative or administrative action permitting voters to register online. As of October 2020, forty states and Washington, DC, have authorized online registration.[99]

Early voting, absentee voting, and voting by mail. Forty-three states and Washington, DC, permit voters to cast ballots in person for a period of days or even weeks before Election Day.[100] Most states have adopted a permissive approach toward absentee voting. As of 2020, thirty-four states and Washington, DC, allow voters to cast an absentee ballot for any reason.[101] Since 2010, nine states have liberalized their laws on filing absentee ballots. As of 2020, five states conduct all elections entirely by mail: Colorado, Hawaii, Oregon, Utah, and Washington. An additional three states—California, Nebraska, and North Dakota—allow counties to choose to conduct elections by mail.[102] Absentee voting, voting by mail, and early voting all significantly expanded in the 2020 election during the pandemic, and for the first time far outnumbered voting in person on Election Day. A May 2021 national poll taken by the Carr Center and the National Opinion Research Center showed that 84 percent of Americans agree that "early voting should be equally available in every state," while 67 percent agree that "every state should allow people to vote by mail."

Same-day registration allows voters to register or update their registration at the voting polls, so they can (re-)register to vote and cast a ballot at the same time. As of 2021, a total of twenty states and Washington, DC, have enacted same-day voter registration. According to the National Conference of State Legislatures, same-day voter registration has increased voter turnout by between 3 percent and 7 percent in states that have adopted it.[103]

Pre-registration. To encourage youth voting, several states have adopted procedures allowing sixteen- and seventeen-year-old citizens to pre-register so that they are immediately eligible to vote when they turn eighteen. Fourteen states and Washington, DC, allow pre-registration beginning at sixteen years old, four states allow it beginning at seventeen, and five additional states specify another age at which a young person may pre-register.[104]

Ranked-choice voting (RCV) is a potential means of broadening representation and reducing polarization. By having voters rank candidates in order of their preferences and elect the candidate with the highest number of total preferences, RCV can broaden representation and reduce polarization. RCV replaces elections where the winning candidate may receive only a plurality of votes (and be opposed by a majority of voters) with elections where the winning candidate receives a majority of voting preferences. As of May 2021, twenty-one jurisdictions, including the state of Maine, have adopted RCV; more than two dozen more were projected to implement RCV in upcoming elections.[105]

Policy Recommendations

- **Restore the Voting Rights Act.** Enact safeguards against voter regulations that have a racially discriminatory impact by reinstating federal government oversight of state or local jurisdictions with a recent or previous history of racial discrimination. These jurisdictions should not be permitted to change their electoral regulations without prior federal approval.

- **Enact Universal Voter Registration.** Enact comprehensive federal voting rights reform to implement universal automatic voter registration. Ensure adequate funding and training for citizen-facing government agencies to include voter registration in the course of their regular processes.

- **Eliminate or Simplify Voter ID Requirements.** Enact federal legislation to establish national standards for voter identification. Fourteen states do not require voter identification, and none of these states have experienced widespread voter fraud. If states do not want to remove ID requirements altogether, they should standardize the issuance of state ID cards to ensure that all eligible voters have an acceptable form of ID. For example, states could issue a state ID card to all residents when they turn eighteen.

- **Authorize Universal Voting by Mail or Early In-Person Voting.** Enact federal legislation to authorize universal voting by mail or early voting in person. Forty-three states and Washington, DC, have already implemented early voting; thirty-four states and Washington, DC, have adopted all-purpose absentee voting by mail, which allows any voter to request an absentee ballot for any reason. States that have not already done so should adopt all-purpose absentee voting and expand early voting periods to at least two weeks before an election. States can also ease access to voting by allowing voters to register at the same time they vote, a practice currently in place in twenty states and Washington, DC.

- **Prevent Automatic Voter Roll Purges.** Enact federal legislation establishing national standards for voter roll purges. States should prevent the automatic purging of voters from state voter rolls. Removing a voter from the rolls should require a transparent procedure and specific evidence showing that the voter is ineligible, and an opportunity for the voter to contest the evidence and proposed removal.

- **Restore Voting Rights for Citizens with Felony Convictions.** Federal and state voting rights should be restored to citizens with felony convictions immediately, and automatically upon their release from prison and voting rights should be restored to people with past felony convictions previously released and living in the community.

- **Implement Ranked-Choice Voting.** RCV increases the representation of voters' interests and reduces polarization. Currently, twenty-one jurisdictions have enacted policies to use RCV, and more jurisdictions should consider changing their voting system to allow voters to express more information about their opinions on electoral candidates.

- **Prevent Partisan Gerrymandering.** Enact federal legislation requiring states to establish independent redistricting commissions to determine the boundaries of congressional districts. Several models have been tried in different states in recent years. While there is no single best model, the Brennan Center for Justice has identified a set of best practices to ensure that redistricting commissions remain impartial and effective, including the following: select commission members from a pool of citizen applicants; include nine to fifteen members on the commission representing the geographic and demographic diversity of the state; establish clear rules and priorities for redistricting before beginning the map-drawing process; hold public hearings on the proposed redistricting map before finalizing it; enact criteria to include equality of district populations, protection against minority vote dilution, geographic contiguity, and compactness; and require that a final map be approved through a consensus mechanism that incentivizes compromise.

- **Reinforce the Responsibility to Vote and Make Election Day a National Holiday.** Voting participation should be made an explicit responsibility of citizenship. Election Day should be moved to Veterans Day to honor citizens who have served their country and increase voter participation by providing for voting in person to be on a national paid holiday and voting by mail to be universally authorized.

- **Amend the Constitution to Abolish the Electoral College.** The Electoral College undermines core democratic values by treating votes unequally, giving them more or less weight based on where voters live; encouraging presidential candidates to focus on a handful of swing states; and potentially enabling a candidate who loses the popular vote to win the presidency.

2

The Corrupting Influence of Money in Politics

When Georgia passed a new voting law in March 2021, restricting voting by mail and other voting practices, several corporations in the state, including Delta Air Lines and Coca-Cola, protested the move as an attack on voting rights, and Major League Baseball announced that it would relocate its All-Star Game from the state. "My advice to the corporate CEO's of America is to stay out of politics. Don't pick sides in these big fights," Senate Minority Leader Mitch McConnell (R-KY) responded at a news conference,[1] decrying a "coordinated campaign by powerful and wealthy people to mislead and bully the American people."[2] But McConnell added: "I'm not talking about political contributions."[3]

Commentators pointed to the minority leader's hypocrisy as a longtime champion of corporate contributions and vocal advocate of the Supreme Court's 2010 ruling in *Citizens United v. FEC*. That controversial decision equated corporations with people, opening the floodgates to give American business unprecedented influence in the American political system on the grounds that money was protected speech. "Mitch McConnell is basically saying that actual corporate political speech on important issues can and should be muzzled by the government but corporate cash contributions to him and others is speech that should be protected by the First Amendment," quipped lawyer Ted Boutrous. "That's nonsensical."[4]

It's not just Republicans like McConnell who have benefited from the expanding role of corporations, unions, and wealthy individuals in politics over the past decade. A report by the nonpartisan group Issue One found that between 2009 and 2020, a dozen "megadonors" contributed more than $3.4 billion—more than 7.5 percent of total contributions, or one in every thirteen dollars. The donors included former New York mayor Michael Bloomberg and casino magnate Sheldon Adelson and were evenly split between Republicans and Democrats.[5]

That eye-popping figure is just the beginning of the tidal wave of cash that has swamped elections in recent years. The 2020 election cycle blew past previous records, with an estimated $14 billion spent on federal races alone—more than twice as much as the 2016 cycle, and more than five times the amount in 2000. In the most recent cycle, Democrats outraised Republicans $4.8 billion to $1.9 billion in the presidential race and $1.2 billion compared to $691 million in congressional races.[6] In 2016, Republicans and Democrats spent about equally on elections, while in 2012, Republicans outspent Democrats.[7]

There is a simple reason for this exponential rise in political expenditures: the Supreme Court's interpretation of the First Amendment to bar the regulation of many aspects of campaign finance. From its first decision on this subject in 1976 to its 2010 ruling in *Citizens United* allowing corporations and other groups to spend unlimited amounts of money on elections, the Court has consistently moved to undercut attempts by Congress to stem the tide of campaign cash, precipitating sharp increases in contributions and spending that have only accelerated in recent years.[8]

The role and influence of money in politics in the United States is having a major negative effect on voting rights. Unlimited and unregulated political funding from major donors to both Democratic and Republican candidates and parties, and to outside groups supporting candidates, limits the rights of voters to participate in the political process, diminishes the value of that right for the average voter, and creates a disincentive for low-income non-donors to vote. At the same time, it promotes disproportionate influence by major donors in the selection of candidates, the election of officials, and the development of public policy. Remedies for these negative consequences include regulation, public financing, and small donor mobilization.

MONEY MATTERS

Money can have an enormous impact on elections. For House races since 2000, the candidate who spends the most money wins 85 to 90 percent of the time—with only slightly lower margins for Senate candidates.[9] That doesn't neces-

"The Supreme Court," Thomas Nast and Tammany Hall. Image via the Smithsonian Center for Learning and Digital Access.

sarily mean that money *causes* the candidate to win—it could also be true that the better candidate attracts more money.[10] Either way, however, donors are not spending all of that money for nothing. According to campaign finance scholars, there is rarely a direct quid pro quo in politics, in which an individual or corporation financially contributes money in order to obtain a particular legislative or regulatory result, which is technically an illegal act.[11] However, contributions by wealthy donors not only help elect candidates whose policies they support, but they also grant access to donors through high-cost fundraisers to pitch their interests in person.

More subtly, argues Harvard scholar Lawrence Lessig, campaign contributions create an "economy of influence," where politicians become so dependent on campaign dollars to run increasingly expensive races that they begin voting for policies they know will make their lives easier next time they have to "dial for dollars" and call to donors to raise cash. That reality has resulted in a system of campaign contributions that is the opposite of free speech: a relatively small number of very wealthy donors, corporations, labor unions, and issue-driven political action committees have an outsized voice when it comes to influencing policy priorities, subverting the very idea of representative democracy.[12]

"Money absolutely matters in the elections for Congress," Lessig told CNBC in 2020. "Candidates for Congress spend anywhere between 30 and 70 percent of their time raising money—and they're raising money not from the average American, they are raising money from the tiniest fraction of the 1 percent. And members of Congress are human. There's no way in which that behavior doesn't make them extremely sensitive to the needs of that tiny fraction of the 1 percent."[13]

Thus an irony has emerged from the Supreme Court's relentless drive to remove any limitations on campaign finance. In its effort to grant more freedom to individuals and institutions to spend money to influence the political system, the Court has actually curtailed the freedoms of all but a small number of very rich donors, leaving the majority of Americans increasingly less able to voice their opinions in politics and undermining the very freedom it has sought to create. Together, these burgeoning manifestations of money in politics have negative consequences for democracy by diluting and discounting the value and votes of the tens of millions of constituents who are not major donors.

Americans seem well aware of this reality. A Hill-HarrisX poll in 2020 found 57 percent of Americans believe that the American political system "only works for insiders with money and power," compared to 32 percent who believe it "works for everyone." (The other 11 percent believe it "works for no one.")[14] A Gallup poll in 2019 found that only 20 percent of Americans were satisfied with the nation's campaign finance laws—a lower percentage than any other issue, including health care, education, and race relations.[15] "Americans are losing faith in our democratic institutions," the nonpartisan election watchdog Issue One wrote in its 2021 donor report. "They see political gridlock and a broken campaign finance system that gives undue influence to billionaires and millionaires across the political spectrum, while the vast majority of ordinary citizens lack a seat at the table."[16]

Americans overwhelmingly want to see reforms made to take money out of politics, according to another 2019 poll by the nonpartisan Campaign Legal Center (CLC). That survey found that a bipartisan majority of 61 percent believe "major changes" need to be made to campaign finance laws; 71 percent want the Federal Election Commission (FEC) to "take a more active role" in enforcement; and 83 percent would like to see disclosure of all donors involved in elections.[17] Despite the widespread public support for campaign finance reform, however, the precedents set by the Supreme Court make wholesale reforms difficult to enact.

THE RISE OF MONEY IN POLITICS

Campaign finance—and efforts to regulate it—has its roots in the mid-nineteenth century. In the first half-century of the Republic, politicians mostly self-funded their campaigns, or sought help from well-connected or wealthy friends. As candidates increasingly solicited donations to fund their campaigns, however, Congress passed its first law on campaign finance in 1867, restricting staff members and officials of the federal government from seeking funding for political campaigns from navy yard workers.[18] As sums raised for elections rose—to a whopping $16 million for William McKinley's 1896 presidential campaign—Congress enacted more comprehensive restrictions during the Progressive Era in the late nineteenth and early twentieth centuries. In 1910, the Publicity Act became the first law to require written public disclosure of all money spent on elections by political parties in House elections. The Act was amended in 1911 to include Senate and primary elections, require political candidates to disclose their spending, and set limits on contributions to candidates and on the amount a campaign could spend. In a pattern that would repeat itself with later efforts to rein in money in politics, however, the Publicity Act was challenged in the Supreme Court, which held in *Newberry v. United States* (1921) that regulations to limit spending in primary elections were unconstitutional.

During the early twentieth century, corporate contributions to federal campaigns were prohibited. Meanwhile, following World War II, Americans became less loyal to political parties, and political communications became more important in the campaign process. This shift was reinforced by the advent of television and mass media. As a result, candidates increasingly looked to sources of technical and media expertise to connect with independent voters and build their base. In this context, corporations, unions, trade organizations, and other special interests formed voluntary associations, known as political action committees (PACs), pooling funds from their members to be contributed to specific candidates. This shift in policy gave rise to the PACs that persist to this day.

A reform period began in the 1970s with the enactment of the Federal Election Campaign Act of 1971, requiring financial disclosure reports for all entities that made political contributions to candidates and for all campaign contributions of more than $100. The Act also established restrictions on spending by candidates on various types of advertising, including broadcasting. The Watergate scandal in 1972 involved secret political funding and campaign finance misuse, sparking more robust reform. In 1974, amendments to the Federal Election Campaign Act included the institution of a federal tax "checkoff" program that allows taxpayers to make voluntary contributions to candidates by reducing their refunds on their income tax forms.[19] These contributions were intended to provide public funds for presidential campaigns, thus offsetting the role of outside donors. The law also imposed new limits not only on contributions, but also on spending in federal elections, and it created the FEC, an independent regulatory agency, to provide oversight in campaign finance in federal elections. In addition to enforcing the Federal Election Campaign Act, the FEC was responsible for receiving and monitoring disclosure reports.

MONEY AS SPEECH

Campaign finance practices have been dramatically impacted by a long line of Supreme Court decisions starting in the mid-1970s that tie campaign finance to the First Amendment. The equation of campaign finance with political speech was first made in 1976 in *Buckley v. Valeo*,[20] a case that challenged the post-Watergate creation of the Federal Election Campaign Act. In its decision, the Court ruled that while limits on *contributions* were permissible to avoid corruption or the appearance of it, restricting *spending* by individuals, groups, or candidates was unconstitutional under the First Amendment. In a 6–3 decision, the majority ruled that "a restriction on the amount of money a person or group can spend on political communication during a campaign necessarily reduces the quantity of expression by restricting the number of issues discussed, the depth of their exploration, and the size of the audience reached." The Court ruled that in the context of a political campaign, spending was equivalent to speech and therefore could not be restricted. As noted by the Center for Responsive Politics, "this distinction between contributions and spending remains a linchpin of campaign finance law" today.

In 1979, in response to restrictions on their contributions to federal campaigns, corporations and unions found a way around contribution limits by contributing to political parties. This "soft money" was not originally directed to campaigns, but rather to "party-building" activities at the local, state, and national levels.[21] There were no limits on such contributions. As this new mechanism for outside groups to contribute to elections emerged, Supreme Court cases delineated a distinction between corporations and nonprofit organizations and their respective rights to make political contributions. Supreme Court decisions in 1986 and 1990 ruled that nonprofit organizations could use specially designated funds (but not funds from their general treasury) for express advocacy, including contributions to fund political ads.[22] Until *Citizens United* in 2010, corporations and nonprofit organizations that received corporate funding were still subject to limits on political contributions.

Despite these restrictions, political soft money contributions continued to expand throughout the 1990s and into the 2000s. Unions and corporations increased their contributions to "party-building" efforts.[23] As these contributions increased, so did the murky nature of their use by the Democratic and Republican parties. Soft money spending skyrocketed in the 1996 election, when it was frequently used for television "issue ads" that were often little more than thinly veiled campaign ads for specific campaigns.[24]

The line became further blurred in 1997, when President Bill Clinton faced criticism for inviting major Democratic donors to stay overnight at the White House.[25] These donors had previously contributed over $5.2 million to the

Democratic National Committee in 1995 and 1996,[26] making the overnight
stays seem like a reward by the administration for these soft-money contributions to the party. These and other revelations led to several subsequent investigations into Clinton's campaign finance practices, including an investigation
by the Department of Justice, but the investigations did not result in charges
against officials at the White House, the Democratic National Committee, or
the Clinton campaign.[27] No legal restrictions on soft money were enacted, and
soft-money contributions continued to rise, from under $243 million in 1996
to more than $457 million in 2000, when political parties outspent candidates
in television advertising for the first time.[28]

DISCLOSURE

As a result of the Supreme Court's interpretation of the First Amendment
equating campaign funding with political speech, Congress was unable
to limit soft money directly. Instead, beginning in 2000, a series of legislative efforts promoted disclosure and transparency requirements as a way to
track campaign finance without triggering potential constitutional issues.
In that year, Congress amended federal tax law to mandate that nonprofit
"issue groups" organized under section 527 of the Internal Revenue Code—
otherwise known as "527s"—publicly disclose their contributions.[29] As entities distinct from PACs, these groups did not have to register with the FEC.
Despite the new rules on disclosure, however, the law did not set limits on
contributions for 527s, provided they did not advocate for a specific candidate's election or defeat.[30]

Additional reforms in 2002 brought further restrictions to outside groups,
including 527s. The Bipartisan Campaign Reform Act, better known as the
McCain-Feingold Act after its primary sponsors in the Senate, Republican
John McCain and Democrat Russ Feingold, banned soft-money contributions to political parties, and restricted hard-money contributions to candidates and issue groups. It also expanded disclosure requirements to include
not only those organizations that expressly advocated for a candidate but also
those that engaged in any communications that named candidates leading up
to an election.[31] These disclosure requirements included the "Stand by Their

Ad" provision, which mandated that federal candidates "approve" and claim responsibility for their advertising content.[32]

THE FALL OF MCCAIN-FEINGOLD

Between 2002 and 2010, a series of Supreme Court and U.S. Court of Appeals cases gradually eroded the McCain-Feingold Act.[33] The plaintiffs in *McConnell v. FEC*, led by then-Senate Majority Leader Mitch McConnell, attacked McCain-Feingold as a violation of the First Amendment, but the Supreme Court largely avoided the constitutional issue in that case.[34] Three later cases were more impactful in challenging the constitutionality of the legislation on freedom of speech grounds. These rulings provided additional precedent to justify challenges to McCain-Feingold and legislation at the state level that sought to mitigate the outsized influence of donors and candidates with more financial resources.

These court decisions collectively served to nullify the McCain-Feingold restrictions on soft money and millionaire candidates.[35] They also weakened the restrictions on electioneering communications, coordinated and independent expenditures, and contribution limitations and prohibitions. Indeed, following the 2007 ruling in *Wisconsin Right to Life v. FEC*, electioneering communications supported by corporations, unions, and nonprofit organizations became more prolific in the 2008 elections.[36] Independent expenditures also ballooned. Furthermore, after *EMILY's List v. FEC* in 2009, soft money was once again used to fund political activities by outside groups in federal, state, and local elections.[37]

In addition, in *EMILY's List v. FEC* and another case the following year, the Court considered efforts to equalize or level the playing field in elections, including the provision of matching funds to less well-financed candidates and restrictions on donor contributions for the sake of "equal voice or influence in the electoral process." The court decisions in these cases reinforced the view that this intended "equalization" is not a "legitimate government objective" and therefore cannot be used as justification for campaign finance regulation.[38] The decisions followed the precedent set in *Buckley v. Valeo* in 1976 that only "combating corruption and the appearance thereof" represents a legitimate government objective and thus a permissible reason for restrict-ing "the quantity of speech." By contrast, "the concept that government may restrict the speech of some elements of our society in order to enhance the relative voice of others is wholly foreign to the First Amendment," and "the Government's interest in equalizing the relative ability of individuals and groups to influence the outcome of elections" does not justify regulation.[39]

OPENING THE FLOODGATES: CITIZENS UNITED

These formulations on freedom of speech and political funding paved the way for the most consequential change to campaign finance law: the Supreme Court's 2010 decision in *Citizens United v. FEC*. In a 5–4 decision, the Court ruled that corporations and other outside groups have a First Amendment right to raise and spend unlimited amounts on elections. The Justices rea-soned that so long as political funding is not given directly to candidates and political spending is conducted independently from them, it is not corrupt.[40] Therefore, following *Buckley v. Valeo* and later decisions, there is no justifica-tion for restricting the First Amendment right of corporations to engage in unlimited fundraising and spending on advertising for and against specific candidates.

The debate among members of the Court over the measure was particu-larly rancorous. In a dissent, Justice John Paul Stevens warned that *Citizens United* "threatens to undermine the integrity of elected institutions across the Nation," adding, "a democracy cannot function effectively when its constitu-ent members believe laws are being bought and sold." Moreover, he argued that the majority misunderstood "corruption" as defined by *Buckley v. Valeo*. The Court, he said, "never suggested that such quid pro quo debts must take the form of outright vote buying or bribes." Granting corporations an unlim-ited ability to contribute money, he argued, would give unhealthy amounts of power to unaccountable institutions which could live on in perpetuity, influ-encing lawmakers and reducing the power of voters.[41]

While the Supreme Court did not overturn the limits on direct contribu-tions to candidates, *Citizens United* had a profound impact on the landscape of campaign finance. Along with a court of appeals decision in the same year, *SpeechNow.org v. FEC*,[42] *Citizens United* opened the door for the rise of the super PAC, able to raise unlimited amounts of money from corporations, unions, and other institutions.[43] The rulings also gave rise to an explosion in political spending by "dark money" groups, which are not required to disclose their donors.[44] In addition, a later Supreme Court ruling in 2014, *McCutcheon v. FEC*, overturned the limit on overall spending by donors, applying similar reasoning that such limits did not serve to protect against corruption and violated freedom of speech.[45]

Following these decisions, there was no limit on the amount a donor may contribute to "all federal candidates, parties and political action committees combined."[46] While donors were still limited in how much they could contribute directly to individual federal candidates, PACs, and party committees, they could now contribute to an *unlimited* number of campaigns, PACs, and party committees. This ruling, in turn, paved the way for joint fundraising committees, making it even easier for donors to contribute to numerous campaigns and committees at once.

UNDERMINING THE DEMOCRATIC PROCESS

In the decade since *Citizens United*, Justice Stevens's warning has come to pass, and the amount of money flooding the political system has become truly breathtaking. As a recent report by the Brennan Center for Justice showed, the 2018 midterm elections saw an unprecedented amount of grassroots activism and organizing that boosted the number of contributions to candidates by small donors contributing less than $200; eventually some 7 million donors totaled $1.8 billion. And yet, those efforts were overshadowed by the vast amounts of money contributed by just a few wealthy individuals; fewer than 3,500 donors each contributing over $100,000 gave almost $2 billion.[47] These increasing inequities are a direct result of the *Citizens United* ruling, and the floodgates to unregulated outside money that it opened.

DOMINANCE OF SUPER PACS

Super PACs have proliferated since 2010.[48] Super PACs may raise and spend unlimited amounts of money pooled from corporations, unions, associations, and individuals, and they may accept funds from any source. While super

PACs cannot directly contribute to or coordinate with candidates or parties, they can utilize the funds they raise to expressly advertise for or against political candidates through independent expenditures in federal races.[49]

Since super PACs are required to disclose their donors to the FEC, it is possible to track the explosion in fundraising and spending by the groups over the last decade. Super PACs raised $829 million in 2012, increasing to over $1.8 billion by 2016, and an incredible $3.4 billion in 2020.[50] While the Supreme Court has ruled that equalization is not a legitimate governmental objective, it is nonetheless important to note participation in super PACs is far from equal. Between 2010 and 2015, fewer than two hundred households funded nearly 60 percent of all spending by super PACs.[51] While these megadonors also contribute to joint fundraising committees, the majority of their contributions are distributed to super PACs by the end of an election cycle.[52]

These trends give rise to a number of concerns regarding super PACs and their role in the democratic process. Super PACs effectively allow for individuals and corporations, and the campaigns to which they contribute, to sidestep limits on direct campaign contributions. While individuals may only donate $2,900 per election to a federal candidate, and corporations may not directly contribute at all, both individuals and corporations may contribute unlimited sums of money to super PACs that can fund communications that specifically advocate for the election or defeat of specific candidates.

This subversion of spending limits increases the risk that wealthy individuals and corporations will have the outsized influence that legislation like McCain-Feingold sought to control. Furthermore, the same issue with the revolving door that fuels criticism of the lobbying industry also holds true for super PACs, particularly those tied to specific candidates. The Campaign Reform Act's restriction on super PACs' coordination with campaigns and parties is thus rendered less effective, as former staff members of such political entities establish and support these outside groups.

In addition, super PACs may engage in a variety of political activities that benefit candidates without those candidates facing any consequences. This concern is particularly salient in the context of attack ads.[53] While dark money groups are relatively more likely to air negative ads, super PACs nonetheless funded more than 33,000 airings of ads in over a dozen key primary states during the 2016 presidential election.[54] Candidates do not have to answer for the rhetoric included in those ads, which critics have equated to misrepresentative smear campaigns.[55]

With the rise in political advertising on social media, super PACs have become even less accountable for their messaging. In the 2020 election cycle, digital media spending rose to $1.6 billion, double the amount in the 2018 midterms, and nearly 20 percent of the total ad spend.[56] Much of that advertising was done on Facebook and supported by super PACs.[57] In a September 2020 report, a nonpartisan campaign watchdog group found examples of hundreds of ads from Republican super PACs that spread false information on social media about Joe Biden's tax and health care plans, among other issues, as well as Democratic ads spreading misleading information about the United States Postal Service.[58]

MEGADONORS AND JOINT FUNDRAISING COMMITTEES

Following the 2014 ruling in *McCutcheon v. FEC* overturning limits on aggregate contributions, megadonors have found new pathways to donate the maximum individual contributions to as many candidates and party committees as possible in a single election cycle.[59] Joint fundraising committees represent a pathway for these donors to do so at one time. As noted by the Center for Responsive Politics, these committees can be created by two or more candidates, PACs, or party committees to share the costs of fundraising and split the proceeds from donations.[60] Joint fundraising committees allow megadonors to write one check that is then distributed across as many candidates and committees as they want.[61]

Joint fundraising committees provide a mechanism for circumventing spending limits. In particular, joint fundraising committees distribute contributions to candidates and state and national party committees. While there are caps on contributions to these candidates and party committees, the condition that a donor's contributions to the state parties are "routed straight to" the national committee effectively provides megadonors the opportunity to exceed the contribution limits to the national party.[62]

While joint fundraising committees were already increasing in popularity before 2014, the Supreme Court decision in *McCutcheon v. FEC* bolstered their use. With the removal of aggregate contribution limits, joint fundraising committees became more valuable to donors as they could involve many, many candidates and party committees. Likewise, these committees could capital-ize on their newfound ability to solicit a given donor for a much larger contri-bution, rather than a greater number of smaller donors. Indeed, there's been a steady increase in both the number of joint fundraising committees and the total amount raised by those committees as of mid-2020, with a notable jump in fundraising levels during presidential election cycles in particular.[63]

THE RISE OF "DARK MONEY"

"Dark money" groups are nonprofit organizations engaged in political spending—for example, social welfare groups, unions, and trade associa-tions that are not required to disclose their donors. These organizations can receive unlimited donations from corporations, individuals, and unions, and they can also raise unlimited contributions from nonprofit organizations and "shell" corporations that are not subject to disclosure requirements.[64]

Some expenditures by dark money groups do not have to be publicly dis-closed or may be obscured in disclosure. While these organizations must report spending on their annual IRS 990 forms, they are allowed to submit nonspecific information regarding their expenditures with major vendors, such as "media services." In this context, it is possible to obscure expendi-tures related to direct political advocacy. Even when these organizations are required to disclose political expenditures to the FEC, expenditures for gen-eral categories like education do not require specification. In addition, some political expenditures are not required to be disclosed to the FEC in the first place, such as issue advertising that does not explicitly advocate for or against the election of a candidate.[65]

The role of dark money groups in elections is growing with each election cycle. In some races, the amount of dark money spent exceeds the amount of funds disclosed. In the 2016 presidential election, outside groups spent over $15 million but only reported $5 million to the FEC.[66] In May 2020, a report by the Wesleyan Media Project and the Center for Responsive Politics found that more than half of the spending on political ads thus far in the 2020 elec-tion had been made by dark money groups.[67] A follow-up in October found that dark money groups had contributed $750 million so far in the cycle—

with more than half of it donated to super PACs, thus obscuring donors to those groups.[68] In summary, dark money groups may pool funds from a range of sources with minimal restrictions and may pursue and fund political activities that serve to influence the decision of a voter without disclosure of the source of the money.[69] This trend means that voters do not have a sense of who is funding the political advertising and other communications they see.

TURNING OFF THE BIG-MONEY SPIGOT

Despite the proliferation of money in politics and the general weakening of campaign finance law by Supreme Court decisions over the past fifty years, actions can be taken today to promote new methods of small-donor and public financing of political campaigns, and to support transparency of political funding and spending.

Major changes have taken place in grassroots political fundraising in recent election cycles. The growth rate of small donor contributions eclipsed the growth rate of big money for the first time in 2018 and again in 2020, although major donors continued to provide the largest amount of total contributions. The rise of technology-powered small-donor fundraising platforms has opened opportunities for new candidates across the ideological spectrum who cannot or do not need to rely on major donors. Small donor-based public financing systems now exist in fourteen states. As described by the National Conference of State Legislatures, "each of these plans requires the candidate to accept public money for his or her campaign in exchange for a promise to limit both how much the candidate spends on the election and how much they receive in donations from any one group or individual."[70] The rise of small-donor fundraising platforms can decrease the power of big money in politics and create opportunities for a wider variety of candidates.

On the issue of transparency, one promising proposal is the DISCLOSE Act, introduced in every congressional session since 2012 to broaden disclosure of political spending. The most recent iteration would require any organization that spends money in elections, including super PACs and nonprofit groups, to disclose donors who have contributed at least $10,000 during an election cycle. The bill also includes provisions to target dark money groups, including regulations intended to impede the use of shell corporations to obscure donors. The bill also expands the existing "Stand by Your Ad" provision by requiring corporations, unions, and other organizations funding political advertising to name their top five funders at the end of television ads.[71]

States have the constitutional authority to require that all groups engaged in political spending in state races disclose their donors. States in which such requirements already exist demonstrate that this approach is effective. For example, nonprofits in California that have been associated with dark money must disclose all donors that contribute funds to their election efforts. Following this change, the state has narrowed the gap between the total amount of outside spending and the amount that is reported.

In today's social media environment, it is crucial that federal and state regulations require the disclosure of donors for digital political advertising, which has risen to nearly 20 percent of total spending, and is predicted to rise even further in coming election cycles.

In addition to improving transparency and disclosure, there are other actions that can close loopholes for candidates and officeholders. While super PACs are required to operate independently from candidates or parties, cracks in the system allow these committees to essentially coordinate with candidates and parties. For example, candidates help to fundraise, conduct polling, and organize events with and for these groups. Reforms to prohibit such coordination have been proposed in federal legislation, namely the Stop Super PAC–Candidate Coordination Act introduced in the House. State and city governments have imposed their own regulations on fundraising coordination.

Because dark money groups do not have to disclose their donors, they can work in direct concert with elected officials. To prevent the role of dark money in both influencing and benefiting elected officials, action at the federal and state levels is needed to require these groups to disclose all major donors. New York City has enacted this requirement for nonprofits controlled by elected officials and has set a limit on contributions from individuals with economic interests before the elected official.[72]

As demonstrated in the evolution of campaign finance law, weak enforcement has hindered effective regulation. As the agency responsible for overseeing campaign finance, the FEC has a key role to play in regulation. However, political stalemates, lack of leadership, and inadequate resources have prevented the FEC from being an effective enforcement agency.[73] In its 2018 agenda for fixing American elections, the Brennan Center for Justice proposed the following reforms to the FEC to address these issues:[74]

- Establish and maintain an odd number of commissioners, one or more of whom is required to be registered as an independent.
- Authorize the Commission's career staff to investigate alleged violations, and expand the Commission's authority in enforcement.
- Appoint one of the commissioners to serve as chair and as its chief administrative officer for a fixed term of four to six years, with sole authority to "hire the staff director and other senior administrative personnel, formulate budget requests to Congress, and manage the agency's day-to-day operations."
- Increase funding to enable the FEC to fulfill its compliance and enforcement responsibilities and to maintain information technology to collect and disseminate data on campaign finance disclosures.

Even though the Supreme Court has established that campaign finance regulation to promote "equalization" is unjustified under the First Amendment, there are nonetheless pathways to help level the playing field. In particular, voluntary public financing allows citizens a greater role in funding elections and is legally permissible under *Citizens United* and other Supreme Court decisions. Examples of existing public financing mechanisms include the following:

- Matching contributions, in which small donations are provided with a multiple match of public funds, as exemplified in New York City.[75]
- Voucher systems, where citizens receive specified amounts of public funding they can direct to their preferred candidates.
- Tax credits for small campaign donations.[76]

While most prominent megadonors are U.S. citizens, the outsized role of money in politics is exacerbated by the influence of foreign funding. Many of the proposals to reform money in politics would target both domestic and foreign actors. Legislation proposed at the federal level includes both comprehensive measures to regulate online advertising and provisions specifically intended to limit foreign influence. In particular, the Honest Ads Act would require sellers of all forms of advertising to make "reasonable efforts" to prevent foreign nationals from purchasing political advertising.[77]

The most comprehensive campaign finance reform is the For the People Act, passed by the House in March 2021 as HR 1. In addition to the bill's voting reforms, HR 1 includes numerous provisions on campaign finance reform, including incorporating the DISCLOSE Act in its entirety. In addition, it would improve disclosure requirements for online advertising; strengthen the Stand By Your Ad Act; and take measures to deter foreign contributions to American elections. Another provision in the bill would effectively end dark money by requiring all political entities donating to campaigns to reveal their donors. The bill would also create a system for public financing by providing a six to one match of contributions up to $200 by citizens, and would establish a pilot voucher program in three states whereby voters could request $25 vouchers from the government to donate to the candidate of their choice.[78] After the House passed HR 1 in February 2021, the Senate introduced its own version of the bill, S 1. The Senate bill has been blocked by Senate Republicans, including Minority Leader Mitch McConnell, who have threatened to filibuster it.

No reforms would be complete without addressing the Supreme Court's ruling in *Citizens United*. Since the decision in 2010, twenty states and more than eight hundred local governments have enacted legislation requesting Congress to pass a constitutional amendment to overturn the decision.[79] HR 1 includes a provision calling for such an amendment. Several forms of the constitutional amendment have been introduced in Congress in the last decade, including the Democracy for All Amendment, most recently reintroduced in January 2021 with bipartisan sponsorship.[80] The proposed amendment would include in the Constitution the following provisions:[81]

> "Congress and the States may regulate and set reasonable limits on the raising and spending of money by candidates and others to influence elections."

> "Congress and the States shall have power to implement and enforce

this article by appropriate legislation, and may distinguish between natural persons and corporations or other artificial entities created by law, including by prohibiting such entities from spending money to influence elections."

Policy Recommendations

- **Require Disclosure of All Political Funding and Spending.** Require full transparency and disclosure of all political fundraising and spending in federal and state elections by candidates, political parties, political action committees, and "dark money groups."
- **Authorize Citizen Funding of Elections.** Enact "clean election laws" for federal, state, and local elections through mechanisms such as voluntary public financing programs, including matching programs, voucher systems, and tax credits that amplify the contributions and power of small donors.
- **Amend the Constitution to Permit Regulation of Money in Politics.** Authorize the regulation of political funding and spending to eliminate the undue influence of money in the U.S. political system by enacting and ratifying a constitutional amendment overturning decisions of the Supreme Court interpreting the First Amendment to bar such regulation.

3

Civic Education: "A Republic, If You Can Keep It"

The societal issues affecting young people in America are overwhelming. Every year from 2009 to 2019, approximately three thousand children and teens were shot and killed by gun violence in the United States.[1] During this decade, anywhere from 10.5 to 16 million children were living below the poverty level.[2] Despite these existential challenges, young people in the United States are not provided with the knowledge and tools to become civically engaged and politically active.

Outside the Constitutional Convention in 1787, Benjamin Franklin was asked what kind of government was being designed, and he famously replied, "A Republic, if you can keep it."[3] Based on the abysmal level of civic education today, that could prove challenging. In 2020, only 51 percent of Americans were able to name the three branches of government, according to a survey conducted by the Annenberg Public Policy Center.[4] Voting rates average in recent decades only about 60 percent in presidential elections and 40 percent in midterms, which places the U.S. below most other democracies in voting participation.[5] In 2019, three out of four Americans believed that public trust in the federal government was declining, according to the Pew Research Center.[6]

The connection between civic education and public trust is key. This connection was starkly clear in the wake of the campaign of lies about voter fraud by President Trump before and after the 2020 presidential election.[7] What has been called Trump's "Big Lie"[8] led to the insurrection at the U.S. Capitol on January 6. If voting is the "defining act of a democracy, it is only meaningful if public deliberation is grounded in veritable information."[9]

LAYING THE FOUNDATION

What is civic education? The *Stanford Encyclopedia of Philosophy* defines civic education as "the processes that affect people's beliefs, commitments, capabilities, and actions as members or prospective members of communities." This broad definition encompasses civic education not only in schools, but also in the family, government, civil society, religious institutions, and the media.[10] The Brown Center on Education Policy at the Brookings Institution divides civic education into three parts: *civic knowledge* (an understanding of government structure and processes), *civic skills* (the capacity to participate in democracy), and *civic dispositions* (attitudes that are important to democratic culture, such as concern for the welfare of others).[11] According to a 2003 report by the Carnegie Corporation of New York and the Center for Information and Research on Civic Learning and Engagement, competent and responsible citizens have the following traits: they are informed and thoughtful, participate in their communities, act politically, and have strong moral and civic values.[12]

Civic education provides students with an understanding of history, contemporary issues, and the democratic process.[13] It teaches respect for democratic values, such as the rights and responsibilities of citizens, as well as an appreciation for a diversity of cultural and political perspectives. A well-rounded civic curriculum includes classroom instruction, discussion of current events, debate about controversial issues, service learning, extracurricular activities, school governance, and simulations of democratic processes. It should include the history of Native American communities, the transatlantic slave trade, and immigration. It should involve the history of cultural and racial diversity in the United States, as well as the contemporary importance of racial equity and justice in promoting anti-racist communities and society. It should cover the history of battles for intellectual freedom, such as the teaching of evolution and the struggle against McCarthyism and blacklisting.

Such curricula have tangible benefits for citizens in a democracy. Citizens who have gained civic education are "four times more likely to volunteer and work on community issues," according to the Campaign for the Civic Mission of Schools and the Leonore Annenberg Institute for Civics. Civic education is associated with an increase in young people monitoring and comprehending the news, thinking critically, voting and discussing political issues, and

William Jennings Bryan (seated at left) being interrogated by
Clarence Seward Darrow during the trial of the *State of Tennessee
v. John Thomas Scopes* about the teaching of evolution, July 20,
1925. Photo by Watson Davis via the Smithsonian Institution
Archives.

feeling confident about their ability to speak publicly and communicate with
elected officials.[14]

The primacy of civic education as a foundation for democracy was recognized by the framers of the Constitution. Thomas Jefferson remarked in
1789, "whenever the people are well-informed they can be trusted with their
own government."[15] Other founders expressed the importance of civic education in ensuring an informed citizenry and creating a shared identity that
could bring together a heterogeneous society. Benjamin Franklin envisioned
schooling as a means of "laying such a foundation of knowledge and ability
as, properly improved, may qualify [individuals] to pass through and execute
the several offices of civil life, with advantage and reputation to themselves
and country."[16] George Washington observed in an address to Congress that
"the assimilation of the principles, opinions, and manners of our country-
men by the common education of a portion of our youth from every quarter
well deserves attention. The more homogenous our citizens can be made in
these particulars the greater will be our prospect of permanent union; and a
primary object of such a national institution should be the education of our
youth in the science of government."[17]

To be an effective tool of democracy, civic education and the schools that
provide it must be equally accessible to all people. The nation was more than
a half-century old before efforts were made to provide universal opportunity

for education. Even after public schools were started in the 1840s, boys could not expect to attend for more than a few years, and girls had no expectations at all. When the Fourteenth Amendment was adopted in 1868, tax-supported schooling was not prevalent in the South, and the education of African Americans was forbidden by law in many states.[18]

Many people were excluded from the vision of the framers, who had viewed civic education as vital for citizenship and democracy. Black educators and activists such as W.E.B. Du Bois, Booker T. Washington, and Mary McLeod Bethune sought in different ways to redress this exclusion by focusing on the educational and racial uplift of African Americans. Civic education for African Americans was linked to the struggle for equality of opportunity and social justice.[19]

For generations of immigrants in the nineteenth and twentieth centuries, the public school represented "the primary teacher of patriotism and civic values. Many came to see the common school as the guarantor of the nation's promise of democracy and freedom."[20] This understanding of the importance of public education led to enactment of the 1862 Morrill Act, which gave each state federal land to establish land grant colleges, and a century later to the 1965 Elementary and Secondary Education Act (ESEA), which extended federal assistance and oversight to public schools.[21]

Students in a classroom.

By the last decade of the nineteenth century, "nearly every American child between the ages of five and thirteen attended school regularly, with the vast majority in schools funded and administered by newly emergent school districts."[22] Civic education became an important part of school curricula as immigrants from many countries and cultures came to the United States.[23] Until the 1960s, courses in civics and government were common in U.S. high schools, and students were taught about the responsibilities of citizenship at local and state levels. Studying problems of democracy encouraged students to discuss current issues and events. In addition, courses on U.S. government focused on the structures and functions of government at the federal level.[24]

Toward the end of the twentieth century, however, "there was widespread concern about whether the [common] schools were continuing to fulfill [their] role" in teaching and promoting civic values.[25] Public schools had seemingly abdicated their earlier responsibilities to serve as providers of civic learning. Policymakers began shifting the focus from social studies toward subjects like math and reading, and schools increasingly saw their role as creating skilled workers more than providing civic skills.[26] Under President Ronald Reagan, the National Commission on Excellence in Education recommended in a well-regarded report, *A Nation at Risk*, that standardized tests be "administered at major transition points from one level of schooling to another and particularly from high school to college or work."[27]

These competing pressures caused public schools to reduce their earlier focus on educating "a nation of immigrants" to become well-informed and civically inclined citizens.[28] By 2011, Kathleen Hall Jamieson, director of the Annenberg Public Policy Center at the University of Pennsylvania, observed that "[a]t a time when the nation is confronting some of the most difficult decisions it has faced in a long time, a lack of high-quality civic education in America's schools leaves millions of citizens without the wherewithal to make sense of our system of government."[29]

DOWNGRADING OF CIVIC EDUCATION

Civic education fell into neglect in the U.S. because of competition from other subjects, such as math and reading. Legislation in 2001 reauthorizing ESEA, "No Child Left Behind," emphasized math and reading assessments, but this meant schools gave less attention to other subjects, such as social studies.[30] In light of civic education's impact on citizens' ability to exercise their rights and participate in their communities, schools should not have to face a tradeoff between civic education and reading and math. A comparison of U.S. Department of Education Schools and Staffing Surveys from 1987 to 1988 (the first year the survey was conducted) and 2003 to 2004 (the years after No Child Left Behind was implemented) showed a reduction in time spent on social studies instruction in grades one through six. Weekly instructional time in history also decreased from 1988 to 2004, and instructional time spent on reading and English Language Arts as well as mathematics increased.[31]

While civic learning was once "woven throughout the curriculum" in elementary schools, by 2010 only a third of teachers reported that they regularly covered civic topics in their instruction. According to a 2011 study, high school courses on the role of citizens and current issues had become "very rare." The study found that there was generally only a single course on U.S. government, typically offered in the eleventh or twelfth grade, not allowing time for students to "build knowledge from year to year" and missing the many students who drop out before senior year.[32] This meant that students were not learning basic democratic values and the skills necessary to understand and engage with diverse communities and differing perspectives.

The decrease in instructional time and requirements for civic education compared to other subjects resulted in a deficiency in civic knowledge, as demonstrated by test scores in the National Assessment of Education Progress (NAEP). In 2014, the average score in civic knowledge for eighth graders was twenty-four points below the proficiency threshold set by NAEP on a scale of zero to three hundred.[33] The NAEP Civics test in 2010 measured the frequency of three civic education practices: discussing current events, debating current issues, and participating in simulations of democratic processes and procedures. A study of the test results found that at eighth grade and twelfth grade levels, students from higher socioeconomic backgrounds were taught more of these practices than those from lower socioeconomic backgrounds. Exposure to civic practices was associated with higher NAEP scores for all groups.[34]

Federal and state requirements and assessments today deemphasize civic education. Studies show there is inadequate classroom instruction nationwide both in civics and in social studies. A 2003 study by the Albert Shanker

Institute found that most state standards in social studies emphasize historical facts and dates for memorization and require more material to be covered than most states and districts allot for civic learning in the classroom.[35]
According to a 2018 study by the Center for American Progress, only nine
states and Washington, DC, required a full year of study on U.S. government
and civics at the high school level. Thirty-one states required only a half-year
of education in civics or U.S. government, and ten states had no civics requirement at all. Only 60 percent of states that require a civics course provided a
"full curriculum," defined as including course materials covering an explanation of democracy, the U.S. Constitution and Bill of Rights, public participation, and information on state and local voting. Moreover, the study found
that many states taught information, not skills, and that no states included
experiential learning or local problem-solving in their civics requirements.
Only Maryland and Washington, DC, required community service in addition to civics coursework for graduation.[36] This unevenness and lack of rigor
indicates that civic learning is not a priority in U.S. education.

The varying state civic education requirements affect not only the quality
of test scores but also the level of youth community engagement. The Center
for American Progress study found that states with robust civics requirements
and learning tended to have the highest rates of youth civic engagement. In
particular, the ten states with the highest rates of volunteerism among young
people ages sixteen to twenty-four had a civics course requirement for graduation and had higher-than-average student scores on the AP U.S. government
exam. In relation to voting, seven out of the ten states with the highest voter
participation rates among youth ages eighteen to twenty-four scored higher
than average on the AP exam. Nevertheless, test outcomes in civic education
lagged behind those for most other subjects nationwide. In 2016, the national average score for the AP U.S. government exam was 2.64, lower than the
average AP score of all but three of the other forty-five AP exams offered by
schools at the time.[37]

IMPLICATIONS OF DISINVESTMENT

Civic education in the United States receives very limited federal funding. Through the early 2000s, the federal government spent approximately

$40 million per year on civic education programs. However, in 2010, Congress changed the funding mechanisms for some programs, shifting funding toward science, technology, engineering, and math, and leaving subjects like civics with inadequate support.

In its budget for the 2011 fiscal year, the Obama administration proposed consolidating smaller programs, including ones related to civic education, into broader funding streams. Programs supporting history, civics, economic education, foreign languages, and the arts would have been combined into a larger funding stream aimed at "effective teaching and learning for a well-rounded education."[38] Even after this downgrading through streamlining, the budget ultimately passed by Congress eliminated the $35 million set aside for civic education.[39]

Between fiscal years 2011 and 2015, there was no federal funding for K–12 education in history or civics. Appropriations earmarked for civic education and federal funding for National History Day, a widely recognized program that increases student participation in historical studies across the country, were eliminated in 2012.[40] This move by Congress to cut funding in the education budget was aimed at consolidating programs and eliminating "wasteful spending." In 2011, Representative Hal Rogers (R-KY), then-Chair of the House Appropriations Committee, said, "[we] have weeded out excessive, unnecessary, and wasteful spending, making tough choices to prioritize programs based on their effectiveness and benefit to the American people. My committee has taken a thoughtful look at each and every one of the programs we intend to cut, and have made determinations based on this careful analysis."[41]

Four years later, there was an unsuccessful effort to reestablish civics in K–12 education in the Every Student Succeeds Act (ESSA), signed into law on December 10, 2015. ESSA included language allowing the Secretary of Education to award grants for "hands-on civic engagement activities for teachers and students" and "programs that educate students about the history and principles of the Constitution of the United States, including the Bill of Rights."[42] ESSA replaced the No Child Left Behind Act and emphasized "college and career readiness, accountability, scaling back assessments, increasing access to preschool and the important role state and local communities play in making their schools successful." ESSA included civics in these accountability systems and funding.[43]

ESSA supported civic education in several ways, including by creating Presidential Academies for Teachers and Congressional Academies for Students of American History and Civics to support the development of teachers and students in civic education. The Student Success and Academic Enrichment Grant Program allowed states and districts to apply for funding for a well-rounded education, and National Civic Activities grants provided funding to promote innovation in civic learning, particularly among underserved populations. However, ESSA authorized but did not appropriate funding to support these activities.[44] In 2017, full appropriation at the authorized amount for ESSA programs would have been $1.6 billion. However, ESSA programs were ultimately allocated a paltry combined $10 million, less than 1 percent of the authorized amount.[45]

The lack of appropriation of funds for civic education from the federal government sends the message that civic education is not important. And without funds, schools are unable to allocate sufficient time to curriculum and teaching in civics, particularly when federal and state policy requires more focus on science, technology, engineering, and math (STEM). In 2019, the federal government allocated almost $3 billion to STEM education.[46] Meanwhile, the U.S. Department of Education's budget for 2019 mentioned civic education only once, in reference to a civics program with a cost of $3.5 million, or 0.1 percent of the STEM budget, that was proposed for elimination.[47] Civic education was no longer a priority.

Americans have fallen far short from what the framers intended in their understanding of participation in democratic governance. The United States has become a nation dotted with "civic deserts," referring to geographic communities without sufficient opportunities for civic engagement. In a 2017 study of millennial voters, approximately 60 percent of rural young Americans and almost a third of suburban and urban young Americans were found to be in communities classified as civic deserts, where there are insufficient opportunities to discuss societal issues and find ways to build shared understanding and platforms for action.[48]

Over the past two decades, according to a study by the RAND Corporation, the phenomenon of "truth decay"—the diminishing role of facts and analysis in American public life—has resulted in the erosion of civil discourse and public disengagement from and suspicion of the political process. Distinctive indicators of truth decay include "increasing disagreement about facts, a blurring of the line between opinion and fact, the increasing relative volume and resulting influence of opinion over fact, and declining trust in formerly respected sources of facts."[49]

CIVIC EDUCATION AND THE LEGACY OF SLAVERY

The history and legacy of slavery are essential aspects of civic education. The 1619 Project, developed in 2019 by journalist Nikole-Hannah Jones, "challenges us to reframe U.S. history by marking the year when the first enslaved Africans arrived on Virginia soil as our nation's foundational date." Originally comprising essays by historians, journalists, and scholars, The 1619 Project was complemented by lesson plans, lesson builders, and other resources developed with the Pulitzer Center to provide materials for teaching about the centrality of slavery in U.S. history and its legacy in contemporary society.[50] The opening paragraph in the *New York Times Magazine* issue devoted to The 1619 Project introduced this perspective:

> 1619 is not a year that most Americans know as a notable date in our country's history. Those who do are at most a tiny fraction of those who can tell you that 1776 is the year of our nation's birth. What if, however, we were to tell you that the moment that the country's defining contradictions first came into the world was in late August of 1619? That was when a ship arrived at Point Comfort in the British colony of Virginia, bearing a cargo of twenty to thirty enslaved Africans. Their arrival inaugurated a barbaric system of chattel slavery that would last for the next 250 years. This is sometimes referred to as the country's original sin, its very origin.[51]

Following its publication, The 1619 Project was criticized by a small group of leading historians and attacked by Republican politicians, who took aim at its stated goal, as described on the project website, "to reframe the country's history by placing the consequences of slavery and the contributions of black Americans at the very center of our national narrative."[52] Critics attacked the project's central thesis that anti-Black racism is pervasive and connects to the nation's history of enslavement.[53] Several efforts have emerged at the federal and state levels to limit or prohibit the use of The 1619 Project in local school curricula and to diminish the central role of slavery in the historical narrative of the United States. While conservative politicians often decry involvement of federal and state government in local school decisions, they have nonetheless targeted this project through federal and state legislation.[54]

The legacy of slavery and its impact on contemporary issues of race are critical subjects for the textbooks used in social studies teaching. Kathleen Hall Jamieson, a democracy expert at the University of Pennsylvania, has observed that "social studies textbooks may not adequately convey the knowledge or facilitate the development of the skills required of an informed, engaged citizenry."[55] In some textbooks, Dred Scott was the only historical Black person featured more than once.[56] A 2017 study by the Southern Poverty Law Center found that 58 percent of polled teachers were not satisfied with how their textbooks taught about slavery, and almost 40 percent said that their state offered little or no support on the topic.[57] The role that The 1619 Project proposed to fill is essential to understanding the centrality of slavery to the historical development of the United States as well as the impact of slavery on current struggles for racial justice.

POLITICAL TENSIONS IN CIVIC EDUCATION

Civic education requires incorporating discussion of diverse perspectives on current local, national, and international issues and events into the classroom, particularly issues that young people view as important to their lives. Students need to learn how to engage productively with the issues and events relevant to the democratic process and how to engage in discussions with people with whom they disagree.

The polarization in our current political climate makes it likely that integrating coursework with the discussion of current events might be framed as "advancing a partisan agenda."[58] Educators have avoided discussing controversial moral and political questions in the classroom out of concern that they will offend certain groups' sensibilities or stray "into areas of discussion that are wholly private prerogatives."[59] One out of four teachers surveyed in 2013 by the Center for Information & Research on Civic Learning and Engagement thought that parents or other adults in their community would object if they taught about politics in their government or civics classes. More than 16 percent said they believed that parents and other adults might object if they taught about elections and voting.[60] Some teachers reported being subject to strict policies against giving any indication of their own opinion on political issues.[61]

Providing nonpartisan education about political topics involves asking students to weigh fact-based evidence, consider multiple perspectives, form and articulate their own opinions, and respond to people who disagree.[62] Research shows that when people engage in discussions about important issues and events with others who disagree, they develop a tolerance for disagreement and build an understanding of the range of views about how best to solve public problems.[63] When civic discussion is discouraged in the classroom, schools are prevented from fulfilling the educational mission of creating informed and participatory citizens. Strengthening civic education, on the other hand, provides a means of bridging polarized views and promoting discourse across political perspectives.

Civic education is the key to democratic governance because it imparts democratic values and encourages participation. According to a 2010 study, completing a year's worth of coursework in U.S. government or civics leads to an increase in a student's propensity to vote in an election after high school.[64]

Democracy is more than just voting and depends on a citizenry that is informed and involved in all aspects of civic life. Informed citizens can better hold their elected officials accountable, engage in productive public discourse, and demand accurate information from the media. Civic education can also help promote equal opportunity by giving every citizen, no matter their socioeconomic status, the tools to be full participants in their own governance. In addition to knowing facts about the U.S. government, active citizenship involves engaging with civil society organizations or participating in social and political advocacy. According to a 2018 study by the Public Religion Research Institute, most Americans did not report high levels of civic engagement and fewer than three in ten respondents said that they had engaged in civic and political activities such as signing an online petition, following a political campaign, contacting an elected official, volunteering for a group or cause, attending a community meeting, or attending a public rally or demonstration in the previous twelve months.[65]

PROMISING DEVELOPMENTS

The high voter engagement and turnout in the 2020 election is a promising development and may be a harbinger of increasing levels of civic engagement. Voters mobilized and organized despite the public health impact of the pandemic, the economic impact on their families, and restrictions on voting in many jurisdictions, with people of color playing an important role in states such as Georgia. Young people were especially active. A pre-election poll and survey conducted by Tufts University found that 83 percent of young people felt that they had the power to change the country. Meanwhile, 79 percent reported that the pandemic had caused them to realize that decisions by elected officials affect people's everyday lives. Approximately a quarter of young people surveyed helped register voters.[66]

Renewed civic engagement and activism is reflected around a broad range of social causes, especially among young people. Survivors of the Parkland school shooting became gun-control activists, creating digital social media campaigns, organizing the March for Our Lives Rally, speaking out for stricter gun laws, and encouraging other young people to get actively involved and registered to vote.[67] In the wake of the water crisis that engulfed Flint, Michigan, community organizations and activists mobilized around concerns of systemic racism and the impact of lead-contaminated water on the health of children and families. One activist, known as Little Miss Flint, was seven years old when the water crisis began; as a teenager, she mobilized people and funding to advocate for safer and better conditions in Flint and similar low-income cities across the United States.[68] Such youth engagement and leadership around public problem solving can both reinforce the relevance of civic education and center future curriculum around the lived experiences of those most excluded and marginalized.

Finally, there are new prospects for federal funding of civic education. In 2021, Senators John Cornyn (R-TX) and Chris Coons (D-DE) announced a bipartisan initiative to invest $1 billion in civics and history education.[69] The Biden administration has called for a grant program for history and civic education "to prioritize instruction that accounts for bias, discriminatory policies in America, and the value of diverse student perspectives."[70] This is a sharp departure from the agenda of the Trump administration's 1776 Commission, which excluded a focus on slavery and racial equity from school curricula. President Biden has dissolved the 1776 Commission and emphasized racial equity as a priority of his administration.[71]

Policy Recommendations

- **Invest in Proven Practices to Improve Civic Learning.** Invest in classroom instruction in government, history, economics, law, and democracy; discussion of current events and controversial issues; service learning and community-service programs; extracurricular activities; student participation in school governance; and simulations of democratic processes.[72]
- **Require and Fund Civic Education.** Enact legislation requiring U.S. history and civics to be taught in all public and private schools, with federal grant programs to support history and civics teachers. Invest in civic education for all ages in all communities through curricula, professional development for teachers, and a federal award program that recognizes innovative civic education initiatives at local, state, and national levels.
- **Broaden History and Civic Education Curricula.** Develop new content and pedagogy for teaching historical subjects related to the denial of rights—such as slavery, Native American removal, racist restrictions on immigration, anti-Semitism, and the political and cultural suppression of minorities and women— in order to promote understanding of the value of diversity and the need for rights to define people's relationships to each other and their government in a democracy.
- **Center Civic Equity and Racial Justice in Civic Education.** Ensure that students of color, students from low-income

communities, and those living in civic deserts are able to avail themselves of civic education, and that such learning is grounded in racial justice and equity.

- **Reimagine Civic Education in a Digital Age.** Use multimedia formats to develop and disseminate curricula. Help young people discern how to assess and evaluate the integrity of online news and civic education sources.
- **Establish a National Trust for Civic Infrastructure.** Following the recommendation of the American Academy of Arts and Sciences in its 2020 report, *Our Common Purpose*, establish a National Trust for Civic Infrastructure as a public-private initiative.[73]
- **Support Civil Society Partners.** Encourage and promote funding for civil society organizations that provide civic education at national, state, and local levels and that can be engaged as partners in school-based civic education programs.

Part II

Equal Protection of Law

4

Bending the Arc Toward Racial Justice

In the years leading up to the Civil Rights Act of 1964, a growing movement for racial justice led by Martin Luther King Jr. and countless activists engaged in direct action calling for the end of racial discrimination in the United States. The Civil Rights Movement was built on decades of struggle and belief, as King expressed it, that "the arc of the moral universe is long but it bends toward justice."[1] In August 1963, King delivered his famous "I Have a Dream" speech at the March on Washington, DC, to 250,000 supporters.[2] Following

Martin Luther King Jr. on the steps of the Lincoln Memorial on the day he delivered his famous "I Have a Dream" speech during the August 28, 1963, March on Washington. Photo via Wikimedia Commons.

the march, civil rights leaders met with President John F. Kennedy to press for civil rights legislation.[3] When President Lyndon B. Johnson signed the 1964 Civil Rights Act into law, his action reflected a decades-long struggle by grass-roots activists and political leaders of the Movement to enact national legislation protecting racial equality. The landmark federal law, which incorporated many of the demands from the March on Washington, prohibited racial discrimination in employment, education, voting, and public accommodations.[4] The Civil Rights Act paved the way for other major federal laws outlawing discrimination in more targeted areas, such as the 1965 Voting Rights Act and the 1968 Fair Housing Act.

Today, the promises of these historic civil rights measures have been hijacked by political efforts to undermine their protection of equal rights and opportunities across racial identities. The era in which the civil rights laws were enacted saw an outburst of state and federal legal action to enforce constitutional rights in the United States. In recent decades, however, obstacles have been imposed to legal remedies against racial discrimination in many areas of society.

Exacerbating the legal obstacles is the social behavior that perpetuates de facto racial discrimination in housing, education, employment, health care, criminal justice, and other areas of life. At its worst, this behavior can cost lives—as the disproportionate killing of Black men and women by law enforcement officers has shown. Racist behavior can also result in individuals perpetrating hate crimes against communities of color—as the spike in racist attacks against Asian Americans and Pacific Islanders during the COVID pandemic demonstrated. The emergence of social advocacy movements such as Black Lives Matter over the past decade and Stop AAPI Hate in recent years is a response to the reality of an America more than half a century after enactment of the civil rights laws that has yet to fulfill the promise of racial equality. The impact of the pandemic has shown how systemic racial discrimination in the justice system, housing, health care, and employment has resulted in higher rates of infection and death and greater economic loss for vulnerable communities of color.

This chapter provides an overview of the continuing struggle for racial justice in the United States. Separate chapters cover racial discrimination in voting, hate crimes motivated by racial bias, and the impact of economic inequality on people of color.

RACE AND THE JUSTICE SYSTEM

No area is more emblematic of racial discrimination than the criminal justice system. The effects of mass incarceration and aggressive, sometimes lethal, police practices are most acutely felt by African Americans, Native Americans, and Latinx Americans.

Policing

Racial injustices rooted in the legacy of slavery and the removal of indigenous people have been perpetrated by law enforcement throughout U.S. history. Policing in the United States has among its early roots the slave patrols of the seventeenth and eighteenth centuries, when White men would patrol the movements of enslaved Black people and inflict violence and summary punishments on enslaved persons who were presumed to be outside the boundaries of the plantation or estate where they were enslaved. In the Jim Crow South, police officers asserted authority to constrain and control the movements of African Americans. Black people were routinely stopped or arrested for offenses that would have been considered trivial had they been committed by a White person. It was common for police officers to hold membership in the Ku Klux Klan or to sympathize with the group's ideology. Police involvement with the Klan became such an issue that in 1871 Congress passed the Ku Klux Klan Act to "prohibit state actors from violating the Civil Rights of all citizens in part because of law enforcement's involvement with the infamous group."[5] The Tulsa Race Massacre of 1921, in which an estimated three hundred Black residents were killed, was carried out by mobs of White men, many of whom had been deputized and given weapons by city officials. The massacre was part of a series of mob violence, lynchings, and massacres that occurred across the nation, beginning in Washington, DC, and Chicago during the Red Summer of 1919.

During the Civil Rights Movement, the advent of mass photography and television coverage brought images of police beatings of predominantly African American civil rights protesters to the larger American and international public. The startling images brought to the public a reality long experienced by African Americans, and played a contributing role in creating the demand for change that culminated in the civil rights legislation of the 1960s.[6]

High-profile cases of police brutality have continued to capture the public's attention. In recent years, police responsibility in the shooting deaths of twelve-year-old Tamir Rice and eighteen-year-old Michael Brown in 2014, the death of Sandra Bland in police custody in 2015, and the shooting of Philando Castile during a traffic stop in 2016, repeatedly brought to public attention the harsh and often deadly tactics used by police against people of color, and the subsequent lack of legal accountability for many police involved in deadly incidents. These cases continue today, with an ever-increasing list of names of African Americans and other people of color, including the 2020 murders of Breonna Taylor and George Floyd.[7]

A 2019 research study found that Black and Native American men are 2.5 times more likely to be killed by police than White men, and Black and Native American women 1.4 times more likely to be killed than White women. Latino men are approximately twice as likely to be killed by police as White men.[8]

People of color are targeted by aggressive policing in locations where they are deemed to be "out of place." Research conducted in 2018 at Northeastern University suggests that "out-of-place" policing can shed light on cases involving the use of lethal law enforcement tactics toward communities of color. The research shows that police rely on the relationship between neighborhood demographics and suspects to identify and police "out-of-place" individuals in predominantly White areas. In other words, "police officers are more likely to treat as suspicious persons who seem out of place in their surroundings. To police officers, race serves as a marker of where people 'belong,' and racial incongruity serves as a marker of suspicion."[9]

Aggressive policing of communities of color is also widespread within their own neighborhoods. Thirteen-year-old Adam Toledo was shot and killed by police near his home in Chicago in March 2021, sparking widespread protests of police violence in Latinx American communities. In 2019, Atatiana Jefferson was shot through the window of her Miami home when police responded to a report from a neighbor that her front door had been left open. In 2018, Stephon Clark was shot while standing in the backyard of his grandmother's Sacramento, California, home, when police mistook his cell phone for a gun.[10]

Policies and criminological theories in the late 1980s and 1990s promoted aggressive police tactics, and the effects are still being felt today. The 1980s "Broken Windows" theory by George Kelling and James Wilson posited that cracking down on smaller-scale infractions like vandalism, public drinking, and loitering prevented more serious crime from occurring in neighborhoods. Critics argued that the vagueness of the social disorders outlined in the theory resulted in too much discretion in enforcement, often leading to increased targeting of racial minorities.[11] The New York City Police Department adopted "Broken Windows" policing and similar controversial tactics like stop-and-frisk, which disproportionately impacted African American and Latino men.[12] Research has since shown that such stops did little to fight crime, but had long-lasting negative effects on young Black students.[13] A 2020 study at the Harvard Kennedy School found that Black middle school students from New York City neighborhoods heavily impacted by stop-and-frisk were more likely to drop out of school and less likely to enroll in college.[14] Former Mayor Michael Bloomberg has since apologized for the practice.

Implicit bias on the part of officials within the criminal justice system and society at large remains a consistent concern. In a 2004 paper published by the American Psychological Association, survey respondents often associated people of color with adjectives such as "dangerous," "aggressive," "violent," and "criminal."[15] These negative stereotypes resurface when people of color enter the criminal justice system. According to a report by the nonprofit research organization The Sentencing Project, "people of color are frequently given harsher sanctions because they are perceived as imposing a greater threat to public safety and are therefore deserving of greater social control and punishment."[16]

The problem of police violence goes far beyond implicit bias or misconduct on the part of individual police officers who are "bad apples." UCLA law professor Devon Carbado focuses on the intersection of Fourth Amendment law and police violence. In an explanation for the frequency of police violence and killings followed by the lack of accountability, Carbado points to "this 'front-end' police contact—which Fourth Amendment law enables" serving as "the predicate to 'back-end' police violence—which Fourth Amendment law should help to prevent."[17] In other words, search and seizure law enables police contact but should restrain police action from resulting in violence.

Just as news photography and television brought the reality of police brutality to American homes during the Civil Rights Movement, technology today plays an important role in documenting and transmitting police interactions with African Americans and other communities of color. The spread of video on mobile phones coupled with access to social media has allowed civilians to record instantaneously and share online any questionable interaction with law enforcement. Many recent shooting deaths were captured by either private cell phone recordings or surveillance cameras. Additionally, many police departments have instituted body cameras on their officers which allow for videotaping of police–civilian interaction.[18] Despite such efforts, modern-day de facto lynchings of African Americans have not abated and the documentation does not always result in accountability or structural change.

The rise of social movements such as Black Lives Matter has brought to national attention the police violence and discrimination faced by African Americans and Latinx Americans. Unfortunately, there has not been a similar level of attention paid to discriminatory policing faced by Native Americans. In a 2014 study, the Centers for Disease Control and Prevention found that between 1999 and 2011, Native Americans were killed by police at a higher rate than African Americans. When looking at the likelihood of being killed by police compared to the overall population, the study found that Native Americans were more likely to be killed by police than any other racial group. Throughout the study's timeframe, Native American men were 3 times more likely to be killed by police than White men compared to 2.5 times for African American men.[19]

Native American deaths at the hands of police are under-reported. The killing of Allen Locke in 2014 was barely reported outside of Rapid City, South Dakota, where it occurred.[20] The same lack of coverage held for the police killings of Native Americans Corey Kanosh in 2012, Mah-hi-vist Goodblanket in 2013, Jeanetta Riley in 2014, Daniel Covarrubias in 2015, and others. Looking at coverage by the top ten U.S. newspapers between May 2014 and October 2015, a study by Claremont University researchers found a consistent lack of coverage of Native American deaths by law enforcement.[21]

Incarceration

The United States incarcerates people at the highest rate in the world, with a disproportionate impact on African American individuals, families, and communities. One in four African American men have experienced incarceration by the age of thirty-five.[22] A study conducted at the University of Illinois at Chicago found that a criminal charge in a county that had high levels of slavery in 1860 was associated with increases in "the risk of pretrial detention, the likelihood of being sentenced to incarceration, and the length of the incarceration sentence."[23]

The legacy of slavery and its aftermath are still present in the incarceration system today. African American men are imprisoned at nearly five times the rate of White men, while African American women are twice as likely to be imprisoned compared to White women.[24] In 2015, African Americans and Latinx Americans accounted for 56 percent of the prison population. These disparities are a result in part of earlier criminal justice policy and sentencing structure that disproportionately affected people of color. In the late 1960s and early 1970s, "law and order" policies such as the 1968 Omnibus Crime Control and Safe Streets Act resulted in an expansion of the crimes that qualified for federal imprisonment and stricter prison sentencing, most notably for drug offenses.[25]

Influenced by initiatives like the "War on Drugs," the 1980s saw a rise of arrests and harsh punishments for these offenses, which were disproportionately applied to African Americans, Native Americans, Latinx Americans, and other persons of color. Despite the discrepancy in arrest and conviction rates, studies show that African Americans use drugs at similar rates as Whites. Between 1995 and 2015, while African Americans comprised only 13 percent of drug users, they accounted for 46 percent of drug arrests by 2005 and 29 percent of arrests by 2015.[26]

Factors beyond disproportionate arrest rates also play a role in exacerbating incarceration rates of people of color. Once taken into custody, defendants face an uphill battle in bail and pre-detention decisions. Financial bail requirements disproportionately affect people of color, who typically have lower economic resources than Whites. Nearly five hundred thousand people in the United States are currently being detained pre-trial. This means that they are awaiting trial and are considered legally innocent. Many are detained because they cannot afford money bail.

Once in front of the court, studies show that such defendants of color often face stricter sentences than their White counterparts for the same crime. "Black and Hispanic offenders—particularly those who are young, male, and unemployed—are more likely than their White counterparts to be sentenced to prison than similarly situated White offenders," according to the nonpartisan research center The Sentencing Project.[27]

A 2016 analysis of prosecutorial outcomes found that communities of color were disadvantaged in charging decisions. People of color were more likely to be charged and prosecuted than White offenders for similar crimes. While the extent of the discrepancy depended on the jurisdiction, region of the United States, and phase of prosecution (e.g., pre-trial or trial), it held constant that "an offender's race and ethnicity did play a significant role in prosecutors' decisions to file a charge or pursue a full prosecution."[28]

In addition to discrimination, limited opportunities in employment, education, and housing often place people of color in vulnerable circumstances that create a cycle of structural disadvantage and exacerbate their overrepresentation within the criminal justice system. A study by The Sentencing Project found that "62 percent of African Americans reside in highly segregated, inner-city neighborhoods that experience a high degree of violent crime, while the majority of Whites live in 'highly advantaged' neighborhoods that experience little violent crime."[29]

Incarceration has negative outcomes for prisoners after their release. A criminal record typically complicates efforts by former prisoners to secure employment, regardless of the type of conviction. In addition, a criminal conviction in many states precludes individuals from voting in federal or local elections. These hurdles, and the general social stigma attached to formerly imprisoned people, further entrench people of color in systemic disadvantages.

While those caught up in the justice system face the primary effects of incarceration, their families and communities also fall victim to the negative impact. In 2017, more than half of those incarcerated were parents of minor children, with African American children more than seven times more likely to have an incarcerated parent than White children. Children and spouses of incarcerated individuals face worse overall health outcomes compared to the general public.[30]

"School-to-Prison Pipeline"[31]

Beginning in the 1970s, the adoption of "zero tolerance" school policies contributed to the rise in disciplinary action against students.[32] The vagueness of what zero tolerance means led to any type of student misconduct, from minor dress code violations to violent action, being subject to discipline.[33] Passage of the 1994 Gun-Free School Act and its vague classification of what constitutes a weapon meant that students faced year-long suspension whether they brought a gun to school or merely made a weapon gesture with their hands.[34] Without review mechanisms to investigate the circumstances of expulsion, students had little recourse to appeal questionable expulsion decisions.[35]

African American and Latinx American students have borne the brunt of these policies. In 2014, the Department of Education found that while African Americans accounted for 16 percent of the school population, they represented 32 percent of students expelled or suspended, 27 percent of referrals to law enforcement, and 31 percent of school-related arrests. In general, African American students were expelled at three times the rate of White students, with African American girls suspended at higher rates across all racial groups.[36] In addition to disciplinary measures in schools, these practices have contributed to the disproportionate incarceration of minority youth, with African American youth five times more likely to be incarcerated than White youth.[37]

Further exacerbating disciplinary outcomes has been the rise in outsourcing student misbehavior to juvenile courts and disciplinary officers. A 2015 report found that schools with student disciplinary resources officers (SROs) had five times more student arrests than schools without, and higher rates of student referral to juvenile correction centers. These referrals expose children to the criminal justice system at an early age.[38] School principals have little input in the SRO hiring process, increasing the probability of hiring an SRO who is a poor fit for the school culture and student body. Principals have been pressured by public officials to allow SROs to be armed because of the perceived danger of school shootings.[39] According to a 2013 report by the Congressional Research Service, only 4 percent of school officials cited the presence of actual violence in school as the reason for hiring an SRO. Instead, 25 percent reported that pressure from media and public officials about the possibility of school violence was their primary motivation for acquiring an SRO.[40]

While SROs are responsible for preventing violence by armed students or intruders, there are troubling reports of aggressive actions toward students by SROs. In 2010, Derek Lopez, a San Antonio fourteen-year-old, was shot to death by an SRO who claimed the student fled after punching another student.[41] In 2013, seventeen-year-old Noe Nino de Rivera suffered a brain hemorrhage when he fell after being tased by an SRO while Rivera was attempting to break up a fight.[42] The SRO was not charged and received a promotion in

2014. In 2015, a Louisville thirteen-year-old was punched by an SRO for cutting the lunch line, and later the same SRO was indicted for putting another teen in a chokehold causing the student brain injury.[43]

Often missing from the discussion about juvenile detention are Native American youth, who can be detained by either tribal, state, or federal authorities. Poor or inconsistent communication among the authorities means that data on Native youth detention are often incomplete.[44] Native youth are disproportionately represented in the juvenile justice system. Even excluding youth in Indian Country facilities, Native Americans comprise 3 percent of girls and 1.5 percent of boys incarcerated in state juvenile detention facilities, despite making up less than 1 percent of the youth population.[45] Similar to African Americans and Latinx Americans, Native Americans often face negative stereotypes of criminality that lead to harsher encounters with law enforcement and sentencing. Compared to White youth, Native youth are more likely to be arrested for low-level infractions like liquor law violations or lack of cooperation with law enforcement. When they are arrested, Native youth are almost twice as likely as their White counterparts to be referred to the adult criminal justice system or out-of-home placements like halfway homes or youth residential treatment centers.[46]

Disproportionately heavy-handed disciplinary action has a far-reaching negative impact on minority youth. In a 2007 study, the Centers for Disease Control and Prevention found that youth transferred to the criminal justice system are 39 percent more likely to be re-arrested for violent crimes—further entrenching them in the criminal justice system, and restricting future employment, education, and housing opportunities.[47]

RACE AND HOUSING

Housing discrimination is one of the starkest examples of systemic racial discrimination in the United States. The problem is rooted in the Jim Crow era and, ironically, was exacerbated during the New Deal by the creation of the Federal Housing Administration (FHA) in 1934. The FHA institutionalized discriminatory housing practices—referred to as redlining—that for generations had effectively excluded people of color, particularly African Americans, from realizing the American Dream of homeownership. On request by the Home Owners Loan Corporation in the 1930s, the FHA identified areas within cities in which the default risk level was deemed sufficiently "safe" to provide loans.[48] The areas deemed riskiest were often communities of color, identified by literally drawing a red line around their borders. Since federal and private mortgage rates were awarded based on the deemed risk of the loan, this left racial minorities with little to no access to mortgages or home-ownership in general.

Even supposedly "race-neutral" legislation had a negative impact on people of color seeking homeownership. The 1944 Servicemen's Readjustment Act, commonly known as the GI Bill, allocated federal aid to help returning World War II veterans "adjust to civilian life in the areas of hospitalization, purchase of homes and businesses, and especially, education."[49] In the case of homeownership, the GI Bill provided federally guaranteed loans for veterans to purchase homes. Yet, African American, Native American, Latinx American, and Asian American/Pacific Islander veterans were unable to take advantage of these benefits since very few banks would lend them the funding to purchase a mortgage.[50] Even if they were to secure a mortgage, their housing options were severely limited. Housing development projects and home-owners' associations either implicitly or explicitly excluded people of color from buying or living in their managed properties. As one report concluded, "FHA was subsidizing builders who were mass-producing entire subdivisions for Whites—with the requirement that none of the homes be sold to African Americans."[51] While White Americans were able to take advantage of growing suburban developments and financial incentives like the GI Bill, African Americans continued to be left behind.

The lack of access to mortgages had a far-reaching negative impact on communities of color. Research in Chicago has shown a negative causal relationship between redlined areas and rates of homeownership, house values, and racial segregation. In a 2019 survey across Chicago neighborhoods, the Federal Reserve Bank of Chicago found that previous redlining could account for 15 to 30 percent of the gap in African American homeownership between redlined and regular neighborhoods. The same study found that 40 percent of the discrepancy in home values could be attributed to redlining practices.[52]

In 1968 Congress passed the Fair Housing Act, which prohibited housing providers, mortgage lenders, and financial institutions from discriminating

against applicants on the basis of race, whether for rental or mortgage properties. Seven years later, the 1975 Home Mortgage Discrimination Act mandated that financial institutions disclose their lending practices in an effort to
further identify and discourage discriminatory mortgage lending practices.

Despite these legislative developments, people of color today continue to
encounter systemic discrimination when seeking housing. In a 2018 randomized experiment, African Americans received lower-than-average response
rates from landlords when inquiring about rental units.[53] A 2012 report by
the U.S. Department of Housing and Urban Development (HUD) found that
people of color often face informal hurdles to securing rental or mortgage
properties. African Americans and Latinx Americans are told of fewer available units compared to Whites when seeking rentals. Even when told of available units, people of color are required to provide more information about
their credit qualifications, have longer wait times for viewings, and are less
often told about rental incentives or discounts compared to non-minorities.
For every three homes a non-minority applicant is shown, African Americans
are shown only two homes, and they are more likely to be shown homes with
physical deformities.[54]

Whether institutionalized or informal, housing discrimination has negative social, financial, and health impacts on communities of color. As indicated in the 2012 HUD report, when searching to buy, people of color are
more likely to be steered by realtors to communities with lower-priced homes
or to areas that reflect their perceived racial identity. This practice, worsened
by the legacy of redlining in certain areas, can further segregate communities
and limit upward mobility in neighborhoods where opportunity is scarce. In
fact, living in segregated areas increases *downward* mobility for children, as
they have less access to quality educational and social support resources.[55]
Additionally, these neighborhoods typically have fewer healthy food options
and less access to quality health services. Residents of poor-quality housing,
often characteristic of low-income segregated neighborhoods, also experience
higher incidents of vermin infestations, lead, and mold, which can lead to
health complications.[56]

Since the appreciation of housing asset values can generate wealth, lack of
access to homeownership has stunted the ability of people of color to build
net worth. In 2016, the median net worth of a White family in the U.S. was

$171,000, compared to $20,700 for a Hispanic family and $17,600 for an African American family.[57] These disparities in wealth are compounded by discrimination in employment and other economic spheres, which further fuels inequality and contributes to the staggering current wealth gap. Richard Rothstein, author of *Color of Law*, concludes that "today African American incomes on average are about 60 percent of average White incomes. But African American wealth is about 5 percent of White wealth . . . most middle-class families in this country gain their wealth from the equity they have in their homes. So, this enormous difference between a 60 percent income ratio and a 5 percent wealth ratio is almost entirely attributable to federal housing policy implemented through the [twentieth] century."[58]

For Native Americans, the issue of housing security is affected by unique circumstances. For decades, Native communities have been fighting against violations of tribal sovereignty and federal encroachment upon tribal lands. Threats to tribal lands are further compounded by the sub-standard housing available within reservations. A 2017 report from the Department of Housing and Urban Development found that tribal communities experience much poorer housing conditions compared to all U.S. households. The report found that 23 percent of households in tribal communities "live in housing with a physical condition problem of some kind," compared with 5 percent of all U.S. households; 16 percent live in overcrowded housing compared to 2 percent of U.S. households. These poor housing conditions are in part due to under-investment from federal agencies and housing resources for Native communities that have "declined more rapidly than for other federal housing programs."[59]

RACE AND EDUCATION

A decade before the Civil Rights Act of 1964, the Supreme Court's landmark decision in *Brown v. Board of Education* initiated the process of desegregating the nation's public schools. The case was brought by African American parents who were forced to send their children to distant segregated schools rather than nearby White schools. The Court's ruling held that public school segregation violated the Fourteenth Amendment's Equal Protection Clause. The ruling mandated that the "separate but equal" doctrine of the Court's 1896

Nine students leave Central High, Little Rock, Arkansas, under U.S. Army escort. Photo via New York Public Library Digital Collections.

decision in *Plessy v. Ferguson* could no longer be applied to public education even if the schools had similar facilities: "Segregation of children in public schools solely on the basis of race deprives children of the minority group of equal educational opportunities, even though the physical facilities and other 'tangible' factors may be equal."[60]

The political backlash to *Brown* was quick and vehement. Open defiance by political leaders of court desegregation orders bolstered de facto segregation and continued to bar African American students from attending desegregated schools. In 1954, 101 members of Congress from southern states signed the "Southern Manifesto," pledging themselves "to use all lawful means to bring about a reversal of this decision which is contrary to the Constitution and to prevent the use of force in its implementation."[61]

Although *Brown* outlawed segregation in public education, it provided neither a roadmap for desegregation nor a timeline for schools to desegregate. The question of "how" to desegregate was the basis for the follow-up 1955 case, *Brown v. Board of Education of Topeka II*. Even here, the Supreme Court was vague in its implementation guidance, stating only that the ruling from *Brown I* should be enforced "with all deliberate speed" under the guidance and recommendation of local education authorities. In the face of vague judicial and legislative guidelines, some school districts started to institute busing to comply with desegregation. Students would be transported to schools outside their regular school zone in an effort to create more racially integrated schools. In response, many White parents revolted against the prospect of their children attending school in predominantly Black neighborhoods.

Despite the 1964 Civil Rights Act and the *Brown* rulings, widespread de facto school segregation and discrimination continue today. A 2019 report found an estimated $23 billion funding gap between public school districts serving the same number of White students and students of color.[62] Since public school funding is based on local property taxes, and neighborhoods of color have lower property values, schools in racial minority areas receive less funding than those in wealthier White neighborhoods. This lack of funding results in lower-quality teaching and instructional materials. A 1998 Brookings study concluded that "schools with high concentrations of low-income and minority students receive fewer instructional resources than others—fewer and lower-quality books, curriculum materials, laboratories, and computers; significantly larger class sizes; less qualified and experienced teachers; and less access to high-quality curriculum."[63]

In recent years, there has been a growth of "charter schools"—schools chartered to receive government funding but permitted to operate independently of the public school systems in which they are located. The asserted goal of the charter school movement is to provide alternatives and opportunities for students for whom the public education system is supposedly failing. A 2017 report by the Associated Press found that most charter schools themselves are highly segregated. "In cities, where most charters are located, 25 percent of charters are over 99 percent non-White, compared to 10 percent for traditional schools."[64] These results are at odds with the goal of offering a better alternative to failing traditional public schools and a better orientation in how to live in contemporary American society.

An historically controversial aspect of race and education is the use of affirmative action in school selection criteria, particularly within higher education. Broadly defined, affirmative action is "a set of procedures designed to eliminate unlawful discrimination among applicants, remedy the results of prior discrimination, and prevent such discrimination in the future."[65] In a 1978 decision in *Regents of the University of California v. Bakke*, the Supreme Court held that it was constitutionally permissible for public higher education institutions to utilize race in their admission criteria. A White student, Allan Bakke, had sued the University of California, Davis (UC Davis) School of Medicine's affirmative action quota policy after he was rejected three times, claiming that the policy violated the equal protection rights of White students. While the Court held that including race in the selection criteria was acceptable since racial diversity was in the interest of the state, instituting formal racial quota systems, like that of UC Davis, was unconstitutional.[66]

This distinction of using race as a *factor* in admission rather than a *cause* of admission would be argued for decades in subsequent Supreme Court cases. Two prominent decisions, *Gratz v. Bollinger* (2003) and *Fisher v. University of Texas* (2016), further differentiated these two criteria and highlighted the need for strict scrutiny of the use of race-based admission methods. In *Gratz*, the Court ruled against the University of Michigan's undergraduate admissions practice of assigning points to applicants based on race. However, in *Fisher*, the Court ruled in favor of the University of Texas, noting that race was just one of many factors assessed and did not on its own sway admission outcomes.[67]

Affirmative action continues to be a contentious issue. Critics argue that past discrimination against students of color does not justify present discrimination against White students and harms the groups it is meant to serve by insinuating that they cannot succeed without affirmative action. There is also the claim that affirmative action discriminates against other communities of color. In 2019, Students for Fair Admissions sued Harvard University in federal court arguing that the school's affirmative action policies discriminated against Asian American applicants.[68] The U.S. District Court and Court of Appeals ruled in favor of Harvard, finding that its admissions process met constitutional requirements.

RACE AND THE LABOR MARKET

Civil Rights activists in the 1950s and 1960s worked to bar racial discrimination in employment. Labor unions and worker rights groups played complementary roles in the larger Civil Rights Movement, with leaders like Martin Luther King Jr. viewing equal access to work as a core requirement of equal protection and equal opportunity.[69] With the signing of the 1964 Civil Rights Act, the country seemed closer to eliminating employment discrimination. Title VII of the Act made it unlawful for employers to discriminate against applicants or employees on the basis of race and mandated that the Equal Employment Opportunity Commission (EEOC) enforce these anti-discrimination protections. In 1965, President Lyndon Johnson issued Executive Order 11246 further specifying that any contractor doing over $10,000 worth of business with the U.S. government was not only barred from discriminating against individuals but was also required "to take affirmative action to ensure that equal opportunity is provided in all aspects of their employment."[70]

As with most issues discussed in this chapter, these legal protections against employment discrimination have been circumvented by continuing de facto discrimination. A 2018 report by the Bureau of Labor Statistics highlighted the inequalities still present in the labor market. Compared to the national unemployment rate of 3.9 percent, Native Americans, African Americans, and Asian Americans and Pacific Islanders faced higher rates of unemployment, with 6.6 percent, 6.5 percent, and 5.3 percent, respectively. African Americans and Latinx Americans continued to have the lowest salaries, with wage disparities across all sectors. While a White full-time employee earned on average $890 weekly, African Americans earned $694, and Latinx Americans earned $680.[71]

People of color have long been at a disadvantage from the beginning of the employment process. Studies conducted in 1990 found that White applicants received 36 percent more employer calls for initial interviews than Blacks and 24 percent more calls than Latinos. A 2017 Harvard Business School study found that there has not been a significant change in these discrepancies even when controlling for other variables such as education and gender.[72] Other studies have shown that resumes of applicants with White-sounding names are 50 percent more likely to receive callbacks than identical resumes with Black-sounding names—an advantage equivalent to having eight more years of work experience.[73]

The EEOC is tasked with fulfilling the mandate of Title VII and the affirmative action requirement of Executive Order 11246. In the fiscal year 2017, the agency received over 28,500 raced-based complaints, excluding those filed at state or local agencies, with a slight decrease to 24,500 complaints in the fiscal year 2018.[74] The magnitude of complaints coupled with lack of EEOC operating resources has made it difficult for the EEOC to carry out its mandate effectively. When adjusted for inflation, the EEOC in 2018 had the same budget as it had in 1980, with less staff, and significantly more complaints to investigate.[75]

Despite the challenges of de facto discrimination and an overburdened EEOC, the affirmative action requirements for government hiring are essential for representation of Black, indigenous, and people of color in government employment. A 2013 Harvard Kennedy School report on state and

local governments that repealed employment affirmative action requirements found that representation of racial minorities decreased. The three
groups most negatively impacted were Asian and African American women
and Hispanic men who respectively saw 37 percent, 4 percent, and 7 percent
decreased representation nationwide within the state and local government
workforce.[76]

SOCIAL MOVEMENTS FOR RACIAL JUSTICE

As racial disparities have increasingly gained public awareness, public activism against racial discrimination has risen dramatically. Following the
murder of George Floyd by a Minneapolis police officer in May 2020, massive protests for racial justice took place in hundreds of cities and towns
across the nation. The unprecedented outpouring of public anger by millions of civil society demonstrators of all races, generations, and socioeconomic backgrounds—undeterred by the coronavirus pandemic—showed
that the demand for racial equality is strong in the United States. Similarly,
a major increase in racist attacks and hate crimes against Asian Americans
and Pacific Islanders during the pandemic stimulated public activism that
led to passage of the COVID-19 Hate Crimes Act in May 2021. Public opinion seems to reflect the increased activism and supports efforts to promote
racial equality. A poll conducted by the Carr Center for Human Rights Policy
and the National Opinion Research Center in May 2021 showed that racial
equality was endorsed by an overwhelming 79 percent bipartisan majority of
Americans.

Black Lives Matter (BLM), a national social movement rallying against
systemic racial discrimination and for criminal justice reform, began in 2013
as a social media reaction to the acquittal of a White man for the shooting
death of fourteen-year-old African American Trayvon Martin.[77] BLM has led
widespread protests against specific cases of police brutality and systemic discrimination within the criminal justice system. During the 2016 and 2020
presidential and congressional campaigns, BLM activism brought racism,
police brutality, and criminal justice reform to the national spotlight, forcing
candidates to explicitly outline their policies on racial justice issues.

SYSTEMIC DISCRIMINATION AND THE COVID PANDEMIC

Examined separately, the racial disparities faced by people of color in each of the areas covered by this chapter are discouraging. The picture becomes even bleaker, however, when one considers how racial discrimination in a particular sector of society can lead to decreased opportunities and poorer outcomes in other sectors. For example, a teen thrust into the criminal justice system at a young age misses out on academic progress which can promote social mobility; her early exposure to juvenile detention is more likely to lead to a criminal record which then limits her employment opportunities, which in turn limits her ability to secure adequate housing and financial resources.

In conversations about racial inequality, it is easy to focus on one aspect of discrimination without recognizing the overall impact that discrimination has on a person's life. The COVID pandemic has provided a unique opportunity to see the entrenched impact that systemic discrimination has on well-being and opportunities for people of color.

During the first year of the pandemic, the prevailing precaution against contracting COVID was to exercise social distancing and limit contact with the public and, if suspected of infection, to practice self-isolation at home. For neighborhoods affected by systemic discrimination, living conditions made these precautions difficult or impossible to implement. People of color are more likely to live in subpar housing and densely populated areas that make social distancing difficult. Some groups are more likely to live in multi-generational households, and the Centers for Disease Control and Prevention reported that these communities found it harder to protect older members who are more susceptible to COVID or to practice home isolation in the event of infection. Furthermore, segregated communities without convenient access to health centers, supermarkets, and other services made it more difficult for marginalized communities to access health care and stock up on food and necessities.[78]

While much of the workforce was required to stay home to slow the spread of COVID, those deemed "essential workers" were required to work and engage with the public. Essential worker positions include workers in health care, food services, mass transit, manufacturing, and maintenance work.[79]

The Centers for Disease Control and Prevention reported that "racial and ethnic minority populations are disproportionately represented among essential workers and industries, and a majority of these workers belong to and live within communities disproportionately affected by COVID-19."[80] Lack of personal protective equipment and extended exposure in public left these workers at greater risk of infection.

Individuals in the prison system, where people of color are disproportionately represented, faced a higher risk of infection. Prisons had a much higher infection rate than the general public because of the close proximity of prisoners and staff.[81] In New York City's correctional facilities, the infection rate of people in custody in May 2020 was over 9 percent compared to an infection rate of 1.77 percent for New York State and 0.43 percent nationally.[82] In the first half of the fiscal year 2020, the New York City Department of Corrections reported that of those in its custody, 55.2 percent were African American, 32.5 percent Hispanic, 7.1 percent White, and 1.5 percent Asian.[83]

Communities of color have generally suffered from higher infection rates compared to the overall population. In Louisiana, where African Americans are 32 percent of the population, they accounted for 70 percent of deaths from COVID by the end of April 2020. In Michigan, African Americans make up only 13 percent of the state population but accounted for 40 percent of deaths from the disease during the same period. African Americans in Chicago were dying at six times the rate of Whites by the end of April 2020, and in New York City, Latinx American and African American individuals were twice as likely to die from COVID than Whites.[84] Nationally, African Americans account for 14 percent of the population, but of the 21,500 coronavirus deaths whose ethnicity was reported by the end of April 2020, 30 percent were African American.[85] Following the outbreak of the pandemic, African Americans, Latinx Americans, and Native Americans were all more likely than White Americans to be infected, hospitalized, or die from COVID.[86]

The discrepancies in infection and mortality rates were especially pronounced within the Native American community. Generally, poor health outcomes coupled with systemic inequality and resource-starved tribal communities left Native Americans more vulnerable to the health and economic consequences of COVID. Native Americans already have a shorter life expectancy, disproportionate disease burden, and more than 1.3 higher mortality rate compared to the general U.S. population.[87] For decades the Indian Health Service (IHS), the Department of Health agency responsible for providing health services to Native Americans and Alaska Natives, has been underfunded.[88]

Lack of federal support in health services led to skyrocketing infection rates within Native tribes. By mid-April 2020, the Navajo Nation had a per capita infection rate ten times higher than the state of Arizona and the third-largest infection rate in the country. With no initial support from the federal government, the Navajo Nation authority had to utilize an estimated $4 million from its own budget in an attempt to slow the spread of infection.[89]

For most communities of color, underlying health inequities and lack of access to health care made them more susceptible to complications from COVID. This was compounded by higher rates of chronic illness within these groups that increased their vulnerability to COVID. Additionally, stigma and distrust toward the health system due to historical discrimination discouraged marginalized communities from seeking medical help and thus further increased their vulnerability to COVID infection and mortality.[90] In summary, the pandemic acted as a magnifying glass exposing the depth of injustice that racial discrimination imposes upon people of color.

LOOKING FORWARD

Policing

Reaction to protests against police brutality and racial discrimination sharply differed between Donald Trump and Joe Biden during the 2020 presidential campaign. Trump ran on a "law and order" platform, dismissing calls to reform the police and attacking the reform movement for promoting anarchy. In contrast, Biden ran on a platform of criminal justice reform that included greater federal oversight of police and an overall focus on mitigating racial discrimination in the justice system.[91] Shortly after his inauguration, President Biden issued an executive order that encouraged states to increase data collection on racial disparities in criminal justice and make evidence-based policy changes.[92] A year after George Floyd's murder, thirty states and dozens of large cities had implemented new rules limiting police restraining tactics.[93] Additional executive action by the Biden White House reinstated oversight responsibilities of the U.S. Justice Department to address racial discrimination and systemic misconduct by state and local police departments and prosecutors' offices.

The George Floyd Justice in Policing Act was introduced in Congress in 2020 and 2021, passed twice by the House of Representatives, and is pending in the Senate. The bill promotes increased police accountability, including transparency and improvement of training and arrest policies. A key provision restricts the application of "qualified immunity" that has shielded police officers from lawsuits for violation of constitutional rights. Another provision authorizes the Justice Department to investigate police departments that demonstrate a "pattern or practice" of racial bias or misconduct. The Biden Justice Department has opened several criminal investigations of police misconduct and civil rights violations. After the conviction of Minneapolis police officer Derek Chauvin for the murder of George Floyd, the Justice Department initiated an investigation of the Minneapolis Police Department for excessive use of force and discriminatory practices.[94]

Housing

Major backsliding in federal civil rights protection occurred during the Trump administration in the area of housing. The Trump administration's Department of Housing and Urban Development (HUD) declined to use its authority to enforce anti-discrimination rules. HUD drastically scaled down federal investigation into allegations of housing discrimination by banks, realtors, insurance agencies, and other private entities.[95]

HUD also proposed to eliminate the "disparate impact" standard in allegations of housing discrimination. From a legal perspective, disparate impact recognizes that housing discrimination against race, gender, or disability "can be unintentional. . . . [O]ften that's the case with race-neutral policies—they can perpetuate segregation and racism."[96] The Supreme Court has upheld the disparate impact standard for assessing discrimination under the Fair Housing Act. Justice Anthony Kennedy observed in 2015 in *Texas Department of Housing and Community Affairs v. Inclusive Communities Project* that "recognition of disparate impact liability under the FHA plays a role in uncovering discriminatory intent: It permits plaintiffs to counteract unconscious prejudices and disguised animus that escape easy classification as disparate treatment."[97]

The election of Joe Biden brought an abrupt halt to Trump's plan to eliminate the disparate impact standard. In January 2021, Biden issued an executive order mandating that HUD review Trump-era changes and proposals to verify their compliance with fair housing practices outlined in the Fair Housing Act.[98] Had the Trump proposal to eliminate the disparate impact standard been adopted, the burden of proof to show housing discrimination would have been significantly raised. This would have effectively absolved private entities of responsibility for discrimination committed as a result of algorithmic or other biases within their selection or reporting mechanisms.[99]

Following his inauguration, President Biden announced plans to expand housing access and eliminate housing discrimination. As his first major legislative initiative, Biden signed into law the $1.9 trillion American Rescue Plan in March 2021. The stimulus package allocated billions of dollars to aid renters and homeowners hit hard by COVID. As part of the law, $21.5 billion was made available to assist low-income renters at risk of losing their housing and $10 billion for mortgage and utility assistance to prevent homeowners from being evicted. An additional $750 million was earmarked for Native American and tribal housing and utility assistance. Other housing assistance in the American Rescue Plan Act included additional funding for housing counseling services, expansion of home loans used by low-income home buyers to purchase and rehabilitate rural houses, and increased assistance for the homeless.[100]

While the American Rescue Plan Act provided immediate stopgap help, the Biden administration also proposed a longer-term solution to the nation's housing crisis. Under the American Jobs Plan proposed in March 2021, federal support would be provided to build or improve housing units for low- and middle-income homebuyers and reinvest in the country's public housing system infrastructure. The American Jobs Plan would also address discriminatory housing practices. Federal grants would be available to jurisdictions that "eliminate exclusionary zoning and harmful land use policies."[101] Restrictive zoning practices inflate housing prices and disincentivize builders from constructing affordable units, often excluding minorities from certain communities.[102]

Education

The Trump administration weakened or eliminated existing policies and guidance that promoted equity across America's schools. Education Secretary Betsy DeVos was a staunch proponent of "school choice" and used her position to support the use of federal funds for private and religious educational institutions.[103] By diverting funds away from public schools, school choice policy disproportionately impacted communities of color in districts already struggling with funding.

The Trump administration put students and teachers at risk during the COVID pandemic by providing no federal funding to assist schools in reopening safely and threatening to withhold federal funds from schools that chose remote learning. This would have most affected schools in majority Black and Latinx districts which heavily depended on federal assistance for funding, in addition to communities facing the most severe negative impact from the pandemic. In contrast, the Biden administration increased education funding to promote school reopening.[104]

In April 2021, President Biden announced his American Families Plan Act to bolster federal support for families and education. The bill provides funding for universal pre-K and kindergarten, teacher training programs, two years of community college education, and funding to improve college affordability for low-income students. The bill also includes federal support for historically Black colleges and universities, tribal schools, and other institutions serving minority students, and funding to improve retention and graduation rates of underserved students.[105]

A NEW CONVERSATION ON RACIAL EQUALITY

The topics of racial equality and systemic discrimination catapulted to the top of the national agenda during the 2020 presidential election. The 2020 primary season saw the most diverse pool of presidential candidates in American history, with two African Americans, one Latinx American, two Asian Americans, and one Samoan American vying for the Democratic nomination. Kamala Harris became the first African American woman and person of Indian heritage to be elected vice president.

The COVID pandemic was the dominant policy issue, but racial justice was also a defining issue of the 2020 election, intersecting other areas such as criminal justice reform, education, affordable housing, and health care. The murder of George Floyd spurred ongoing national protests and calls to action to end discrimination against African Americans, not only in law enforcement but across all sectors of society. Social media allowed for greater scrutiny of discrimination against people of color, amplifying calls for nationwide reckoning for racial justice.[106]

Data from the July 2020 Harvard Carr Center/Institute of Politics national poll showed encouraging trends on the perceived importance of racial justice among Americans. Majorities of Republican (52 percent), Democratic (67 percent), and Independent (54 percent) respondents agreed that "racial diversity makes the U.S. stronger." Across all political affiliations, 77 percent agreed that equal treatment of all citizens is necessary for the country to reach its full potential and 81 percent believed racial equality is "very important to being an American today." Similar results were reported in the May 2021 Carr Center national poll.

Despite the immense structural barriers to racial equality outlined in this chapter, as well as the deep political polarization of the country today, public opinion surveys suggest that Americans are increasingly interested in understanding issues of racial discrimination and inequality. Social awareness and mobilization around police brutality, systemic discrimination, and racial injustice have initiated a national conversation and begun to engage public officials in policy debates to address these issues. Scholars in recent decades have developed an influential theory that "race is not a natural, biologically grounded feature of physically distinct subgroups of human beings but a socially constructed category that is used to oppress and exploit people of color."[107] The theory posits that racial discrimination is not simply the product of individual bias but is embedded in legal systems and policies. As the theory becomes more influential, reflecting growing social awareness of the roots of discriminatory practices, it also faces attack by the same political forces that continue to resist civil rights reform and the movement for racial justice.

Policy Recommendations

- **Require Opportunity Impact Statements.** Require all publicly funded programs and projects to publish opportunity impact statements to ensure anti-discriminatory practices and equal access and opportunity for communities of color.
- **Reform Law Enforcement and Strengthen Public Safety.** Public safety reforms should be designed and implemented to redefine law enforcement, increase funding of social services, abolish "qualified immunity" (which shields police officers from accountability through civil liability), demilitarize the police, prohibit chokeholds and "no-knock" unannounced searches, eliminate racial discrimination in policing, and bar police unions from blocking disciplinary actions against police officers. Public safety reform requires shifting the necessary funds to social service agencies to perform non-law-enforcement functions currently assigned to police, such as mental health care, drug treatment, homeless assistance, community mediation, and restorative justice. Public safety and racial justice should be advanced by making greater investments in communities that have been ravaged by violence and a discriminatory justice system.
- **Reduce Mass Incarceration.** Review and reform federal and state sentencing codes and procedures to reduce mass incarceration and provide alternatives to imprisonment. The United States is an international outlier on incarceration, holding 22 percent of the world's prisoners with only 4 percent of the world's population. The United States imprisons more than two million people in federal and state prisons and jails, 56 percent of whom are Black, Latinx American, or Native American.
- **Enact Legislation Allowing Proof of Disparate Discriminatory Impact.** In cases seeking remedies for racial discrimination in housing, employment, education, and health care, allow

proof of the racially disparate impact of policies and practices on communities of color, and eliminate the requirement of proving that racial discrimination was specifically intended by those responsible for the policies and practices that caused it. Congress should enact explicit, actionable disparate impact protections in areas like criminal justice and environmental siting where inadequate protection against racial discrimination now exists.

- **Reform Education Funding.** Establish federal requirement to disconnect public school funding from local property taxes and provide federal funding to eliminate disparities in school district zones resulting from differential property tax bases.
- **End Employment Discrimination.** Strengthen federal anti-employment discrimination enforcement and increase funding for job training programs and access to employment community services.
- **End Housing Discrimination.** Strengthen federal authority to oversee local officials and private parties on fair housing practices and improve renter protections to prohibit discrimination based on public assistance status.
- **Provide Community Development Investment.** Provide public community development investments in African American and Native American communities that have historically been denied economic opportunity and equality as a result of federal policies such as slavery, removal, land seizure, and redlining.
- **Establish a National Truth Commission** to acknowledge, document, and recommend remedies for historic and continuing systemic racism in the United States.

5

The Ongoing Struggle for Women's Rights

On January 21, 2021, Kamala Harris stood on the steps of the U.S. Capitol and took her oath of office as vice president of the United States. A few hours later, she spoke about being the first woman elected to the vice presidency: "In many ways, this moment embodies our character as a nation," she told a crowd assembled on the National Mall. "It demonstrates who we are. Even in dark times, we not only dream, we do. We not only see what has been, we see what can be."[1]

The ascension of women to the highest offices in the land has long been deferred. Hillary Clinton as the Democratic presidential nominee in 2016 won the popular vote by 3 million votes but lost the Electoral College to Don-

Women's March on Washington, January 2017. Photo by Roya Ann Miller via Unsplash.

ald Trump.[2] In 2020, a record number of 118 women were elected to the U.S. House of Representatives. There are now twenty-four women in the Senate. Despite these victories, however, a woman has not yet been elected president.[3]

Political representation matters. It ensures that women are influential in political decisions, that their interests are represented, and that the legitimacy of government is enhanced.[4] Political representation can address overlapping barriers to equality that women continue to face, such as wage discrimination and unequal access to comprehensive health care. Women are 35 percent more likely than men to live in poverty.[5] Persistent sexual violence against women at home, work, or in educational settings impacts women's health, well-being, and economic outcomes.[6]

SETTING THE LANDSCAPE

Women's rights battles today are rooted in America's past. In 1769, the British colonial government denied women the right to "own property in their own name or keep their own earnings," making women dependent on their male relatives or husbands for survival.[7] British laws were based on the ancient legal concept of coverture, which "held that no female person had a legal identity."[8] Coverture influenced many aspects of women's lives, including denying women the right to enter certain professions and barring legal recourse for marital rape victims.[9] The principle of coverture continues to influence how women's rights to equal protection and personal autonomy are perceived; it wasn't until 1993, for example, that all fifty states had at least some form of law criminalizing marital rape.[10]

Starting in the nineteenth century, women activists increasingly challenged societal perceptions and the law. In 1848, suffragists organized the Seneca Convention, calling for women's equal rights and the right to vote.[11] After more than seventy years of activism, women won the right of franchise with the ratification of the Nineteenth Amendment in 1920. While the amendment was widely celebrated, it failed to enfranchise most Black female voters, continuing to shut out millions of women from the vote until the passage of the Voting Rights Act of 1965.[12]

Broader exclusion of Black women and the failure of gains from women's suffrage for Black women led to the development of a Black feminist and inter-sectional movement that drew upon the historical and current traditions of Black women leaders and social movements to put pressure on the women's movement and Civil Rights Movement to be more inclusive. Twentieth-century activists and academics such as Audre Lorde, Patricia Hill Collins, and Kimberlé Crenshaw, and organizations such as the National Black Femi-nist Organization and the Combahee River Collective highlighted the need for the women's movement to be anti-racist and intersectional and created new narratives around solidarity with Black women.

The rise of the women's movement advanced gender equality during the 1960s and 1970s. Following decades of activism, Congress finally responded by enacting a series of laws increasing equal protection for women, including:

The Equal Pay Act (1963), banning "sex-based wage discrimination between men and women in the same establishment who perform jobs that require substantially equal skill, effort and responsibility under similar work-ing conditions."[13]

Title VII of the Civil Rights Act of 1964, prohibiting "employment dis-crimination based on race, color, religion, sex and national origin."[14]

Title X of the Public Health Service Act (1970), authorizing grants that help increase health care access by funding "comprehensive family planning and related preventative health services. . . . [It] is designed to provide access to contraceptive services, supplies, and information. By law, priority is given to persons from low-income families."[15]

Title IX of the Education Amendments Act (1972), establishing that "no person in the United States shall, on the basis of sex, be excluded from partici-pation in, be denied the benefits of, or be subjected to discrimination under any education program or activity receiving Federal financial assistance."[16] Protections apply to any educational institution receiving federal funding, including schools, universities, museums, and libraries.

The Equal Employment Opportunity Act (1972), amending Title VII of the Civil Rights Act of 1964 to increase the authority of the Equal Employ-ment Opportunity Commission (EEOC) to pursue enforcement litigation in cases of employment discrimination. The Act expanded Title VII protections to include public and private employers and labor organizations with fifteen or more members.[17]

The Pregnancy Discrimination Act (1978), forbidding "discrimination based on pregnancy when it comes to any aspect of employment, including hiring, firing, pay, job assignments, promotions, layoff, training, fringe benefits, such as leave and health insurance, and any other term or condition of employment."[18]

The Family and Medical Leave Act (1993), providing "employees with up to 12 weeks of unpaid, job-protected leave per year, also requiring that their group health benefits be maintained during the leave."[19]

The Violence Against Women Act (1994), creating guidelines on domestic violence cases for the criminal justice system and authorizing federal funding "to programs that prevent domestic violence, sexual assault, dating violence and stalking." The Act also funded "shelters, community programs and studies tracking violence against women."[20]

The Clery Act (1990), requiring higher education institutions to publicly report campus safety policies, publish campus crime statistics in accordance with federal guidelines, and support crime victims.[21]

The Affordable Care Act (2010), expanding public access to affordable health insurance, including provisions governing gender equality in preventive services and access to extended Medicaid eligibility, supporting service delivery methods that lower health care costs, and increasing insurance eligibility and coverage for services and medications.[22]

Congress established the principle of equal protection in the workplace via the Equal Pay Act of 1963 and Title VII of the Civil Rights Act of 1964. The Supreme Court elaborated on these legislative principles by expanding women's access to unemployment benefits, interpreting Title VII to prohibit sexual harassment that creates a hostile work environment, holding that Title VII includes same-sex workplace harassment,[23] and protecting the right of pregnant employees to receive unemployment compensation during the third trimester and the six weeks following birth.[24] Interaction between Congress and the Supreme Court was demonstrated in a 1976 Supreme Court decision that an employee benefits plan "excluding disabilities arising from pregnancy does not constitute sex discrimination under Title VII."[25] In response, Congress passed the Pregnancy Discrimination Act in 1978.

Abortion is among the most contentious women's rights issues the Supreme Court has addressed. The Court's decisions have both expanded and restricted the right to have a medically safe abortion. In *Roe v. Wade* (1973), the Court held that the choice to have an abortion is protected by the right to privacy in the Fourteenth Amendment, which includes "a woman's qualified right to terminate her pregnancy." *Roe v. Wade* also established criteria for states to regulate abortions, with increasing regulatory power for states during the final two trimesters. Regardless of the trimester, the Court held that state laws could not interfere with preserving the mother's life or health.[26]

The Court shifted from the trimester system to a fetal viability analysis with its decision in *Planned Parenthood of Southeastern Pennsylvania v. Casey* (1992), which established that "a state may not prohibit any woman from making the ultimate decision to terminate her pregnancy before viability."[27] This change allowed states to regulate and prohibit abortions at an earlier stage than *Roe v. Wade*. It also increased focus on what constitutes fetal viability. The *Casey* decision introduced a new "undue burden" standard on which state restrictions on abortion are evaluated.[28] An "undue burden . . . exists, and therefore a provision of law is invalid, if its purpose or effect is to place substantial obstacles in the path of a woman seeking an abortion before the fetus attains viability."[29] The Supreme Court's vague definition of "undue burden" allowed states and lower courts to interpret the standard subjectively, creating opportunities for states to pass restrictive laws. The "undue burden" standard increased the ability of states to restrict abortion access and therefore weakened *Roe v. Wade*.[30]

Following *Casey*, the Supreme Court decided a number of cases that further defined reproductive rights under the undue burden standard. In *Casey*, the Court expanded abortion access when it established under that standard that a state may not require a married woman to notify her husband that she is having an abortion.[31] Eleven years later, the Court used the undue burden standard to restrict abortion access when it upheld restrictions on the late-term medical procedure covered under the 2003 Partial Birth Abortion Ban Act,[32] except to ensure the health of the mother.[33] In 2016, the Court used the standard to establish that states may not create arbitrary licensing and facility requirements, such as requiring the physician to have admitting privileges at a hospital within a thirty-mile radius, or requiring abortion clinics to comply with ambulatory surgical center standards.[34]

In a number of cases, the Supreme Court has upheld legislation restricting the use of public funds to perform abortions at both federal and state levels. In 1980, the Court upheld the Hyde Amendment, which "bans the use of federal funding for abortions except in the case of rape, incest, or a threat to the life of the pregnant person."[35] This ban includes Medicaid, which serves many low-income women. In 1989, the Court also upheld state-level restrictions on funding abortions.[36] In both cases, the Court decided that restricting public funding did not preclude a woman from obtaining an abortion at her own expense. These decisions and subsequent rulings drastically reduced abortion access for low-income women, with some states making medically safe abortion practically inaccessible to them.

The Supreme Court has also influenced how publicly funded programs can communicate to patients about family planning. The Court ruled in 1991 that the Department of Health and Human Services (HHS) could set regulations prohibiting funding for counseling or referrals for family planning. The Court ruled that these regulations, frequently referred to by opponents as "gag rules," were not a violation of the First Amendment.[37]

The Supreme Court decision in *Roe v. Wade* has faced sustained conservative political backlash for decades.[38] The religious right, a Christian socially conservative political movement, was mobilized in the early 1970s in response to strictures on religiously based private schools.[39] The religious right expanded its platform to include anti-abortion organizing in 1978. Its public opinion campaign, which used strategies like televangelism and radio preachers, helped recruit people to join the religious right while shaping their opinions on core issues like abortion.[40] The religious right mobilized voters to campaign for the election of presidential candidates opposed to abortion, including Ronald Reagan, George W. Bush, and Donald Trump;[41] these presidents, in turn, shaped the composition of the federal judiciary by nominating judges opposed to abortion.[42] In 2018, President Trump nominated and the Senate narrowly confirmed Supreme Court Justice Brett Kavanaugh, who has publicly praised the dissenting justices in *Roe v. Wade* and has sided with lower court decisions exempting employers from contraceptive coverage. The Trump appointments of Kavanaugh, Neil Gorsuch, and Amy Coney Barrett to the Supreme Court have increased the likelihood of decisions further restricting access to contraception and abortion. A large number of cases challenging *Roe* are headed to the Court or have already been granted review. A decision by the Supreme Court overturning Roe or further restricting a woman's right to autonomous decision-making on issues of abortion would fly in the face of public opinion in the United States. According to a nationwide poll conducted in July 2020 by the National Opinion Research Center at the University of Chicago as part of this study, 72 percent of Americans support "a woman's ability to choose and make decisions affecting her body and personal life."

WOMEN'S RIGHTS TODAY

In recent years, policies advancing women's rights have been rolled back, resulting in fewer protections against discrimination and broader harm across many policy issues. Women today continue to experience major inequalities ranging from wage discrimination to health care disparity to insufficient protection against sexual violence.

Women and the Workplace

Although women make up nearly half of the workforce, they experience unequal pay, with disparate impacts across race. For example, Hispanic women earn 54 cents to the dollar for White men, Black women earn 62 cents, and White women earn 79 cents.[43] Unequal pay affects women across other identities as well, particularly working mothers, who, according to the National Women's Law Center (NWLC), are typically paid 69 cents for every dollar paid to working fathers for full-time, year-round work.[44] Transgender women see their pay fall by nearly a third following their gender transitions, while transgender men see a slight increase.[45]

Factors contributing to the wage gap include discrimination, differences in the types of jobs that women perform, differences in hours worked, availability of paid family and maternal leave, and childbearing.[46] The Pew Research Center found that 42 percent of women report experiencing "discrimination on the job because of their gender."[47] Women's hours and ability to work full-time are also affected by the increased burden of caregiving and home responsibilities.[48] Studies show that women perform approximately twice as much unpaid domestic work daily as men.[49]

Women are more likely to experience career disruptions due to unpaid caregiving responsibilities,[50] illustrating the importance of providing paid family leave. Currently, the Family Medical Leave Act only covers up to twelve weeks of unpaid leave,[51] making the United States one of a few countries without a national paid family leave policy.[52] Some jurisdictions, including California, Massachusetts, New Jersey, Rhode Island, New York, Washington, and Washington, DC, have expanded forms of paid family and parental leave.[53]

In recent years, women have experienced both progress and setbacks in employment rights resulting from legislative changes and administrative decisions. In 2019, the EEOC ruled companies may not discriminate during recruitment in online marketing. Three companies were accused of discriminating against women when using a feature of Facebook marketing that pushed recruitment to only male-identifying Facebook users. After the EEOC ruling, Facebook agreed to change its credit, housing, and marketing advertisement criteria to better prevent discrimination on the basis of sex.[54]

In 2016, the EEOC announced a new transparency rule requiring companies with one hundred or more employees to collect and report data on pay by race, ethnicity, and gender.[55] Reporting was contested and delayed by the Trump administration, but after taking office, President Biden vowed to reinstate it and support legislation to reduce pay inequity. In April 2021, the House of Representatives passed the Paycheck Fairness Act, which would strengthen the Equal Pay Act of 1963 by placing the burden on employers to show that differentials in pay by gender are not a result of discrimination.[56]

The Trump administration rolled back anti-discrimination protections for women in the workplace. In 2017, the Federal Communications Commission (FCC) voted to remove some of the rules that support diversity and competition in broadcast media ownership, undermining access to ownership opportunities for women and people of color. In 2019, the Centers for Medicare and Medicaid Services (CMS) issued a rule preventing homecare workers from using a payroll deduction to pay union dues and benefits.[57] Since most homecare workers are women of color, this rule had a disproportionate racial and gendered impact.

The coronavirus outbreak disproportionately affected women in vulnerable front-line occupations. According to a *New York Times* analysis, women hold nearly 90 percent of nursing and other health support positions, as well as 66 percent of jobs at grocery stores and fast-food counters, and "nonwhite women are more likely to be doing essential jobs than anyone else."[58] Women were also more likely to bear the burden of unpaid caregiving during the pandemic, reducing their ability to hold full-time employment.[59] According to the National Women's Law Center, at the beginning of 2021, more than 2.3 million women had left the workforce since the start of the pandemic. The effects were particularly pronounced on women of color, with about 20 percent of Black and Latinx American women experiencing food insecurity and 30 percent being late on rent.[60]

Women and Anti-Poverty Assistance

American women are 35 percent more likely to live in poverty than men,[61] and are more likely to head single-parent households.[62] This data highlights the importance of applying a gendered lens when designing and altering anti-poverty programs. Women are more likely than men to apply for assistance under anti-poverty programs such as the Supplemental Nutrition Assistance Program (SNAP). Nationwide, 63 percent of SNAP recipients are women. White women make up 35.7 percent of the total, while African Americans and Hispanics are 25.1 percent and 16.7 percent, respectively.[63]

In 2018, President Trump signed an executive order directing agencies to increase work requirements for federal assistance programs.[64] After lawsuits by several states, a federal judge prevented the rule from going into effect in light of the coronavirus pandemic.[65] In April 2021, President Biden dropped the government's opposition to the lawsuit and rescinded the rule changes, which resulted in more than $1 billion in additional aid to 25 million low-income families.[66]

In response to the economic hardship brought about by the pandemic, President Biden worked with Congress in early 2021 to pass the American Rescue Plan Act (ARPA) through budget reconciliation on a party-line vote. The plan earmarked $1.9 trillion for economic stimulus, including provisions that benefited low-income women and families. For example, the plan increased the amount of the Child Tax Credit to $3,000 per child ($3,600 for younger children), and instituted monthly credit payments starting in July 2021. The White House estimated that this expansion would lift 4.1 million children above the poverty line and reduce child poverty by 40 percent. The plan also increased the amount of the Earned Income Tax Credit (EITC), which disproportionately benefits low-income women of color, and included direct funding for childcare and increases in tax credits for childcare expenses.[67]

Women and Health Care

Leyila,[68] a working single mother from rural Kansas, is at high risk of experiencing an aggressive form of uterine cancer. She has had difficulty obtaining health care access and affording the preventive screenings essential for early detection. Lacking health insurance, "she struggles to feed and clothe her two children, making the extra expense of a doctor's visit nearly unsustainable." She has not had a screening in five years because of the cost and distance from a federally subsidized health clinic.[69] Leyila is among millions of low-income women who struggle to access and afford health care. Compared to men, a higher share of women forgo health care because of cost barriers.[70]

Women experience additional barriers beyond cost in accessing health care. Women in the LGBTQ community report being denied medical treatment and experiencing disrespect when seeking medical aid.[71] Black women tend to receive "lower-quality health services, including for cancer, HIV, prenatal care and preventive care."[72] Women living in rural communities often have to travel long distances to receive medical care.[73]

Leyila's struggles highlight the importance of legislation such as Title X of the Public Health Service Act, which funds preventive health services. The program requires that priority is given to patients from low-income families.[74] While Title X improves health access and affordability for many low-income women and families, it has become a target of partisan conflict around women's health, particularly in terms of reproductive freedom. These partisan debates significantly influence health care access and affordability for low-income women to services including contraception, medically safe abortion, and maternal mortality.

The United States has one of the highest maternal mortality rates among industrialized nations. According to the Centers for Disease Control and Prevention (CDC), "the majority of lives lost—approximately three out of five—could have been saved if the mothers had access to better medical care."[75] Maternal mortality is also an area of significant racial disparity, with Black women 3.3 times more likely and Native women 2.5 times more likely to die a pregnancy-related death than White women.[76] In response to these statistics, Congress in 2018 passed the Preventing Maternal Deaths Act, which sought to improve national data collection on this issue and enable agencies to increase efforts to reduce the maternal mortality rate.[77]

On a more general level, the Affordable Care Act (ACA) increased women's access to health care services in several key ways. The ACA reduced insurance costs for low-income households[78] and also expanded Medicaid eligibility. After the enactment of the ACA, an additional 20.4 million women were able to access preventive care, and the uninsured rate for women fell by 39 percent. Notably, the ACA reduced gender-related health care barriers including higher premiums and preclusion from insurance due to preexisting issues like pregnancy, infertility, or chronic health conditions due to sexual violence.[79]

The ACA included a contraceptive coverage mandate, which required most private health insurers to cover contraceptive costs.[80] In addition to individual benefits, contraceptive access has been shown to increase the number of women in the workforce.[81] It also reduces reliance on public assistance, decreases the number of children born into poverty, and narrows the pay gap.[82]

The contraceptive coverage mandate in the ACA raised the question of whether employers should be required to provide contraceptive coverage if doing so was contrary to their religious beliefs. In the 2014 case *Burwell v. Hobby Lobby Stores Inc.*, this issue reached the Supreme Court, which ruled 5–4 in favor of a religious exemption for the employer.[83] In 2020, the Trump administration expanded the types of institutions that can file for "religious exemption" or "moral objection" under the ACA to include nonprofits, for-profit entities that do not have publicly traded ownership interests, higher education institutions, health insurance issuers, and in certain cases, individuals.[84] This change allowed qualifying employers to exclude contraceptive and sterilization coverage in their health insurance plans. Groups claiming exemption were not required to apply,[85] making it more difficult to ensure the exemption is not misused and impacting women's health and society more broadly. President Biden has stated that his administration will rescind the exemptions to the ACA contraceptive mandate.[86]

Title X of the Public Health Service Act has long played an essential role in health care access for millions of low-income families.[87] One of Title X's biggest providers has been Planned Parenthood, which until 2019 served 40 percent of Title X patients, and in some states was the only provider of such services.[88] The religious right has opposed federal funding for Planned Parenthood because some clinics provide medically safe abortions.[89] In 2019 the Trump administration issued rules restricting Title X funding from being used to promote, make referrals for, or support medically safe abortion. This substantially impacted Planned Parenthood, which chose to withdraw from Title X rather than follow the new regulations.[90] In states where Planned Parenthood was the only Title X recipient, the group's decision to withdraw meant the state would no longer receive Title X funding. An estimated 876 clinics closed nationally following this change, reducing health care access for many low-income families and women.[91] In April 2021, President Biden announced plans to rescind the Trump rule by fall 2021.[92] In addition, ARPA earmarked $50 million for Title X's family planning funding, with no restrictions on abortion services.[93]

According to a 2019 Pew Research Center poll, 70 percent of Americans are opposed to overturning *Roe v. Wade* and 61 percent believe abortion should be legal in all or most cases. In addition, 59 percent of Americans express greater concern that some states are making abortion too difficult to obtain, as opposed to 39 percent concerned that states are making it too easy.[94] The general state legislative trend, however, has been to increase restrictions on access to abortions. According to a report by the Alan Guttmacher Institute, states enacted fifty-nine abortion restrictions in 2020, in contrast to thirty-five laws to expand or protect abortion.[95]

Among the new restrictions passed are laws that ban abortion in all or most circumstances. As noted by the *Journal of the American Medical Association,* "statutes often fail to grant exceptions for rape or incest, or for the woman's physical and mental health."[96] States have enacted restrictions on gestational age, type of procedure, or rationale for the abortion.[97] Some states have included new criminal penalties for physicians and patients.[98] The courts have struck down or enjoined many of these restrictions from going into effect, but these efforts illustrate repeated efforts to overturn legislation and Supreme Court decisions establishing women's rights to a medically safe abortion. These efforts are coming to a head as the Supreme Court considers the constitutionality of state legislation effectively overturning or drastically restricting women's reproductive rights. A notable exception that expands reproductive rights occurred in 2019 at the state judicial level in Kansas, where the state supreme court issued a ruling to guarantee access to medically safe abortion under the state constitution. The court's ruling was based on the right to personal autonomy guaranteed by the Kansas Constitution's Bill of Rights.[99]

Women and Domestic Violence

Approximately 80 percent of domestic violence survivors are women.[100] They often experience severe consequences, harming their health and well-being as well as that of other household members. According to the CDC, approximately 41 percent of female victims and 14 percent of male victims of intimate partner violence (IPV) experience physical injuries.[101]

Measuring domestic violence is difficult because these acts are underreported due to the highly personal nature of the crime. Among the reasons why someone may not report domestic violence are fear of further violence, fear of having one's sexual identity exposed, a history of abuse, shame, financial dependence, psychological manipulation, cultural or religious beliefs, language barriers, immigration concerns, children, and love.[102] The experience of sexual and other forms of domestic violence varies depending on a woman's identity in relation to the dominant culture, which may also influence whether victims choose to report domestic violence.[103] For example, a Black woman "may fear that calling the police will subject their partners to racist treatment by the criminal justice system."[104] For undocumented female immigrants, the fear of deportation or family separation may similarly prevent reporting.[105]

Of the relatively few domestic violence incidents that are reported to the police, 67 percent were committed by a relative, and 54 percent were committed by an intimate partner.[106] Despite the lack of reporting, statistics show women from certain demographic groups experience higher rates of violence, especially from their intimate partners. Multiracial, Native American, and Black women reported higher rates of IPV, including sexual violence, physical violence, and/or stalking.[107] According to the American Psychological Association, women with disabilities have a 40 percent higher rate of IPV.[108] For female immigrants, domestic violence rates are as high as 49.8 percent.[109] Rates of IPV are also higher within the LGBTQ community, with 43.8 percent of lesbian women and 61.1 percent of bisexual women having experienced IPV and/or stalking, compared to 35 percent of heterosexual women.[110] The *Journal of Women's Health* found that women living in small rural towns reported IPV at a rate of 22.5 percent, compared to 15.5 percent for women living in urban and suburban areas.[111]

Federal and state criminal law against domestic violence has been strengthened over the last four decades. In 1984, Congress passed the Family Violence Prevention and Services Act (FVPSA), which funded support services and shelters for victims of domestic violence and their children.[112] Two years later, Congress passed the Federal Sexual Abuse Act, which "criminalized marital rape on all federal lands." By 1993, every state had some type of marital rape law on record,[113] although seventeen states still have exemptions that define rape narrowly.[114] In 1994, Congress passed the Violence Against Women Act (VAWA), providing increased protections and federal funding for programs serving victims of domestic violence.[115] The 2013 VAWA Reauthorization included new protections for lesbians, immigrants, and Native American women assaulted by non-tribal residents while on tribal lands.[116]

VAWA expired on February 15, 2019.[117] That same year, the House passed a new version of the law with bipartisan support, but it was blocked in the Senate, primarily because of a provision that allowed law enforcement to take away the guns of domestic abusers.[118] According to the *American Journal of Public Health,* women are five times more likely to be murdered in domestic violence situations when abusers have access to a gun.[119] Gun rights advocates, however, opposed the bill, arguing that "the new provision is 'too broad and ripe for abuse.'"[120] With support from President Biden, the House once again passed a VAWA reauthorization bill in March 2021.[121]

Women and Educational Institutions

In the past two decades, sex- and gender-based harassment and assault have received increased attention in educational institutions, particularly on college campuses. According to the 2019 Association of American Universities Survey on Sexual Assault and Misconduct (AAU Survey), 25.9 percent of female undergraduates report experiencing "nonconsensual sexual contact by physical force or inability to consent or stop what was happening," compared to 6.8 percent for male undergraduates. In addition, 59.2 percent of women reported experiencing sexual harassment, compared to 36.2 percent of men,[122] highlighting the gendered nature of these issues, as well as the frequency with which these incidents occur at higher educational institutions.

Title IX of the Education Amendments Act prohibits discrimination on the basis of sex in "any education program or activity receiving Federal financial assistance."[123] The Clery Act further requires higher education institutions to publish policies and data on campus crimes.[124] As a result, schools receiving federal funds are required to have procedures for addressing sex- and gender-based harassment and assault, and to report statistics on sexual assault and harassment on campus.[125]

A school-based process and data transparency requirements offer some benefits for victims. First, unlike the police, schools are legally required to adjudicate and respond to every student report.[126] They are also able to respond more quickly and implement accommodations including mental and sexual health support and dorm transfers. Victims may also be more comfortable with using college processes than reporting incidents to the police, due to mistrust in the justice system, self-blame, fear of the accused, and shame. A report from the Center for Public Integrity (CPI) on campus sexual assaults found that while most victims report to their schools, "95 percent do not end up reporting the incident to the police."[127]

The federal government has gone back and forth on regulations defining sexual harassment. In 2011, the Obama administration published a letter expanding the definition of sexual and gender-based harassment under Title IX, shifting the standard of evidence from "clear and convincing evidence" to a lower "preponderance of evidence."[128] In 2017, the Trump administration's Department of Education (DOE) withdrew the 2011 guidelines and announced a new rulemaking process, releasing its final rules in May 2020.[129] The new rules significantly altered how schools handle accusations of sexual harassment and assault. Some of the specific changes included redefining criteria for sexual harassment more narrowly, requiring schools to allow a third-party cross-examination of the complainant and the respondent during a live hearing, and allowing schools to choose between the "preponderance of evidence" standard and the "clear and convincing" standard.[130] In response, attorneys general from eighteen states filed lawsuits against the DOE to block the changes. In the spring of 2021, President Biden directed the DOE to review the policies with the aim of revising them.[131]

Gender equity in higher education also involves big questions around gender disparities in science, engineering, and math training, laboratory work, and the retention of staff and faculty, with hostile work environment, lack of institutional support, and pressures related to family duties as major causes of continuing inequity.

Women and Civil Society Movements

Historically, civil society movements have spurred women's rights successes, including voter enfranchisement and increased protections in the workplace, education, and other settings. One of the recent driving forces to advance women's rights has been the rise of new social activism, including a renewed effort to ratify the constitutional Equal Rights Amendment (ERA) and the #MeToo movement against sexual violence and harassment.

Many women's rights advocates believe that adding the ERA to the Constitution would establish universal equality on the basis of sex and protect against the rollback of federal protections for women's rights.[132] ERA proponents argue that it could help eliminate pay inequality and discrimination and advance other positive developments in areas such as domestic violence and sexual harassment and protection against discrimination based on pregnancy.[133] ERA opponents argue that current U.S. law is sufficient for protecting gender equality,[134] and cite concerns that the ERA could threaten family structures, render restrictions on abortion procedures unconstitutional, and encroach upon religious beliefs.[135]

By 1982, thirty-five states had ratified the ERA, three short of the thirty-eight required for ratification. In the following years, Tennessee, Nebraska, Kentucky, Idaho, and South Dakota rescinded their ratification, reducing the number of approvals to thirty. Meanwhile, Nevada (2017), Illinois (2018), and Virginia (2020) added their ratifications, bring the approvals to thirty-three. Based on a precedent set after the Civil War, when states were not permitted to rescind ratification of the Fourteenth and Fifteenth Amendments, ERA proponents argue that states cannot rescind ratification, and that therefore the number of state ratifications has reached the required thirty-eight. At the same time, Alabama, Louisiana, and South Dakota are suing to block

Women's Equal Rights Parade, 1977. Photo by Warren K. Leffler and Thomas J. O'Halloran via Library of Congress.

the ERA's certification on the basis that the ratification deadline has passed.[136] In response, the House of Representatives passed a bill in 2020 removing the earlier deadline.[137] In January 2021, the Senate introduced a similar measure, co-sponsored by Democratic senator Ben Cardin and Republican senator Lisa Murkowski.[138]

On January 21, 2017, activists across the globe held the first Women's March as a response to the anti-women's-rights rhetoric of the 2016 U.S. presidential campaign. Organizers held the event the day after Donald Trump's presidential inauguration "to tell the new administration that on Day 1, 'women's rights are human rights.'" Millions of women peacefully demonstrated in multiple cities in January 2017, followed by smaller protests throughout the year.[139]

In 2006, the #MeToo movement was founded by Tarana Burke to support low-income and people of color who are victims of sexual abuse. The movement sparked national activism in the wake of sexual harassment and assault allegations against film producer Harvey Weinstein, who was found guilty of criminal sexual assault and rape in 2020.[140] As a result of the attention focused on high-profile figures accused of sexual misconduct, the movement gained a broad audience, with millions of women sharing their experiences of sexual assault and harassment in their personal lives and the workplace.[141] According to the NWLC, in the years since #MeToo was launched nineteen states and New York City have passed laws on workplace harassment, sexual harassment, and assault.[142]

The recent role of Black women in voter education, registration, and mobilizing, as well as in other social movements surrounding police abuse and violence and immigration justice, underscores the importance of intersectional lenses in advancing women's rights.

The ongoing struggle for women's rights aims to move the United States to a future where women receive equal pay for their work, have access to affordable health care, are safe from sexual violence and harassment, and have equal rights legally guaranteed by the U.S. Constitution.

Policy Recommendations

- **Strengthen Women's Rights in the Workplace.** Establish childcare for working parents, protect pregnant workers from discrimination, and provide three-month paid parental leave. In addition, mandate fair pay and pay equity, include low-wage workers and domestic workers under minimum wage laws, and prohibit government contractors from firing employees whose identities or choices do not conform to the employer's religious views.

- **Expand Women's Access to Anti-Poverty Assistance.** Abolish work requirements and expand eligibility and funding for federal anti-poverty assistance programs. Permanently expand Child Tax Credit eligibility so that single mothers living in poverty can access benefits.

- **Protect Women's Access to Health Care.** Guarantee women's right to choose when to bear children, protect access to contraceptive services and medically safe abortion services, expand pregnancy coverage in federal health insurance programs, and provide federal funding for programs to decrease preventable maternal deaths.

- **Expand Protection Against Sexual Violence and Harassment.** Define "sexual harassment" as "unwelcome conduct of a sexual nature," amend the Violence Against Women Act to include provision expressly banning marital rape in federal law, and update the legislative definition of "sex" to include people who are transgender or gay.

- **Ratify the Equal Rights Amendment.** Complete the process of amending the Constitution to affirm that "equality of rights shall not be denied or abridged on account of sex." The Equal Rights Amendment would ensure that women's rights have full constitutional protection and cannot be curtailed by judicial, legislative, or administrative decisions.

- **Ratify the International Convention on the Elimination of All Forms of Discrimination Against Women.** The Convention is the international counterpart to the Equal Rights Amendment. It has been signed but not yet ratified by the United States.

6

Living Queer History:
The Fight for LGBTQ Rights

TIMOTHY PATRICK MCCARTHY*

Queer people have always been here—since antiquity, they have lived across communities and intersections of every class, color, creed, condition, and country. Lesbian, gay, bisexual, transgender, and queer (LGBTQ) people have often been victims of personal prejudice, social and cultural stigma, and legal and political discrimination.[1] This has certainly been the case in the modern era, the same time that "human rights" has gained currency and frequency as a rallying cry for various struggles and peoples seeking freedom, equality, and justice. That is not a coincidence: as the formal infrastructure of human rights *and* state-sanctioned homophobia expanded simultaneously in the middle of the twentieth century, so, too, did the modern movement for LGBTQ+ rights in the United States first emerge.[2] This "paradox of progress"—the persistent battle between progress and prejudice—is a key characteristic of the history of social justice movements, including those for queer liberation and rights.[3]

During this time, major advances in LGBTQ rights have been driven principally by queer people themselves—with the help of key allies—through community organizing, institution-building, and resource mobilization. Both major U.S. political parties—Democrats *and* Republicans—have long histories of advancing policies that are hostile to LGBTQ people and their rights,

---

*Lecturer on education at the Harvard Graduate School of Education; award-winning historian, educator, and activist; New Press books include *The Radical Reader* and *The Indispensable Zinn*.

and only recently have Democrats begun to more fully embrace what could be called a pro-LGBTQ agenda.

In the meantime, LGBTQ people have created change through a combination of "outside" politics—cultural work, public advocacy, and protest—that has changed over time, and "inside politics"—advocacy in legal, legislative, and electoral realms. The latter strategy, while increasingly successful, has also led to certain compromises that sometimes privilege the already relatively privileged in the LGBTQ community and further marginalize the already marginalized.

GENERATIONS OF QUEER RIGHTS

In 1948, groundbreaking sexologist Alfred Kinsey published *Sexual Behavior in the Human Male*, his then-controversial study that found that 4 percent of men identify as "homosexual" while 37 percent engaged in at least one "homosexual act."[4] Kinsey's research induced something of a "heterosexual panic" that led to increased efforts to police, punish, and purge gay people. That same year, a group of discharged veterans living in New York City organized the Veterans Benevolent Association (VBA) to provide legal assistance, employment support, and social outlets for gay and lesbian veterans discharged during or immediately after World War II, one of the first LGBTQ organizations in the United States.[5]

While the immediate post-war era was a period of dramatic change in the lives of LGBTQ people, including the proliferation of "homophile" organizations and more public protests, many historians locate the "origin" of what we now call the modern LGBTQ movement in the United States in the Stonewall rebellion that exploded in late June 1969. Since then, there have been three interwoven generations of LGBTQ lived experiences that have profoundly shaped the movement—and vice versa.[6]

- The first is the **Stonewall generation**, encompassing the late 1960s and 1970s, when LGBTQ people became increasingly politicized in the face of more concerted and oppressive forms of discrimination. This was a period marked by protest and pride, when queer people fought back more forcefully against normative constraints on gender and sexuality and came out more fully to celebrate their differences. These were the *politics of liberation.*

- The second is the **AIDS generation**, encompassing the 1980s and 1990s, when LGBTQ life was dominated by the AIDS epidemic. This was a period marked by death and disease, when gay men, especially, were viewed by many in society as "deviant" and "dangerous," a moral and mortal threat to mainstream America. It was also a time when the broader queer community came together to care for each other and mourn with one another and to act up and speak up in the face of the mounting death toll and its root causes. These were the *politics of loss.*

- The third is the **marriage generation**, encompassing the 1990s to the present, when the LGBTQ movement reoriented its work to focus on the struggle for equal rights through more formal, institutional channels. This has been a period marked by appeals to law and legislation, whereby many queer people have sought mainstream acceptance through a process of becoming "normal," most especially around the struggle for military service and marriage equality. These are the *politics of love.*

These three generations constitute somewhat distinct sets of lived experiences for LGBTQ people. Like all histories of "outsider" groups, this is a story about the tensions between rejection and acceptance, pride and prejudice, difference and assimilation, political power and second-class citizenship, the denial of and demand for equal rights.

THE STONEWALL GENERATION

More than fifty years ago, around 1:20 a.m. on June 28, 1969, a group of plainclothes police officers raided the Stonewall Inn, a popular gay bar located on Christopher Street in New York City's West Village. Raids on gay bars were a common practice of surveillance and violence at that time—but this one lit the fire. Lucian Truscott, who covered the Stonewall rebellion for the *Village Voice*, characterized it this way: "The forces of faggotry . . . rallied Saturday night in an unprecedented protest against the raid and continued Sunday

Stonewall Inn. Photo via New York Public
Library Digital Collections.

night to assert presence, possibility, and pride until the early hours of Monday
morning."[7]

Stonewall was hardly the first confrontation between state authority and
LGBTQ citizens. In many ways, however, it was the most spectacular and sustained, involving thousands of ordinary people—diverse in color, class, and
conviction—who participated in six consecutive nights of violent resistance
against police repression and so much else.[8] As the pioneering gay historian
Martin Duberman describes it, "Stonewall is the emblematic event in modern
[queer] history . . . an empowering symbol of global proportions."[9]

THE AIDS GENERATION

For queer people, the 1980s and 1990s were the deadliest of decades, when
the "AIDS plague," as the late Larry Kramer prophetically put it, constituted a
"Holocaust" for gay people.[10] On June 5, 1981, the Centers for Disease Control
and Prevention (CDC) reported that in the period between October 1980 and
May 1981, five homosexual men were treated for a rare combination of symptoms at three different hospitals in Los Angeles. On July 4, 1981, the CDC

reported that twenty-six cases of Kaposi sarcoma had been reported among gay men, with eight fatalities. On July 27, 1982, the term *AIDS*—Acquired Immune Deficiency Syndrome—was used for the first time to describe the growing health crisis.[11]

That year, 463 HIV/AIDS-related deaths were reported, and the crisis only grew over the decade: 1,508 deaths reported in 1983, when HIV was first isolated by French researchers; 3,505 in 1984, when San Francisco closed down the city's bathhouses; 6,972 in 1985, when the Food and Drug Administration (FDA) licensed the first HIV test; 12,110 in 1986, when Ronald Reagan first mentioned AIDS in public; 16,412 in 1987, when AZT, the first drug to treat AIDS, was approved by the FDA at an annual cost of $10,000; 21,119 in 1988, when the AIDS Coalition to Unleash Power (ACT UP) ramped up its radical protests; 27,791 in 1989, when the National Institutes of Health (NIH) finally invited AIDS activists to participate in discussions about research and treatment; and 31,538 in 1990, when Ronald Reagan failed to apologize for his administration's earlier handling of the AIDS epidemic, claiming that "we did all we could at the time" during the two terms of his presidency. The total number of reported deaths that decade was 121,318, and those numbers continued to climb during the 1990s. In 1995, the worst year of the crisis, 54,670 people died of AIDS.[12]

Throughout it all, the CDC was a voice in the wilderness, as most of the medical establishment either dismissed the disease or denigrated its victims. The dean of a leading medical school remarked, according to award-winning writer Randy Shilts, "At least with AIDS, a lot of undesirable people will be eliminated."[13] Reverend Jerry Falwell Sr., co-founder of the Moral Majority and leader of the religious right, which helped promote the rise of the Reagan presidency, often repeated this popular refrain: "AIDS is the wrath of God upon homosexuals."[14]

This toxic climate of professional malpractice, religious mendacity, and political malfeasance led LGBTQ activists to establish their own public health organizations, such as the Gay Men's Health Crisis, Queer Nation, and ACT UP—whose ubiquitous cry "Silence=Death" became a symbol of the age—to occupy the front lines of the increasingly lethal culture war. AIDS was an example of how lethal it can be when prominent academics, religious leaders, political officials, and everyday citizens allow stigma and prejudice to infect their social conscience and public policy.

Co-founder of STAR, Marsha P. Johnson, protesting for gay students at New York University, 1970. Courtesy of the New York Public Library.

ACHIEVEMENTS OF THE MOVEMENT

After centuries of discrimination and abuse, the birth of LGBTQ activism in the twentieth century secured fundamental rights and freedoms for LGBTQ people. In some of these major conflicts and campaigns, LGBTQ people fully achieved their goals, while in others, they achieved partial victories.

The Right to Advocate Freely

In the 1950s, magazines such as *ONE* and *The Ladder* began circulating nationwide, allowing the idea of an LGBTQ movement to reach every state in America. The magazines provided vital and unique resources for a community of people that were in hiding and yet needed to find each other to push forward.[15] A year after a U.S. District Court judge in 1956 ruled that the magazine *ONE* was not mailable because "its filthy and obscene material was obviously calculated to stimulate the lust of the homosexual reader," the U.S. Supreme Court reversed this ruling, sending a powerful message to the nation: homosexuality was not unspeakable.[16] As a result, the case, *One, Inc., v. Olesen*, established that speech regarding homosexuality was constitutionally protected. LGBTQ people gained the right of freedom of expression and, most notably, the right to engage in advocacy.

The Right to Sexual Relations and Intimate Relationships

Until 1963, homosexual relations were criminalized in every state in the United States. Although these laws explicitly banned homosexual sex, their message was much broader, declaring homosexuality immoral and categorizing homosexual relationships as crimes against nature.[17] The federal government used the laws as excuses to deny employment and security clearances to gays and lesbians. LGBTQ people were often denied custody of their children, even when their children were put in danger by separation. The stigmatization of LGBTQ people as criminals served to perpetuate the discrimination that often manifested as an eviction notice, a termination of employment, or a punch in the face.

Repealing these criminal laws took decades of struggle, advocacy, and organizing by LGBTQ activists. In *Bowers v. Hardwick* (1986), the Supreme Court upheld the constitutionality of sodomy laws as a legitimate tool to prevent an "infamous crime against nature" that was "a deeper malignity than rape."[18] Advocacy by LGBTQ rights activists following this decision forced the Court to reimagine sodomy laws as an affront to the constitutional rights of LGBTQ people, reducing the number of state sodomy laws to only thirteen.[19] Finally, in *Lawrence v. Texas* (2003), the Supreme Court declared all sodomy laws in the United States an unconstitutional exercise of authority in regulating morality. Speaking for the majority, Justice Anthony Kennedy stated that "when sexuality finds overt expression in intimate conduct with another person, the conduct can be but one element in a personal bond that is more enduring." His words signaled to the nation the legitimacy of homosexual relationships and affection and enshrined the right of LGBTQ families to be acknowledged and respected equally under the law.[20]

The Right to Same-Sex Marriage

In 1970, Richard Baker and James McConnell were denied a marriage license when the Minnesota Supreme Court ruled they were unable to marry because they were of the same sex.[21] On appeal, the U.S. Supreme Court ruled that because marriage was an institution regulated by the states, there was no federal standing for an appeal, thus throwing the fight to the state level.[22] After decades of activism, legal recognition of same-sex couples began with domestic partnership rights in San Francisco (1989) and Washington, DC (1992), and a Hawaii Supreme Court ruling (1993) that denying same-sex couples marriage rights violated the Equal Protection Clause of the Fourteenth Amendment.[23] The national backlash was swift. Congress passed the Defense of Marriage Act (DOMA) to deny same-sex couples federal benefits, signed into law by President Bill Clinton in 1996. Two years later, voters in Hawaii approved a state constitutional amendment banning same-sex marriages.

The debate began to shift in 2003, when the Massachusetts Supreme Court legalized same-sex marriage in *Goodridge v. Department of Public Health*, and activists and organizers mounted a successful campaign to prevent the legislature from rolling back the ruling. Despite a backlash, in which eighteen states passed bans on gay marriage, LGBTQ activists began to turn the tide from 2008 to 2012, winning marriage equality in ten states and Washington, DC. After winning reelection in 2012, President Obama became the first sitting president to announce his support for same-sex marriage. In 2013, the U.S. Supreme Court ruled DOMA unconstitutional and then with *Obergefell v. Hodges* in 2015 the Supreme Court ruled that all bans on same-sex marriage were unconstitutional, effectively making gay marriage legal throughout the United States.[24]

The right to same-sex marriage extends far beyond the legal benefits that the institution provides, since those rights could have been granted through civil unions and other domestic partnership rights. The right that is acknowledged in marriage is the "status that everyone understands as the ultimate expression of love and commitment."[25] In their decision, the Supreme Court sent a powerful moral signal of inclusion of gays and lesbians in society, recognizing the "equal dignity" of same-sex relationships.[26]

The Right of LGBTQ People to Immigrate to the United States

Until 1990, the United States was the only country in the world that excluded visitors and potential migrants because of their sexual orientation. A provision in the Immigration and Nationality Act of 1952 allowed the U.S. government to deny immigration rights to people afflicted with a "psychopathic person-

ality." The term was used to deport, deny naturalization, and prohibit entry into the country for countless LGBTQ people. When the Immigration and Nationality Act was updated with a package of immigration reforms in 1990, gay activists mobilized their allies in Congress and the ban was removed.[27] After the Supreme Court declared DOMA unconstitutional in 2013, U.S. citizens and permanent residents further gained the ability to petition to adjust immigration status for their same-sex spouses.[28]

The Right to Be Protected from Identity-Based Police Harassment

For much of the twentieth century, the police were the LGBTQ community's most harmful foe.[29] Entrapment and witch hunts of gay people were dangerous police tactics that destroyed the lives of many LGBTQ people. Plainclothes officers would often frequent gay establishments and cruising places to lure gay men into propositioning them, swiftly leading to an arrest. If such an arrest was made public, it was almost certain that these men would lose not only their jobs but also the love and support of their families.[30]

The 1969 riots at the Stonewall Inn were a direct reaction to abusive policing against LGBTQ people in New York City, in turn inspiring a new generation of groups such as the Gay Liberation Front (GLF) and the Gay Activists Alliance (GAA), which achieved remarkable success in ending entrapment and raid practices throughout the 1970s, 1980s, and 1990s. As police harassment of white LGBTQ people diminished during that time, bar raids and entrapment have largely become practices of the past. Nevertheless, police harassment of LGBTQ people continues to disproportionately affect transgender people of color, who police often profile as sex workers. A 2014 study from Columbia University found that LGBTQ youth of color are "endemically profiled as being engaged in sex work, public lewdness, or other sexual offenses."[31]

The Right to Be Protected from HIV/AIDS

The U.S. government has made substantial investments starting in 1990 to protect the country from HIV/AIDS.[32] Enraged by the silence and indifference of the federal government throughout the 1980s, ACT UP and other activist groups were relentless in bringing public attention to the epidemic, staging "die-ins" at the New York Stock Exchange and the FDA, coupled with strategic outreach to leaders and doctors in the field. Their activism transformed the way that HIV/AIDS research was being conducted, winning access to experimental treatments and succeeding in pushing the government to mount the counteroffensive against HIV/AIDS.[33]

Passed in 1990, the Ryan White CARE Act established programs that provide HIV/AIDS treatment to low-income, uninsured, and underinsured people.[34] The first National HIV/AIDS Strategy was released in 2010 and focused on reducing HIV infections, improving health outcomes of people living with HIV/AIDS, and addressing HIV-related inequities.[35] In February 2020, the Trump administration launched a new initiative to reduce new HIV infections by 90 percent by 2030.[36] In April 2021, Joe Biden declared an additional $267 million in funding for AIDS research and prevention as part of his 2022 budget request, after campaigning on the goal of eliminating the epidemic entirely by 2025.[37]

The Right to Participate in Political Life

According to the Victory Institute's Out for America project, there were 992 openly LGBTQ elected officials in the United States as of May 2021, composing 0.19 percent of total elected officials nationwide; this list includes two governors, eleven members of Congress, fifty-five mayors, and 593 local officials. Expansion of LGBTQ rights has been almost entirely championed by the Democratic Party; out of all the politicians Victory Institute identified, 73 percent are Democrats, and 3 percent are Republicans.[38] The inclusion of LGBTQ people in American politics was a hard-fought victory; before the energized activism of the 1970s, LGBTQ people were considered the "untouchables of society."[39] In 1974, Kathy Kozachenko became the first openly gay or lesbian person to become an elected official in the United States by winning a spot in the Ann Arbor City Council.[40]

President Bill Clinton was the first president to appoint openly LGBTQ people to serve in the federal government, totaling up to 140 openly LGBTQ appointees during his two terms. After hundreds of further LGBTQ appointments by George W. Bush and Barack Obama,[41] Donald Trump became the first president to appoint an openly LGBTQ person to a cabinet-level position by tapping Richard Grenell as Acting Director of National Intelligence.[42] In 2020, Pete Buttigieg became the first openly LGBTQ person to win a primary contest for the presidential nomination in the Iowa caucuses, and was later appointed as Joe Biden's Secretary of Transportation, the highest-profile appointment of an LGBTQ person to date.[43] Biden also appointed Rachel Levine Assistant Secretary of Health, the first openly transgender person to win approval of the U.S. Senate.[44] Despite the gains in this area, LGBTQ individuals still face underrepresentation in the political system. By 2020, no openly transgender person has served as a member of Congress. No openly LGBTQ person has served as a justice of the Supreme Court, or as vice president or president.

The Right to Be Protected Against Discrimination

After decades of activism to pass nondiscrimination ordinances, a landmark 1996 Supreme Court case, *Romer v. Evans,* overturned an amendment to the Colorado state constitution that prevented gays, lesbians, and bisexual people from being protected by such laws. Writing for the majority, Justice Anthony Kennedy stated that the amendment served no purpose except animosity against a class of people, with the intended purpose to "make them unequal to everyone else."[45]

Currently, twenty-two states and Washington, DC, protect LGBTQ people on the basis of both sexual orientation and gender identity; Wisconsin's nondiscrimination law includes sexual orientation but excludes transgender protections. Meanwhile, twenty-two states cover domains such as employment, housing, and public accommodations. Across the country, some jurisdictions have also included protections in credit and education.[46] Despite numerous attempts, however, a federal law to protect LGBTQ people nationwide has yet to be enacted.[47]

The Right to Be Protected from Hate Crimes

On October 28, 2009, President Barack Obama signed into law the Matthew Shepard and James Byrd Jr. Hate Crimes Prevention Act, which expanded the 1969 federal hate crimes law to include crimes based on bias against the victim's gender, sexual orientation, gender identity, or disability. The law provides funding and federal assistance to state, local, and tribal jurisdictions to investigate and prosecute hate crimes,[48] and sends a clear signal that crimes against LGBTQ people must be brought to justice.

The Right to Be Free from Stigma of Mental Illness
and Protected from Conversion Therapy

In the United States, homosexuality and gender dysphoria are no longer medically classified as mental illnesses; the American Psychiatric Association (APA) removed those associations from the Diagnostic and Statistical Manual of Mental Disorders (DSM) in 1973 and 2012, respectively.[49] Similarly, so-called conversion therapy that attempts to change a person's sexual orientation or gender identity through psychological or spiritual intervention has been banned in twenty states, and partially in North Carolina, where it is banned for youth.[50] Nonetheless, today twenty-nine states still allow such practices.

The Right to Serve Openly in the Military

Today, openly gay, lesbian, and bisexual people can serve in the military without fear of expulsion. In his 1992 campaign, Bill Clinton promised to let gay Americans serve openly in the military. Once in office, however, he received fierce opposition to removing the ban by the Chairman of the Joint Chiefs of Staff, Colin Powell. In 1993, a compromise between Powell and President Clinton resulted in "Don't Ask, Don't Tell," a policy that allowed gay Americans to serve so long as they did so in the closet. The new policy, however, continued the discriminatory persecution of LGBTQ people. By 2009, thirteen thousand LGBTQ people had been expelled from the military under the policy, which stayed in place until its repeal in 2011 by President Barack Obama. In 2016, Secretary of Defense Ashton Carter extended the repeal to transgender Americans, but President Trump announced after he took office that the military would no longer allow transgender people to serve.[51] In January 2021 President Biden signed an executive order allowing transgender people to serve openly in the military under their self-identified gender, with full protection against discrimination.[52]

The Right to LGBTQ-Inclusive Education

In July 2020, Illinois became the fourth state to require schools to teach about LGBTQ history and contributions of LGBTQ people to other areas of study; California, New Jersey, and Colorado previously adopted similar laws. The first law of this kind to pass in the nation was the FAIR Education Law in California, signed by Governor Jerry Brown in 2011.[53] The exclusion of LGBTQ history from school textbooks is a symptom of longstanding discrimination against LGBTQ people, robbing them of their history and heroes. Fewer than 25 percent of U.S. students learn about LGBTQ-related topics in school. Six states have laws barring LGBTQ education in the classroom.[54]

CURRENT STRUGGLES

Despite legal, social, and political progress over the last fifty years, the struggle for LGBTQ rights in the United States remains an ongoing and contested project. To this day, nearly two-thirds of LGBTQ residents across the country have reported experiences of discrimination.[55] At the same time, a wide range of laws and policies (or a lack thereof) continue to restrict the civil rights of LGBTQ communities. Even though LGBTQ advocates have registered significant achievements, such as same-sex marriage and the decriminalization of homosexuality, there is a deficit of robust federal policies supporting LGBTQ equality. States, cities, and towns have become battlegrounds for progress, leaving some LGBTQ people with fewer rights than others simply as a result of their zip code.[56]

Certain subpopulations of LGBTQ people are uniquely vulnerable to the current lack of protections and face additional and distinct barriers to equality.[57] LGBTQ people of color, undocumented LGBTQ people, low-income LGBTQ people, and LGBTQ people living with disabilities face intersecting forms of discrimination that further threaten their health and well-being. Additionally, as LGBTQ rights have advanced over the last century, they have faced pushback from conservative leaders and religious communities, who often cite federal overreach, religious freedom, and the exercise of free speech as the basis for repealing or precluding LGBTQ rights.

Recently, vestiges of stigma and age-old anti-LGBTQ arguments, such as concerns about LGBTQ adults harming children, have been reinvigorated, especially levelled against transgender and nonbinary communities, as rights for these communities have gained more visibility. While transgender and nonbinary communities carry a long legacy of advocacy and activism, these communities have at times been left out of mainstream LGBTQ organizing. A notable example of such exclusion occurred in 2007, when a weakened version of the

Employment Non-Discrimination Act, including protections based on sexual orientation but not gender identity, was introduced in hopes that narrowing its scope would make it more likely to pass Congress. Some LGBTQ advocacy organizations saw the move as a necessary short-term concession that would precede a fully inclusive bill once the political timing was right. Other organizations decried the move as leaving behind transgender and nonbinary communities.[58]

Nondiscrimination

LGBTQ people are not protected from discrimination at the federal level or in most states. Only twenty-three states and Washington, DC, explicitly include sexual orientation or gender identity or both as protected characteristics in their nondiscrimination statutes. Further, these statutes vary widely in what they cover. The Williams Institute recently estimated that nearly half of all LGBTQ people in the United States lack protections from discrimination in employment, education, housing, public accommodations, and credit—roughly 6.5 million people.[59]

Even though there is bipartisan support for LGBTQ nondiscrimination protections,[60] the Equality Act—a bill updating the Civil Rights Act to prohibit discrimination based on sex, sexual orientation, and gender identity—has failed to pass Congress each year since it was introduced in 1974.[61] In 2021, the bill passed the U.S. House of Representatives on a mostly party-line vote of 224–206, but it has not been taken up by the Senate.[62] LGBTQ nondiscrimination protections have been threatened at the state and local levels. In 2015, Houston, Texas, voters defeated a local ordinance that would introduce nondiscrimination protections based on fifteen different protected characteristics, including sexual orientation and gender identity.[63]

Particularly controversial has been the right of transgender people to use public restrooms according to their gender. In 2016, North Carolina's House Bill 2 (HB 2) became the first state law to address restroom access for transgender people. The law required individuals to use restrooms that aligned with their sex assigned at birth and was a direct reaction to a Charlotte City Council Ordinance 7056, which allowed individuals to use the restroom that corresponded to their gender identity. HB 2 was ultimately repealed after a national outcry from LGBTQ rights advocates and allies, including a letter from the Obama administration Department of Justice indicating it breached a number of federal civil rights laws.[64] Other jurisdictions, however, have attempted to pass such "bathroom bills." Massachusetts attempted in 2018 to repeal gender-identity protections, but gender identity was ultimately protected within the state's broader nondiscrimination law.[65]

Opponents of nondiscrimination protections often rely on fear-based arguments, asserting that these bills would allow men to enter women's restrooms and assault women and girls. This argument has been extensively debunked by studies. For example, a 2018 study comparing localities in Massachusetts with and without transgender public accommodation ordinances found no link between the ordinances and reported incidences of sexual assault; in fact, the incidence of sexual assault in bathrooms was "exceedingly rare."[66] In another study, one in four transgender youth reported being sexually assaulted in the past year, with transgender youth more likely to experience sexual assault when using bathrooms according to their sex assigned at birth rather than their sexual identity.[67]

A lack of public accommodation protections has been shown to have a negative impact on the mental and physical health of transgender individuals. According to the 2015 U.S. Transgender Survey conducted by the National Center for Transgender Equality, 59 percent of transgender people avoided using a public restroom in the previous year for fear of discrimination, and nearly one-third (32 percent) limited the amount they ate and drank in order to do so.[68] Despite bipartisan support for LGBTQ nondiscrimination protections more broadly, there is a vast partisan divide when it comes to "bathroom bills"; 59 percent of Republicans are in favor of bills that require transgender individuals to use bathrooms that correspond with their sex assigned at birth, while only 30 percent of Democrats favor such bills.[69]

In 2017, a conflict between nondiscrimination and religious freedom was thrust onto the national stage in a Supreme Court case, *Masterpiece Cakeshop Ltd. v. Colorado Civil Rights Commission.* The owner of Masterpiece Cakeshop had refused to design and bake a cake for a gay couple, claiming that doing so violated his religious beliefs,[70] and the Supreme Court ruled in favor of the baker. Polling data show that Americans are closely divided on the use of religious grounds as a basis for LGBTQ discrimination.[71]

Employment

LGBTQ people in the United States are not uniformly protected from employment discrimination. Only twenty-two states explicitly prohibit discrimination on the basis of sexual orientation and gender identity in their state employment nondiscrimination laws.[72] In the other twenty-eight states, it is legal to fire a worker because of LGBTQ status. Data show the extensive effects of LGBTQ discrimination in the workplace. Sixteen percent of LGBTQ workers have reported losing a job because of their sexuality, gender identity, or gender expression. In addition, 18 percent of LGB people and 30 percent of transgender people have reported being denied jobs or promotions due to their LGBTQ status.[73]

During the Obama administration, the Department of Justice issued guidelines that expressly interpreted gender identity as falling within sex discrimination under Title VII.[74] In October 2017, however, the Trump administration released a memo reversing an Obama-era interpretation of Title VII of the Civil Rights Act of 1964, removing a barrier to potential discrimination against transgender employees.[75] In August 2018, the Department of Labor issued a directive exempting contractors from federal nondiscrimination laws if they conflict with their religious beliefs.[76]

In June 2020, the Supreme Court gave a major victory to LGBTQ rights when it ruled in *Bostock v. Clayton County* that sexual orientation and gender identity are protected under existing federal laws prohibiting sex discrimination.[77] In a 6–3 decision, the Court held that gender and sexual identity were included in the Civil Rights Act ban on discrimination in employment based on sex. Writing for the majority, Justice Neil Gorsuch observed that it was "impossible to discriminate against a person for being homosexual or transgender without discriminating . . . based on sex." On his first day in office, President Biden signed an executive order implementing the decision across the federal government.

LGBTQ YOUTH

LGBTQ youth are more likely to face adverse social outcomes than their non-LGBTQ peers. The 2016 Youth Risk Behavior Survey[78] found LGB youth are almost three times more likely to seriously contemplate suicide than their heterosexual peers, and almost five times more likely to attempt suicide.[79] Another 2016 study found that transgender youth are also at significantly higher risks of suicide, with almost half of transgender youth reporting that they have contemplated suicide in the past year.[80]

In a 2017 National School Climate Survey, the Gay, Lesbian and Straight Education Network (GLSEN) found that about 60 percent of LGBTQ students reported experiencing LGBTQ-related discriminatory policies at school. Examples of such policies included being prevented from wearing clothes considered "inappropriate" based on students' legal sex, being prohibited from discussing or writing about LGBTQ topics in school assignments, and transgender and nonbinary students being required to use a bathroom of their legal sex.[81]

In addition to hostile school climates, LGBTQ youth are also at risk of experiencing so-called "conversion therapy," the harmful and debunked practice of attempting to change an LGBTQ person's sexual orientation or gender identity.[82] Many reports and studies have documented the link between adverse outcomes for LGBTQ youth and conversion therapy and hostile school climates.[83] In response, LGBTQ youth organizations have advocated to ban conversion therapy nationwide, make school curricula LGBTQ-inclusive,[84] and expand anti-bullying and nondiscrimination protections for LGBTQ students.[85]

The Trump administration rolled back policies aimed at protecting the LGBTQ youth population. It rescinded Obama-era guidance on Title IX of the Education Amendments of 1972 that interpreted discrimination on the basis of sex to include gender identity. This meant that under Title IX, transgender students have the right to be treated according to their gender identity, including accessing bathrooms, participating in dress codes, and using their correct name and pronouns.[86] In 2018, the Trump administration Department of Education announced that it would no longer investigate complaints from transgender students unable to access the bathroom aligned with their gender identity.[87] In 2020, the Department's Office for Civil Rights concluded that a Connecticut transgender-inclusive athletic policy violated civil rights law, effectively using Title IX to prohibit transgender youth from participating in sports.

After taking office, President Biden vowed to roll back discrimination against transgender Americans. Biden announced in an April 2021 speech, "To all the transgender Americans watching at home, especially the young people who are so brave, I want you to know that your president has your back," calling for Congress to pass the Equality Act to protect LGBTQ people from discrimination.[88]

The rights of LGBTQ youth are being threatened at the state level. The Equality Federation is currently tracking hundreds of anti-LGBTQ bills across the country, the majority specifically targeting transgender youth and making it more difficult for them to access medically necessary health care, such as puberty blockers.[89] A 2020 study in the journal *Pediatrics* added to a growing evidence base linking gender-affirming care for transgender youth to lower rates of suicide.[90] In 2021, an unprecedented slate of bills in state legislatures targeted participation of transgender youth in sports, as well as other bills attacking gender-affirming medical care and other protections. After eight states passed laws or issued executive actions against transgender youth in the first few months of the year, the Human Rights Campaign's Alphonso David declared that 2021 was on track to "become the worst year for state legislative attacks against LGBTQ people in history," asserting that such laws are an "attempt to erase transgender people and attempt to make LGBTQ people second-class citizens."[91]

HEALTH CARE AND HUMAN SERVICES

LGBTQ people face a range of health risks and disparities. For example, men are at higher risk of HIV and STDs, especially among communities of color; LGBT people are more likely to smoke and have higher rates of alcohol use, other drug use, depression, and anxiety; LGBT people have higher rates of behavioral health issues; and transgender individuals experience a high prevalence of HIV and STDs, victimization, and suicide.

As the National LGBT Health Education Center explains, "there are no LGBT-specific diseases or illnesses. . . . [T]hese health issues are mostly related to the stigma and discrimination experienced by LGBT people in their daily lives—including at school or work, in public spaces, or at health care settings."[92] Research has shown that LGBTQ people in the United States encounter significant barriers to accessing health care, including difficulty finding providers who are knowledgeable about LGBTQ health care needs, discriminatory treatment from providers or insurers, and foregoing care altogether for fear of mistreatment.[93]

In 2019, the Trump administration Department of Health and Human Services (HHS) proposed a rule to roll back Obama-era regulations protecting LGBTQ people from discrimination by federally funded health providers, programs, and insurers.[94] The Obama-era regulations explicitly stated that discrimination on the basis of sex stereotyping and gender identity was prohibited under Section 1557, the nondiscrimination provision of the Affordable Care Act (ACA). HHS finalized its rule in June 2020, but three days later, the Supreme Court ruled in the *Bostock* case that gender identity was protected under the federal government's definition of discrimination by sex, leading a federal judge to invalidate the rule.

CRIMINAL JUSTICE, VIOLENCE, AND IMMIGRATION

LGBTQ people, especially transgender people of color, are disproportionately likely to be victims of violent hate crimes.[95] Despite the passage of the federal Shepard-Byrd Hate Crimes Prevention Act in 2009, state-level hate crimes legislation remains a patchwork: fourteen states do not include sexual orientation and gender identity in their hate crimes statutes, and three states have no statutes at all.

Many areas of the country still allow the use of "gay/trans panic defenses" to justify anti-LGBTQ violence. According to the American Bar Association, these defenses "seek to partially or completely excuse crimes such as murder and assault on the grounds that the victim's sexual orientation or gender identity is to blame for the defendant's violent reaction."[96] These defenses are condemned by LGBTQ rights advocates, but they remain legal in forty states.[97]

LGBTQ people, specifically transgender people, also face heightened violence in prisons and jails. Transgender people are more likely than cisgender people to be assaulted in prison, and they are more likely to be assigned to solitary confinement as a result.[98] Solitary confinement has been linked to serious psychological health consequences.[99] Research has documented the increased risk that transgender people face in sex-segregated facilities. Studies show that transgender women who are incarcerated in male settings are at heightened risk of rape and sexual assault as a result of their gender identity.[100]

Under the Trump administration, the Federal Bureau of Prisons approved new guidelines instructing staff to house inmates according to their biological sex.[101] These guidelines reversed Obama-era guidelines that encouraged staff to rely on gender identity instead.

LGBTQ advocacy organizations continuously raised concerns about the Trump administration's anti-immigration policies. These groups argue that policies that restrict immigration into the United States have an outsized effect on LGBTQ people who are fleeing anti-LGBTQ violence from other countries.[102]

DATA COLLECTION AND IDENTITY DOCUMENTATION

Demographic data collection on LGBTQ people is widely inconsistent across the United States and within state and local settings. For example, the Behavioral Risk Factor Surveillance Survey, the largest health survey in the world, only includes LGBTQ demographic questions in thirty-two states.[103] LGBTQ advocates argue for inclusive data collection as a critical tool for quantifying and addressing disparities among LGBTQ communities.[104]

Transgender and nonbinary people who seek to change their names and gender markers are frequently subjected to excessive requirements. Eleven states require individuals to formally publish a name-change announcement, often in a local newspaper.[105] This outdated practice exposes transgender people to potential harassment and violence by making their gender transition public. Many states place extensive burdens on transgender and nonbinary individuals to change their gender marker, including the provision of a court order, a letter from a medical provider, and proof of surgery. Advocates have fought for and won "self-attestation" policies in many states by arguing that existing policies violate the individual's right to privacy.[106]

Federal data collection practices in recent years have threatened LGBTQ inclusion and representation. Under the Trump administration, the Census Bureau removed proposed questions on LGBTQ demographic data in the 2020 American Community Survey.[107] According to ProPublica, several federal agencies and LGBTQ advocates favored the inclusion of these questions to better understand the needs of LGBTQ communities. Under the Trump administration, HHS removed a proposed question about sexual orientation from its Administration for Community Living survey. This survey helps inform federal funding for programs for people with disabilities. Many condemned the move.[108]

Policy Recommendations

- **Pass the Equality Act.** Ban discrimination against LGBTQ people nationwide. The Equality Act would amend existing civil rights laws to provide consistent and explicit protections for LGBTQ people in employment, housing, credit, education, public spaces and services, federally funded programs, and jury service. By explicitly including sexual orientation and gender identity in federal civil rights law, LGBTQ people will be afforded the same protection as race, sex, and other explicitly covered characteristics.
- **Appoint High-Level Federal Officials.** Nominate openly LGBTQ people to serve in presidential cabinet-level positions and as Supreme Court justices and federal judges.
- **End Family and Health Care Discrimination.** Require federally funded adoption agencies to provide service to LGBTQ couples and families, expand existing resources to support LGBTQ elders and people living with HIV/AIDS, and expand the Affordable Care Act to fully cover LGBTQ-related health needs, including HIV/AIDS medication, hormone treatment and sex-reassignment surgery, mental health services, and elder care.
- **End Employment and Workplace Discrimination.** Enact the Do No Harm Act, which amends the Religious Freedom Restoration Act to clarify that discrimination on the basis of race, sex, or LGBTQ status by individuals or organizations claiming

infringement of their religious liberty is prohibited as an unfair
burden on the exercise of the constitutional right to equal protection.

- **End Discrimination in Schools.** Require public schools to prohibit discrimination against LGBTQ students, issue clear federal and state mandates and guidelines for LGBTQ-inclusive
  curriculum, ensure that transgender students are protected
  from bullying and allowed access to bathrooms and other
  facilities consistent with their gender identity, and require that
  the history and practice of the "gender binary tradition" are
  addressed explicitly in schools so that gender diversity is fully
  accepted and no longer considered "abnormal."

7

Rights of Individuals with Disabilities

Nearly 61 million Americans have a disability, making the group the country's largest minority.[1] People with disabilities cut across race, gender, sexual orientation, and political party, making the experience of disabilities something that affects people of all walks of life. Since people with disabilities are disproportionately older, they also have made up an expanding share of the general population as the U.S. population has aged. In fact, unlike other more fixed identities, any person can become disabled at any time, due to severe injury, illness, or trauma. While only 11 percent of people ages eighteen to sixty-four reported having a disability in 2017, 35 percent of people ages sixty-five and over reported having one, illustrating the fluid nature of disability status.[2] Indeed, as Emory law professor and disability rights expert Ani B. Satz has said, the vulnerability to disability is something that is both universal and constant, making it a fundamental part of the human condition.[3]

Individuals with disabilities have experienced discrimination for much of our nation's history, facing animosity, isolation, degradation, unemployment, and inappropriate institutionalization. Starting in the 1970s, a new movement for disability rights led to increased awareness and legislative action, starting with the Rehabilitation Act of 1973. That movement continued with the enactment of the landmark Americans with Disabilities Act of 1990 (ADA), which protects people with disabilities as a matter of civil rights, and prevents discrimination against individuals with disabilities in employment, public services, and places of public accommodation.

Even with this progress, people with disabilities still often lack meaningful accommodation to allow them access to civic and social spaces. Legal accommodation targeted to specific spaces and contexts leaves disability protections fragmented overall, often failing fully to address individuals' specific needs and experiences.[4] According to recent statistics, approximately 75 percent of people with disabilities are unemployed, and those who are employed earn, on average, at least 30 percent less than people without disabilities.[5] People with disabilities are also twice as likely to live in poverty, and more likely to experience higher health care costs.[6]

Due to these myriad challenges, seemingly neutral policies can have unintended consequences. For example, policies that make public assistance contingent on employment disproportionately burden individuals with disabilities, who are less likely to be employed. Recent policies enacted under the Trump administration eroded some past protections and exacerbated barriers across a range of issue areas, from health care to immigration.

Disability advocates took hope from the election of Joe Biden, who reversed many of these policies within a few weeks of taking office.[7] Biden has been open about his own disability, a speech impediment that he has had since childhood, and he was the second president in U.S. history (after Barack Obama) to mention the word "disability" in his victory speech.[8] During his campaign, Biden promised to enforce civil rights for individuals with disabilities, strengthen their economic security, and expand access to health care, education, housing, and transportation.[9] Protecting the rights of people with disabilities requires both reinstating protections and expanding accommodations to better allow participation in all aspects of society.

SETTING THE LANDSCAPE

According to the ADA, a disability is a "physical or mental impairment that substantially limits one or more major life activity." Those activities include "caring for oneself, performing manual tasks, seeing, hearing, eating, sleeping, walking, standing, lifting, bending, speaking, breathing, learning, reading, concentrating, thinking, communication, and working."[10] While the ADA does not list all covered disabilities, examples include motor impairment, blindness, deafness, psychological disorders, learning disabilities, and certain illnesses such as HIV.[11] People covered under the Act include those with a "record of such an impairment," such as someone with cancer who is now in remission. They also include those "regarded as" having a disability by others.[12] For example, a person with a severe burn may not experience physical impairment but may be denied employment based on appearance.[13]

Broad protections for individuals with disabilities have been in place only for the past three decades. Before that, the federal government and the American public mistreated people with disabilities, through a combination of misinformation, ignorance, fear, and stigma. Laws in many states allowed involuntary sterilization of people with intellectual impairments and mental disorders. Many municipalities banned people with physical disabilities from public spaces due to their appearance.[14] Federal law lacked protections for people with disabilities against employers, schools, and landlords who denied them accommodations and access to services. The lack of federal protections meant very few cases on disability rights came before the Supreme Court before the 1970s, and in the rare cases that did, the Court upheld mistreatment. In *Buck v. Bell* (1927), the Supreme Court notoriously upheld a Virginia law legalizing sterilization for individuals "afflicted with hereditary forms of insanity, imbecility, etc."[15]

A disability rights movement emerged following World War II, when returning veterans insisted on government rehabilitation services and vocational training. Starting in the 1960s, parents and advocates sought

Vietnam War veterans protest against the war at the 1972 Republican National Convention. Photo by Owen Franken/Corbis via Getty Images.

Advocates, including Justin Dart (right), marched to spur passage of the ADA. Photo by Tom Olin.

deinstitutionalization and educational opportunity for children with disabilities.[16] In the 1970s, disability rights activists, inspired by the Civil Rights Movement, pushed for more broad-reaching legislation to end discrimination. The first of these laws was the 1973 Rehabilitation Act, which prohibited "discrimination on the basis of disability" by federal agencies and contractors.[17] Despite this success, school boards and local transit authorities pushed back on the legislation with claims of increased costs and reduced efficiency—arguments that would become common in attacks on disability protections.[18]

In the 1980s, Congress increased protections for institutionalized persons and gave the Justice Department authority to investigate allegations of institutional abuse and mistreatment.[19] More broadly, however, many forms of discrimination against people with disabilities remained legal until the passage of the ADA in 1990. Decades after other landmark civil rights legislation, the ADA finally "guarantee[d] equal opportunity for individuals with disabilities in public accommodations, employment, transportation, state and local government services, and telecommunications."[20]

The ADA passed with broad bipartisan support, indicative of the wide-ranging impact of disabilities across society.[21] Over time, however, the Supreme Court chipped away at its protections by narrowing the definitions of conditions considered disabilities, and how severe and pervasive they had to be to merit accommodation.[22] Even so, disability advocates won a major court victory in 1999 with the Supreme Court decision in *Olmsted v. L.C.*,[23] establishing a standard for community-based services and increasing independence for people with disabilities.[24]

In 2008, Congress effectively overturned several Supreme Court decisions narrowing disability protections by passing the ADA Amendments Act (ADAAA)—a rare instance in which Congress actually expanded rights that had been limited by the courts.[25] Similar to the ADA, the ADAAA passed with bipartisan support, uniting lawmakers across party lines. Among other changes, the law expanded the list of major life activities subject to impairment.[26] It also expanded coverage for temporary disabilities, such as an accident that substantially limits mobility.[27] Coverage for such disabilities depends on the length of time and severity of the impairment. For example, the ADAAA would not cover a short-term illness, but would cover a severe injury that prevented an individual from being able to walk for several months.[28]

Bipartisan support for disability rights faltered in 2012 when the Senate voted against ratifying the United Nations Convention on the Rights of Persons with Disabilities, an international treaty establishing worldwide standards for disability protections. Despite a dramatic visit to the Senate floor to encourage ratification by the Republican Party's 1996 presidential nominee, Bob Dole, the vote fell short of the required two-thirds majority.[29]

Stigmatization of people with disabilities was exacerbated by harmful rhetoric from former President Trump. During the 2016 presidential campaign, Trump publicly mocked a reporter with physical disabilities during a political rally.[30] In 2018, he described the Paralympics as "a little tough to watch too much,"[31] and in 2019, he derided Greta Thunberg, a sixteen-year-old climate change activist with Asperger syndrome, declaring on Twitter that she needed to "work on her anger management problem."[32] Each of these comments sparked public backlash, but revealed a disregard for people with disabilities by the former president.

CURRENT POLICIES

Despite the gains of recent decades, people with disabilities continue to face significant disparities and discrimination in a wide range of areas, including health care, employment, education, poverty, housing, transportation, immigration, and voting.

Health Care

People with disabilities face, on average, higher health care needs than others. More than one-third of people with disabilities have ten or more doctor's visits in a year, compared to six for those without disabilities. They are also more likely to require hospitalization, at 19 percent compared to 5 percent for people without disabilities. At the same time, however, they are less likely to have access to medical care,[33] due to factors including lack of mobility, lack of knowledge by health care providers, and lack of protections in administrative policies, procedures, and practices.[34]

The ADA mandates that people with disabilities be given equal access to health care programs and facilities. Putting this requirement into practice, the 2010 ADA Standards for Accessible Design codify specific requirements for the physical structures of offices and clinics; the Affordable Care Act expanded those requirements to include furnishings and equipment. Nevertheless, studies have uncovered widespread gaps and failures in providing proper access to care. A survey of more than four hundred wheelchair users, for example, found 73.8 percent encountered barriers during primary-care visits, and 54.1 percent said their care was incomplete. Another study found 93 percent of examination rooms failed to meet at least one ADA requirement. These and other gaps in providing proper facilities and diagnostic equipment limit care for individuals with disabilities and leave them vulnerable to poor health outcomes.[35]

Individuals with disabilities face significant hurdles in the cost of health care. The $13,492 average annual cost of health care for a person with a disability is approximately five times that of a person without a disability, $2,835. Average out-of-pocket costs are twice as high, $1,053 compared to $486. As a result, people with disabilities are more than twice as likely to delay needed medical care, and three times as likely not to seek care.[36]

The Affordable Care Act, passed in 2010, significantly increased health care coverage through subsidized health insurance exchanges and expansions in Medicaid,[37] covering 30 percent of all adults with disabilities and 60 percent of children with disabilities.[38] Medicaid is the primary form of health insurance funding services and supports such as personal care assistants, transportation services, lifts in homes, and durable medical equipment such as wheelchairs.[39]

In 2012, however, the Supreme Court limited the ACA's Medicaid expansion, with a majority of the Court concluding it was "unconstitutionally coercive of states."[40] Since that decision, twelve states have decided against expansion,[41] creating major disparities for people with disabilities between states.[42] In addition, in 2018, the Trump administration allowed states to enact work requirements for adult Medicaid enrollees. This decision disproportionately affected people with disabilities, according to a study by the Center on Budget and Policy Priorities,[43] since individuals with disabilities are less likely to work. While people with disabilities may be exempt from work requirements if they receive Supplemental Security Income (SSI) or Social Security Disability Insurance (SSDI),[44] their eligibility depends on a more stringent standard—"inability to engage in any substantial gainful activity" for at least twelve months.[45] Moreover, nearly 60 percent of all adult Medicaid enrollees with disabilities do not receive SSI.[46]

Soon after his election, President Biden began the process of eliminating work requirement rules in states that had adopted them.[47] The new administration also sought to improve home and community-based health care services, announcing $400 billion in proposed funding for those services in the American Jobs Act, the infrastructure plan proposed in April 2021.

Since the onset of the pandemic, some people who contract COVID have had severe symptoms for months, impairing their ability to work and perform other life tasks. People with "long COVID" have obtained disability benefits for their condition, aided by patient advocacy groups that have pushed to have it recognized as a chronic disease that fits the definition of a disability under ADA guidelines.[48]

Employment

In 2012, William Pierce applied for a police job in Iberia Parish, Louisiana. After receiving a job offer, he disclosed his status as HIV-positive, noting "it didn't affect his ability to perform his duties." Following his disclosure, the sheriff rescinded the job offer.[49] Pierce sued the sheriff's office and filed an ADA claim with the Equal Employment Opportunity Commission (EEOC) for discrimination on the basis of disability.[50] The EEOC found that Pierce's case had merit, and the sheriff's office settled out of court for $90,000.[51]

Pierce's case illustrates how the ADA's employment protections prohibit both public and private employers from discriminating against people with disabilities in hiring, firing, compensation, and other employment procedures for organizations with at least fifteen employees.[52] However, employment discrimination cases are often unsuccessful, and many people with disabilities do not qualify for protection. Only 38 percent of adults ages eighteen to sixty-four with disabilities are employed.[53] According to research by the Bureau of Labor Statistics, people with disabilities are almost twice as likely to hold part-time work, and are more likely to work in lower-wage occupations.[54] Discrimination remains a major barrier to employment. A Rutgers University study found that fictional cover letters citing a disability received 26 percent fewer responses from employers.[55]

A current trend that could mitigate barriers for some people with disabilities is increased telework, which can remove issues with difficult commutes and office settings lacking sufficient accommodations.[56] While the ADA includes working remotely as a reasonable accommodation, employers are not required to provide this accommodation if it poses undue hardship for the employer or gets in the way of the job's essential functions.[57] However, significant increases in telework resulting from the coronavirus pandemic may make employers more open to allowing work from home. An analysis by the Pew Research Center found that 40 percent of jobs at the start of the coronavirus pandemic could potentially be performed via telework, including 62 percent of jobs requiring a bachelor's degree or higher.[58] Other studies have shown that telework can actually boost productivity.[59]

Not all people with disabilities can benefit from remote work, and such practices may also unintentionally lead to segregation between workers with disabilities at home, and workers without disabilities at the office. Furthermore, the remote-work trend creates challenges in terms of digital accessibility. Many websites and apps are not accessible for people with visual impairments, which may restrict their ability to work remotely. Rates of technology adoption are lower among people with disabilities. A Pew Research Center poll found 67 percent computer ownership among adults ages eighteen to sixty-four with disabilities, compared with 84 percent for those without. This technology-adoption disparity would prevent many people with disabilities from engaging in remote work.[60]

In recent years, states have done more than the federal government to create initiatives to increase employment opportunities for people with disabilities by improving workplace recruitment, accommodations, and retention. Maryland, for example, provides a benefit to people with disabilities seeking public sector employment by increasing their selection test score by five points.[61] Massachusetts established a statewide fund designed to finance accommodations for employees with disabilities. Vermont and Minnesota offer employment trial periods to incentivize managers from public agencies to recruit and hire people with disabilities. While these trial periods might be perceived as an additional barrier to employment, they also challenge employer perceptions about people with disabilities by allowing them to demonstrate that they can effectively handle the work. In Minnesota, this program has contributed to a 40 percent increase in employment of people with disabilities in the state workforce since 2015.[62]

Education

The United States has come a long way in improving educational equity for children with disabilities over the last half-century, but significant disparities remain. According to a Department of Education Report, in 1970, only one in five children with disabilities was educated in U.S. schools. Many states explicitly excluded children who were deaf or blind, or who had emotional issues or cognitive disabilities.[63] The official decision not to offer public education to these children impacted all aspects of their lives, especially their future work opportunities and incomes.

The first major piece of legislation establishing equal protection for people with disabilities in educational settings was Section 504 of the Rehabilitation Act (1973), which restricted discrimination, the denial of benefits, and exclusion of people with disabilities from federally funded programs and activities.[64] The equal protection established by Section 504 was strengthened in 1975 by the Education for All Handicapped Children Act (EHA), which required public schools accepting federal funds to "provide equal access to education for children with physical and mental disabilities." The law required schools to develop individual plans with parental input to educate children in the "least restrictive environment."[65] That meant that children with disabilities would learn with their peers, aiming to combat a history of segregating children into separate learning environments.

In 1990, Congress reauthorized and renamed the EHA as the Individuals with Disabilities Education Act (IDEA) and has since reauthorized it and expanded it multiple times. Today, IDEA makes "a free appropriate public education" available to all children with disabilities, as well as providing grants to states to improve special education[66] and to institutions of higher education for research, technology development, and training.[67]

These laws established two types of educational plans for students with disabilities. A 504 plan accommodates students in regular classrooms without additional federal funding.[68] An individualized education plan (IEP), on the other hand, assesses the individual student's academic achievement and functional performance, establishes annual goals, describes how progress will be measured, and lists the additional services the child will receive.[69] The IEP requires a more formal administrative process than a 504 plan,[70] and results in additional funding from the federal government.[71]

While 504 plans and IEPs are designed to help students with disabilities, parents and their children often face confusing barriers. A recent study in the *Northwestern Journal of Law & Social Policy* found that many parents "do not know their rights under the IDEA, do not feel competent to be equal team members, have anxieties about bringing due process claims, and cannot get legal assistance."[72] These issues can cause parents to struggle with advocating for their child and having a say in their child's education.

According to the National Center for Education Statistics, IDEA served approximately 7.3 million students, making up 14 percent of the enrolled public school population during the 2019–20 school year. The most commonly reported type of disability was a specific learning disability (33 percent), followed by a speech or language impairment (19 percent), other health impairment (15 percent), autism (11 percent), and developmental delay (7 percent).[73]

Students with disabilities are disproportionately subject to punitive disciplinary measures. According to a 2014 report by the Disability Rights Education and Defense Fund, they were more than twice as likely to receive an out-of-school suspension. In addition, while students with disabilities represented 14 percent of the school population, they included 25 percent of those involved in school-related arrests, and 75 percent of all students physically restrained at school. These statistics contribute to the school-to-prison pipeline that disproportionately impacts students with disabilities and students of color. According to the Disability Rights Education and Defense Fund, 85 percent of children in juvenile detention had some disability making them eligible for special education, but only 37 percent were receiving assistance.[74]

These challenges affect student outcomes, including high school diploma attainment and college graduation rates. In 2018, students with disabilities were less likely to attain a high school diploma, 83 percent compared to 92 percent. The gap in attaining a bachelor's degree was even larger, at 16 percent and 38 percent, respectively.[75]

In 2017, President Trump signed an executive order "to alleviate unnecessary regulatory burdens,"[76] which led Department of Education Secretary Betsy DeVos to rescind seventy-two guidance documents that protected students with disabilities.[77] Despite pleas from disability rights groups to keep the guidance documents in place, the department claimed that the documents were "outdated, unnecessary, or ineffective."[78]

Immigration

While immigration to the United States is an arduous and restrictive process under any circumstances, people with disabilities and their families face additional barriers in entering, settling, staying, and applying for naturalization in the United States as immigrants.[79] A number of recent policy and legal changes have increased barriers to immigration for people with disabilities. In 2019, the Department of Homeland Security (DHS) changed its regulations on admission based on whether a person was likely to become a "public charge," dependent on government assistance.[80] The rule included Medicaid, the main source of health insurance for people with disabilities, affecting their ability both to enter the country and to receive a green card. A study conducted by the Kaiser Family Foundation concluded that the regulation would lead to decreases in participation in Medicaid and other programs among immigrant families and their U.S.-born children beyond those directly affected by the new policy.[81] In response to these concerns, DHS insisted that it "did not codify this final rule to discriminate," but rather "to better ensure that aliens subject to this rule are self-sufficient."[82] Despite legal challenges, the new regulations went into effect in February 2020.

The Trump administration increased restrictions on the ability of immigrants with disabilities to stay in the country. In August 2019, the administration eliminated a longstanding "medical deferred action" program, which allowed immigrant families to remain in the United States if at least one member of the family had a serious or life-threatening health condition, including a disability, and was receiving medical treatment.[83] The program had protected families from deportation.[84] With the elimination of the medical deferred action program, immigrants and their families began receiving written notifications that they were required to leave the country within thirty-three days.[85] The people affected by this policy include children with disabilities who were born in the United States but whose parents, on whom they rely to access needed health care, are immigrants. For these and other immigrants, deportation to a country with inadequate medical services represented a virtual death sentence.[86] Following widespread condemnation, the Trump administration reinstated medical deferred action in September 2019.[87]

Adequate services are lacking for immigrants with disabilities who are otherwise fully qualified to apply for citizenship. An internal report published in 2018 found persistent, "systemic" gaps in accommodations provided by U.S. Citizenship and Immigration Services (USCIS) for people with disabilities in taking the required citizenship test, including multiple issues related to sign language interpreters.[88]

Poverty, Housing, and Transportation

Disabilities are both a cause and consequence of poverty. The 25.9 percent poverty rate for working-age Americans with disabilities is nearly two-and-a-half times higher than the rate for people without disabilities. Half of all working-age adults who experience at least one year living below the poverty rate have a disability, and nearly two-thirds of those experiencing longer-term poverty have a disability.[89]

These high rates are due to a confluence of factors, including higher unemployment and workplace discrimination, educational barriers, and higher health care costs. Poverty is exacerbated by barriers to housing and transportation. People with disabilities struggle to meet housing costs, with 41 percent of all households that include a person with a disability unable to afford housing, an estimated 14.4 million households. These challenges often lead to homelessness; at least 43 percent of U.S. adults who have stayed in a shelter for individuals experiencing homelessness had a self-reported disability.[90]

Transportation difficulties are a challenge for people with disabilities. Adults with disabilities are more than twice as likely as those without disabilities to report having inadequate transportation. Strikingly, of the almost 2 million people with disabilities in the United States who never leave their homes, more than a quarter (560,000) stay at home because of transportation difficulties.[91] In one study, only about a quarter of surveyed adults with disabilities indicated that they had good options for public transportation.[92]

People with disabilities may qualify for a number of public assistance programs to alleviate their poverty. The largest are the SSDI and SSI programs, which cover health care costs;[93] however, the process for qualifying for these programs is burdensome, requiring a total and permanent disability, and the majority of people with disabilities do not qualify. Individuals with disabilities may be eligible for public assistance programs, including the Supplemental Nutrition Assistance Program (SNAP). A 2019 study by the Urban Institute found that over one-quarter of SNAP participants report "a functional or work limitation," a proportion that has remained relatively constant for more than a decade.[94] Requirements for SNAP are less stringent than those for SSDI and SSI, allowing it to serve a broader subset of people with disabilities.[95]

Housing discrimination against people with disabilities is generally prohibited. The Fair Housing Act of 1988 contains protections for people with physical and mental disabilities, making it illegal to discriminate in the sale, rental, and financing of housing or other housing-related transactions on the basis of their disability. Discrimination includes "rejecting or refusing to negotiate with individuals seeking housing or housing-related services," or "misrepresenting or limiting housing opportunities" based on a person's disability. The Act provides that multifamily housing built after March 1991 must include accommodations such as wheelchair ramps and must allow residents to make changes necessary for access and enjoyment.[96] In addition, the Act subsidizes rental housing with access to supportive services for people with disabilities.

The program provides interest-free capital advances and subsidies for operations to nonprofit developers of affordable housing for persons with disabilities and offers rental assistance to state housing agencies.[97]

Finally, in terms of transportation, Title II of the ADA prohibits discrimination on the basis of disability in public transportation services, and mandates accessibility accommodations for new public transit vehicles and stations.[98] However, instead of promoting increased accessibility in mass transit, the Department of Transportation has "effectively maintained a separate-but-equal vision of public transportation," funding programs that provide accessible alternatives to mass transit rather than enabling people with disabilities to use existing and more robust transportation networks.[99]

Voting

In the 2020 presidential election, an estimated 35.4 million Americans with disabilities were eligible to vote, comprising approximately one-fifth of the electorate. People with disabilities face barriers to voting and are therefore less likely to vote, particularly in person.[100] In 2018, just over one-fourth of people with disabilities indicated that they were not registered to vote due to "permanent illness or disability." Among those who were registered but did not vote in the 2018 midterm elections, 41 percent responded that "illness or disability" was the reason for not voting.[101]

These statistics demonstrate the need to improve the voting infrastructure to facilitate voting by people with disabilities. A 2013 research report found that the most common problems were difficulty with reading or seeing the ballot or understanding how to vote or use voting equipment.[102] These difficulties have persisted even as voter turnout among people with disabilities has increased, from 43 percent in 2010 to 49 percent in 2018.[103] Voting rates by people with disabilities increased again during the COVID pandemic, when widespread voting by mail allowed greater participation by those with mobility issues and other disabilities. Nearly 62 percent of people with disabilities voted in 2020, compared to 56 percent in the 2016 presidential election. However, the turnout gap between people with and without disabilities remained largely unchanged, and a move by many states to restrict mail-in voting could erode these gains.[104]

As suggested by surveys of individuals with disabilities, the accessibility of polling places is a principal barrier. In the 2016 presidential election, the Government Accountability Office (GAO) evaluated 178 polling places, finding that 60 percent had at least one potential impediment, such as "steep ramps located outside buildings, lack of signs indicating accessible paths, and poor parking or path surfaces." Just under two-thirds failed to provide a voting station with an accessible voting system that ensured the casting of a "private and independent vote." The GAO noted that some of these voting stations could not accommodate wheelchairs, forcing wheelchair users to require the assistance of another person to cast their vote.[105] In the 2018 midterm elections, people with disabilities were more likely than the general voting population to cite transportation problems as a reason for not voting.[106]

The barriers to voting accessibility reveal a significant gap between practice and law. Federal law generally requires polling places for federal elections to be accessible to all voters and have an accessible system for casting ballots.[107] The ADA requires state and local governments to ensure people with disabilities are fully able to participate in the voting process, including voter registration and early voting.[108] In addition, the Voting Rights Act of 1965 allows any voter requiring assistance to be supported by a person of their choice.[109] Other federal legislation has specific requirements pertaining to accessibility. The Voting Accessibility for the Elderly and Handicapped Act of 1984 requires that each state and local government responsible for conducting elections ensure that all polling places for federal elections are accessible to "handicapped" and elderly voters.[110] In addition, the Help America Vote Act of 2002 requires "at least one accessible voting system . . . at each polling place in federal elections."[111] States have also gradually increased their accessibility requirements. Between 2000 and 2016, the number of states requiring accessibility standards increased from twenty-three to forty-four.[112] Despite these legal improvements, however, thirty-one states in the 2016 election reported experiencing challenges in ensuring accessibility in polling places.[113]

The increase in voting restrictions and requirements in recent years has placed a disproportionate burden on people with disabilities.[114] State laws surrounding voter competence, identification, and incarceration have limited electoral participation.[115] Because people with disabilities are less likely to drive and therefore often do not have a license, laws that require official identification for voting are more burdensome for these individuals.[116] In addition, because of the challenges experienced by people with disabilities related to mobility and transportation, the closure of polling places has also limited their voting.[117]

Policy Recommendations

- **End Employment and Workplace Discrimination.** Eliminate subminimum wage for people with disabilities, provide additional incentives for employers to hire people with disabilities, require employers to report data on hiring of people with disabilities, increase workplace protections for people with disabilities during times of national emergency (e.g., the COVID pandemic), address complaints of workplace discrimination at federal agencies, and evaluate the representation of people with disabilities throughout federal and state agencies.
- **Improve Supports for Students with Disabilities in Schools.** Increase educational support for remote and in-school learning by students with disabilities during times of national emergency (e.g., the COVID pandemic), expand educational support for mental-health-related and cognitive disabilities, prohibit seclusion of students with disabilities, and increase the supply of special education teachers.
- **Improve Access to Health Care.** Expand Medicaid eligibility for persons with disabilities, streamline the application process for Supplemental Security Income (SSI) and Social Security Disability Insurance (SSDI), and remove the mandatory waiting period for Medicare benefits for persons with disabilities who are approved for SSDI.
- **Increase Assistance to Address Poverty, Housing, and Transportation Needs of People with Disabilities.** Remove work requirements for anti-poverty programs for people with disabilities, provide equal access to housing support programs to

persons with disabilities, increase funding to provide accessible public transportation systems, and expand transportation access.

- **Protect Voting Rights.** Increase funding and make necessary upgrades for accessibility of polling places and provide accessible absentee ballots for persons with disabilities.
- **Ratify Convention on the Rights of Persons with Disabilities.** The international convention has been signed but not yet ratified by the United States.

8

Economic Inequality and the Freedom from Want

"Liberty," President Franklin D. Roosevelt declared during the Great Depression, "requires opportunity to make a living—a living decent according to the standard of the time, a living which gives man not only enough to live by, but something to live for."[1] In his 1941 State of the Union Address, Roosevelt proclaimed that "freedom from want" is essential to the survival of American democracy.[2] This was not a partisan claim. Roosevelt's observation was echoed two decades later by President Dwight D. Eisenhower, who remarked that "as long as we allow conditions to exist that make for second-class citizens, we are making of ourselves less than first-class citizens."[3]

The United States today faces unprecedented economic, environmental, and public health challenges that require its democratic institutions to develop policies to secure the promise of freedom from want. These challenges have

Unemployment Council pickets, before 1936. Photo by Aaron Siskind via Smithsonian American Art Museum.

the potential to redefine the role of government in providing equal access to public goods and services. The COVID pandemic had a devastating impact on the economy. At a time of public health emergency and mass unemployment, the pandemic required government to support and provide equal access to basic necessities such as health care, housing, education, and environmental protection. As the nation struggled to control the pandemic and stabilize the economy, the public and private sectors needed to work together to create a new social contract that included all citizens. Some initial steps were taken but partisan polarization and institutional gridlock have so far prevented transformative change from occurring.

Long before the outbreak of the pandemic, it was clear that existing policies were failing to secure the freedom from want. After decades of public disinvestment and burgeoning inequality, many Americans were being left behind. Now, after the pandemic-related economic slowdown, inequality of opportunity has become increasingly visible, as Americans have struggled to maintain and regain their livelihoods.

The Carr Center's July 2020 national poll shows that bipartisan majorities of Americans believe that rights of equal access to basic necessities of life are "very important," but that these rights are not "very secure." Eighty-five percent believe that "the right to quality education" and "the right to clean air and water" are "very important," while only 17 percent believe these rights are "very secure." A similar result (83 percent to 10 percent) is shown for "the right to affordable health care."

Despite broad public support for rights of equal access to these basic necessities, government institutions have been hard-pressed to secure them. Since the early 1980s, politically dominant economic theories have restricted government spending and regulation. As a priority was put on private economic activity, the federal government reduced its role in supporting public education, health care, and housing. Now, with the nation struggling to overcome the long-term effects of the pandemic, the stage may be set for a significant shift. Enactment of a massive $1.9 trillion COVID relief package in March 2021 and the $1 trillion bipartisan legislation in November 2021 to rebuild the nation's physical and social infrastructure and provide millions of new jobs are indications that such a shift may be taking place. The infrastructure plan has broad popular support. The Carr Center's May 2021 national poll showed that 83 percent of Americans "agree or somewhat agree" that the United States "will only remain a global leader if it invests in updating its infrastructure."

The nation's ineffective early response to the pandemic and the subsequent economic and racial crises have caused people to think differently about the role and responsibility of government in securing rights. In our July 2020 poll, a supermajority of respondents (84 percent) reported that "events in recent months have made me think differently about the role and responsibility of government to protect the rights of all Americans." Eighty-five percent also say they now "think differently about the responsibility Americans have to our fellow citizens."

LEGAL FRAMEWORK

A right of equal opportunity and access to public goods and services is rooted in the promise of "Life, Liberty, and the pursuit of Happiness" made by the Declaration of Independence, marking the concept of equality as a founding principle.[4] Nearly a century later, during the nation's "second founding" after the Civil War,[5] the Fourteenth Amendment to the Constitution guaranteed equal protection of the law. These foundational commitments articulated the principle from which a right of equal access is derived, including access to education, health care, housing, and environmental protection.

Throughout American history, the concepts of liberty and equality have been intertwined. Liberty requires a delicate balance between the power of the state and freedoms of society.[6] With the near collapse of the American economy during the Great Depression, the federal government undertook a significantly greater role in ensuring the rights of equality while maintaining the principle of liberty. Emphasizing that "necessitous men are not free men," President Franklin D. Roosevelt articulated a "New Deal" agenda for government support of the basic necessities of life.[7]

The New Deal policies persisted throughout the post-war era. The United States played a role in the drafting of the American Declaration of the Rights and Duties of Man and the Universal Declaration of Human Rights (UDHR). The UDHR, adopted by the United Nations (UN) in 1948, enshrined political and social rights including the right to an adequate standard of living and the right to social security, human dignity, and development.[8] The U.S.

relationship to these new rights was complicated by political resistance from proponents of restricted government spending and limited economic regulation, as well as opponents of international law as an imposition on national sovereignty.

Current trends in health care, education, housing, and environmental protection reflect increasing disparities in opportunity. Public policy in recent years has centered around the promotion of macroeconomic growth but has done little to guarantee individual and societal well-being. The private sector's focus has been on maximizing shareholder value, sometimes at the expense of employees and consumers. These policies have exacerbated the inequality of access to public goods and services among significant portions of the population, who lack the agency and the opportunity to sustain themselves.[9]

The COVID pandemic provided a graphic illustration of why civil and political rights are inseparable from economic, social, and cultural rights. The right to life implies a right to health, a right to food, and a right to work. Food insecurity was a growing national problem even before the pandemic, and the national food bank network estimates that one in four children needed food assistance in 2020.[10]

Citizens wearing protective masks form lines to receive free food from a food pantry run by the Council of Peoples Organization on May 8, 2020, in the Midwood neighborhood of Brooklyn, New York. Photo by Andrew Lichtenstein/Corbis via Getty Images.

The right of equal access to public goods and services is framed in this chapter by the following interconnected values:

- *Equal opportunity:* for individual development and the basic freedom to pursue it.
- *Agency to utilize equal opportunity:* the government can protect the agency of individuals to develop their own capacities and provide equal opportunity for them to lead productive and fulfilling lives.
- *Equal opportunity for future generations:* as well as today's generation.
- *Human dignity:* recognized through self-worth and security.[11]

SHRINKING PUBLIC ASSETS

Health Care

Since the 1930s, the United States has extensively debated the extent to which health care is a right of every American. This right gained traction when President Roosevelt in his 1944 State of the Union Address called for a "Second Bill of Rights," including "the right to adequate medical care and the opportunity to achieve and enjoy good health."[12] In response, the federal government began incrementally to provide and expand access to basic health care services.

Through the creation of Medicare, Medicaid, the Children's Health Insurance Program, and most recently, the Affordable Care Act (ACA), the United States has taken steps to ensure low-income and otherwise vulnerable residents have access to basic health services.[13] These federal initiatives have been supplemented by state programs that provide additional resources for health care, but many states have declined to expand the eligibility for Medicaid authorized by the ACA, which has left millions of low-income and chronically ill Americans without access to health care. With millions of uninsured Americans, many regional and local hospitals across the United States have closed or are in danger of closing due to the high cost of medical care and a high proportion of rural uninsured and underinsured people.[14]

Successive administrations have attempted unsuccessfully to implement policies to control the growth of health care costs to families and individuals while ensuring greater access to health care services. Millions of Americans continue to lack health care coverage. In 2018, approximately 13.7 percent of Americans, many of whom are members of historically marginalized groups, did not have health insurance.[15] At the same time, health care costs have continued to skyrocket, reaching approximately $3.6 trillion in 2018, from $255 billion in 1980.[16] When measured as a percentage of gross domestic product, U.S. spending on health care dwarfs that of other developed nations, growing from 8.9 percent of GDP in 1980 to 17.7 percent in 2017.[17]

The enormous growth in the costs of health care, and the inability of millions of Americans to access it, have become sharp points of political contention. While the Republican Party has traditionally promoted private competition to control costs, the Democratic Party, along with many health experts, has advocated for greater public support for those who lack private health insurance.[18] Despite the attempts of several administrations, comprehensive health care reform did not pass Congress until 2010, with the enactment of the ACA. Unanimously opposed by congressional Republicans, the comprehensive reform package extended health care coverage to millions of Americans.[19]

Even with this expansion of coverage, patient outcomes in the United States continued to lag those of other developed nations.[20] While mortality rates fell from 1,184 per 100,000 people in 1980 to 840 in 2017, they remained above the "comparable country average" of 691. At the same time, the United States trailed other developed nations in access to physicians, and has seen a 33 percent increase in suicide rates since 1999, compared to a global decline of 30 percent since 2000.[21]

While these disparities in access and outcomes affect all Americans, they most significantly impact communities of color. Following the COVID outbreak, research has shown that Black, Latinx American, and tribal communities have been disproportionately affected by the pandemic. Data from New York City in April 2020 showed that Blacks were overrepresented among hospitalized patients, and mortality rates among Black and Latinx Americans significantly outpaced those of Whites and Asians.[22] These disparities in cases and mortality rates can be largely attributed to inadequate access, as Latinx American individuals are approximately three times more likely than Whites not to have health insurance, and Blacks almost twice as likely to be uninsured.[23] At the same time, chronic diseases continue disproportionately to burden communities of color, with Blacks experiencing higher rates of chronic disease and chronic stress from systemic inequality.[24]

Inequality of opportunity and access has long been a hallmark of the American health care industry. Yet, before the COVID outbreak, the Trump administration sought to repeal critical provisions of the ACA, while presenting alternatives that independent studies predicted would cause millions of Americans to lose their coverage.[25] After numerous failed attempts to repeal the ACA, the Trump administration instead sought to nullify portions of the statute through separate legislation and regulation.[26] As part of the Tax Cuts and Jobs Act of 2017, the administration repealed the individual mandate, which required every American to have health insurance or be penalized.[27] In addition, the administration issued new rules allowing states to impose work requirements for Medicaid and stopped the reimbursement of insurance carriers that waive deductibles for low-income individuals.[28] During the Trump administration, the uninsured rate increased from 10.9 percent to 13.7 percent at the end of 2018. In absolute terms, these policies left more than 7 million additional people without health care coverage, many of whom were low-income, younger individuals, and women.[29]

Across the United States, communities economically decimated by the outbreak of COVID continued to face inequitable and insufficient access to health care services. Despite the ACA, current policies have resulted in significant increases in premiums and a decline in enrollment within the health care exchanges. These policies have exacerbated the barriers to health care faced by large portions of the nation.

Education

Education is a public good primarily provided by state and local institutions. While the Constitution does not explicitly guarantee a right to education, there are many references by the nation's early leaders to the importance of education. Thomas Jefferson observed that "[w]here every man is able to read, all is safe."[30] Jefferson's statement reflects the founders' belief that American democracy depended on an educated citizenry.

The founders recognized the need for citizens to be educated in order to strengthen their capacity for self-government. The importance of education was highlighted in 1787, when Congress, in the Northwest Ordinance, provided that "knowledge, being necessary to good government and the happiness of mankind, schools and the means of education shall forever be encouraged."[31]

The United States has never lived up to this ideal. In its landmark 1954 ruling in *Brown v. Board of Education*, the Supreme Court struck down the "separate but equal" doctrine that had governed racially segregated public education as a violation of the Equal Protection Clause of the Fourteenth Amendment.[32] In an opinion for a unanimous Court, Chief Justice Earl Warren wrote that education "is required in the performance of our most basic *public responsibilities. . . . It is the very foundation of good citizenship.*" Having recognized the link between education and democracy, the Court ruled that a state must provide education to all its students "on equal terms."[33]

Despite the promise of *Brown v. Board*, millions of American children today continue to be deprived of access to quality public education. Continuing inequities in public schools reinforce racial and economic disparities. Referred to as the 'great equalizer' by Horace Mann, public education is now at the root of the socioeconomic inequalities that permeate the United States.[34] Low-income communities and communities of color have continued to experience significant barriers in accessing public schools. Despite these trends, until recently the federal government has shown little indication that it is prepared to implement a comprehensive strategy for improving outcomes among the nation's most disadvantaged students.

Inequalities in public education are rooted in the nation's reliance on local control. Across the United States, public schools are overseen by local and state governments, with school boards playing a key role in implementing the curriculum. While local control is intended to maintain proximity to communities, it has resulted in chronic inequalities in funding, which have exacerbated disparities in student outcomes. With the decentralization of public education, communities have traditionally relied on property taxes to fund local schools. Yet, in 2019, the average White family held approximately ten times more wealth than the average Black family.[35] These economic disparities have played a key role in sustaining the significant concentration of underfunded public schools in predominantly Black and Latinx American communities.[36]

The lagging performance of the nation's public education system has drawn bipartisan criticism. With the release of the report *A Nation at Risk* in 1983, the Reagan administration drew public attention to what it termed the nation's "unilateral educational disarmament."[37] Since then, various initiatives, such as No Child Left Behind, have contributed to a rapid shift toward standards-based assessment. While intended to improve student outcomes within the nation's historically underserved communities, the impact of these initiatives in narrowing existing disparities in student outcomes has been limited.[38]

Across the United States, students continue to face inequality in academic opportunities and outcomes. These disparities affect students in every region, and they are particularly felt within communities of color. In 2018, 89 percent of White students completed high school, as compared to 81 percent of Latinx American and 79 percent of Black students.[39] At the same time, test scores among students in low-income, rural, and minority communities continued to trail those in affluent and predominantly White communities.[40]

The disruptions in educational instruction resulting from the pandemic lifted the veil on the chronic inequities in access and opportunity throughout the nation's public schools. As local and state institutions imposed social distancing requirements, millions of children were left without access to reliable internet or technological devices.[41] With many children in rural and low-income communities experiencing the adverse impact of the digital divide, existing funding and political structures failed to equitably meet the needs of all children. While disparities in access to broadband internet have long been a source of concern, the impact of COVID amplified the urgency of equipping students with the technological resources they need to compete in a competitive and globalized economy.

Housing

The federal government has historically played a role in the provision of safe, decent, and affordable housing for low-income families. In 1934, Congress responded to the Great Depression by creating the Federal Housing Administration (FHA). President Roosevelt lamented in his second inaugural address that "one third of a nation [is] ill-housed, ill-clad, [and] ill-nourished."[42]

After the end of World War II, FHA programs helped finance military housing for returning veterans and their families. Throughout the following decades, the FHA contributed to the production of millions of units of privately owned apartments for elderly, handicapped, and lower-income Americans.[43] However, the model of high-density public housing "projects" was increasingly questioned as these became stigmatized as centers of poverty, crime, and segregation. In 1974, the Housing and Community Development Act effectively ended most new construction of public housing.[44]

Before the passage of anti-discrimination housing legislation in the late 1960s, government and private institutions regularly engaged in the racially segregating practice of "redlining." Through this form of lending discrimination, racial minorities were denied the opportunity to purchase a home in certain communities.[45] In other instances, people of color were also denied loans on the basis of their race, which contributed to gaping wealth disparities.

In a 2019 report, the National Law Center on Homelessness and Poverty demonstrated how rising rents, stagnant wages, historically low rental vacancy rates, and the severe decline of federally subsidized housing have collectively led to a critical shortage of affordable housing units in the United States.[46] Here, as with education, significant disparities are apparent across the nation. Expert studies have demonstrated how historic and ongoing displacement, exclusion, and segregation continue to prevent people of color from obtaining and retaining their own homes and accessing safe, affordable housing.[47]

Throughout the post-war era, the concept of homeownership was a key element of the American Dream. For many Americans, the prospect of owning a home symbolized entry into the middle class and, by extension, embodied the core ideal of what it means to be an American. Yet, in communities around the country, the prospect of homeownership has become increasingly out of reach, particularly with the economic disruptions caused by the pandemic.

Increasing home prices have significantly outpaced any increase in wages. With the growth of wages now lagging the growth of housing costs in 80 percent of housing markets,[48] an individual working full-time must now earn approximately $17.90 per hour to afford a one-bedroom apartment. Yet, with the federal minimum wage largely stagnant at $7.25 per hour, many families have found themselves locked out of a highly competitive housing market. As 43.5 million Americans continue to experience poverty,[49] the federal minimum wage has proven inadequate, with approximately 11 million Americans paying more than half of their income in housing.[50]

To put these challenges into perspective, an individual earning the federal minimum wage would have to work approximately 103 hours per week, on average, to afford a one-bedroom apartment at the fair market rate. There are few alternatives for families in this situation, as only 1 percent of counties have a housing market that the nonprofit National Low Income Housing Coalition considers affordable for those earning the minimum wage.[51]

Shortages of affordable housing are exacerbated by existing federal policy. Decades of chronic underinvestment in renovating existing public housing, and a tepid rate of new construction, have contributed to the national shortage of 7 million affordable housing units.[52] The federal government has decreased spending on low-income housing assistance as a percentage of GDP and non-defense discretionary spending.[53]

These policies have contributed to an affordable housing crisis that impacts communities across the United States. As the purchasing power of the minimum wage has steadily eroded, more Americans have been experiencing challenges in accessing affordable housing.[54] Without a comprehensive policy response from the federal government and with limited support from local and state governments, there are now only thirty-seven affordable and available housing units for every one hundred extremely low-income households.[55]

While many Americans have found the prospect of homeownership increasingly out of reach, communities of color have been disproportionately hit by the affordable housing crisis. In 2019, over half a million individuals experienced homelessness on any given day.[56] Approximately 40 percent were Black and 22 percent were Latinx American.[57] These statistics show that policy failures at the local, state, and federal level have not only exacerbated existing shortages of affordable housing but have also disproportionately impacted historically marginalized and underserved communities of color.

Environmental Sustainability

The United States was an early leader in developing concepts and strategies around environmental sustainability. In a 1907 address to Congress, President Theodore Roosevelt observed that "the conservation of our natural resources and their proper use constitute the fundamental problem which underlies almost every other problem of our national life. We must maintain for our civilization the adequate material basis without which that civilization can not exist. We must show foresight, we must look ahead."[58]

The modern era of federal environmental policy was launched during the administration of President Richard Nixon. The National Environmental Policy Act (NEPA) of 1969, the first major federal environmental law, committed the United States to sustainability, declaring a national policy "to create and maintain conditions under which man and nature can exist in productive harmony, and fulfill the social, economic and other requirements of present and future generations of Americans."[59] Congress then established a statutory foundation for the United States Environmental Protection Agency (EPA), stating that it is the responsibility of the federal government to "use all practicable means . . . to improve and coordinate Federal plans, functions, programs, and resources to the end that the Nation may fulfil the responsibilities of each generation as trustee of the environment for succeeding generations."[60] The NEPA and subsequent congressional declarations established a broad national framework for protecting the environment.

There are numerous other federal and state environmental and sustainability laws that drive environmentally sound business and governmental practices, including the Clean Air Act, Clean Water Act, Resource Conservation and Recovery Act, Comprehensive Environmental Response, Compensation, and Liability Act, and Toxic Substances Control Act. Through these statutes, the federal legal framework supports a definition of sustainability that includes economic, environmental, and social elements.

The Trump administration pursued an aggressive strategy of rolling back existing environmental protections. In doing so, it embraced what it called a "business-friendly" agenda that was opposed by some businesses as detrimental to the long-term interests of the private sector.[61]

Under its then-administrator Scott Pruitt, the EPA abandoned its focus on implementing data-driven policies. In 2017, despite overwhelming scientific evidence demonstrating the threat of climate change, the Trump administration withdrew the United States from the Paris Climate Accord.[62] The EPA embarked on what observers called "an unprecedented attempt to delete or bury credible scientific information they find politically inconvenient."[63] Under Pruitt's pressure the EPA removed references to terms such as fossil fuels, greenhouse gases, and global warming. In addition, in a step toward fulfilling President Trump's campaign promise to abolish the EPA,[64] the administration proposed a 31 percent budget reduction for the agency.[65]

During the Trump administration, ninety-eight environmental rules and regulations were either repealed or relaxed. Nearly half of the rollbacks impacted emissions or drilling standards.[66] These impacts were disproportionately felt by low-income families and communities of color. Historically, people in low-income and predominately minority communities have had greater exposure to toxic pollution, with predominantly Black communities being exposed to significantly higher levels of industrial air pollution than White communities and experiencing a greater risk of premature death from particle pollution.[67] These disparities are rooted in socioeconomic factors, including dynamics in the housing market and disparities in access to health care.

In response to the Trump rollbacks of environmental protection, the Biden administration brought the United States back into the Paris Climate Accord and began to pursue policies of weaning the nation away from fossil fuel production and consumption and toward investment and use of renewable energy.

Fiscal Policy

Each of the critical challenges discussed in this chapter requires a robust and comprehensive response from federal, state, and local governments. The federal government has been constrained by recent fiscal policies.[68] These policies, which include tax reform initiatives that reduce tax revenues and largely benefit affluent individuals and large corporations, have limited the federal government's ability to invest in programs that promote equal access to public goods.

Starting in the Reagan administration, throughout the last four decades the United States has enacted tax reform initiatives championed as tools of economic growth that have disproportionately favored the wealthy. These initiatives have significantly reduced the tax burden on corporations and high-income individuals and, through their adverse impact on the federal deficit, laid the groundwork for significant cuts to discretionary spending.

The most recent of these initiatives is the Tax Cuts and Jobs Act of 2017. Among its significant provisions, the Trump tax reform package doubled the estate tax exemption, repealed the individual mandate of the Affordable Care Act, and reduced the corporate tax rate from 35 percent to 21 percent.[69] Before the outbreak of the COVID pandemic, these provisions were projected to reduce federal revenue by approximately $1 to 2 trillion between 2018 and 2025.[70]

The Trump administration prioritized reducing the tax burden on individuals and corporations while also pursuing an aggressive campaign to reduce discretionary federal spending. The administration proposed significant reductions in allocations to the Department of Education, and despite having failed to repeal the Affordable Care Act, it undermined various provisions of the statute through regulation. In doing so, the Trump administration signaled its intention to continue a fiscal policy that placed greater priority on reducing taxation than investing in public services.

The Biden administration has begun to reverse the Trump policy by following an aggressive strategy of investing in public goods. Funding these initiatives will require an effort to alleviate the chronic tax evasion that now deprives the federal government of one out of every six dollars that are owed in federal taxes.[71] In addition to proposing reform of the current tax laws—for example, by increasing the corporate tax rate—the Biden administration is seeking to strengthen enforcement of existing tax policies in order to create revenues for investing in public goods and services.[72]

There is no shortage of proposals for addressing the inequities facing American society. In most proposed solutions the federal government plays a central role in expanding and promoting equal access to public assets. If the United States is to make significant progress toward securing the freedom from want, the federal government must invest in public goods such as health care, education, housing, and environmental protection that are basic necessities of life.

ROLE OF THE PRIVATE SECTOR

The private sector serves as an engine of economic growth and job creation in the United States and is therefore a crucial participant in creating public goods and services. Corporations have the capacity to support or undermine the right of equal access. During the COVID crisis, the role of the private sector in maintaining services and providing employment came under scrutiny.

Some businesses played a critical role in responding to the pandemic, providing everything from rubber gloves and ventilators to diagnostic tools and the development of vaccines. Other companies were accused of damaging practices including exposing staff to unnecessary health risks, refusing paid sick leave, exploiting low-wage workers, engaging in share buyback programs, and paying large shareholder dividends while firing employees and closing plants.[73] The majority of dividends generated from these corporate practices have gone to higher-income Americans: according to data from the Internal Revenue Service, 69 percent of all dividends are paid to taxpayers with incomes over $200,000.[74]

Low-wage workers bore the brunt of the pandemic, risking their well-being while working to implement public health protocols and keeping essential service industries running. Twenty-four percent of U.S. civilian workers, or roughly 33.6 million people, had no paid sick leave during the early peak of the pandemic, according to the federal Bureau of Labor Statistics. Of those whose wages were $10.80 per hour or less, 69 percent had no paid sick leave. And only 27 percent of childcare workers and food preparation workers had access to paid sick leave.[75]

The COVID-related surge in unemployment claims exposed massive failures in the U.S. labor market. Job creation alone is not the answer to economic revival and poverty alleviation. Equitable growth requires *decent* jobs, where people can work in safe conditions and be paid fair wages. Government regulation is essential for preventing or minimizing negative social and environmental impacts of the labor market and ensuring that corrective remedies are provided to those harmed by unsafe working conditions.

In addition to providing jobs, goods, and services, the private sector contributes to the tax revenues necessary to finance public infrastructure and public services. However, 55 percent of the foreign profits of U.S. multinationals are currently booked in tax havens. Profit centers are disconnected from the places where firms employ workers and produce goods and services.[76]

Beyond the fiscal constraints imposed by the loss of corporate tax revenue, there are also misalignments between corporate shareholder value and public responsibility. The controversy surrounding the accident record of the Boeing 737 Max is a leading example. In the decade before the multiple accidents that resulted in numerous fatalities, Boeing allocated significant resources to shareholder buybacks, while its investment in research and development remained relatively flat.[77]

The private sector has the capacity to develop innovative solutions to acute and emerging societal challenges, such as the COVID pandemic and climate change. There are many business opportunities where profit-seeking and human and environmental sustainability objectives closely align.[78] The public and private sectors have complementary and often overlapping roles, and corporate responsibility should be a key component of providing equal access for all members of society to the basic necessities of life.

Workplace Problems and Rising Inequality

The private sector and government both have critical and interconnected roles to play in alleviating working poverty and in responding to social and economic challenges. Precarious livelihoods, lack of access to affordable health care, homelessness, and joblessness are growing concerns for millions of Americans. At the same time, Americans are experiencing rising inequality, as increasingly large proportions of the wealth generated in the United States ultimately end up in the hands of the wealthiest people. Since 1973, American productivity has increased by 77 percent, but hourly pay has grown by only 12 percent.[79]

According to the U.S. Census Bureau, about 40.6 million people, or 12.7 percent of the nation's population, lived below the poverty level in 2016.[80] Of these individuals, 7.6 million were classified as the "working poor," with 3.4 million full-time wage and salary workers.[81] The federal minimum wage has been stagnant at $7.25 per hour since 2009.[82] This is a poverty wage and has an effect on wages for millions of jobs. Overall, 58.3 million workers (43.7 percent) earn under $15 per hour, and 41.7 million (31.3 percent) earn under $12 per hour.[83] New employment opportunities increasingly take the form of insecure gig work, temporary contracting, or day labor, which is less likely to provide basic social benefits like health insurance.

Wealth inequality is rising in the United States. While the overall economy has grown significantly since the 1970s, the top 10 percent of earners received 87 percent of all income growth. The top 1 percent received 56 percent of all income growth from 1975 to 2006.[84] Over the last four decades, the labor share of income declined from 66 percent to 58 percent, and the average real wage of workers declined over a period in which total income in the United States almost tripled.[85] The combination of rising income and savings inequality has fueled further wealth inequality.

Labor unions provide an important structural avenue for improving the ability of the U.S. economy to create decent jobs. Unions in the United States have historically been champions of a range of laws that apply to and protect working people, including the minimum wage, occupational health and safety, paid sick leave, and equal employment opportunities.[86] Unions equip workers with the bargaining power they need to negotiate improvements to their working conditions and protect against exploitation.

Experts have highlighted attacks on freedom of association and fierce opposition on the part of employers when employees try to organize at their workplace.[87] Right-to-work laws have also undermined the strength of trade unions. In 2019, the percentage of wage and salary workers who were members of unions dropped to 10.3 percent, down from 20.1 percent in 1983, when the U.S. Bureau of Labor Statistics started reporting the figures.[88]

Finally, the United States has embraced automation and globalization with greater alacrity and fewer restrictions than almost any other nation. Deterioration in pay and job stability as a result of automation has been particularly acute in the U.S. over the past forty years.[89] Displaced workers whose jobs are offshored or automated receive relatively little protection or support.

Corporate Responsibility

Over the last three decades, the idea that businesses have social responsibilities has entered mainstream discourse and is increasingly the subject of political debate. Securing the freedom from want cannot be addressed by government alone—the private sector has a critical role to play; indeed, the private sector's own long-term success depends on its willingness and ability to take on a greater role in addressing social issues.

Historically, corporations were granted protected legal status because they served the public interest as well as a private interest. Indeed, early corporations were considered to be quasi-public entities.[90] For hundreds of years, most corporations were created to build and manage infrastructure projects that today would be considered public goods, such as highways, bridges, and canal systems. Corporations were regarded as a form of social institution. From the New Deal era through the post-war period and into the 1970s, it was widely accepted that in addition to making money for shareholders, "the corporation has other purposes of perhaps equal dignity: the satisfaction of consumer wants, the provision of meaningful employment opportunities, and the making of a contribution to the public life of its communities."[91]

A massive shift in thinking about the purpose of the corporation occurred in the early 1970s, typified by Chicago School economist Milton Friedman's edict that the sole social responsibility of a business was to increase profits.[92] Friedman's view, reflected in mainstream economic opinion, was that business decision-makers had an obligation to *maximize shareholder value.* For several successive decades, the doctrine of shareholder value maximization was almost unassailable. But in the wake of the 2008–2009 financial crisis, the pendulum started to swing in the other direction.

Earlier moments had already called the doctrine into question. South African apartheid became an important flashpoint in debates in the United States over the social responsibility of business. For many Americans, businesses that operated or invested in South Africa were regarded as complicit with a racist apartheid regime illegal under international law. Businesses that invested in South Africa became the targets of activist campaigns.[93] During the 1980s, more than 150 universities in the United States divested from companies that had investments and carried on business in apartheid South Africa.[94] The anti-apartheid consumer boycott gained support across the United States and around the world, ultimately colliding with the doctrine of shareholder value maximization. In the end, the apartheid regime fell.

The push for corporate responsibility intensified during the 1990s, but resulted primarily in voluntary, ad-hoc, and philanthropic efforts that did not produce new corporate governance structures or cultures to better align with social priorities or needs. In the following decade, calls for a more systemic and institutionalized corporate responsibility increased.[95] With rising inequality, climate disruption, rising health care costs, and the middle-class American Dream unattainable for many Americans, the demand for corporate responsibility entered the mainstream.

A recent example of the mainstreaming of corporate responsibility occurred in the summer of 2019, when the U.S. Business Roundtable (an organization of CEOs from more than two hundred of the country's largest corporations) issued a statement on "the purpose of a corporation," in which it rejected Friedman's shareholder value-maximization principle and endorsed a broader stakeholder principle. The Business Roundtable statement announced a commitment by the CEOs to "lead their companies for the benefit of all stakeholders—customers, employees, suppliers, communities and shareholders."[96]

Achieving progress in equal access to public goods and services will require a transformation of corporate finance and financial regulation. To address workplace problems, workers must be treated as ends in themselves, not simply as a means for generating profits for shareholders. A move in this direction would be the recognition that employees are *investments* rather than *expenses*. Employees comprise the company's *human capital* and ought to be managed accordingly (as a long-term capital investment, rather than an annual business expense). In 2019, the Investor Advisory Committee of the Securities Exchange Commission recommended that companies be required to disclose aspects of their "human capital management." The committee stated that "[t]oday's companies are increasingly dependent on their workforces as a source of value creation" and that, "for many of the most dynamic companies, human capital is their primary source of value."[97]

CONCLUSION: EQUAL ACCESS TO EXPANDED PUBLIC ASSETS

Communities across the United States continue to experience the adverse impact of chronic inequities in accessing the public goods and services that are the essential necessities of life. At the same time, the COVID pandemic has caused unprecedented health and economic challenges that are disproportionately burdening racial minorities and other vulnerable populations.

Protecting public health and rebuilding the economy remains, primarily, the responsibility of government institutions. However, providing equal access to public goods and services and addressing the inequities documented in this chapter will require comprehensive public and private sector collaboration. The government must work with the private sector, trade unions, civil society actors, and communities to create initiatives that deliver long-term wealth "in human, natural, social, and material assets."[98]

Ironically, Milton Friedman once wrote in a different context: "Only a crisis—actual or perceived—produces real change. When that crisis occurs, the actions that are taken depend on ideas to develop alternatives to existing policies, and to keep them alive and available until the politically impossible becomes politically inevitable."[99] With the nation reeling from a series of social and economic challenges, now is the time to implement ideas, develop alternatives to existing policies, and forge a new path aimed at securing the dignity, agency, and opportunity of all Americans. These ideas should provide the United States with the basis for a new social contract to guarantee equal access to the public goods and services that are essential for life, liberty, and the pursuit of happiness.

Policy Recommendations

- **Establish Fiscal Policy to Promote National Investment in Public Assets.** Enact a framework for government taxing and spending policy that promotes equality of access and opportunity in education, health care, housing, and the environment; enact tax reform that establishes graduated tax responsibility based on income and net worth, with tax incentives for private sector initiatives that would complement government fiscal policy in promoting equality of access and opportunity in education, health care, housing, and the environment; enact comprehensive relief to protect equality of access and opportunity during the COVID pandemic and similar emergencies.

- **Promote Equal Access to Health Care.** Transition to a health care system that provides universal access to affordable health care; provide funding for health care programs targeted at minorities and low-income groups at risk of developing COVID or other chronic diseases; reduce the national shortage of physicians by expanding federal funding for residency training.

- **Promote Equal Access to Education.** Reform public education funding by disconnecting the funding of local public schools from local property taxes and expanding federal funding to eliminate disparities among school districts resulting from differential property tax bases; establish universal prekindergarten education; increase federal support for intervention programs that provide academic resources for at-risk youth; increase federal funds to states that provide residents with free or substantially subsidized access to public universities and community colleges; target federal funds to high school science, technology, engineering, and mathematics (STEM) and civics programs and students pursuing postsecondary degrees in STEM and civics; invest in trade and technical schools.

- **Promote Equal Access to Affordable Housing.** Expand funding for low-income housing, including new construction and renovation; increase federal mortgage assistance and relief programs; expand the Earned Income Tax Credit to assist low-income homebuyers and renters; develop a programmatic strategy to address homelessness.
- **Promote Equal Access to a Safe Environment.** Develop a comprehensive strategy for transitioning the nation away from fossil fuels while investing in renewable energy; promote environmental justice by protecting vulnerable populations and communities from toxic and hazardous materials and other forms of environmental degradation; prohibit private and public entities from exploiting resources for economic gain within federal and state designated public lands; invest in maintaining critical physical and digital (e.g., broadband) infrastructure.

Part III

Due Process of Law

9

Giving Justice Its Due

How can the public be protected from crime while protecting the rights of the accused? That is the major public policy question in criminal justice. The answers given by politicians seeking to be "tough on crime" often reflect bias against the accused and misunderstanding of the facts.

Starting with the Nixon administration in the early 1970s, and gaining steam throughout the next decade, the prevailing view on criminal justice was that "tough on crime" laws make crime rates go down. That sentiment drew on a belief that criminals were not being sufficiently punished for their offenses, and that sentences should be increased—including mandatory minimums and "three strikes laws"—to remove criminals from communities and deter others from committing crimes. The incarceration rate more than tripled between 1980 and its peak in 2008, from 310 to 1,000 people incarcerated per 100,000 adults, for a prison population of 2,310,300. Today, the United States leads the world in incarceration at 1.8 million people, or 551 per 100,000, a rate more than four times that of comparable democracies in western Europe.[1]

The "get tough" policies had at best minimal impact on deterring crime. While crime rates fell in the 1990s and early 2000s, studies have found little relationship between the crime rate drop and higher rates of incarceration—accounting for less than 25 percent of the drop during the 1990s and 0 percent in the 2000s. In fact, the studies found that prison time actually increased an individual's proclivity to commit crimes, and some states with the highest increases in incarceration rates also had the smallest drop in crime.[2]

Given the high cost and limited effectiveness of increased imprisonment policies, states began pushing through limited reforms to reduce sentences and release offenders to community supervision. The crime rate decline continued as deincarceration and community supervision increased. Community supervision policies focused on reducing recidivism—the likelihood that a released prisoner would re-offend and return to incarceration—through drug treatment and reentry programs. Between 2007 and 2017, the Brennan Center for Justice found that thirty-four states reduced *both* crime *and* incarceration, decreasing prison populations and making communities safer. Massachusetts, for example, decreased crime by 40 percent during that period, at the same time reducing those incarcerated for nonviolent drug offenses by 45 percent.[3]

Small steps toward reform were also taken at the federal level. In 2018, a bipartisan coalition succeeded in passing legislation that made minor improvements in federal sentencing practices. The new law, The First Step Act, applied only to the 150,000 federal prisoners, a small percentage of the 1.8 million total prisoners in the United States. While it began to reform sentencing and prison conditions, the law left out many other aspects of the criminal justice system that trample on rights of due process.

On any given day there are nearly 7 million people directly involved with the U.S. corrections system—including arrests, pre-trial detention, sentencing, incarceration, probation, and parole.[4] At each stage of the process, there are issues of rights, including widespread discrimination and systemic racism that result in unequal justice for people of color. In addition to issues of equal protection, individuals caught up in the criminal justice system also face issues of due process—the constitutional requirement that authorities respect defendants' rights to be treated fairly when accused, tried, and convicted of a crime.

The U.S. Constitution protects the right to due process of law through the Fifth and Fourteenth Amendments. These provisions are intended to prevent the government from arbitrarily depriving individuals of life, liberty, or property. Government officials in many cases, however, have overridden these rights in the name of tougher enforcement at each stage of the criminal justice process. For example:

- Misconduct in **policing** can lead to violations of due process before an arrest is even made.

- Following arrest, **pre-trial detention** can unfairly deprive individuals of liberty as they are held because of an inability to pay bail.
- Once a verdict is reached, an arbitrary and poorly functioning **sentencing system** that relies on plea bargaining and mandatory minimum penalties can leave individuals serving unfairly long sentences.
- **Incarceration** may lead to cruel treatment through solitary confinement and other extreme forms of punishment, and prisoners are often exposed to violence from other prisoners.
- Upon **reentry**, former prisoners face barriers to reintegrating with society including limited employment opportunity, housing disqualification, bars on immigration, and voting disenfranchisement.
- **Juveniles** are often transferred to the adult system, where they are harshly punished.
- Exacerbating these problems is a growing **private prison system** that has created an economic demand for incarceration and cost cutting, reducing prisoner welfare.

Reform of the criminal justice system must take into account each stage of the process, respecting the due process rights of individuals throughout their interaction with the system while at the same time bringing criminals to justice and improving overall public safety.

JUSTICE DEFERRED, STEP BY STEP

Policing

Since the beginning of the tough-on-crime approach, and in particular the "war on drugs," law enforcement has become increasingly militarized. This process began with a policy signed into law by President Lyndon Johnson, the Omnibus Crime Control and Safe Streets Act of 1968, which provided federal funds to local governments to obtain military resources to control potential riots.[5] Fifty-four years later, nearly 90 percent of cities in the United States with populations above fifty thousand have paramilitary police units known as SWAT (Special Weapons and Tactics) teams.

After the 9/11 attacks in 2001, the Department of Homeland Security began to disburse billions of dollars in grants to local governments for counterterrorism and counter-drug programs.[6] This distribution of military equipment led to an increase in aggressive tactics by police: in 1980, SWAT teams were deployed three thousand times in U.S. cities, and by 2015 they were deployed more than fifty thousand times.[7] The increasing militarization of police has gone hand in hand with racial disparities in enforcement. A Maryland study found that SWAT deployments concentrated on minority neighborhoods, even when they had controlled for crime rates between minority and non-minority neighborhoods. The study found that "more heavily militarized policing in those areas had little effect on public safety, but did erode public trust in police among residents."[8]

Despite numerous states legalizing or decriminalizing marijuana in recent years, many police practices instituted during the "war on drugs" continue. Arrests for drug-related crimes peaked in 2006 at 1.9 million.[9] While there was a small decline between 2006 and 2015, the rate started to increase again in 2016; at the same time, arrests for violent crime and property crime continued to decline.[10] In 2018, 40 percent of drug-related arrests were for marijuana offenses, 92 percent of which were for simple possession.[11] Heroin and cocaine, on the other hand, only amounted to a quarter of the drug arrests in 2018. Marijuana arrests come at a high cost, with no clear correlation to public safety. The American Civil Liberties Union (ACLU) estimates that the annual cost of enforcing marijuana possession laws is $3.6 billion.[12]

Racial profiling is another abusive police practice. One study reviewed camera footage of over 100 million police vehicle stops across the United States by local and state police, revealing a persistent bias in the rate at which White drivers were stopped compared to Black drivers, who were 1.4 times more likely to be pulled over. The rate significantly decreased in Colorado and Washington after those states legalized marijuana, cutting down on drug searches during traffic stops.[13] A study of racial profiling in the Los Angeles Police Department found that "a Black person in a vehicle was four times more likely to be searched by police than a White person, and a Latino was three times more likely." However, "Whites were found with drugs, weapons or other contraband in 20 percent of searches, compared with 17 percent for

Blacks and 16 percent for Latinos. The totals include both searches of the vehicles and pat-down searches of the occupants."[14]

Pre-Trial System

Once the police have made an arrest, the court holds a pre-trial hearing to determine if the person should be released on bail while awaiting trial. Currently, there are nearly half a million people in the United States held in detention awaiting trial, mostly at the state and local level;[15] in fact, there are twice as many people in state and local jails awaiting trial than the entire number of people incarcerated in the federal prison system.[16] According to the Bureau of Justice Statistics, those awaiting trial now constitute 65 percent of jail inmates and 24 percent of the prison population.[17] Since the early 2000s, these percentages have been increasing, despite an overall decrease in crimes and arrests. According to a 2018 report by the Brookings Institution, the average defendant who is unable to afford bail spends anywhere from fifty to two hundred days in detention.[18]

Pre-trial detention can be necessary to ensure public safety by detaining some potentially violent offenders who may pose a risk of harm to society. For most defendants, however, monetary bail impinges on their rights to due process and a speedy trial if they are unable to meet the bail amount. Many of these prisoners remain in jail for weeks or months before trial, maintaining their presumption of innocence but facing punitive conditions while incarcerated.

The median bail for a felony is approximately $10,000, a figure out of reach for many defendants, and in some cases, defendants are unable to pay even a low bail of a few hundred dollars.[19] The bail system is intended to prevent anyone who is a flight risk from disappearing while awaiting trial, but cash bail disproportionately impacts people in poverty.[20] Many studies have found that the vast number of defendants return to face trial without financial incentive, making monetary bail unnecessary. On the other hand, detention can wreak havoc on the lives of individuals, costing them employment and putting a strain on their relationships,

There are racial disparities as well. For example, a study found that a county in Texas is "34 percent more likely to detain Black defendants compared to

White defendants."[21] In New Orleans, a 2018 study found that Black offenders are more likely than Whites to be required to pay bail, that the amount is usually higher, and they are less likely able to afford bail and therefore more likely to be incarcerated before trial.[22]

As increasing attention has been brought to bear on the issue of bail, some states have moved to reform their systems. In 2018, an appellate court in California found the state's system of cash bail unconstitutional because it discriminated against defendants with less money; the ruling required judges to consider a defendant's ability to pay in setting bail. A few months later, the state passed a new law to end its system of cash bail entirely, replacing it with an algorithm to determine which defendants to hold before trial based on safety risk.[23] The law, however, was overturned by voter referendum in the November 2020 election—opposed by both "law and order" adherents and left-wing activists who feared it placed too much emphasis on the risk-assessment algorithm.[24]

Other jurisdictions, including Washington, DC, and New Jersey, have also taken steps to reform their monetary bail systems. In 2019, the New York State Legislature instituted a measure to eliminate cash bail requirements for most misdemeanors and nonviolent offenses. As a result, the state saw its jail population decrease by as much as one-third. In early 2020, however, the legislature reversed course in a backlash against reform, passing a new law that allows a judge to order a person to be held on bail in certain circumstances.[25]

Evidence suggests that the current pre-trial system is not only contributing to further inequalities and inefficiencies in the system, there are also fiscal costs associated with the system.[26] Average daily costs of inmates vary widely depending on location—for example, as low as $48 in Cherokee County, Georgia, or as high as $571 in New York City. Overall, Brookings estimates that the cost of pre-trial detention, along with lawyers and other pre-trial expenses, amounts to $38 billion a year.[27]

Sentencing

Once a federal trial has been concluded, a convicted defendant is sentenced by a judge based on guidelines by the U.S. Sentencing Commission, an independent, bipartisan agency that is part of the judicial branch. Congress created the Sentencing Commission in 1984 to reduce disparities in sentencing across the United States.[28] From the moment of their promulgation, however, judges, lawyers, and criminal justice advocates asserted that the Commission's guidelines take away the judge's ability to determine a fair sentence based on the particular circumstances of the defendant and the crime and, in particular, disregard the role such factors as substance abuse disorders, trauma, and adverse childhood experiences play in criminal offending.

Several states have adopted their own assessment tools to determine a prisoner's sentence based on a computer algorithm intended to determine whether the offender is likely to commit another crime. Courts can reduce or waive a sentence when the data says the offender is unlikely to re-offend, but the algorithm can lead to harsher punishment when it predicts the opposite and is racially skewed.

In Wisconsin, for example, Eric Loomis pleaded guilty in May 2013 for attempting to flee a traffic officer and taking a car without the owner's permission. Data from a system called Correctional Offender Management Profiling for Alternative Sanctions suggested he would re-offend when released, leading the judge to consider a harsher sentence. Loomis appealed the sentence to the Wisconsin Supreme Court, in part because the methodology used to produce the algorithm was not disclosed to the Court or to the defendant. The Court upheld the ruling based on the fact that the judge did not rely solely on the assessment tool's recommendation, but only used it as a factor in the decision. As an analysis from the Brookings Institution pointed out, however, the ruling raises a "troubling paradox": either the tool played no part in the decision, rendering it useless, or it had some impact on the judge's ruling, raising constitutional concerns about the lack of transparency in the process.

Eric Loomis's case was not unusual. Defendants subjected to algorithm-based risk assessment are often denied access to the information input into the system that leads to the sentencing results.[29] This may violate due process rights when defendants do not have access to the data or methodology that determines their sentence.[30] Initially, the argument for using algorithms was based on the idea that artificial intelligence tools reduce human bias and decrease the number of people incarcerated by only focusing on those who truly pose a risk. Studies, however, call into question that premise, creating concern that algorithmic risk assessment could increase bias, exacerbating existing racial disparities.[31]

Plea Bargaining

A critical challenge in the sentencing process is that the overwhelming majority of criminal cases never come to trial. Approximately 98 percent of federal criminal cases in 2018 resulted in a guilty plea, reached by "plea bargaining," with only 2 percent going to trial and less than 1 percent resulting in an acquittal. Rates in state courts are similar, with cases rarely proceeding to trial.[32]

While plea bargaining does not necessarily violate due process rights, it can become a problem if it is overused because the system is burdened with a high number of cases.[33] High caseloads raise issues concerning adequate legal representation allowing lawyers to present their case and make informed decisions about the trial. In cases where a defendant cannot afford a lawyer, the court appoints a public defender who may be overburdened with cases and unable to devote sufficient time and resources to those cases. As with pre-trial detention, the system punishes the poor, who are not able to afford adequate representation. The possibility of a mandatory minimum sentence, should the defendant be convicted at trial, too often coerces pleas of guilty, whether or not the defendant is in fact guilty as charged.

Mandatory Minimum Sentencing for Drug Offenses

Mandatory minimums set specific penalties for the conviction of a crime, which then triggers a sentence regardless of other facts in the case.[34] The most common of these at the federal level involve drug and trafficking offenses, with minimum sentences of five to ten years depending on the amount of possession, under the Anti-Drug Abuse Act of 1986.[35]

The requirement for judges to impose a minimum sentence based on the charges brought by the prosecutor removes a judge's discretionary power. While recent federal legislation limits the use of mandatory minimum sentencing for low-level drug offenses, these sentences continue to be used, resulting in individuals with drug-related offenses serving lengthy prison terms without regard to the particular circumstances of their cases and too often coercing defendants to plead guilty.

Capital Punishment

The federal government suspended executions in 2003. In July 2020, it performed its first execution in seventeen years. The Trump administration went on to carry out another dozen executions before the end of its term. Currently, twenty-three states and Washington, DC, have abolished the death penalty and three states are subject to their own moratorium imposed by the governor.[36] However, twenty-seven states, mostly in the South and the West, continue to use capital punishment.

Constitutional challenges to capital punishment are principally based on two issues: the potential to inflict severe pain and the potential to execute a wrongfully convicted person. Practical challenges involve the high cost of the execution procedure. According to a study in 2012, approximately 3 percent of executions in the United States are botched in some way. Those rates vary by method, with more than 7 percent of lethal injections going wrong. These failed executions, the study found, usually resulted from a breakdown in protocols, and had the potential to inflict extreme pain. Death penalty opponents argue that such pain is a violation of the Eighth Amendment's prohibition against "cruel and unusual punishment."[37] In several cases in recent years the Supreme Court has ruled in 5–4 decisions that the use of lethal injections is constitutional.[38]

Given the irreversibility of capital punishment, one might assume that only individuals convicted of serious offenses without any shred of doubt would be subject to execution. That is not the case. A 2014 study found that at least 4 percent of individuals sentenced to death could have been exonerated.[39] In fact, since 1973, 185 people on death row have been exonerated for wrongful convictions, including inadequate defense, misused forensic data, false confessions, and eyewitness misidentification.[40]

Costs of capital sentences vary from state to state, but studies demonstrate that death penalty trials are more costly than non-capital trials. A Seattle University School of Law study found that each death penalty case cost the state of Washington an additional $1 million a year over cases where the death penalty was not sought.[41] A study by the Kansas Judicial Council found that it cost four times as much to defend a death penalty case as a non-death-penalty case.[42] These higher costs are associated with the extended trial in capital cases, the automatic appeal that is required, and the cost of execution.

Incarceration

While the 1.8 million people currently incarcerated in the United States represent a two-decade low, it is still far above the 330,000 people held in jails and prisons in 1980, in both absolute and relative numbers. The dramatic rise in incarceration resulted from a series of legislative and judicial policy changes in the 1980s and 1990s:

- In 1982, Congress passed the Violent Crime and Drug Improvements Act, increasing enforcement and penalties for drug offenses.[43]
- In 1984, President Reagan signed into law the Comprehensive Crime Control Act, which introduced the U.S. Sentencing Commission and increased penalties for drug-related offenses.[44]
- In 1988, the Supreme Court reinstated the federal death penalty.
- In 1990, the Crime Control Act increased penalties for juveniles, including raising the maximum term of imprisonment for some violent offenses.[45]
- In 1994, President Clinton signed the Violent Crime and Law Enforcement Act, increasing funding for police officers, instituting a federal three strikes sentencing mandate, providing grants to states

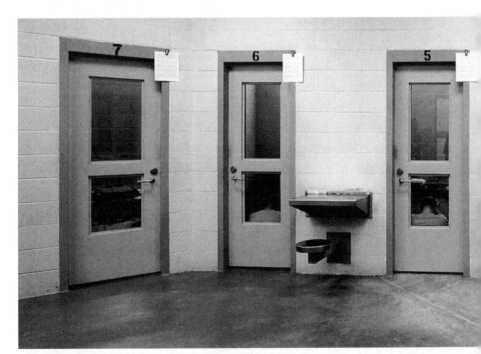

Young men sit in their cells at the Juvenile Detention Center in El Paso, Texas. Photo by Richard Ross.

to build prisons, and requiring inmates to serve 85 percent of their sentence.[46]

As the number of incarcerated people rose with these policies, so did government spending on the criminal justice system, which grew to $296 billion by 2016.[47] Prisons alone cost more than $80 billion per year, accounting for the second-fastest-growing category in state budgets, second only to Medicaid. The average yearly cost of a prisoner's confinement ranged per state from $14,000 to $69,000, with a national average of $33,000.[48]

While incarceration can have an impact on public safety and crime reduction, it also has diminishing returns as the number of people imprisoned increases.[49] Crime rates have steadily declined since the 1990s.[50] Many factors have been linked to that decline, including changing demographics, anti-crime technology, private security, an improving economy, and even reduction in exposure to lead, which has been correlated with aggressive behavior in children.[51]

Demonstrators call for abolishing jails and prisons outside the Manhattan Detention Complex. Photo by Andrew Lichtenstein/Corbis via Getty Images.

Incarceration rates, however, have at best a weak correlation with crime rates, which were already starting to drop as more people were imprisoned in the early 1980s.[52]

This limited correlation, combined with the high cost of maintaining correctional institutions, fueled bipartisan efforts to reform the criminal justice system beginning in the mid-2000s. The call for reform resulted from a unique convergence of factors, including efforts by liberals to reduce harsh punishment and increase racial equity, concerns from deficit hawks about the high costs of prisons, and a push from evangelical Christians for rehabilitation and forgiveness. One key figure bringing these divergent factions together was Charles Colson, a former Nixon administration official who became a "born-again Christian" during several months in federal prison for his role in the Watergate scandal. Upon release, he founded the Prison Fellowship, which ministered to prisoners and advocated for criminal justice reform.[53] Colson's record as a high-ranking conservative politician, and moral credibility as an evangelical, attracted others in the conservative sphere to take on the cause of justice reform.[54]

In 2003, President George W. Bush invited Colson to the White House to present findings showing a correlation between prison rehabilitation programs and lower rates of recidivism, leading to a focus on correctional policy reform both in the Bush administration and in Congress. In 2004, Bush launched the Prisoner Reentry Initiative, connecting released prisoners with faith-based and community organizations to help them find work and resources to transition back to life after prison, a program made permanent with the 2007 passage of the Second Chance Act.[55] Many states with fiscally conservative governments, including Texas and Indiana, initially led the way on reform. The Obama administration continued these efforts with a push to reform sentencing laws. At the same time, nonprofit organizations including the Pew Research Center, the Vera Institute of Justice, the Brennan Center for Justice, and the Brookings Institution played a key role in gathering data and evidence to show the efficacy of correctional policy reform in reducing costs and incarceration rates, while also improving public safety.

Despite such efforts, the prison system in the United States continues to be overburdened, leading to prisoners in many states being held in poor conditions that threaten their mental and physical health, safety, and human dignity. Prisons in Mississippi, for example, are under pressure to reform cruel conditions of confinement that resulted in deaths of prisoners. The Department of Justice has opened an investigation. At the same time, lawsuits for civil rights and constitutional violations point to unsanitary conditions, unclean water, rodents and other pests, inadequate medical care, and gang violence that led to the deaths. The Republican chairman of the Mississippi House Corrections Committee blamed the state for relying too heavily on incarceration and not investing enough in programs that incentivize reduced prison time and reentry programs.[56]

Mississippi's corrections department is emblematic of poor state-level prison conditions nationwide. A Department of Justice investigation in April 2019 found prison conditions in Alabama unconstitutional, violating the Eighth Amendment prohibition against cruel and unusual punishment. The report found that Alabama prisons have the highest suicide rate in the nation, three times the national average, as well as some of the highest rates of homicide and rape.[57] The Justice Department attributes the conditions to understaffing and overcrowding, with Alabama at an average occupancy rate of 182 percent. High suicide and homicide rates have also been reported in other state prisons, including Florida, Mississippi, Arizona, and Texas. In South Carolina, a gang dispute in 2018 sparked one of the deadliest prison riots in decades. Seven inmates were killed, and seventeen others were wounded in a series of fights.[58]

Advocates for prison reform have also criticized exploitive prison labor. Prisoners reportedly earn as little as 4 cents per hour for their labor. Prisoners are in coercive labor situations where power dynamics leave workers without bargaining power.[59] Prisoners are also used for dangerous work with few resources, such as fighting California fires where they are paid $1 per hour.[60]

Solitary confinement is another policy resulting from the "tough on crime" approach of the 1980s and early 1990s.[61] Most prisoners in solitary confinement spend twenty-three hours a day locked in their cells, without personal phone calls or physical contact. Recently, some states have moved away from solitary confinement based on concerns that it might constitute cruel and unusual punishment, as well as the high cost of operating solitary confinement facilities.[62] A 2015 lawsuit settlement in California severely limited solitary confinement in the state. Other states, including Colorado, New Jersey, and New York, have banned long-term solitary confinement (e.g., more than fifteen consecutive days), and eleven states have limited its use.[63]

The COVID pandemic has brought attention to health conditions within prisons. By May 2021, the Marshall Project reported approximately 400,000 COVID infections—more than one in every five prisoners—and 2,680 deaths of prisoners in state and federal prisons and local jails.[64] Reports found that prisoners were often not informed about infections and transmission.[65] Some prisoners who died from COVID were awaiting trial and unable to pay bail.[66]

In response to the virus, some states took steps to reduce their prison populations through a variety of methods, including legislation, executive orders by governors, court orders, and policy changes by corrections departments and parole boards. Significant efforts included legislation in New Jersey to release three thousand prisoners with less than a year left on their sentences; a governor's order in North Carolina to release 3,500 prisoners in response to an NAACP lawsuit over prison conditions; and a federal policy change resulting in the release of 24,000 prisoners by the U.S. Bureau of Prisons. Most efforts to reduce prison populations during the pandemic, however, have been modest.[67]

After incarceration, key challenges impact former prisoners' ability to reintegrate into society. These include difficulty in obtaining employment, housing, government benefits, and dealing with immigration status, as well as felony disenfranchisement.

An estimated 70 million Americans with a criminal record face difficulties in obtaining employment.[68] A study in the *American Economic Review* found that "even fairly minor felony records have large negative effects on employer callbacks."[69]

Felony disenfranchisement results in millions of citizens with a criminal record being excluded from voting.[70] One out of every forty-four American adults could not vote in the November 2020 election because of a criminal record—an estimated 5.2 million Americans, with a higher likelihood for racial minorities. Most of the individuals who are ineligible to vote are not in prison and have already served their time. Only seventeen states restore the right to vote after a convicted felon is released. In others, the right to vote is restored when a former prisoner completes probation or parole. In eleven states, former prisoners are permanently barred from voting, at least for some types of offenses. In two states, Maine and Vermont, prisoners retain the right to vote while incarcerated.[71]

Juvenile Detention

In 2019, law enforcement agencies in the United States made an estimated 696,600 arrests of children under the age of eighteen.[72] As of 2017, the Department of Justice reported a total of 43,580 juvenile offenders held in detention centers. Of that, approximately 12,600 were held by private facilities and 935 were inmates in adult jails. The number of juveniles in detention reached its peak in 1999 at 107,493 and has declined since.[73] Youth of color are disproportionately represented in the juvenile system (including adult sentencing) and stay for longer periods of time than White youth.[74] Children and youth held in adult prisons have limited access to education and rehabilitative services appropriate for their age and development.

Trying children as adults began in the late 1990s, as the now-discredited myth that some children were vicious "superpredators" took hold, leading to the mantra "adult time for adult crime." In 2001, a report by the U.S. Surgeon General found that there was no evidence that children in the 1990s were more frequent or vicious offenders than children in previous years.[75]

Research has established that children's brains are less mature than those of adults, and that juveniles tend to be more impulsive and have less control than older people. Psychologists have argued that juveniles should not be subject to the same punishment as adults for the same crimes.[76] Other studies have shown that there is limited or no deterrent effect of severe punishment of children. Long sentences for children may negatively impact their psychological development, creating negative future consequences for both the children and society. Among other issues, juveniles tried as adults are five times as likely to experience sexual assault in prison.[77] Based on these findings, the U.S. Supreme Court has ruled in four separate cases since 2005 that children cannot be treated as adults and sentenced to life without parole. The Court found that children are "constitutionally different" than adults and should not receive the harshest punishment, mandatory life without parole.

Several states have refused to resentence adults serving life sentences who were originally sentenced as juveniles to mandatory life without parole.[78] In April 2021, there were 1,465 people serving sentences of life without parole for crimes committed as juveniles.[79] In 2021, the U.S. Supreme Court issued a surprise ruling that rolled back rights for juvenile offenders when it ruled 6–3 that a state judge could sentence a juvenile convicted of murder to life without parole, so long as the judge understood that he had the discretion not to do so. Writing for the majority, Justice Brett Kavanaugh asserted that "the states make those broad moral and policy judgments in the first instance when enacting their sentencing laws, and state sentencing judges and juries then determine the proper sentence in individual cases."[80]

Juvenile detention is very costly, with the average cost for incarcerating a young person between $35,000 and $64,000 a year. Reform advocates argue that the money would be better spent on rehabilitative or early intervention programs that could keep young people out of prison. A year of Head Start, for example, costs $4,300 per child a year.[81]

Private Prisons

Between 1980 and 2013, the federal prison population increased by 800 percent, a faster rate than the Bureau of Prisons could accommodate, leading to the use of private prison facilities. By 2013, when the prison population reached its peak, 15 percent of the federal prison population was housed in private facilities.[82] States also relied on the use of private facilities to accommodate the dramatic increase in state prisoners.

While private prison advocates have argued that private companies are able to house prisoners more efficiently, critics have pointed out that the need to profit off prisoners provides exactly the wrong incentives, encouraging prison companies to cut corners on food, staffing, rehabilitation programs, and other costs. The Department of Justice Inspector General found in 2016 that private prisons had a 28 percent higher rate of prisoner-on-prisoner assaults, and twice the number of assaults on prisoners by corrections officials compared to federally run facilities.[83] After large-scale criticisms of conditions in private prisons, as well as a decrease in the number of prisoners, the Justice Department announced in August 2016 that it would gradually phase out the use of private prisons in the federal prison system.[84]

With the election of Donald Trump, however, the private prison ban was reversed in 2017. According to the Bureau of Prisons statistics, about 128,063 people were housed in private prison facilities in 2018, including both federal and state prisoners, about 8 percent of the total prison population,[85] most in facilities owned by the two main private prison companies, GEO Group and CoreCivic (formerly known as Corrections Corporation of America).[86] Upon inauguration, President Biden signed an executive order in January 2021 phasing out the federal use of private prisons, although they still remain in operation for state prisoners.[87]

The challenge with privatization is not just the facilities but also the other related private industries. For example, the prison phone industry earns an estimated $1.2 billion per year, with calls costing up to $25 for a fifteen-minute local call since these companies operate as monopolies. Privatized prison health care generates $1.4 billion in annual revenues and has been the subject of 660 separate malpractice lawsuits over five years.[88]

REFORM MOVEMENT

To begin to address inequities and other flaws in the criminal justice system, bipartisan efforts have been undertaken to reduce the economic and social costs of the system and restore basic due process rights.

Recent Reforms

The First Step Act (FSA), signed into law by President Trump in December 2018, expanded job training and other programs aimed at reducing recidivism rates among federal prisoners. The FSA also modified mandatory minimum sentencing and expanded early-release programs.[89] While the FSA applied only to federal prisons, it provided states with a roadmap of options they could adopt to reform their systems.[90] The Act mandated a Risk and Needs Assessment system that matches people in prison to programs supporting their rehabilitation. To incentivize participation, prisoners earn ten days of Earned Time Credit for every thirty days of programming. The Act also scaled back some components of the 1994 Crime Bill, eliminating mandatory "three strikes" life sentences for drug offenses, commuting the sentences of thousands of prisoners serving harsh sentences for crack cocaine convictions, giving judges discretion to sentence below mandatory minimums, and requiring the Bureau of Prisons to place those convicted of crimes in facilities within five hundred miles of their families. The FSA also improved a compassionate release process for terminally ill and elderly prisoners, allocating $375 million for programs and classes. The Act increased Good Time Credit, banned placing juveniles in solitary confinement, provided women with hygiene products free of charge, and banned the shackling of pregnant women, women in labor, and women postpartum.

Since the FSA was enacted in December 2018, it has resulted in the release of approximately three thousand prisoners, and sentence reductions for another two thousand—the majority of them Black men. Parts of the legislation dealing with prison conditions and rehabilitation have not been implemented. These issues involve programs that are understaffed and underfunded, with the Justice Department providing only $75 million of the estimated $300 million needed to properly fund programming.[91] In addition, data has shown that most of the reductions in prison populations have occurred from the drop in new admissions rather than release of existing prisoners. In April 2021, Senators Dick Durbin (D-IL) and Chuck Grassley (R-IA) co-sponsored the bipartisan First Step Implementation Act to expand sentencing reform and make more of the FSA's provisions retroactive to existing prisoners.[92]

Advocacy organizations for criminal justice reform have been working to identify issues and lobby members of Congress for changes. For example, the Justice Action Network promoted legislation to eliminate solitary confinement and prevent pregnant women from being shackled.[93] Social justice movements have drawn attention to mass incarceration and racial disparity. The Black Lives Matter movement has focused on police reform.

On the state level, both Republican- and Democratic-led states have enacted reforms.[94] Between 2008 and 2016, thirty-six states reduced imprisonment rates, and all but one of them (Alaska) reduced crime rates as well—often by double digits.[95] Texas implemented prison reform, starting in 2005 with a decision not to build new prisons because of high costs; expanding drug and alcohol treatment, mental health, and other rehabilitative programs in prisons; and closing eight state prisons.[96]

Other states have enacted similar reforms. Starting in 2015, Minnesota determined that a major driver of prison admissions was technical violation of probation. The state made changes, reducing prison reentry from technical violations and saving on the cost of building new facilities.[97] In 2015, South Dakota passed comprehensive reform legislation, including incentives for diversion programs as a default response for many lower-level offenses. After three years, the sentencing of youth to juvenile detention dropped by 63 percent. In 2017, Kansas reformed its juvenile detention system, with children convicted of a misdemeanor with no prior offense entering a diversion program instead of a juvenile facility. By the end of 2018, the program had resulted in $30 million of savings, with projections of $72 million by 2022.[98]

In 2020, several states passed laws increasing accountability for law enforcement. For example, Colorado passed bipartisan legislation to eliminate qualified immunity for police officers, restrict the use of deadly force, and mandate data disclosure. New York repealed measures shielding officers' disciplinary records. Virginia became the third state to ban no-knock warrants, and states including Connecticut, Iowa, Minnesota, and New York banned the use of tactics such as neck restraints and chokeholds.

States also enacted adult sentencing reforms. In 2020, North Carolina passed its own First Step Act, retroactively reducing sentences for prisoners convicted of low-level drug offenses. By the end of 2020, fifteen states had legalized marijuana use through legislation or ballot initiatives, reducing a major driver of prison admissions for nonviolent offenders. Oregon voters went a step further, adopting a ballot initiative decriminalizing possession of *all* drugs including cocaine, heroin, and methamphetamine, punishing possession of small amounts with fines rather than prison.

Six states have recently adopted a system to automatically expunge convictions for low-level crimes, including marijuana convictions, allowing for smoother reentry after release from prison. Another half-dozen states have taken steps to end felony disenfranchisement, restoring voting rights to previously incarcerated or convicted people.[99]

Positive reforms such as these have in recent years continued to decrease prison populations on both the state and federal levels, while allowing for the more humane treatment of those involved in the criminal justice system, and at the same time improving public safety. If bipartisan cooperation could continue, the criminal justice system in the United States could begin to return due process rights to those involved in all aspects of the system.

Policy Recommendations

- **Reform Law Enforcement and Strengthen Public Safety.** Public safety reforms should be designed and implemented to redefine law enforcement, increase funding of social services, abolish qualified immunity (which shields police officers from accountability through civil liability), demilitarize the police, prohibit chokeholds and no-knock unannounced searches, eliminate racial discrimination in policing, and bar police unions from blocking disciplinary actions against police officers. Some police funding should be redirected to social service agencies that can better perform non-law-enforcement functions currently assigned to police, such as mental health care, drug treatment, homeless assistance, community mediation, and restorative justice. Public safety and racial justice would be advanced by making greater investments in communities ravaged by violence and the discriminatory justice system.

- **Reduce Mass Incarceration.** Review and reform federal and state sentencing codes and procedures to reduce mass incarceration and create alternatives to imprisonment, establish procedures for the early release of prisoners during the COVID pandemic and similar public health emergencies, expand the release of nonviolent offenders, and create increased opportunities for home confinement under the federal First Step Act.
- **Reform Sentencing Laws and Practices.** Eliminate federal and state mandatory minimum sentencing, treat drug abuse as a rehabilitation issue not requiring imprisonment, decriminalize marijuana use, and abolish the death penalty.
- **Reduce Pre-Trial Detention.** Eliminate federal and state cash bail in most cases and limit the use of pre-trial detention to violent crimes where the defendant is a direct threat to public safety.
- **Reduce Juvenile Detention.** Develop federal and state programs to shut down the "school-to-prison pipeline," implement diversion and rehabilitation programs for juveniles who have committed nonviolent offenses, prohibit the charging of juveniles as adults and holding them in adult facilities, and resentence prisoners serving long prison sentences that were imposed when they were juveniles.
- **Ban Private Prisons.** Ban the private operation of prisons and detention centers on both state and federal levels.

10

Building Bridges, Not Walls:
Refugees and Asylum-Seekers

"Give me your tired, your poor,
Your huddled masses yearning to breathe free,
The wretched refuse of your teeming shore.
Send these, the homeless, tempest-tost to me,
I lift my lamp beside the golden door!"

These lines from Emma Lazarus's poem, "The New Colossus," engraved on the base of the Statue of Liberty, capture the vision of the United States as a beacon of hope and opportunity for millions around the world. For centuries, waves of migrants and refugees have come to the United States seeking economic opportunity and freedom from oppression. While many found what they desired, many others encountered persecution, resentment, and xenophobia. In the case of the millions of Africans whose migration was forced, who were kidnapped and part of the transatlantic slave trade, they and their descendants' experiences in enslavement were marked by brutal, degrading, and inhumane treatment.

Tensions over competing visions of immigration, and between inclusion and exclusion, mark most of the history of the United States. While U.S. laws on immigration have varied over the decades and centuries, government policies have been influenced by public opinion and have shaped public perception of newcomers.[1]

Laws passed in the late nineteenth century and first half of the twentieth century actively discriminated against Asian immigrants, favored literate immigrants from western Europe, and numerically restricted the number of individuals who could seek refuge in the United States.[2] In the decades that followed World War II and the Holocaust, the Civil Rights Movement contributed to changes in U.S. law and policy, including ratification of international agreements protecting asylum-seekers from persecution, ending quotas based on nationality, and affirming constitutional protections for migrants seeking entry.[3] At the same time, however, xenophobia continued to find purchase in the public sphere, with caps on immigration from Mexico and Latin America, as well as scapegoating of immigrants.[4] Today, while U.S. laws provide tools to advance due process rights for immigrants and reflect a legal basis for a rights-oriented vision, there remains a huge gap between aspiration and reality, especially with the exclusionary and cruel policies and practices of the Trump administration that were developed and implemented with little regard for U.S. and international law, and continued challenges presented by the Biden administration.

NATURALIZATION AND NATIVISM: AN INTERTWINED HISTORY

The Naturalization Act of 1790 was the first law passed by Congress regulating who could be become a citizen. It allowed any "free White person . . . of

Naturalization ceremony.

A group of immigrants traveling aboard a ship celebrate as they catch their first glimpse of the Statue of Liberty and Ellis Island in New York Harbor. Photo by Edwin Levick/Getty Images.

a good character" who had been in the United States for at least two years to apply.[5] The first U.S. Census took place later that year, with the English comprising the largest ethnic group and with one in five Americans being of African descent. German and Irish immigration in the early and middle parts of the nineteenth century was followed by increased immigration from eastern and central Europe later in the nineteenth century.[6]

In a climate of racial violence against Chinese immigrants, an 1854 Supreme Court decision, *People v. Hall*, ruled that Chinese immigrants—similar to African Americans and Native Americans—could not testify in court, thereby rendering them unable to seek redress and justice.[7] Later, the Chinese Exclusion Act of 1882 barred Chinese people from immigrating to the United States, reflecting a backlash against Chinese immigrants working in a range of sectors including the railroads, mining, and agriculture. This law represented the first in U.S. history to "place broad restrictions on certain immigrant groups."[8]

The Immigration Act of 1891 expanded restrictions, and included "[a]ll idiots, insane persons, paupers or persons likely to become a public charge, persons suffering from a loathsome or a dangerous contagious disease, persons who have been convicted of a felony or other infamous crime or misdemeanor involving moral turpitude, [and] polygamists."[9] The first immigration station, Ellis Island, opened in 1892 and received over 12 million immigrants between 1892 and 1954.[10]

Xenophobia at the beginning of the twentieth century and the start of World War I led to further restrictions. The Immigration Act of 1917, also known as the Asiatic Barred Zone Act, prohibited immigration from most Asian countries and established an English literacy requirement.[11] The Immigration Act of 1924 limited the entry of immigrants through a quota by nationality at the time of the 1890 census, favoring immigrants from western and northern Europe.[12] During World War II, the United States accepted 125,000 German refugees, most of whom were Jewish. More broadly, an estimated 180,000 to 220,000 refugees from Europe, mostly Jewish and from central and western Europe, immigrated to the United States between 1933 and 1945. Overall, the United States accepted more refugees seeking to escape Nazi persecution than any other country. Despite this role, the low quotas set under the Immigration Act of 1924 meant that the United States accommodated only a small percentage of people attempting to flee the Holocaust. Jewish people from eastern Europe had very little chance of emigration, and the vast majority were killed by the Nazi regime.[13]

It was not until the passage of the Immigration and Nationality Act of 1965 that Congress opened immigration to a range of other nationalities, ending the prior system that privileged immigrants from the United Kingdom, Ireland, and Germany.[14] The Migration Policy Institute, a non-partisan think tank, noted that "[b]uilding on a campaign promise by President Kennedy, and with a strong push by President Johnson amid the enactment of other major civil-rights legislation, the 1965 law abolished the national-origins quota system." President Johnson signed the bill at the foot of the Statue of Liberty, a year after the 1964 Civil Rights Act and the same year as the 1965 Voting Rights

Act. This legislation served as the impetus to move the United States from a restrictive and exclusionary vision to an inclusive and multicultural one.[15]

Since then, the pendulum has swung again in the opposite direction, and restrictive legislation has focused on reducing immigration, reducing access to benefits for immigrants, increasing border surveillance and security, and, in recent years, reducing refugee levels.[16] Despite these restrictive public policies and legislative rollbacks, the United States is still on a path of racial and demographic diversification, with no racial or ethnic majority group projected by the year 2055, according to the Pew Research Center.[17] In summary, the history of immigration to the United States has been defined by oscillation between inclusion and exclusion, expansion and rollback.

Obligations Under the U.S. Constitution and International Law

The Fifth and Fourteenth Amendments to the U.S. Constitution provide safeguards against arbitrary abridgement of fundamental rights to life, liberty, and property without due process of law, a principle that at its core ensures individuals can contest arbitrary or wrongful acts by the government through the judicial process. On issues of immigration, the Supreme Court has established in the last century that procedural due process protections extend to foreign migrants seeking entry to the United States.[18] Moreover, America's adherence to the 1951 United Nations Refugee Convention binds it to international treaty obligations to secure the rights and safety of asylum-seekers.[19] (While the United States has not signed the Convention itself, its obligations under the treaty arise from signing the 1967 Protocol to the Convention.[20])

The 1951 Refugee Convention and the subsequent 1967 Protocol Relating to the Status of Refugees set out binding obligations requiring nations to protect refugees seeking asylum. The Protocol defines a refugee as an individual who, "owing to well-founded fear of being persecuted for reasons of race, religion, nationality, membership of a particular social group or political opinion, is outside the country of his nationality and is unable or, owing to such fear, is unwilling to avail himself of the protection of their country . . . or to return to it. This definition emphasizes the protection of [these] persons from political or other forms of persecution."[21] As the 2011 handbook to the Convention from the United Nations High Commissioner for Refugees (UNHCR) explains, the standard for persecution includes "a threat to life or freedom" and other "serious violations of human rights" based on one's identity or beliefs.[22]

The United States defines refugees in accordance with the UNHCR definition as individuals fleeing their own countries because of persecution or fear of persecution due to race, religion, nationality, and/or membership in a social group or political opinion. Individuals may apply for refugee status only from outside the United States; asylum-seekers are individuals seeking refugee status who are already in the United States or at a port of entry.[23] Under the 1951 Convention, the United States must guarantee refugees protection from being returned to conditions of persecution ("non-refoulement"), as well as access to courts and the possibility of assimilation and naturalization.[24] Of course, many of the conditions causing vulnerable people to flee their countries of origin today are markedly different and much broader than the fear of persecution as conceived seventy years ago, raising questions about whether the international definition of a refugee as well as U.S. laws and policies need to adapt and expand to address these changed circumstances.

The United States acceded to the Protocol in 1968, binding U.S. law to the responsibilities it sets forth.[25] Under the Supremacy Clause of the U.S. Constitution, international treaties made pursuant to the Constitution's procedures are part of the "supreme Law of the Land."[26] Accordingly, the United States has a constitutional obligation to secure the rights of refugees as articulated by the Refugee Protocol.

One of the most crucial rights, affirmed as a cornerstone of international refugee law, is the right of refugees not to be returned to a country where they face serious threats to their lives or freedom.[27] In today's context, there is an urgent need to improve the asylum system by shifting away from restrictions that generate and incentivize the creation of migration "crises" to an approach that preventively addresses the predictable need for mobility and equalizes access to legal mobility across races, classes, and genders.

Over the course of the nineteenth through twenty-first centuries, the U.S. Supreme Court has recognized executive and legislative discretion in matters of immigration where national sovereignty is concerned.[28] Yet even under this degree of deference, the Court has consistently held that immigration policies, such as deportation procedures, are subject to constitutional scrutiny.[29] Measures such as indefinite detention without recourse to judicial or administrative review are unconstitutional regardless of the legal status of the individuals detained.[30] In *Yamataya v. Fisher* (1903), a case reviewing the U.S. government's deportation authority, the Supreme Court recognized that procedures for deporting immigrants within the country or at the border require a hearing of some kind.[31] In its ruling, the Court rejected the position that the executive branch "may disregard the fundamental principles that inhere in 'due process of law' as understood at the time of the adoption of the Constitution."[32] In other words, executive discretion cannot justify the denial of a fundamental liberty such as due process of law.

The century-old precedent set in *Yamataya* was reaffirmed and strengthened in *Reno v. Flores* (1993), which addressed the detention and release of unaccompanied minors. In this case, several justices concurred that detained children have "a constitutionally protected interest in freedom from institutional confinement," and they may generally be released only to a parent, legal guardian, adult relative, or another person designated by a parent or guardian, or otherwise guaranteed "a suitable placement . . . in a facility designed for the occupancy of juveniles."[33] In the words of Supreme Court Justice Antonin Scalia, "it is well established that the Fifth Amendment entitles aliens to due process of law in deportation proceedings."[34] The decision reinforced the principle that immigrants are entitled to procedural fairness in asylum proceedings and to substantive rights in their treatment, on account of their personhood and human dignity, once inside the United States. However, in practice, the way in which asylum proceedings are conducted is anything but procedurally fair.[35]

In the more recent case of *Zadvydas v. Davis* (2001), the Supreme Court held that indefinite detention of immigrants was unconstitutional and ruled that the Fourteenth Amendment's due process protection applies to all individuals "whether their presence is lawful, unlawful, temporary, or permanent."[36] Furthermore, the Court acknowledged that while Congress may exercise discretion over matters of immigration, Congress must still "choose a constitutionally permissible means of implementing" that power.[37] The decision reaffirmed the due process safeguards for all persons on U.S. soil regardless of their immigration status.

Reaffirming rights and responsibilities in the context of migration requires the United States to reverse exclusionary and cruel policies and develop an inclusionary approach that can create a humane and just immigration system. An important starting point for such an approach is around the U.S.-Mexico border and migration from the Northern Triangle.

BORDERLANDS: MEXICO AND THE NORTHERN TRIANGLE

The Northern Triangle—comprising the Central American countries of Honduras, El Salvador, and Guatemala—is racked by poverty, food insecurity, the legacy of civil war, and violence, with murder rates in Central America among the highest in the world.[38] According to the Council on Foreign Relations, "[t]o a certain extent, Central America's predicament is one of geography—it is sandwiched between some of the world's largest drug producers in South America and the world's largest consumer of illegal drugs, the United States." U.S. intervention during bloody civil wars in the region contributed significantly to destabilization and violence, while U.S. demand for drugs such as cocaine "buttresses the case for increased U.S. responsibility."[39] The roots of U.S. intervention in Latin America go much further back, to the Monroe Doctrine issued by President James Monroe in 1823 and the Roosevelt Corollary issued by President Theodore Roosevelt in 1904, according to which the United States could intervene in the internal affairs of a Latin American country in the case of wrongdoing by its government.[40]

While migration in the 1990s and 2000s largely consisted of adults coming from Mexico looking for work, over the last decade there has been a shift to unaccompanied minors and families from the Northern Triangle who are seeking asylum.[41] U.S. policy has largely been reactive over the decades in response to migration flows until the Trump administration came into office.

Deter, Detain, and Deport

President Trump made the issue of immigration and the border a signature rallying cry of his election campaign, deriding Mexicans and insisting on the construction of a border wall to stem migration.[42] Numerous policies and executive orders, some well-known and some hidden, were enacted during his term that demonized, stigmatized, and deterred migrants.[43]

Asylum Ban

One of the most egregious attempts to deter asylum-seekers was the Trump asylum ban. In November 2018, the Trump administration issued a presidential proclamation banning individuals who do not present themselves at a point of entry from applying for asylum, even if they had legitimate claims of credible fear.[44] The ban was implemented through an interim final rule (IFR) allowing for immediate implementation without the regular notice and comment period usually mandated for significant regulatory changes.[45] However, the U.S. Court of Appeals upheld an injunction against the asylum ban in February 2020 in *East Bay Sanctuary Covenant v. Trump*, on the ground that the government's ban unlawfully precluded migrants who use an explicitly authorized method of entry from asylum.[46]

In July 2019, the administration introduced yet another IFR banning all individuals, including children, who have traveled through another country to reach the United States from applying for asylum. This transit-country rule was, in effect, an asylum ban barring non-Mexican asylum-seekers from entering the United States through the southern border.[47] The administration's rationale was based on an assertion that the United States should not be the first provider of refuge to asylum-seekers if there are closer countries that may offer protection. This rationale flies in the face of the reality confronted by migrants from Central America, who do not often have safe proximate countries where they can seek safety from violence and repression.[48]

In order to further tighten the transit-country rule, in 2019, the Trump administration started to push for "safe third country" asylum cooperation agreements with Mexico and Central American countries to preclude asylum applications in the United States by refugees who transited through those countries to reach the U.S. border. By designating neighboring states as "safe third countries," the Trump administration sought to use them as buffer zones against unwanted flows of asylum-seekers. According to U.S. law, the elements of a "safe third country" are that a bilateral or multilateral agreement must exist; the lives and freedom of refugees would not be threatened there on account of "race, religion, nationality, membership of a particular social group, or political opinion"; and refugees would have "access to a full and fair procedure for determining a claim to asylum or equivalent temporary protection."[49]

While Mexico rejected such an asylum cooperation agreement, the Trump administration succeeded in entering into agreements with Guatemala in July 2019, and El Salvador and Honduras in September 2019. The agreements required all asylum-seekers arriving at the U.S. southern border who previously passed through any of these countries to be transferred there to pursue asylum.[50] Human rights advocates, however, contended that these countries not only are incapable of protecting their own citizens from persecution but also lack adequate systems for adjudicating asylum claims.[51] At the time of the agreement, the U.S. Department of Homeland Security (DHS) touted El Salvador as "a leader in countering human smugglers, traffickers, transnational criminal organizations, and gangs."[52] On the other hand, the State Department warned potential visitors to El Salvador to reconsider travel or exercise increased caution when traveling to the country due to crime. In 2019 and still as of 2021, the description of the country on the State Department website reads, "Violent crime, such as murder, assault, rape, and armed robbery, is common. Gang activity, such as extortion, violent street crime, and narcotics and arms trafficking, is widespread. Local police may lack the resources to respond effectively to serious criminal incidents."[53]

In another effort, a "metering" policy introduced by President Trump in 2018 restricted the number of individuals who can make asylum claims at any port of entry along the U.S.-Mexico border. Anyone who sets foot in the United States is by law guaranteed the ability to request asylum. However, as a result of the metering policy, asylum-seekers were forced to put their names on a list and return to Mexico to wait in dangerous, unstable conditions until it was their turn to file their asylum claim. Moreover, they must then return to Mexico to wait months and even years for their case to be granted a hearing with a judge.[54]

While the metering policy meant that asylum-seekers were made to wait in Mexico until their hearing, subsequent policies by the Trump administration reinforced this approach through additional restrictions.[55] In particular, the administration's contradictorily titled Migrant Protection Protocols (MPP) forced asylum-seekers to wait in Mexico not only to await their hearings, but for the duration of their immigration proceedings.[56] In its first thirteen months, MPP required approximately sixty thousand migrants to wait in Mexico while their cases were processed in the United States.[57] While waiting for a chance to be heard in immigration court, these migrants struggled to find safe and stable shelter and faced dangerous conditions of violence, extortion, and other crimes.[58] As of June 2019, five months after MPP was enacted, only about 1 percent of people returned to Mexico under the protocols had been able to secure legal representation in their court cases.[59] In addition, the program was associated with numerous instances of family separations.[60] This initiative violated international refugee law.[61] The Biden administration announced a suspension of new enrollments in MPP effective January 21, 2021,[62] and officially ended the program in June 2021.[63]

The Biden administration has also made efforts to deter immigration since coming into office. Notably, Vice President Kamala Harris told Central Americans considering migrating to the United States "do not come" while speaking at a press conference in Guatemala.[64] Additionally, Vice President Harris further emphasized that the United States would "continue to enforce [its] laws and secure [its] border."[65] Advocates have criticized the administration's message, noting that it ignores the reality that people flee because they do not have the option to stay in their country of origin.[66] Furthermore, while the Biden administration has promised to tackle the root causes of migration, such as corruption, the administration's message appears to overlook the ways in which U.S. policy has created or exacerbated the root factors that cause individuals to migrate.

Taken as a whole, both the Trump and Biden administrations' actions have demonstrated disregard for evidence supporting the reasons why many Central Americans flee their home countries, including gang violence, gender-based violence, and extreme poverty. Some of these conditions have been exacerbated by historical and current U.S. policies in the region, including engineering political coups that heavily destabilized Central America during the Cold War era and Trump-era policies that helped political elites and authoritarian rulers in the region to dismantle anti-corruption and democratic governance efforts.[67] The United States has a moral and legal responsibility to provide refuge to victims fleeing threats of violence, particularly threats that it helped to instigate.

Family Separation and Detention of Children

The most notorious of President Trump's immigration policies was the separation of migrant children from their parents and caregivers at the border. As undocumented asylum-seekers were apprehended and imprisoned on arrival, their accompanying children under the age of eighteen were "handed over to the U.S. Department of Health and Human Services (HHS), which shipped them miles away from their parents and scattered them among 100 Office of Refugee Resettlement shelters" and other sites across the United States. These youth included infants and toddlers.[68] According to the American Civil Liberties Union (ACLU), nearly 20 percent of youth separated from their families between July 2017 and June 2018 was younger than age five.[69]

In detention facilities, young children experienced a range of degrading conditions, lacking adequate hygiene supplies and sleeping arrangements and barred from even touching their own siblings.[70] In addition, long-term separation and detention of families produces stress and trauma, the kind that can permanently affect youth's biology and brain development, according to the American Academy of Pediatrics.[71] Separated children and unaccompanied minors were also often subject to rampant abuse, according to reports during and predating Trump's separation policy. The federal government received more than 4,500 complaints about the sexual abuse and harassment of detained immigrant children by both staff and fellow detainees from October 2014 to July 2018, with an increase in complaints while the Trump administration's family separation policy was in effect. Of the 1,303 cases considered the gravest, 178 included accusations of sexual assault of children by adult staff members, including allegations of kissing, fondling, and rape.[72]

Following nationwide criticism, President Trump signed an executive order officially ending the family separation policy in June 2018, except in cases where there was concern that the parent represented a risk to the child.[73] However, according to an October 2019 report by the House Committee on Oversight and Reform, more than one thousand additional children were separated from their parents after the official end of the separation policy.[74] In addition, Border Patrol agents continued to justify and enforce separation, often using vague or unproven allegations of low-level offenses that would not normally lead to a loss of parental custody.[75]

The total number of children separated from their families since the early implementation of family separation in July 2017 is estimated to be more than 5,400.[76] Disconcertingly, "DHS itself doesn't have an accurate database for tracking children whom officials have separated from their parents," which makes mitigating the effects of this policy all the more difficult. In April 2018,

DHS reportedly did not know the location of 1,475 migrant children, and even after the end of the separation policy, in September 2018, the agency could not account for 1,500 youth.[77] Nongovernmental organizations such as the Texas Civil Rights Project have worked to track down separated migrant children, relying on sparse documentation and independent investigation, such as interviews with parents.[78]

In addition to this cruel policy of family separation and detention, the Trump administration introduced a de facto measure that prolonged the detention of asylum-seekers for as long as their cases were being processed. In mid-2019, data from Immigration and Customs Enforcement (ICE) revealed that the agency had detained nearly nine thousand immigrants who were found to have a credible or reasonable fear of persecution or torture, demonstrating the need for increased scrutiny of the agency's approach to detention.[79]

Deportation by Any Means

Summary removal procedures, which allow for the deportation of migrants without a hearing before an immigration judge, undermine due process and unlawfully curtail the rights of asylum-seekers and migrants. According to the American Immigration Council, individuals who are subject to expedited removal are rarely informed of their right to counsel or given the chance to contact counsel. In such cases, expedited removal often fails to account for whether individuals are eligible to apply for lawful status. The procedures for deporting noncitizens in such a summary manner, without higher-level oversight, can lead to arbitrary or erroneous deportations. Noncitizens have no avenue to appeal an official's decision to deport via expedited removal.[80]

Prior to the Trump administration, the use of expedited removal was limited to border regions, broadly defined as within one hundred miles of any U.S. border, and to individuals apprehended within fourteen days of entering the country. In January 2017, the Trump administration dramatically expanded the scope of expedited removal by decreeing through executive order that the procedure could be applied to all individuals anywhere in the United States who cannot prove they have been continuously present in the country for the previous two years.[81] The executive order was implemented in July 2019 following a notice by DHS.[82] This change in procedure placed undocumented individuals in a fast-track deportation process, without the opportunity to plead their case in front of an immigration judge or to seek help from an attorney.[83]

In 2020, the Trump administration introduced two new expedited removal programs, the Prompt Asylum Case Review (PACR) program and the Humanitarian Asylum Review Program (HARP). Respectively targeted at Central American migrants and Mexican migrants, these two similar programs aimed at concluding asylum claims—and removing individuals who did not meet eligibility criteria—within ten days, precluding time for detailed screenings and the arrangement of legal counsel.[84] In early February 2021, President Biden ordered DHS to stop implementing these programs.[85]

Additionally, in March 2020, the Trump administration began using an obscure U.S. health law, referred to in the media as "Title 42," to turn away migrants, including asylum-seekers, during the COVID pandemic. The administration used the law to expel asylum-seekers at the U.S. border en masse under the guise of preventing the spread of COVID, despite expert opinions that the expulsions had no legal or scientific basis as a public health measure.[86] From March 2020 to April 2021, more than 642,000 individuals were expelled as a result of this application of Title 42.[87] Under Title 42, DHS collects asylum-seekers' biometric information, makes a record of the encounter, and expels the individual without giving them the chance to claim asylum. This policy was made possible by an agreement the administration struck with the Mexican government, under which the United States can expel asylum-seekers to Mexico; those not returned to Mexico have been summarily returned to their home country.[88] Although the Biden administration has criticized the previous administration's immigration policies,[89] the Trump-era policy was still in effect as of November 2021.

Additionally, for those individuals who were able to reach the United States, the standards for assessing credible fear were significantly heightened by the Trump administration, increasing the risk that they would not pass their credible fear interview and possibly be deported. Under international law, individuals must have a "well-founded fear of being persecuted for reasons of race, religion, nationality, membership of a particular social group, or political opinion" in order to be considered refugees and granted corresponding rights and protections.[90] Modeled after this standard, U.S. immigration law requires asylum-seekers to establish a well-founded fear of returning to their home country in order to advance their asylum claims. When asylum-seekers first enter the United States, they are guaranteed the right to a credible fear interview with a trained asylum officer from the U.S. Citizenship and Immigration Services (USCIS). This interview offers the first screening of asylum claims at the border, and passing the screening allows immigrants to continue pursuing their claims before a judge.[91]

In 2017, USCIS made it more difficult for asylum-seekers to pass their credible fear screening when it removed previous guidance that in cases of "reasonable doubt" regarding the outcome of a determination of credible fear, a migrant "likely merits" a positive determination and thus would still be eligible to proceed with an asylum claim. In place of this language, USCIS instead added that reasonable doubt may be considered as a screening standard.[92]

In 2018, then-Attorney General Jeff Sessions reversed a longstanding immigration court opinion granting asylum to victims of gangs and domestic violence and declared the need for stricter scrutiny of credible fear claims at the border. In response, USCIS issued further guidance to its officers to comply with Sessions's unprecedented interpretation, requiring migrants who often lack formal education and knowledge of U.S. law to present complete legal claims immediately after crossing the border.[93] These policies increased the risk of erroneously deporting asylum-seekers back to situations in which they face physical harm or death. As a result of the Trump administration's changes to the credible fear process, the rates of positive credible fear determinations for women and children fleeing violence decreased from 97 percent to fewer than 10 percent between July and November 2019 at the family detention center in Dilley, Texas.[94] However, in June 2021, Attorney General Merrick Garland vacated two key decisions issued under the Trump administration—*Matter of A-B-* and *Matter of L-E-A*—thereby "restor[ing] access to asylum for many people fleeing persecution abroad," including survivors of domestic and gang violence.[95]

BUILDING BACK BETTER

The Biden-Harris administration has repudiated some of the Trump-era restrictive immigration policies, but it has not developed an approach that addresses the changing landscape and context in which migration occurs and some of its policies and rhetoric have been highly exclusionary. The new administration took several immediate and important steps to repeal and repudiate Trump-era directives, including sending a reform bill to Congress and signing several executive orders to reverse some of the most inhumane policies, while continuing to follow a restrictive approach to migration at the southern border.[96] The horrific images of vulnerable Haitians seeking asylum in Del Rio, Texas, being met by border guards on horseback with whips, shocked the nation, and Vice President Harris's and President Biden's words to Central Americans—"do not come"—ran counter to the U.S. values, traditions, and policies surrounding asylum.

If the United States is to develop a more responsive and rights-respecting immigration system, U.S. refugee policy must comply with U.S. treaty obligations to secure the safety of refugees. In addition, the United States should strengthen the procedures and resources for fairly and accurately adjudicating asylum and refugee claims.

Improving Access to Justice

Processes that are speedier, fairer, and respecting of immigrant rights and due process not only can benefit individual migrants and families but also can improve the functioning and accountability of government immigration institutions.

Access to legal counsel significantly alters outcomes for immigrants and asylum-seekers. A national study of over 1.2 million deportation cases between 2007 and 2012 found that immigrants with legal representation "fare[d] better at every stage of the court process." Immigrants with legal counsel were four times more likely to be released from detention after a custody hearing than those without counsel. Represented immigrants were also nearly eleven times more likely to seek relief such as asylum than those who did not have representation; only 3 percent of those without counsel pursued relief. Moreover, even among immigrants who were detained, "those with representation were twice as likely as unrepresented immigrants to obtain immigration relief if they sought it"; this disparity was even greater among immigrants who were never detained. Such differences in outcomes imply that there are many individuals who are detained and denied relief due to a lack of counsel. Despite the importance of counsel, the vast majority of immigrants facing removal do not have access to court-appointed legal representation. Without being provided an appointed attorney, immigrants can struggle to pay for counsel and, if they are detained, to access counsel from behind bars. In the same study of outcomes from 2007 to 2012, only 37 percent of all immigrants were able to secure legal representation in their removal cases.[97]

In March 2018, Attorney General Sessions eviscerated asylum-seekers' due process rights in immigration courts by issuing a ruling that immigration judges could deny applicants asylum without a hearing if they find their written asylum submissions do not demonstrate prima facie eligibility.[98] This runs contrary to longstanding precedent that asylum-seekers have a due process right to a hearing.[99] The vast majority of asylum-seekers are not able to secure legal counsel to assist them in filing detailed applications, and many of them do not speak English.[100] It is unrealistic to expect them to know which of the many details of their persecution claim are most relevant to complex U.S. asylum laws. A study estimated that the cost of providing pro bono counsel for all indigent individuals in removal proceedings would be offset by significant savings in federal expenditures on detention and other outlays such as transportation and foster care.[101]

Addressing Judge Shortage and Case Backlogs

An additional problem that confronts due process in immigration courts is the severe shortage of immigration judges. Particularly as spending and focus on immigration enforcement have sharply increased, the underfunding of immigration courts throughout the country has limited the number of judges hearing cases and has resulted in huge backlogs of cases, with average delays in hearings of over a year and a half. Between 2003 and 2015, for example, immigration court backlogs increased by 163 percent as more cases were filed than could be completed.[102] This trend has become steeper in recent years, as immigration court backlogs have risen to unprecedented levels—doubling in five years from four hundred thousand in 2014 to eight hundred thousand by 2019.[103] This backlog is primarily a result of government immigration enforcement, rather than asylum applications. As immigration judges become overworked, their ability to give every case due diligence is hindered. Furthermore, as immigrants wait for their cases to be processed, many remain in detention, separated from family members. According to the American Immigration

Council, some with valid claims ultimately give up their right to a hearing due to prolonged delay.[104]

In 2018, the Department of Justice announced new evaluations of immigration judges based on how many cases they close and how fast they hear cases. These evaluations required finishing cases within three days when an immigrant is in detention or within ten days when the immigrant is not detained. That arbitrary timetable can present problems in cases in which asylum-seekers are psychologically traumatized by their experiences and unfamiliar with English and the nuances of U.S. law. In addition, they often lack the education or the ability necessary to obtain counsel, let alone quickly to produce evidence and witnesses. By prioritizing quantity over quality, this policy violates the due process right of immigrants to have a fair and reasonable hearing in court.[105]

In addition to threatening the integrity of the courts and the rights of immigrants, the Trump policy did not impact the backlog of immigration cases. When President Trump assumed office, the backlog of pending deportation cases was approximately 540,000; as of early 2021, the backlog had increased to 1.3 million, with an average wait for a hearing date of fifty-four months. Despite the Trump administration generally portraying immigrants as criminals, nearly all cases in the backlog as of 2021 (98.2 percent) involved immigration violations, such as not going through a legal port of entry or overstaying one's visa, not criminal offenses.[106]

To address the case backlog and failure of due process, the Biden administration should dedicate resources to the staffing needs of immigration judges and a plan to meet those needs.[107] For fiscal year 2020, the Executive Office of Immigration Review (EOIR), which oversees the nation's immigration courts, requested a budget of $673 million, including funds to increase its staffing to 3,761 positions.[108] By comparison, in 2020, the Internal Revenue Service (IRS) had $12.3 billion in operating costs and 75,773 full-time equivalent staff.[109] However, it will not be enough on its own to merely increase immigration courts' funding and staffing levels without also making changes to the immigration court system. The administration should also increase the vetting and training of immigration judges to ensure that they are adequately qualified.[110] Finally, it should avoid micromanaging and politicizing immigration courts, in order to reduce pressures on immigration judges and increase morale.[111]

Ending Abuses and Impunity at the Border

Following the creation of U.S. Customs and Border Protection (CBP) under DHS in 2003, serious problems emerged in accountability for due process violations at the border.[112] Between 2009 and 2014, "at least 214 complaints were filed against federal agents for abusing or mistreating migrant children." However, according to DHS records, only one employee faced disciplinary consequences as a result of a complaint.[113] In a broader range of abuse cases adjudicated between 2012 and 2015, roughly 96 percent of the 1,255 cases of reported abuse resulted in a decision of "no action" against the agent accused of misconduct. These cases involved allegations of a range of types of abuse, including physical and sexual assault, theft of property, verbal abuse, and denying medical care to children.[114]

The Trump administration further enabled this climate of impunity and abuse by granting CBP more powers that further shielded it from public scrutiny. In January 2020, the administration designated all of CBP a "security agency," which placed it on par with intelligence agencies and curtailed its transparency. Effectively, the new classification exempted the names of all CBP employees from Freedom of Information Act requests or other public disclosures, limiting the ability of the media and citizens to gauge the full scope of misconduct within the agency or to challenge misconduct by Border Patrol agents.[115] Serious allegations against CBP continued to surface during the Trump administration—including sexual assault of children,[116] trafficking of firearms,[117] and pursuit with moving vehicles of people crossing the border.[118]

Expanding Refugee Admissions

In 2019, Trump cut the number of openings for U.S. refugees by nearly half—reducing the already diminished limit from thirty thousand to eighteen thousand; by contrast, the Obama administration had allowed 110,000 refugees to be admitted in 2016.[119] This cap was by far the lowest ceiling for refugee admissions since the U.S. began setting caps on refugee admissions in 1980.[120] Yet even this low figure misrepresented the number of slots available for some refugees, as the Trump administration prioritized openings for certain groups of individuals, such as those fleeing religious persecution.[121] President Biden announced that his administration would increase the refugee cap to 62,500 for fiscal year 2021, with the goal of 125,000 in future years, in keeping with his vision that the "United States Refugee Admissions Program embodies America's commitment to protect the most vulnerable, and to stand as a beacon of liberty and refuge to the world."[122] Following the chaotic withdrawal of the United States from Afghanistan, the Biden administration must include eligible Afghans fleeing Taliban persecution, many of whom provided assistance to the United States, in its new Refugee Admissions Program.

Addressing Structural Racism in the Immigration System

The history of U.S. immigration is rooted in exclusionary laws and discrimination against immigrants from Asia, Africa, and Latin America. This thread continues with today's immigration policies and practices. Immigration in prior decades and centuries from Europe took place with few, if any, restrictions or repercussions: "from the early 1900s through the 1960s, millions of predominantly White immigrants entered the country unlawfully, but faced virtually no threat of apprehension or deportation," observed Charles Kamasaki of the Brookings Institution. "Over the past half century, the immigration enforcement system has grown from just a few hundred border guards to what the Migration Policy Institute calls a 'formidable machinery' larger than all other federal law enforcement agencies *combined*, further augmented by state and local police agencies."[123]

In addition to the deeply anti-Mexican and Central American policies and practices of immigration enforcement, historical legacies of racial favoritism permeate the current immigration system. The Naturalization Act of 1790, the country's first citizenship law, reserved the privilege of citizenship for free Whites only, explicitly excluding not only all immigrants of color, but also Africans who were enslaved or free.[124] The legacy of the country's founding and history is reflected in continuing elements of exclusionary racism in the immigration system. According to the American Bar Association, data from DHS show that "immigrants of African descent are more likely to be detained and deported than other immigrants."[125] The unique plight facing Black asylum-seekers and refugees is best captured by the 2020 case of Cameroonian men who had fled persecution in Cameroon and sought asylum in the United States, "only to be detained indefinitely in a facility in the deep

South run by a for-profit corporation that has long been accused of human rights abuses."[126]

Accountability for Private Actors

Private businesses and corporations are engaged as contractors in the U.S. immigration system in myriad ways, from operating detention centers to conducting surveillance of asylum-seekers at the border. Because these private actors often operate in the shadow of state agencies and officials, they are held to lower levels of scrutiny and oversight, and their complicity in violations of due process is often overlooked.

Private prisons have become the federal government's default facilities for detaining undocumented immigrants, housing as much as three-quarters of the population of detained migrants.[127] Private prison contractors reap significant profits from the detention of migrants at the border, asylum-seekers awaiting immigration court, and individuals in deportation proceedings. Between January 2017 and June 2019, ICE spent more than $480 million in contracts with GEO Group and more than $331 million with CoreCivic, both for-profit prison companies.[128] Payments from ICE accounted for 20 and 25 percent of these companies' profits in fiscal year 2018, respectively.[129] In December 2019, ICE signed new contracts for detention facilities with these entities, with a five-year contract with CoreCivic worth $2.1 billion and two fifteen-year contracts with GEO Group collectively worth $3.7 billion.[130]

As of January 2020, 80 percent of immigrants in detention were housed in facilities owned and/or operated by private companies.[131] These companies' emphasis on maximizing profit and lack of accountability make them particularly prone to abuse. A 2020 report by the ACLU, Human Rights Watch, and the National Immigrant Justice Center found that newly built private facilities were more likely to be located in remote locations, with decreased access to attorneys and increased likelihood that immigrants lose their cases. In addition, the report found "sordid," unhygienic conditions, with inadequate food and water, overcrowding, physically violent staff, and lack of medical and mental health treatment.[132] Among the 172 recorded deaths of detained immigrants in ICE custody taking place between October 2003 and July 2017, at least fifteen were housed in one private detention center, the CoreCivic-operated Eloy Federal Contract Facility in Arizona.[133] A whistleblower also came forward in 2020 alleging that a gynecologist at the Irwin County Detention Center in Georgia, which is run by the private company LaSalle Corrections, engaged in medically unnecessary procedures. According to the complaint, the gynecologist's conduct amounted to sexual assault and included an "alarmingly high" number of hysterectomies on women who may not have understood the procedure.[134] The whistleblower further alleged that she referred to the gynecologist as "the uterus collector," in light of the gynecologist's reputation for performing a high number hysterectomies.[135]

Despite assurances by President Biden that he would end for-profit detention centers, he had not taken action as of September 2021.[136] Following his inauguration, President Biden signed an executive order aiming to end the use of "privately operated criminal detention facilities," but the order did not extend to facilities for the detention of immigrants.[137] Talks between the Biden administration and GEO Group about contract renewal will serve as an indicator of whether the administration will fulfill its promise.[138]

Oversight of Surveillance Technology

Technology companies are increasingly contracted to surveil, investigate, and arrest undocumented migrants, with no oversight over their invasive mass collection of data. Palantir Technologies, a data-analytics firm valued at $20 billion in 2020,[139] provided software to support a program to target people who directly or indirectly help unaccompanied minors cross the border into the United States.[140] Developed and implemented in 2017, the "Unaccompanied Alien Children Human Smuggling Disruption Initiative" was a plan for "the identification, investigation, and arrest of human smuggling facilitators, including, but not limited to, parents and family members."[141] Under the program, once an unaccompanied minor was located by an ICE investigator, immigration agents were instructed to log the child's arrival in Palantir's Investigative Case Management (ICM) system. Within this system, agents could access intelligence from the Drug Enforcement Administration, the FBI, and other federal and private law enforcement agencies. According to the program plan, if "sufficient information on parents or family members is obtained" through this intelligence, a case would be created and "[teams would] be available to . . . contact suspected sponsor/parent or family members to identify, interview, and, if applicable, seek charges against the individual(s) and administratively arrest the subjects and anybody encountered during the inquiry who is out of status."[142]

Previously, after minors arrived at the border unaccompanied, their family members would be able to come forward and claim their children, be reunited, and then go through the immigration process. Under the Palantir-supported program, ICE conducted background checks through ICM on family members claiming children, deterring them from doing so, and consequently resulting in longer periods of detention for children.[143] By the end of the roughly three-month "domestic enforcement phase of the initiative," ICE reported that the program had resulted in 443 administrative arrests.[144]

There appears to be a bipartisan consensus around technological surveillance and smart borders. In his first day in office, President Biden proposed legislation to "prioritize smart border controls" and invest in technologies to surveil the border and beyond, with a focus on screening for and detecting illicit activity.[145] Proponents of creating a "smart border" have noted that using new technology to secure the border will be significantly cheaper than constructing a physical wall and won't force the government to take land for the construction of a physical barrier that will render portions of land unusable.[146] However, civil rights groups, including the ACLU and the Electronic Frontier Foundation, have expressed concerns about the use of border surveillance technology. In particular, groups have noted that the technology will force migrants to seek remote and dangerous migration routes and open a pathway to infringements on civil rights.[147] Additionally, advocates have raised concerns that increased use of border surveillance technology will threaten privacy rights without adequate safeguards or clear security benefits.[148]

Oversight of DNA Testing

Since 2019, private companies have been assisting DHS in DNA testing at the border to investigate familial ties and relationships. In May of that year, DHS launched a pilot DNA testing program to "identify and prosecute groups of individuals posing as families in an effort to target human smuggling." The testing involved a cheek swab and provided results in about ninety minutes on average.[149] Following the pilot program, DHS continued using DNA testing and expanded this procedure to more locations along the border.[150]

Although the DNA testing has been represented as voluntary, families are presented with consent forms stating that opting out of the testing could influence ICE's decision to separate families in immigration detention. The Electronic Frontier Foundation has concluded in a report that this practice is coercive, and that the testing does not take into account families with children who are not biologically connected to parents, such as adopted children and stepchildren.[151] It is also unclear whether immigrants have the opportunity to review or challenge the accuracy of their tests.[152]

Policy Recommendations

- **Secure Due Process at the Border.** Reform the border control system: mandate accountability and transparency of U.S. Customs and Border Protection; issue broad "credible fear" guidance for assessing asylum claims; require asylum claims raised in removal proceedings to be fully reviewed and, if plausible, referred to an immigration judge for determination; and curtail expedited removal at the border.
- **Secure Humanitarian Protections.** Reform the asylum system: bar the separation of migrant children from their families; prohibit the return of refugees to conditions of persecution; end the ban on asylum claims of refugees coming through transit countries; overturn the designations of Guatemala, El Salvador, and Honduras as "safe third countries"; establish federal court review of "safe third country" designation procedures; reinstate the Temporary Protected Status (TPS) program for refugees fleeing war, famine, or natural disasters; reinstate the Deferred Action for Childhood Arrivals (DACA) program; and provide pathways to permanent residence and citizenship for TPS and DACA recipients.
- **Secure Due Process in Immigration Proceedings.** Reform the immigration court system: increase the number of immigration judges; transfer immigration courts from the federal executive

to the judicial branch; implement a right to government-funded counsel for indigent noncitizens eligible for relief from removal, in addition to unaccompanied children and migrants with mental disabilities; provide access to qualified interpreters to facilitate communication with immigrants who have difficulty understanding procedures; end the detention of immigrants charged with non-felony offenses; address racial discrimination in the immigration system; and end the expedited removal of immigrants already in the United States, unaccompanied minors, and migrants with mental disabilities.

- **Establish Accountability and Transparency for Private Contractors.** Provide congressional oversight of private contractors performing immigration functions; ban private detention facilities; and oversee private contractors' surveillance of asylum-seekers.

11

Gun Rights and Public Safety

In March 2018, hundreds of thousands of young people walked out of school and marched at their local statehouses and at the U.S. Capitol in Washington, DC, to advocate for stricter controls on gun sales and ownership. The March for Our Lives was initially organized by students at Marjory Stoneman Douglas High School in Parkland, Florida, where a school shooting had killed seventeen students. With more than a million participants, the marches were collectively the largest-ever protest against gun violence.[1]

During the year following the mobilization, twenty-six states passed sixty-seven laws to strengthen protections against gun violence, in efforts led and supported by both Democratic and Republican public officials. Among them

Teens for Gun Reform, an organization created by students in the Washington, DC, area, in the wake of the shooting at Marjory Stoneman Douglas High School in Parkland, Florida. Photo by Lorie Shaull.

were laws increasing waiting periods and establishing higher minimum ages to purchase firearms.[2] Despite these state law changes, at the national level, no federal gun safety legislation was enacted following the protest. A measure passed by the House of Representatives to require background checks for private gun sales at gun shows and over the internet died in the Senate.[3] In fact, no major gun safety legislation has been passed by Congress in decades. These trends reflect the crisis of gun safety in the United States. Despite overwhelming support for protecting public safety through increased regulation of gun sales and ownership, federal efforts to improve gun safety have been repeatedly stymied by an uncompromising stance by gun lobbyists, led by the National Rifle Association. Debate over the meaning and requirements of the Second Amendment has resulted in gun rights lobbyists asserting claims of a right to own firearms that is virtually unfettered. Yet, the United States far exceeds other countries in firearm-related fatalities, including suicides, homicides, and accidental deaths.

Despite the extent of gun violence and the frequency of high-profile shootings, the Second Amendment has yet to be balanced at a national level with the responsibility of government to protect the public safety of its citizens. The Carr Center's July 2020 national poll demonstrates that Americans are seeking this balance: 50 percent believe that "a right to bear arms" is "very important," while a much larger 81 percent believe that a "right to personal safety" is also "very important." An April 2021 Pew Research Center poll found that 53 percent said "gun laws . . . should be more strict," compared with 32 percent who said they were "about right" and 14 percent who said they "should be less strict." There was a distinct partisan divide on these issues, with 80 percent of Republicans against tightening gun laws, while only 19 percent of Democrats felt similarly.

There is room for compromise. Many policies that could help control gun violence would have minimal impact on the vast majority of law-abiding gun owners. A bipartisan supermajority of 87 percent of respondents in the Pew survey, for example, supported limiting gun purchases by persons with mental illness. A similar majority of 81 percent of respondents supported closing the "gun-show loophole" that allows for the private sale of guns without background checks. Even on more controversial issues, such as banning high-capacity magazines and assault-style weapons, majorities of 64 percent and

63 percent, respectively, supported tighter regulations. While there was a partisan divide on these proposals, they commanded the support of a significant minority of Republicans, 41 percent, and 37 percent, respectively.[4]

The growing consensus over the need for "common-sense" gun laws to regulate the sale and ownership of firearms stands in sharp contrast to the incendiary rhetoric of the National Rifle Association, which has sounded the alarm in recent years that gun safety advocates are coming to "take away" guns. The high level of bipartisan support for reasonable gun laws implies that there is a middle ground that can be achieved to limit gun violence in the United States, while upholding the Second Amendment right of responsible ownership and use of firearms for hunting, sport shooting, and personal protection.

While still well below historic highs, those increases represent a disturbing trend. Every day in America, an average of more than one hundred people are killed with firearms and more than two hundred more are shot and injured.[5] On average, there has been a mass shooting of four or more people every day since 2014.[6] After decades of falling violent crime rates, 2020 saw a 25 percent rise in firearm murder rates, according to FBI data.[7] A 2021 report by the nonpartisan Council on Criminal Justice found that rates of homicide increased throughout the coronavirus pandemic, surging in early summer, which the report's authors attributed to the strains of the pandemic on vulnerable populations, coupled with a decline in violence prevention efforts by police and public health institutions preoccupied with the pandemic.

Data suggest that increased availability of firearms was a factor in the rise of gun violence. Gun assaults rose 7.4 percent between the declaration of a public health emergency in March 2020 and the end of the year. At the same time, there was a massive increase in the purchase of firearms during the period of social uncertainty at the outbreak of the pandemic—with a 64 percent increase in purchases between March and May 2020, representing an additional 2.1 million guns.[8] Purchases stayed high throughout the summer during the social unrest in the wake of George Floyd's murder and the ensuing protests; overall, at least 20 million guns were sold legally in 2020, up from 12 million the previous year—the highest year ever for firearm purchases.[9] Some researchers have associated the increase in firearms sales with increases in gun violence, citing the higher ratio of assaults involving firearms during the year.[10]

A string of high-profile mass shootings in Atlanta, Georgia; Boulder, Colorado; Orange, California; and other locations renewed attention on gun availability as a contributing cause of the violence. Calling gun violence an "epidemic and an international embarrassment," President Biden issued a half-dozen gun regulations through executive action, but Congress failed to pass any changes in gun laws.[11]

GUN OWNERSHIP AND GUN VIOLENCE

Gun ownership in the United States dwarfs that of other wealthy nations. According to the latest estimates, there are 393 million civilian-owned firearms in the United States in a population of 332 million—many more guns than people.[12] In fact, the U.S. rate of gun ownership is 119 guns for every one hundred thousand people, nearly four times as high as the next highest wealthy country, Canada, which has approximately thirty-five guns for every one hundred thousand people. Those numbers increasingly diminish for European countries, such as Germany, which has less than twenty guns per one hundred thousand people; and the United Kingdom, which has less than five. At the bottom of the list is Japan, which has 0.3 guns per one hundred thousand people.[13]

Despite the prevalence of gun ownership in the United States, guns are not spread proportionately throughout the country. In fact, only three in every ten Americans own a gun.[14] Of these gun owners, 32 percent own a single gun, while 37 percent own between two and four, and 29 percent own at least five. In other words, the majority of guns are concentrated in a relatively small percentage of the American populace.[15]

A majority of gun owners cite personal protection (67 percent) as their primary reason for owning a gun, while smaller numbers cite hunting (38 percent), sport shooting (30 percent), gun collecting (13 percent), or employment (8 percent). Gun owners in urban and rural locations are equally likely to cite protection as their primary reason for ownership. According to a Pew Research Center report, the spike in gun sales in 2020 was due not only to anxieties over the coronavirus lockdown, but also to increased concerns during the social unrest and protests that followed the killing of George Floyd.[16] While gun ownership is higher among conservatives, this spike actually occurred in more liberal states that were initially harder hit by the coronavirus lockdown.[17]

Along with the high rates of gun ownership in the United States are the high rates of gun violence. Each year, 39,000 Americans are killed by guns.[18] Almost half of Americans (44 percent) know someone who has been shot, intentionally or accidentally.[19] Not surprisingly, the United States has a higher rate of firearm fatalities compared to peer nations, with a rate of 11.9 per one hundred thousand people—four times as many as the next highest nation, Switzerland, which has 2.8 deaths per one hundred thousand people.[20] An analysis of mortality data from the World Health Organization in 2010 found that Americans were twenty-five times more likely to die from gun-related homicide, and eleven times more likely to die from gun death of any kind, than citizens of other wealthy, industrialized nations.[21]

Contrary to news reporting that tends to focus on shootings of one person by another, the clear majority of gun deaths are actually self-inflicted: 61 percent of gun deaths are suicides, whereas only 35 percent are homicides.[22] Correspondingly, the biggest predictor of a completed suicide is access to a gun; such access triples the probability that a suicide attempt will result in death.[23] The suicide rate in the United States steadily rose by 35 percent in the twenty years from 1999 to 2018, when it reached a record high of 14.2 per one hundred thousand people.[24] After a slight drop in 2019, many public health observers feared that the rate would rise again during the pandemic due to increases in depression—as well as the spike in gun sales. However, preliminary data shows that the rate of suicide actually declined by 6 percent, which researchers attribute to a "rally together" effect during the coronavirus pandemic, coupled with increased acceptability of seeking help.[25] Nevertheless, understanding the prevalence of suicide as a major portion of gun violence has the potential to re-contextualize the purpose of gun ownership and regulation. Despite the fact that a majority of gun owners cite protection as their reason for owning a gun, guns in fact are not frequently used for self-defense. According to an analysis of data from the National Crime Victimization Survey, people defended themselves with a gun in less than 1 percent of crimes from 2007 to 2011.[26]

Homicidal gun deaths have a disproportionate effect on communities of color. African Americans are ten times more likely than Whites to be murdered with a gun.[27] In addition, White-on-Black killings are more likely to be ruled justifiable homicide, at 17 percent compared to 2 percent overall.[28]

Additional concerns around gun violence are related to domestic violence and hate- and bias-driven attacks, both of which are exacerbated by access to firearms. In domestic violence situations, an abuser's access to a gun increases the likelihood that the victim will be killed by five times.[29] Firearms also exacerbate hate- and bias-driven crimes, indicated by the lower level of hate crime fatalities in countries with stricter gun laws.[30]

Numerous lobbying groups advocate for different positions on gun rights and regulation. The National Rifle Association (NRA) is the leading pro-gun-rights lobbying organization. Seven percent of gun owners are NRA members. The NRA currently advocates against all forms of gun regulation. Founded in 1871, the NRA was initially established as a sportsman's organization to advocate for hunting and shooting safety, even lobbying for limits on gun trafficking.[31] After the Gun Control Act of 1968 was passed in response to the assassinations of President Kennedy, Martin Luther King Jr., and Robert F. Kennedy, the NRA gradually transformed itself into a lobbying organization, taking a position against restrictions on gun ownership.[32]

The key moment in the NRA's transition occurred in May 1977, during the organization's annual meeting in Cincinnati, Ohio. A wing within the organization led by current NRA president Harlon Carter surprised the membership with a strident stance on gun laws. In a meeting lasting until 4 a.m., the splinter wing succeeded in removing the chief executive and many other senior leaders, replacing them with Carter and other leaders whose primary focus was on gun rights.[33] Since that incident, known as the Revolt in Cincinnati, the group has taken an uncompromising position, advocating for unfettered gun ownership. With aggressive recruiting, the group grew its membership from less than one million members to more than five million today. Like many lobbying organizations, it has frequently made campaign contributions to lawmakers who support its anti-gun-regulation stance. What makes the NRA a particularly potent organization is its membership, which it mobilizes to take retribution at the polls against any lawmaker who supports gun regulation. The ability to compel votes based on a single issue has made the group a feared political force.[34]

No More Guns student lie-in at the White House to protest gun laws. Photo by Lorie Shaull.

Numerous gun safety lobbying groups, such as the Giffords Law Center, Brady United Against Gun Violence, and Everytown for Gun Safety, work to counterbalance the NRA's message. These organizations were often founded in the wake of major gun violence, and produce research about the consequences of gun violence in the United States. The most recent entry into gun-control activism is the student-led group March for Our Lives, formed after the Marjory Stoneman Douglas mass shooting in Parkland, Florida. Since the initial march that gave new visibility to gun-control issues, the founders have turned the group into an ongoing nonprofit organization that advocates for gun regulation, especially in state legislatures.

THE SECOND AMENDMENT: WHAT ARE THE RIGHTS?

The debate over firearms is centered around the Second Amendment, which is split into a prefatory clause, "A well-regulated Militia, being necessary to the security of a free State," and an operative clause, "the right of the people to keep and bear Arms shall not be infringed."[35] Considering these two clauses separately has led to different interpretations of who can exercise this right and who is responsible for regulation. The Second Amendment stems from

English common law, which provided a right to bear arms for self-defense and protection of collective or individual security.

The Second Amendment has historical ties to the institution of slavery. Some slave-owning founders viewed the amendment as a way to protect the system of slavery, seeing the need for states to have militias in order to prevent enslaved people from escaping.[36] After the Civil War, the Fourteenth Amendment granted citizenship rights to formerly enslaved people, including a right to bear arms for self-defense.[37]

The prefatory clause indicates on its face that the right to bear arms is a collective right that exists in the context of a militia, whereas the operative clause indicates that the right to bear arms is an individual right given to the people. In *United States v. Miller* (1939), the Supreme Court affirmed that Congress could regulate the interstate sale of sawed-off double-barrel shotguns. This gave a right of regulation to the federal government, based on the argument that this particular type of gun did not relate to the "preservation or efficiency of a well-regulated militia."[38] Since sawed-off double-barrel shotguns were not related to a collective militia, Congress was permitted to regulate their use. This framed the right to bear arms as a collective, rather than an individual, right and seemed to open the door to the regulation of firearms that are not related to their collective use. The Court held that unless the firearm in question "has some reasonable relationship to the preservation or efficiency of a well-regulated militia, we cannot say that the Second Amendment guarantees the right to keep and bear such an instrument."[39]

The prevailing legal interpretation of the Second Amendment has shifted over time. Prior to the 1990s, the predominant view was that the Second Amendment was intended to be a collective right, with some scholars identifying it as specifically intended for individual states to have militias. Since then, there has been a movement among legal scholars (including a few prominent liberals) to view the right to bear arms as an individual right. This shift, however, does not preclude reasonable government regulation, which has had long-standing support among legal scholars.[40]

The changing view of the right to bear arms was reflected in *District of Columbia v. Heller* (2008).[41] This case was brought by a police officer to challenge the Firearms Control Regulations Act of 1975, a Washington, DC, law that banned handguns. The plaintiff sought the right to bear handguns for use in self-defense, and the Supreme Court ruled that the handgun ban was unconstitutional. The decision effectively reversed *Miller* in defining the right as an individual right not related to a collective "well-regulated militia." This case focused on the operative clause of the Second Amendment and stated that the prefatory clause did not limit the right to bear arms as a collective right. The opinion states that there is a "guarantee of an individual right to possess and carry weapons in case of confrontation."

Heller was a 5–4 decision, and the dissenting justices argued that the ruling by the majority did not preclude gun regulation. Justice Stevens in his dissenting opinion stated that the right to bear arms is not an unlimited right, and Justices Souter, Ginsburg, and Breyer joined his opinion. Even Justice Scalia, arguing for the majority, wrote that the Second Amendment right to bear arms is not absolute. He noted that while guns in common use at the time of the founders—single-shot handguns and rifles—cannot be banned, modern weapons such as military-style assault weapons were not known by the founders and are therefore not within the meaning of the Second Amendment. The government can therefore put reasonable restrictions on how such weapons are sold and owned.[42] Additionally, because the case was brought against Washington, DC, a federal jurisdiction, the decision leaves open the possibility that states could regulate firearms under the Second Amendment. Finally, the decision did not address whether the Second Amendment provides an individual right to bear arms outside of the context of handgun possession within the home for self-defense.

Two types of regulation have been addressed by the courts since the *Heller* decision: "concealed carry" and "stand your ground." Concealed carry allows an individual to carry a weapon, generally on their person, in a concealed fashion. This has been an area of significant regulation with differences across states, and the Supreme Court has not yet ruled on the regulation of concealed carry laws. States vary from unrestricted (no permit required), to shall-issue (permit required, but issuance of permit involves no discretion), to may-issue (permit required and not essentially universally provided), to no-issue (no concealed carry).

A century before *Heller*, the Supreme Court actually addressed concealed carry obliquely in *Robertson v. Baldwin* (1897), which held that "the right of the people to keep and bear arms (Article 2) is not infringed by laws prohibiting the carrying of concealed weapons."[43] Specific concealed carry laws have been addressed by federal circuit courts, where decisions have been split between allowing states to maintain may-issue policies to requiring shall-issue or looser policies.

In early 2021, the Supreme Court agreed to take up its first gun-rights case in more than a decade. The case, *New York Rifle & Pistol Association v. Corlett*, concerns a challenge to a New York State concealed carry law that requires citizens to obtain a license in order to carry a concealed firearm outside the home. The law, which was upheld in lower court rulings, requires "proper cause" for the license, demonstrating that the carrier, for example, is on their way to hunting or target practice, or needs a gun for protection in their job—for instance, as a store owner or a bank employee transporting money. (Six other states have similar laws.) The case, expected to be heard in the fall of 2021, is the first gun-rights case since the appointment of Justices Brett Kavanaugh and Amy Coney Barrett, who have previously expressed an expansive view of the Second Amendment's right to bear arms, and are part of the emerging 6–3 conservative majority on the Court.[44]

The second type of regulation considered by the Supreme Court since the *Heller* decision is "stand your ground." Stand-your-ground laws permit proactive self-defense with no duty to retreat, even if safe retreat is possible. Different states have set different limits on when someone has this right, from the "castle doctrine," which restricts the right to one's own home, to applying stand your ground in any public space. These laws came under national scrutiny in 2012, in the wake of the fatal shooting of Trayvon Martin in Florida by George Zimmerman. Zimmerman, a member of a community watch organization, claimed that he shot Martin in self-defense under Florida's stand-your-ground law. Zimmerman was acquitted of second-degree murder and manslaughter. Racial bias is often evident in justifiable homicide cases like Zimmerman's, where White-on-Black cases are more likely to be found justifiable than Black-on-White cases.[45] This raises concerns about the expansion of stand-your-ground laws and opens these laws up to scrutiny for their potentially discriminatory nature. The Supreme Court has not ruled on the constitutionality of stand-your-ground laws in the context of racial discrimination.

GOVERNMENT RESPONSIBILITY TO PROTECT PUBLIC SAFETY

Responsibility for the protection of public safety is shared by state governments and the federal government. The protection of "life, liberty and the pursuit of happiness" expressed in the Declaration of Independence is a founding principle of both governments. At the international level, U.S. ratification of international human rights treaties, such as the International Covenant on the Elimination of All Forms of Racial Discrimination (ratified in 1994) and the International Covenant on Civil and Political Rights (ratified in 1992), extends "the right to life and bodily integrity"[46] from international law into U.S. federal and state law. Federal and state government responsibility to protect citizens under these treaties could theoretically compel the United States to reduce gun violence through regulations on gun use and ownership.

The Supreme Court has ruled that government is required by the U.S. Constitution to protect citizens from *government* violence, but not from *private* violence. In *DeShaney v. Winnebago County Department of Social Services* (1988), the Supreme Court found that state governments did not have a responsibility to protect individuals from private violence under the Due Process Clause of the Fourteenth Amendment. In this case, four-year-old Joshua DeShaney's mother had sued the Winnebago County Department of Social Services for failing to protect her son from his father's abuse, thereby depriving him of physical safety. The Supreme Court, in a 6–3 ruling, found that, while the Due Process Clause "forbids the State itself to deprive individuals of life, liberty, and property without due process of law, its language cannot fairly be read to impose an affirmative obligation on the State to ensure that those interests do not come to harm through other means."[47] The *DeShaney* decision does not preclude federal or state governments from regulating guns *proactively* with the aim of preventing violence in general.

Federal Regulation

For nearly a century, the federal government has gone back and forth between waves of more restrictive and less restrictive regulation of firearms. The first national gun regulation law was the 1934 National Firearms Act (NFA), which established firearm-related taxes and required that certain types of weapons be registered. This law was challenged in the *Miller* case and upheld by the Supreme Court, in a ruling that the Second Amendment does not guarantee a right to own and carry a sawed-off double-barrel shotgun.[48] As noted, the *Miller* decision was premised on the argument that such a weapon "does not have a reasonable relationship to the preservation or efficiency of a well-regulated militia." This decision focused on the prefatory clause of the Second Amendment and supported the constitutionality of federal gun regulation. The NFA remains part of federal firearms law. An additional law was passed in 1938, the Federal Firearms Act (FFA), which added a licensing requirement for manufacturers, importers, and sellers, and restricted gun ownership to purchases from licensed sources.

These two laws constituted the primary federal firearms regulation until the 1968 Gun Control Act (GCA). The 1968 law incorporated the 1934 NFA and portions of the 1938 FFA. The GCA maintained licensing requirements for gun sellers but did not address the possibility of unlicensed individuals making private sales. It also defined groups of people who were not permitted to own guns, including convicted felons, underage people, those having severe mental illnesses, and those with convictions of misdemeanor domestic violence.

The legislative trend shifted away from restrictive regulation with the 1986 passage of the Firearm Owners Protection Act (FOPA). This law protected gun owners and dealers by prohibiting a national database of "firearms, firearms owners, or firearms transactions or disposition," and limited federal compliance inspections to once a year. It loosened the definition of what constitutes a gun seller that would require a federal license. It also laid the groundwork for the gun show loophole by legalizing offsite sales by licensed gun dealers. It loosened some regulations on types of sales and weapons, such as the sale and transfer of ammunition, and tightened others, such as the sale of parts for silencers and a prohibition against civilians owning machine guns. Finally, it created provisions permitting the transport of guns from states with looser gun laws through states with stricter gun laws.

The regulatory trend shifted again toward gun restriction with the 1993 Brady Handgun Violence Prevention Act, named for another victim of gun violence, James Brady, who was shot during an assassination attempt on President Reagan. The Brady Act established the National Instant Criminal Background Check System (NICS) and required a background check for any gun purchase from a licensed dealer. This regulation leaves space for purchases made from unlicensed sellers of guns, online purchases, and sales made by dealers at gun shows when background checks are not required. Shortly after enactment of the Brady Act, Congress passed a ban on assault weapons as part of the Violent Crime Control and Law Enforcement Act. This law, enacted in 1994, prohibited the manufacture, transfer, or possession of assault weapons (certain semi-automatic weapons and those with large-capacity magazines) for civilian use. The bill contained a ten-year sunset provision set for 2004, at which time the ban was not renewed.

The assault weapons ban faced two legal challenges but was upheld both times. First, it was challenged under the Commerce Clause in *Navegar, Inc. v. United States*. Two gun manufacturers who produced restricted semi-automatic weapons claimed that the assault weapons ban was a regulation that exceeded Congress's authority to regulate interstate commerce under the Commerce Clause.[49] In 1997, a federal appeals court upheld the law and the Supreme Court then declined to hear the case,[50] leaving open the feasibility of limited gun regulation under the Commerce Clause, as long as possession of a gun could be tied to interstate commerce.

Secondly, the assault weapons ban was challenged under the Equal Protection Clause in *Olympic Arms v. Buckles*. The premise of this case was that, because other weapons that had not been prohibited were functionally equivalent to assault weapons, those weapons should be considered equal, and therefore permitted. A federal appeals court held that this argument was not legitimate under the Equal Protection Clause, which "protects against inappropriate classifications of people, rather than things."[51] The court also stated that the assault weapons ban was a rational prohibition. State-level assault weapons bans that have gone into effect after the 2004 sunsetting of the federal assault weapons ban have been upheld by state courts.[52]

After the passage of the Violent Crime Control and Law Enforcement Act in 1994, Congress once again changed course toward a more permissive attitude, passing several amendments and laws limiting gun regulation. In 1996, the Dickey Amendment prevented the Centers for Disease Control and

Prevention (CDC) from advocating for or promoting gun control—stymying the consideration of gun violence as a public health issue. The year 2020 was the first year since the passage of this amendment that money was allocated to conduct research on gun-related deaths and injuries. The research is being done by the CDC and the National Institutes of Health (NIH).[53]

In 2003 and 2005, Congress passed other laws protecting gun manufacturers and dealers. The 2003 Tiahrt Amendment prohibited the Bureau of Alcohol, Tobacco, Firearms, and Explosives (ATF) from releasing data about where criminals procure firearms to anyone other than law enforcement. The 2005 Protection of Lawful Commerce in Arms Act prevented gun manufacturers and dealers from being named in civil suits involving crimes committed using guns made by those manufacturers or purchased from those dealers.

Another recent shift in gun regulation came in the wake of the 2017 Las Vegas mass shooting. After a long line of mass shootings, advocates attempted unsuccessfully to pass a law banning bump stocks—gun stocks that allow semi-automatic rifles to fire more rapidly. However, in response to bipartisan public outcry, the Department of Justice (DOJ) reclassified bump stocks as machine guns, rendering them illegal. As this case shows, discretionary regulation through the DOJ may be another avenue for future shifts in gun regulation.

In March 2021, several mass shootings increased pressure on the new administration of President Joe Biden to push for increased gun-regulation measures. In Atlanta, Georgia, a shooter murdered eight people, most of them Asian women, at a series of shootings at spas in the city. In Boulder, Colorado, a man shot and killed ten people, including a police officer, with a semi-automatic handgun with an arm brace at a supermarket. Following these incidents, in April 2021, President Biden announced new executive actions to control access to guns.

The most substantive measure was an order to the DOJ to control the proliferation of so-called ghost guns, which can be ordered and assembled from kits without a license or background check. Another measure placed additional strictures and licensing requirements on arm braces such as the one used in Boulder, which can make a pistol more accurate. Another directed the DOJ to create a model red flag law, which could be passed by states to allow law enforcement to temporarily remove firearms from people "who may present a danger to themselves or others."[54]

Despite these measures, Biden acknowledged that he had only limited authority to promulgate gun regulation through executive action. The House of Representatives passed a pair of bills to expand background checks, including closing the gun show loophole, as supported by a strong majority of Americans, but the Senate has failed to take up the legislation.[55]

State Regulation

Each state has its own set of gun regulations, which has made a complex patchwork of different laws throughout the United States. The ability of states to adopt their own laws makes the concept of regulation quite complex, as guns cross state borders. A gun purchased in a more permissive state can be used in a stricter state.

Nevertheless, according to the CDC, every state with tougher gun laws has lower gun deaths than states with lax gun laws. Massachusetts has enacted the strictest gun violence prevention laws, including background checks, gun safety training, safe storage, an assault-weapon ban, and a red flag law. Since 1994, Massachusetts has reduced the rate of gun deaths by 40 percent and now has the lowest gun death rate and lowest cost of gun violence of any state in the nation.[56] Other northeastern states with similarly strict laws also see low rates, while the highest rates of gun violence are found in southern and western states, which have the most permissive gun laws.[57] Certain types of laws are enforced against anyone who is physically present in a state, whereas other laws, such as concealed carry permits, are generally recognized across states based on residency.

States differ widely on gun regulation. In terms of licenses, permits, and registration, some states require gun owners to have a permit in order to purchase a gun, to have a license to carry the gun, and to register the gun.[58] Other states have none of these restrictions. On background checks, twenty-two states and Washington, DC, have stronger laws than those set out in the federal Gun Control Act of 1968 and the Brady Act.[59]

There are differences in how strictly the federal government and states regulate gun possession in the context of domestic violence. Federal law limits gun possession in cases of spouses, parents, or cohabitants who have been convicted of domestic violence, but does not limit gun possession by dating partners or stalkers.[60] Some states have instituted such regulations. This issue is particularly relevant today, with studies showing an increase in domestic violence due to the coronavirus pandemic, creating a particularly dangerous situation in cases where there is a weapon within reach of an abusive partner.[61]

Concealed and open carry laws are also an area of major regulatory difference, with some states requiring permits for concealed and/or open carry and others not requiring any permit.[62] There are state-by-state differences in what types of guns and ammunition are allowed. Some states have placed limits on certain types of weapons, including assault weapons, semi-automatic guns, and certain magazines. Some states also have additional restrictions on bump stocks, which are legal restrictions separate from the DOJ reclassification in 2018.[63] There is also a federal law restricting ownership age to eighteen, and some states have additional restrictions setting the limit at twenty-one for at least some types of weapons.[64]

A final type of state law that is an area of particularly active debate today is the extreme risk protection order,[65] also known as a red flag law. These laws permit the removal of guns from someone deemed by a judge or another authorized official to be at extreme risk of committing a crime of violence or to pose an extreme risk. These laws are under scrutiny for mandating removal of weapons from owners without adequate due process.[66]

All of these laws show that it is possible to balance the right to own and use firearms with legal regulations to protect the safety of the public. A renewed commitment to pass such laws on both the state and federal levels could increase gun safety and save lives across the country.

Policy Recommendations

- **Focus on Areas of Consensus.**[67] Opinion polling has revealed several areas in which there is bipartisan consensus for gun regulation.

  More than 90 percent of Democrats and Democratic-leaning Independents and 85 percent of Republicans and Republican-leaning Independents support laws prohibiting persons with mental illness from buying guns. Tying this consensus to widespread concern over the prevalence of suicides in cases of gun violence could help build consensus establishing stricter gun-purchasing regulation. A second area of consensus is closing the loophole that allows gun purchases at gun shows and in private sales without background checks. Ninety-two percent of Democrats and 70 percent of Republicans support such a measure. This demonstrates that the public understands the need to balance gun rights with government responsibility to protect public safety.

Polls show that up to 60 percent of Americans consistently support stricter gun laws, particularly in the wake of mass shootings. Large percentages are concerned about gun violence. Narratives created by lobbyists often mislead public perceptions about what is politically viable, but recent polling demonstrates that there are in fact areas of consensus. This consensus, together with the history of constitutionally acceptable gun regulation, demonstrates that additional regulation is feasible and necessary.

- **Focus on States and Replicate the Successful Model Set by Massachusetts.** While there is broad support on certain issues that make federal legislation possible, many states have been successful arenas for passing gun legislation. As previously discussed, Massachusetts provides a model for other states to replicate. State regulations are broad-ranging, reflect public opinion, and have a strong legal basis for constitutionality based on previous court cases. While guns can travel across state borders and reduce the efficacy of state regulation, states with stricter laws see lower gun violence.[68] Polling done on the state level can provide state legislatures with a better picture of what gun laws might be most appropriate in particular states. This type of polling could also help hold lawmakers more accountable to the public interest and encourage them to uphold their responsibility for public safety, rather than being responsive only to gun lobbyists.

A potentially limiting feature of state regulation is preemption law.[69] Preemption is a statewide law that limits local initiatives. Such laws can nullify municipal ordinances, thereby preventing cities and other municipalities from having more restrictive gun laws than the state as a whole. In states with effective, well-supported gun legislation, this is not a problem, but in states with permissive gun legislation, preemption ties the hands of local governments. Overturning preemption laws makes city and municipal regulation feasible.

- **Reframe the Issue.** In order to be more effective, advocates of increased gun control must reframe the issue. In considering a framework where government and citizens at the local, state, and federal levels have both rights and responsibilities, the concept of gun control is simplistic and unnecessarily contentious and should be replaced by gun safety laws and gun violence prevention laws. The Second Amendment provides a right to keep and bear arms, and the Supreme Court's interpretation that this is an individual right is unlikely to change in the near future. However, this right does not supersede the importance of other rights and responsibilities: the right to life requires gun safety, citizens have the responsibility to hold government accountable for public safety, and the government is responsible for protecting its citizens.

    In thinking about security, it is worth noting that many people carry guns for self-defense and see guns as a form of protection and security. Gun ownership and gun safety can be seen as two sides of the same coin. Gun ownership is not an unlimited right. This right must be balanced and contextualized. Framing the debate in terms of gun safety and gun violence prevention rather than taking away guns brings it closer to public concerns about reducing gun violence, while still allowing for responsible gun ownership. The overall message should be that gun safety advocates want to enact and enforce effective gun violence prevention laws and regulations within the context of Second Amendment rights.

- **Balance Gun Rights with Gun Regulation.** Guns should be treated like other inherently dangerous products such as automobiles, requiring safety training, safe storage, and renewable licensing and registration. The Biden administration and other elected officials at the federal and state levels should take the lead in calling for legislation that balances Second Amendment rights with the protection of public safety. Gun regulation can be formulated that protects both the constitutional right to bear arms and public safety.

- **Ban Categories of Gun Sales and Restrict Gun Ownership.** Federal and state legislation should ban the sale and ownership of military-style assault weapons and high-capacity ammunition magazines; ban the purchase and ownership of guns by persons with mental illness, individuals under age twenty-one, and domestic partners with domestic violence misdemeanor convictions (the "boyfriend loophole"); and require gun owners to store guns in locked containers unless the gun is in their direct control.

- **Regulate the Sale and Manufacture of Guns.** Federal and state legislation should require background checks for all gun sales, including at gun shows, online, and in private sales; mandate a one-week waiting period for gun sale approval; require the Justice Department to publish the identities and locations of gun dealers who have sold guns that have been used in crimes; and repeal federal law protecting gun dealers and manufacturers from liability in civil suits for death or injury resulting from the use of guns they sold or manufactured.

- **Institute a Federal Gun Buyback Program.** The federal government should establish a program to buy back guns from private owners in order to reduce the enormous size of the national arsenal of 393 million guns now privately owned in the United States.

- **Expand Research and Polling on Gun Violence.** The federal government should support research and polling on gun violence in the United States in order to provide a scientific basis and public opinion support for establishing the balance of gun rights and public safety in gun regulation.

Part IV

Speech, Media, and Belief

12

Speech, Lies, and Insurrection

The right to free expression is at the foundation of American democracy. For more than two centuries, freedoms of speech and the press have been bulwarks against tyranny. Until recently, the greatest threat to these foundational freedoms was government censorship. Today there is a new threat—disinformation spread through powerful technologies that have the capacity both to democratize and undermine free expression. Digital technology is transforming our notions of freedom of speech. Stories about social media giants wielding algorithms to target disinformation flood the news. Controversies about facts and truth raise questions about the responsibilities of government, corporations, media, and citizens to protect the integrity of speech.

The stakes are high. Donald Trump's lies about voter fraud in the 2020 presidential election gained traction through social media, and were repeated and amplified for months after his defeat at the polls until they spurred an

Tear gas outside the United States Capitol on January 6, 2021. Photo by Tyler Merbler.

attempted violent insurrection at the Capitol. The former president has become a symbol of a new era in political speech, as have the social media platforms he utilized to stimulate and consolidate his political base. On January 21, 2021, Facebook, Twitter, and YouTube announced that they were suspending the former president's accounts because he had used them to encourage political violence. This momentous decision constituted a new form of censorship, not by government, but by social media companies that had come to dominate the new communication landscape.

In the midst of technological revolution, freedom of speech is facing and posing far-reaching challenges. Declining trust in institutions, including the media, has contributed to a lack of reliable means for testing information, allowing disinformation to have free rein. This trend has contributed to the rise of what some have called a "post-truth era" in which facts are increasingly disputed, especially when connected to political agendas.[1]

THE RISE OF "FAKE NEWS"

Before the Trump presidency, the term "fake news" was used to refer to false news stories spread by hoax and propaganda campaigns. This was a lay term for what today is known as disinformation, defined as the deliberate spread of false or misleading information to deceive and influence public opinion. It is a subset of misinformation, which also includes the unintentional spread of falsehoods due to ignorance or negligence. Today, misinformation takes many forms, ranging from false statements from politicians to unverified claims about health products to altered photos and videos.

During his first year in office, President Trump appropriated the term "fake news" to attack the press, claiming that major news outlets were perpetrating disinformation when they criticized him.[2] Using social media, especially Twitter, as his principal means of official communication, Trump broadcast his claims directly to the public without intermediation by the press. According to a 2018 analysis of his Twitter communication, Trump used the term "fake news" as a political tactic to cover his own mistruths, distance himself from negative reporting, and weaken the press as an institution entrusted with holding him and others in power accountable.[3]

In addition to making claims that unfavorable reporting was false information, the former president aimed his attacks at the press as an institution.

With these claims, he sought not only to detract from particular stories but to discredit the mainstream media entirely. For example, on October 29, 2018, he referred to the press on Twitter as "the true enemy of the people,"[4] claiming that journalists and news media companies are responsible for spreading distrust in American society.[5]

The former president's divisive attacks on the mainstream media escalated from claims of illegitimacy to unrestrained animosity toward critical news outlets. On September 2, 2019, Trump tweeted that in his re-election bid in 2020, the "real opponent is not the Democrats . . . our primary opponent is the Fake News Media."[6]

The repetition of these claims had a strong negative impact on trust in the mainstream media among Americans, dividing along party lines. In 2017, the Knight Foundation polled nineteen thousand Americans on the issue of "fake news" and found that 42 percent of Republicans and 17 percent of Democrats considered news stories that cast a politician or political group with which they agree in a negative light to be "fake news" even when the information was accurate.[7] Growing distrust of the media, especially among conservatives, challenges the media's role as a primary check on political power.

President Trump was the source of a continuing stream of false information throughout his presidency. According to PolitiFact, as of October 2020, 71 percent of his claims that warranted investigation by the organization were either "mostly false," "false," or "pants on fire."[8] While all political leaders embellish or spin the truth to some extent, Trump's lies differed from lies told by previous presidents in that they often contradicted established facts.[9] The erosion of agreed-upon facts made reasonable political discourse increasingly difficult. As one researcher observed, "If there are no agreed-upon facts, then it becomes impossible for people to make judgments about their government or hold it accountable."[10] These falsehoods, paired with the former president's attacks on the press, created a vast official landscape of disinformation and misinformation in which freedom of speech is hijacked and distorted beyond recognition.

DECLINING TRUST AND INCREASING POLARIZATION

Public trust in the mainstream media has been slowly and steadily declining since the late 1970s, when trust in many major institutions started to wane.[11]

According to a periodically updated Gallup poll, the widening divide in trust in news media has developed along partisan lines.[12] With the White House creating a narrative that pits the administration against the mainstream media, Americans are left in the middle to pick sides.[13]

The landscape of news media has changed significantly in the past two decades. Digital news sources and social media platforms have increased the speed of information-sharing, giving rise to a twenty-four-hour news cycle. In an age in which breaking news is available instantaneously through social media and cable television, mainstream media have lost their role as the primary disseminator of facts and have become instead a source of news analysis. According to Michael Schudson of the Columbia Journalism School, "the old days of ritually objective news reporting (he said/she said) are not gone but have been reduced in importance from the 1970s on, as mainstream outlets have increasingly emphasized analysis in news coverage—not quite so much 'who, what, when, where' as 'why.'"[14]

It is increasingly difficult for journalists to keep up with the speed of information-sharing on social media while maintaining strong journalistic integrity. As news events and imagery are posted on social media by unvetted sources in real time, newsrooms are enhancing their efforts on fact-checking and investigative journalism.[15] Although investigative journalism is slower and more expensive to produce than opinion and headline news, it plays a critical role in uncovering information to hold powerful parties accountable to the public. For example, investigative reporting led to the headline discoveries regarding the Ukrainian corruption that led to the first Trump impeachment trial.[16]

By shifting to a more narrative style, the news is, by nature, filtered through the lens of journalists and editors. This does not mean that mainstream media produce "fake news." Their narrative analysis is mitigated by professional journalistic standards for objective news-gathering. As news consumers interpret the narrative style of reporting, however, it is not surprising that Americans would seek their own values and worldviews in the stories they consume, projecting their own partisan biases.

The behavioral economics concept of confirmation bias would suggest that news consumers are likely to seek out and believe information that confirms their preexisting beliefs. The same phenomenon persists on social media, creating ideological filter bubbles that are perpetuated by social media content algorithms.

During the past several decades, the United States has seen a rise in political polarization as a measure of increasing ideological differences between parties. The Pew Research Center's 2014 report concludes that "[w]hen responses to questions [on political values] are scaled together to create a measure of ideological consistency, the median Republican is now more conservative than nearly all Democrats (94 percent), and the median Democrat is more liberal than 92 percent of Republicans."[17] The news media consumed by these constituencies reflect the growing partisan divide.

IDEOLOGICAL CLASHES

As political values have become increasingly polarized, the exercise of free speech has become similarly polarized. In recent years, protests on college campuses have often been linked to partisan antipathy toward ideologically extreme campus visitors. Students across the country have staged protests in response to visiting campus speakers with whom they have ideological differences or whose policies or actions they denounce. In many cases, the visiting speaker was blocked from speaking either before arriving or even after the event had begun.

There are many examples of this phenomenon from the past decade, ranging from the cancellation of small events to large events that escalated in some cases to violence. In 2014, the threat of student protests caused commencement speakers Christine Lagarde and Condoleezza Rice to withdraw from speaking at Smith College and Rutgers University, respectively.[18] In 2017, students at Middlebury College protested a visiting speaker, Charles Murray, who had been invited to campus by a conservative student group. Protests blocked the speech from taking place and devolved into physical attacks against the speaker and a Middlebury professor while they were attempting to leave the site.[19] The protesters claimed that their efforts did not deny Murray's right to speak, but only his use of the university's platform. The university countered that its platform was available to the speaker because he was invited by students. Two years later, Middlebury College cancelled a visit from Ryszard Legutko, a conservative politician from Poland, because of concerns about maintaining the safety of the event and a counter-event planned by student protesters.[20] These incidents exemplified the conflict that can occur over the First Amendment rights of ideologically opposed groups on campus.

Ideological tension is a foundation of a healthy democracy. College administrators have typically avoided any action that would censor speech from any side, except incendiary hate speech or speech that incites violence. Preserving this tension while protecting students and speakers from physical danger has often come at a high financial cost to colleges. In 2017, for example, the University of California at Berkeley spent more than $2.5 million on security for controversial visitors.[21]

Promoting differences of opinion is a central rationale for protecting free speech. In settings in which power differentials deter, suppress, or punish dissenting opinions, free speech is curtailed. In 2016, NFL quarterback Colin Kaepernick began kneeling during the national anthem before each game as a protest of police brutality against people of color. Although Kaepernick gained support from many fellow NFL players, he faced resistance from NFL team owners, fans, and President Trump. Those who condemned the protest claimed that kneeling during the national anthem showed a lack of respect for the country's armed forces. Kaepernick was denied a contract with the NFL for the following season. His case illustrates the influence that power structures can have on an individual's right to free expression. Kaepernick's protest did not interfere with his ability to perform his football duties, but his public expression cost him his job.

During the summer of 2020, mass protests broke out across the country in response to incidents of police brutality against Black Americans, particularly the murder of George Floyd by a Minneapolis police officer.[22] The public response gave renewed energy to the Movement for Black Lives with an emphasis on ending police brutality. The movement highlighted police violence and pushed for changes in a policing system that reinforced violence against Black people. This created a division between protesters and police that led to numerous instances of suppression of the First Amendment right to assembly. For example, on June 1, 2020, peaceful protesters in Lafayette Square, adjacent to the White House, were forcibly cleared from the area by National Guard and Park Police through the use of "smoke canisters, irritants, explosive devices, batons and horses."[23] A few minutes later, President Trump walked through the park so that he could pose for a photo in front of St. John's Church, across the park from the White House.

As protests against racism continued across the country, the Trump administration escalated its confrontational response. In Portland, Oregon, after nightly protests for more than a month, federal agents were deployed to the city to suppress the demonstrations. The federal agents were militarized, using tear gas and other physical tactics against protesters, in some cases pulling them into unmarked vans and detaining them without probable cause.[24] The federal forces were sent into the city under the auspices of restoring order and protecting federal property, but city and state officials opposed the federal presence on the ground that it would stimulate further unrest.

Racist expression is protected under the Constitution. While racist speech is objectionable to most Americans, its legal censure is permissible under the First Amendment only when it is likely to stimulate violence, or where it exposes hateful intent behind a connected criminal act that allows for a higher penalty than the act alone would receive. In recent years, several students at universities have been expelled for posting racist videos online. These expulsions show the tension between efforts to curtail racist speech and the First Amendment protection of speech.[25] The authorities in these cases justified the decision to expel the students on the basis of maintaining a safe educational environment for all students, but critics argued that the expulsions crossed the line into illegal censorship.[26]

WHISTLEBLOWERS

One of the principal functions of speech freedom in a democracy is to provide a channel for dissent. Whistleblower protections create an important defense for those who seek accountability for government action from inside the government. The Whistleblower Protection Act of 2007 protects government employees from retaliation when they make a "protected disclosure" of government wrongdoing.[27] The legislation protects the right to free speech to promote government accountability.

On August 12, 2019, a whistleblower within the intelligence community filed a complaint that alleged that President Trump had tried to arrange a quid pro quo deal with the president of Ukraine to investigate his political opponent former Vice President Joe Biden. As the investigation into this claim proceeded, the Trump administration and its supporters in Congress repeatedly demanded that the whistleblower's identity be revealed despite protections in the Whistleblower Protection Act protecting the individual from retaliation.[28]

The whistleblower was not the only government employee who was a target of retaliation during and after the Trump impeachment hearings. The president fired several government employees who had testified or otherwise participated in the hearings in the course of their duties or pursuant to a court order, including Intelligence Community Inspector General Michael Atkinson,[29] U.S. Ambassador to the European Union Gordon Sondland, and Ukraine policy officer on the National Security Council Lt. Col. Alexander Vindman. Several other high-level officials who cooperated with the impeachment inquiry were removed from their posts, including former U.S. Ambassador to Ukraine Marie Yovanovitch and former top U.S. envoy to Ukraine Bill Taylor.[30] Retaliatory tactics like this discourage future whistleblowers from coming forward and demonstrate the importance of the whistleblower protections that exist in the federal government.

Earlier attacks on whistleblowers have occurred during previous administrations. In 2010, NSA senior executive Thomas Drake provided unclassified documents to a *Baltimore Sun* reporter preparing an article on NSA domestic spying. Drake was initially charged with crimes under the Espionage Act for allegedly bringing the documents home, but the charges were dropped.[31] Under the Obama administration, prosecution of suspected leakers under the Espionage Act increased. Prior to the administration, only three press leaks had ever been tried under the Espionage Act, but during the Obama years, eight cases were prosecuted.[32] The Espionage Act traditionally targeted only spies who serve foreign governments, but the new interpretation of the law has targeted whistleblowers who leak information to journalists.[33] In 2019, the government indicted Julian Assange, the publisher of Wikileaks, for publishing whistleblower leaks of classified documents revealing criminal conduct by U.S. military officials in Afghanistan. While the case raised complex issues, pitting national security against government accountability, editors of the *Washington Post*[34] and the *New York Times*[35] criticized the indictment as a dangerous precedent for holding journalists and publishers criminally liable for publishing leaked information about government misconduct.

SOCIAL MEDIA TRANSFORMATION OF SPEECH

The rise of social media has transformed the ecosystem through which information and opinion are disseminated. With social media outpacing print newspapers as a news source for Americans,[36] more than two-thirds of adults report getting their news through social media.[37]

In the traditional press model, publishers present professionally developed stories and information to consumers. Polarized press and false information have always been a reality in the media ecosystem. Until the advent of social media, however, professional journalists, in theory and often in practice since the 1960s, sought to provide "fair and balanced" information. Social media have had a significant impact on the way traditional media function. According to a 2010 study, 60 percent of mainstream journalists use social media as a source in their research.[38] The emergence of broadcast and cable propaganda outlets such as Fox News, Breitbart, and One America News Network, has exacerbated the polarization of traditional media,[39] and the rise of social media without the gatekeeping function of traditional journalism has further complicated the search for facts and truth on which the integrity of the democratic process depends.

The power of social media lies in platforms' ability to amplify and suppress content based on the calculations of powerful, proprietary machine-learning algorithms. These tools vary in the ways they prioritize different kinds of content across a variety of metrics. With this technology, social media platforms can become ideological echo chambers, can amplify false information, and can provide a platform for destructive disinformation campaigns.

At the same time, the rise of social media has democratized access to platforms for sharing and spreading ideas and information. Social media's democratization of speech has created an unprecedented capacity for grassroots mobilization and has lifted voices who lack access to traditional forms of communication and power. It has broken down barriers that had kept individuals from being able to engage more widely in political, social, and cultural activities. The platforms provide a mechanism for users to come together around common interests, facilitating new forms of collective action.

According to a 2018 survey by the Pew Research Center, about half (53 percent) of American adults had engaged in some form of civic activity on social media within the previous year.[40] The examples in the survey include both online and offline activities and a wide range of actions.[41] In addition to this increase in civic engagement, social media have provided a platform for large-scale organizing by civil society activists across the political spectrum.[42] The March for Our Lives led by high school students against gun violence was organized through social media, bringing thousands of students together from across the country. Started in 2018 by students from Marjory Stoneman Douglas High School in Parkland, Florida, who experienced firsthand gun violence in schools, the student gun-control movement used social media to organize the largest single-day protest against gun violence in history, with as many as a million protesters demonstrating across the globe.[43] Similarly, the #MeToo movement harnessed the power of collective action on social media by creating visibility of the broad pervasiveness of sexual harassment. Activists for conservative causes like gun rights and anti-abortion action have also used social media to organize, as have pro-Trump activists.

Critics argue that social media have created a culture of "slacktivism," a pejorative term used to describe the low-cost, low-impact activism of supporting causes through social media (e.g., sharing posts by advocacy organizations, using political hashtags, or signing an online petition). Movements like #MeToo, Black Lives Matter, and March for Our Lives, however, have shown that social media can be a powerful tool for mass group mobilization both online and off. Author Clay Shirky argues that the power of social media to mobilize social movements is not only that the technology strengthens tactical organizing capacity, but also that social media platforms change the competitive landscape by empowering traditionally under-resourced movements compared to incumbents.[44] There are examples of social media playing a leading role in movements against authoritarian regimes, from the Arab Spring in the early 2010s[45] to the Umbrella Movement in Hong Kong, where social media was referred to as an "insurgent public sphere."[46] These movements benefited both from the power to organize in mass numbers, the anonymity that platforms provide which protects protesters from state retribution, and the speed with which stories can be shared. On the other hand, the movements were threatened by government surveillance targeting protesters through increasingly sophisticated online surveillance tools.

In a Pew Research Center survey about political engagement on social media, Black and Hispanic survey respondents stated that social media were very important for their ability to engage in civic activity—more important than for non-minorities, in part because mainstream media outlets often did not sufficiently cover minority interests.[47] This finding suggests that social media are playing an important role in redistributing access to the tools of civic engagement and applying pressure on elected officials.

The reality, however, may be different when seen through the eyes of social media critics. A 2020 internal audit commissioned by civil rights organizations with Facebook's cooperation stated that Facebook has failed to protect civil rights on the platform.[48] The auditors contended that Facebook's decision to protect freedom of speech at the expense of other protections such as nondiscrimination has had a detrimental effect on civil rights. The Facebook civil rights auditors were also concerned with Facebook's decision to exempt politicians' speech from fact-checking and community standards violations. The auditors cited a specific instance in May 2020 in which President Trump posted statements on Facebook and Twitter regarding the protests for racial justice following the murder of George Floyd. The president wrote, ". . . These THUGS are dishonoring the memory of George Floyd, and I won't let that happen. Just spoke to Governor Tim Walz and told him that the Military is with him all the way. Any difficulty and we will assume control but, when the looting starts, the shooting starts. . . . "[49] This statement would ordinarily have been flagged by Facebook's Violence and Incitement Community Standard as it references a call to action against a particular group of people. However, Facebook allowed the post to remain on the platform because it served as "a warning about impending state action," which is not prohibited by the Violence and Incitement Community Standard.[50]

DOMINANT PLATFORMS

During the past decade, the public has relied increasingly on social media for news and political information. Although television is still the most popular source for news, social media surpassed print newspapers in 2017 in percent of the population using the platform for news, with the gap widening in 2018.[51] With the increase of time and engagement on social media, digital platforms have a growing impact on the political information ecosystem.

Social media platforms are not legally responsible for monitoring the content of speech that users post or promote. Traditional news outlets are liable for defamatory material that they publish, but since social media are not considered publishers, they are exempt from this form of accountability. Social media providers are free from content liability as a result of the Communications Decency Act, Section 230 (CDA Section 230), which states, "No provider or user of an interactive computer service shall be treated as the publisher or speaker of any information provided by another information content provider."[52]

Section 230 originated in the early days of the internet in 1996, when lawmakers were promoting self-regulation among tech companies. The law was precipitated by a case in which a financial firm had sued a bulletin-board website for libel after a user of the site accused the firm of fraud.[53] The website moderators claimed that their site functioned like a library, which is not liable for the content of the books it provides to the public. The court found that the platform was more like a publisher because the moderators had edited posts to remove objectionable language and were thus acting like the editor of a newspaper. In response to this ruling, Congress enacted Section 230 to free internet platforms from liability for content while preserving the "Good Samaritan" principle that encourages sites to conduct some degree of content monitoring (for example, to remove foul language or obscenity). The sponsors argued that this provision maintained freedom of speech on the internet by distinguishing platforms from publishers. Under this theory, internet platforms serve as hosts for users to post content for which the users are independently responsible. While internet platforms may curate content to better the community, they are not obligated to do so.

Today, the conversation around Section 230 has been turned on its head. Critics of the legislation argue that companies are using the provision as a shield to protect them from accountability for their decisions about curating the content on their platforms. This curation includes decisions about what information is to be promoted on the site as well as decisions about what algorithms will engage more users. The critics are divided along partisan lines:

conservatives argue that sites like Facebook have censored conservative content, while liberals argue that the platforms should be required to take a stronger stand against disinformation and hate speech.[54]

Social media platforms have largely refrained from content curation, except for removing certain types of speech that violate community standards such as hate speech, calls for violence, and solicitations of sex. In the era of false information in the public sphere, there is mounting pressure for social media to address the spread of disinformation online. However, social media companies have been unwilling to take on the responsibility for being the arbiters of truth, citing freedom of speech as their guiding principle.

The norm is for platforms to rely on the "marketplace of ideas." This refers to the idea that valuable content will beat out less valuable content through forces akin to the "invisible hand" of the unregulated market. Mark Zuckerberg has invoked the marketplace of ideas in defense of Facebook's 2019 decision not to fact-check political speech. The theory is that counterspeech is the remedy for undesirable speech; that is, more speech is a better remedy than restricting speech.

In response to the "marketplace of ideas" theory, both conservative and liberal proponents of social media regulation argue that the freedom from liability enjoyed by social media platforms under Section 230 threatens the information ecosystem.[55] They propose that platforms be treated like publishers, subject to the same defamation and libel law that governs newspapers and other traditional media outlets. These laws would provide an incentive to reject user posts that would constitute defamatory or libelous material, creating an effect similar to the traditional gatekeeping function of the mainstream media. Opponents of changing Section 230, such as the Electronic Frontier Foundation, argue that treating social media companies as publishers would incentivize the companies to screen their users, diminishing marginalized voices who benefit from the unregulated platforms.[56] In addition, smaller social media sites would not have the resources to monitor content at scale, and the internet might become less receptive to innovation.[57]

Filter Bubbles

Because ad-driven digital platforms sell eyeballs and engagement, the algorithms they use maximize targeting for likely interest and emotional responses. The platforms are designed to show users the content that will be most relevant to them, and analysts have commented on the tendency of social media to reflect back to users and reinforce their own biases.[58] This phenomenon, known as a "filter bubble," is similar to the sociological concept of an echo chamber, in which people surround themselves with others who share similar views; a filter bubble is an algorithmic reinforcement of the echo chamber phenomenon.

Filter bubbles exist in a media landscape which provides news and political information with an ideological slant that can be amplified among ideologically aligned circles on social media. In a study of filter bubbles on Twitter, researchers found that the willingness to engage with media from the opposing political viewpoint was not equally distributed across the political divide. Conservative Twitter users were more likely to follow media accounts from left-leaning sources than liberal users were to follow equally right-leaning media accounts.[59]

Research into the polarizing effect of social media has produced mixed findings. A 2016 study found that the use of social media and search engines was correlated with an increase in mean ideological separation, but the study also found that social media users were exposed to an increase in diverse views.[60] A 2018 Pew Research Center study found that 14 percent of U.S. adults said that their views on an issue had changed because of something they had seen on social media in the past year.[61] These findings suggest that social media may increase users' exposure to information from competing ideological sources, but the studies are not conclusive. In addition, Facebook's own research found that while users are most likely to share content that aligns with their own political ideology, they are exposed to a wider range of differing opinions due to the weak-tie relationships that Facebook surfaces, which are more likely to differ from one's closer, strong-tie circle.[62]

Psychological concepts about information processing have been used to analyze how users experience the information they encounter on social media. Confirmation bias studies demonstrate that individuals are more likely to accept as valid information that confirms what they already believe to be true about the world than information that contradicts it.[63] This implies that in "the marketplace of ideas" in which users are expected to evaluate conflicting perspectives, confirmation bias will skew a person's views toward their preexisting ideology.

Political Speech

As we have seen, social media have become a primary source of news for many Americans. The platforms that host news content reflect the changing political landscape, and their own policies determine the parameters of the information ecosystem.

In 2019, Facebook controversially announced that the company would exempt speech content posted by political entities from the fact-checking mechanism that it applies to other forms of speech on the platform.[64] Facebook executives argued that their platform should not be the arbiter of political speech even when statements include false information. Facebook's stance was that the marketplace of ideas and a free press can effectively police political speech by allowing voters the opportunity to assess politicians' messages.

But the marketplace can only function when it includes a healthy, free press able to fulfill its fact-checking function and inject critical responses to false political speech. Fact-checking depends on the capacity of resource-strapped journalists to analyze the veracity of claims in the vast number of political ads hosted by social media. Even assuming that such a fact-checking system is feasible, there is no guarantee that social media news consumers will be reached by corrective information and that they will update their understanding of the information based on fact-checking.

Facebook's announcement of its political ad policy was met with widespread criticism. News outlets, advocacy groups, politicians, and hundreds of Facebook employees denounced the policy, claiming that enhancing the spread of false information by politicians was harmful to democratic integrity. In a defiant example, Adriel Hampton, a political activist from California, registered to run for governor in the 2022 election, openly stating that he would run ads on Facebook with false information.[65] Facebook quickly responded by rejecting Hampton's false ads, claiming that his political candidacy was illegitimate. Other politicians also took part in testing Facebook's policy by posting obviously false information in ads. The ads were permitted on the platform under the new policy, including one by presidential candidate

Elizabeth Warren protesting the policy.[66] The critics argued that Facebook's policy allows politicians to freely spread and promote false information without recourse.

Following the backlash against Facebook's political ad policy, Twitter announced in 2019 that it would prohibit paid political speech on its platform. In a Twitter thread about the decision, CEO Jack Dorsey explained that political advertisers were employing "machine learning-based optimization of messaging and micro-targeting, unchecked misleading information, and deep fakes" with "increasing velocity, sophistication, and overwhelming scale," making it impossible for the company to adequately police the messaging to prevent inaccuracy and manipulation.[67] While many praised Twitter's policy, the decision had significant collateral consequences. For example, a freeze on political advertising—especially the low-cost, targeted advertising available through social media—tends to favor incumbent candidates because less established campaigns will have fewer financial resources to employ on more expensive paid advertising.[68] Additionally, Twitter faced criticism for its lack of clarity about what its policy would mean for advertising around issues-based advocacy on climate change, women's rights, and other major public topics.[69]

Meanwhile, the White House incorporated Twitter into its official platform, as President Trump used his @realDonaldTrump personal account on the social media service for communicating with the public instead of the White House @POTUS account. In 2019, a federal appeals court ruled that President Trump violated the First Amendment by blocking Twitter users who were critical of him from following his account.[70] The court pointed out that "[t]he salient issues in this case arise from the decision of the President to use a relatively new type of social media platform to conduct official business and to interact with the public. We conclude . . . that the First Amendment does not permit a public official who utilizes a social media account for all manner of official purposes to exclude persons from an otherwise-open online dialogue because they expressed views with which the official disagrees."[71] Because the president was making significant statements to the public through Twitter, the court concluded that it was unconstitutional for him to bar his critics from access to that information. White House lawyers appealed the decision, arguing that Trump's account was personal, not official. The Supreme Court dismissed the case in April 2021 on the grounds that Trump was no longer in office.

While president, Trump was often criticized by civil liberties advocates for using his Twitter account to advocate violence against individuals—a violation of the platform's policies—and to spread misinformation. In the lead-up to the 2020 election, Twitter labeled several tweets as containing "potentially misleading information about voting processes," and hid another, saying it violated terms on "glorifying violence." However, Twitter made the latter tweet visible, on the grounds that "it may be in the public's interest" to see the communications of the president.[72]

These actions represent the difficulties social media platforms have faced in maintaining community standards on the one hand and allowing for communications that had essentially become official government speech on the other. Twitter took definitive action after the January 6 attack on the Capitol building by violent supporters of Donald Trump attempting to overturn the 2020 election. Citing several tweets by Trump after the attack it said were "likely to inspire others to replicate the violent acts," Twitter permanently banned Trump from the platform under its policy against inciting violence.

In a statement, Twitter articulated the difficult balancing act it faced, saying that "our public interest framework exists to enable the public to hear from elected officials and world leaders directly"; however, "these accounts are not above our rules entirely, and cannot use Twitter to incite violence, among other things." It left vague, however, exactly what other communications by officials would not be tolerated.[73]

Following Twitter's announcement, other social media platforms including Facebook, Instagram, YouTube, Reddit, and even Shopify also banned Trump.[74] Facebook left open the possibility that Trump could be reinstated, pending a decision by the company's Oversight Board, experts in law, freedom of expression, and human rights from around the world.[75] In May 2021, the board ruled that the platform was right to ban the former president, since the president's support of the January 6 rioters created a "clear, immediate risk of harm." However, the board said that the company's indefinite suspension was "a vague, standardless penalty," and it gave Facebook six months to either lift the ban or make it permanent.[76] The decision pleased no one, and was condemned by commentators as well as Trump supporters and opponents, who

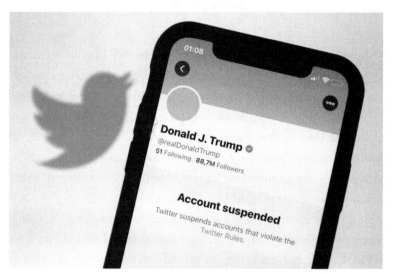

Twitter suspended Donald Trump's account because of violating the app rules. Image by Jakub Porzycki/NurPhoto via Getty Images.

criticized the lack of resolution, and called into question the wisdom of leaving momentous issues of free speech in the hands of an unelected "supreme court" appointed and supported by Facebook, while effectively absolving the company from accountability for its decision.[77] The reality and danger is that a private company is making influential decisions about speech based on its own rules, whims, or market analyses.

FIXING A BROKEN SYSTEM

First Amendment rights are at a turning point as the information and speech landscape is transformed by the technological revolution. The landscape in the past was determined by journalistic norms and trust in media institutions. Today, the democratization of the new information ecosystem relies largely on the assumption that truth will prevail in the marketplace of ideas. With the rise of disinformation campaigns and the loss of public trust, this laissez-faire system may no longer be sustainable. Regaining control of the media landscape will require change from all stakeholders—the media, the government, social media platforms, and consumers—focusing on a mixture of external regulation, self-regulation, and media literacy education.

The current system is riddled with weaknesses. Traditional information gatekeeping is too slow and too centralized to keep up with the pace of technological change, and the "marketplace" incentives that drive social media platforms do little to censor false information before it spreads. The business model of "surveillance capitalism," a term coined by Shoshana Zuboff to describe the market for data capture and manipulation, creates a misalignment in incentive structures between the objectives of the public sphere and the interests of private corporations that control the vast majority of online speech.[78]

The public interest must be the guiding principle for rebuilding the broken information ecosystem. According to media scholar Ethan Zuckerman, this will require inserting public interest values into the design of the public sphere through a "digital public infrastructure." This infrastructure would create spaces within the digital landscape in which public interest values are prioritized over commercial interests.

Integrating the public interest directly into the design of digital services would be similar to what occurred with radio in the early twentieth century and with TV broadcast decades later. In a leading example, President Kennedy's federal communications commissioner, Newton Minow, concerned in 1961 about the "vapid content" provided by private broadcasting companies, sought ways to create public interest broadcasting to fill "holes in educational, news, and civic programming—areas left underserved by the market." By the early 1970s, public service television and radio broadcasters like PBS and NPR were bringing *Sesame Street* and *All Things Considered* to the American public.

As technology sociologist Langdon Winner has observed, technology is a product of the political, economic, and cultural context in which it is designed.[79] As such, public interest should shape the course of technological progress. It is equally important that principles of transparency and accountability provide oversight of the practices of social media companies in the future of a regulated internet.[80]

The traditional media landscape relied on a system of checks enforced by the press and public opinion to hold government and private actors accountable. In the new system, a similar degree of oversight would monitor what is currently considered proprietary. For instance, the algorithms that govern what information is promoted and what is suppressed on social media are considered proprietary and therefore inaccessible to anyone outside the companies. Because these algorithms play a major role in shaping the information ecosystem, however, accountability requires transparency to allow the public to understand how algorithms can be used in order to safely and responsibly protect freedom of speech and the information users consume.

Regulating Content?

One category of potential regulation would alter or repeal the liability protection given to tech companies for their content under CDA Section 230. The debate over Section 230 is wide-ranging, spanning the analysis of downstream effects on free speech, the effects on the information ecosystem, the practical design of legislative changes, and the feasibility of implementation.[81] Those in favor of modification or repeal cite the contrast between the editorial responsibility of traditional media companies and the freedom from liability enjoyed by tech companies. While repeal might be an extreme solution to fight the spread of disinformation, other options include modification through judicial or legislative means, including adding restrictions in certain contexts.

One such restriction, enacted in 2018, is the Stop Enabling Sex Traffickers Act (SESTA). This amendment states that internet platforms are treated like publishers and are liable for any activity on the platform that advertises sex work, thus exempting such content from Section 230.[82]

Opponents to further restriction of Section 230 argue that it could have grave consequences for freedom of speech online and that legislative and judicial bodies lack the technical competence to effectively implement and enforce broader modifications.[83] Enforcement of standards, they argue, would be more proficiently and flexibly handled by the tech companies themselves.

Whatever the fate of the Section 230 protections, self-regulation of tech companies could and should be expanded. Policies of self-regulation could mirror some proposals for external regulation, including transparency and limiting of micro-targeting. With the speed of technological innovation, it may be difficult for external regulation to keep up with shifting trends and usage of social media. Iteration and testing would be useful for optimizing self-regulation.

As the controversy over Facebook's quasi-self-regulatory Oversight Board shows, however,[84] such governing bodies may prove to be unable to control the spread of false information on the site. Some argue that this Oversight Board should adhere to international human rights standards rather than rules that have been internally designed by the company.

In addition to self-regulation by social media companies, the traditional media need to be clear with the public about the way that their industry has changed in light of the new information ecosystem. This shift has occurred within the framework of standards of journalistic integrity. A 2019 Pew Research Center study found that a majority of adults believe that traditional news media have the greatest responsibility for addressing false information in the news.[85] This indicates that it is incumbent upon the press to articulate the role that the traditional media play in the new information landscape in order to partner with other stakeholders to help address the problem of misinformation and disinformation.

Developing the capacity of media consumers to evaluate conflicting information within the marketplace of ideas is critical for the information ecosystem to function effectively under the principles of free speech and media freedom. Currently, the education system does very little to educate students to think critically about media consumption. A Pew Research Center study found that Americans are generally unable to discern what kinds of statements are factually based and which are opinions.[86] Additionally, another study indicated that people have difficulty parsing truth from a range of information sources.[87]

In a rapidly changing media environment, people need to learn how to navigate through the vast amounts of information that they encounter every day. This includes learning digital competencies as well as the tools of critical analysis required to understand biases. Media literacy scholars emphasize that there is an important distinction between teaching the technical skills for working in digital spaces and the critical comprehension of media in an interdisciplinary fashion.[88]

Policy Recommendations

- **Create a Digital Public Infrastructure.** Enact federal legislation to establish a public interest mandate for for-profit social media platforms, requiring digital platform companies to support the development of digital spaces designated for public use, and requiring these companies to develop standards of interoperability, data portability, and data openness.
- **Provide a Funding Mechanism for Public Interest Uses of Social Media.** Through federal and state legislation, subsidize innovation to reinvent public functions that social media have displaced, for example, by taxing digital advertising to create a public social media fund to support experimental approaches to public social media platforms and new forms of investigative journalism, as recommended by the American Academy of Arts and Sciences in its 2020 report, *Our Common Purpose.*
- **Require Social Media Transparency and Accountability.** Enact federal legislation to require social media platforms to operate with transparent procedures in order to allow researchers, oversight officials, regulators, and journalists to understand how and for what purposes social media algorithms are designed, and to establish oversight and accountability measures to require algorithms to be used safely and responsibly to promote freedom of speech and protect against racial, gender, religious, disability, or LGBTQ discrimination.
- **Promote Media Literacy.** Develop media literacy education to assist media consumers to evaluate information and navigate the rapidly changing marketplace of ideas. Media literacy is critical for a democratic information system to function effectively under the principles of free speech and media freedom in the midst of technological change.

13

Religious Freedom and Civil Rights

The complicated relationship of religion and government predates the founding of the United States. The Founders grappled with the problem for years before compromising on the final language of the First Amendment. Even then, the issue was far from settled: the United States has struggled since its founding to reconcile the right of religious freedom with the reality of governing a pluralist democracy with an increasingly diverse population.

Today, a struggle over the scope of religious freedom is taking place in politics, the courts, and across American society. Claims of religious freedom are increasingly receiving preferential treatment in judicial decisions when religious beliefs come into conflict with other rights. That is particularly true for women's reproductive rights and the rights of individuals to non-discrimination on the basis of their sexual identity, both of which are under attack by opponents claiming a superior right to religious freedom.

At the same time, a controversy has emerged over the meaning of the Establishment Clause of the First Amendment, in which recent Supreme Court cases have pitted the prohibition on establishment of religion against the right of religious free exercise. The central question over religious rights today is how to strike an appropriate balance between rights when they come into conflict. This question has troubled the American republic since its formation.

FREEDOM AND INTOLERANCE

While it may seem self-evident that religious freedom and the separation of church and state are core rights and responsibilities in the United States, this has not always been the case. Throughout American history, a tension has existed between the ideal of religious freedom and the practice of governance and the protection of other rights.

A common narrative of the country's founding tells the story of two groups—the Pilgrims and Puritans—seeking religious freedom after persecution in England. But the real story is more complex. While the narrative of a search for religious freedom holds true for the seventeenth-century Pilgrims, the Puritans have a somewhat different story. The Puritans fled England not only for religious freedom, but also to establish a state in which their own version of Christianity was the law of the land.[1] Their mission was to create a Puritan society based on the principle of a pure populace. Practitioners of other faiths, such as Quakers or Baptists, were banned from living in Massachusetts, under threat of brutal punishment.

The concept of "religious liberty" in colonial America was born out of circumstances in the Massachusetts Bay Colony, where its denial was the norm. Some Puritans, such as Anne Hutchison and Roger Williams, rejected Puritan doctrine and challenged this denial.[2] Williams made a revolutionary argument that the civil authorities of Massachusetts should not be involved in matters of religion, and that religious tolerance was not only a moral precept, but also a requirement of civil society.[3]

In the eighteenth century, James Madison and Thomas Jefferson led the development of religious liberty, advocating for religious diversity and disestablishment of any one official denomination. Madison succeeded in including a religious freedom clause in Virginia's new Declaration of Rights, inspired by the persecution he had witnessed Virginia's Baptists suffer at the hands of the colony's Anglican establishment.[4] Madison's clause read: "religion . . . and the manner of discharging it, can be directed only by reason and conviction, not by force or violence; and therefore all men are equally entitled to the free exercise of religion."[5] Later, other colonies adopted similar language.[6] Madison argued that governments should take an entirely hands-off approach to religion, neither helping nor hindering it.[7]

In 1789, the Constitution of the United States forbade the use of religious tests for public office in the national government, a necessary accommodation given the diverse array of Christian denominations the colonies represented.[8] In arguments over the Bill of Rights, Madison again led efforts to secure religious free exercise and disestablishment.

The debate over the First Amendment came down to two questions: whether the national government could support religion and whether individual states could regulate religion as they saw fit.[9] After a lengthy debate in the House of Representatives, Madison succeeded in barring the national government from supporting religion. The final wording of the religious freedom section of the First Amendment provides that "Congress shall make no law respecting an establishment of religion, or prohibiting the free exercise thereof."[10] During a second debate in the Senate, however, states were granted the right to regulate or support religion within their borders.[11] Not until 1868, with the passage of the Fourteenth Amendment, did states also become subject to the Bill of Rights and its prohibition on religious establishment.

The United States has long struggled to live up to these ideals. First and foremost, Protestant Christianity was the de facto established religion of the new republic. American Christians pressured Native Americans to assimilate to their traditions via indoctrination in U.S. government-funded boarding schools and prohibitions on practicing their native religions.[12] They prevented African American enslaved people—approximately one in five of whom were Muslims—from practicing their native religions and often forcibly converted them.[13]

Nativist movements victimized Catholics and excluded them from mainstream politics for nearly two centuries, culminating in the anti-Catholic Know-Nothing Party, which ultimately placed three representatives in Congress by the mid-1850s.[14] States discriminated against Mormons, including an infamous incident where the governor of Missouri gave an order in 1838 that all Mormons be either expelled or "exterminated."[15] Jewish Americans faced discrimination throughout American history and, around 1900, began to be depicted as a racial threat, culminating with the lynching of Jewish businessman Leo Frank in Atlanta in 1915.[16] American Muslims have regularly faced negative stereotypes portraying them as "violent and hedonistic."[17] In the anti-Chinese fervor in the late nineteenth and early twentieth centuries, Buddhism came to be regarded not as a religion, but as a "dangerous cult."[18] These and many other examples of past religious discrimination continue to color the current debate over the right to religious freedom.

PARSING THE FIRST AMENDMENT

"Congress shall make no law respecting an establishment of religion, or prohibiting the free exercise thereof."[19]

These sixteen words consist of two independent but interrelated clauses: the "Establishment" Clause and the "Free Exercise" Clause. At a minimum, the first clause prevents the government from declaring any one faith to be the official religion of the United States or any individual state or municipality. Throughout history, the courts have generally interpreted it to mean governments cannot directly support religion—including promotion, encouragement, or financing.[20] In the words of the Supreme Court, that requires a "benevolent neutrality" on the part of the government,[21] in which government allows religious exercise but prevents government sponsorship.[22] A seminal 1971 Supreme Court case, *Lemon v. Kurtzman*, provided the opportunity to put this balance into action, creating the so-called Lemon test, whereby a government policy must meet three criteria to be considered constitutional under the Establishment Clause: It must (1) "have a non-religious purpose; (2) not end up promoting or favoring any set of religious beliefs; and (3) not overly involve the government with religion."[23] Since then, recognizing that the Lemon test is perhaps too rigid in some cases, the Supreme Court has experimented with different interpretations of "neutrality," but has never managed to precisely define what is and is not "establishment."[24]

The Free Exercise Clause prohibits the government from interfering with the private religious beliefs of American citizens. There are, however, circumstances in which practices stemming from those beliefs may be proscribed.[25] This battle has played out frequently in the legislative arena and in the courts. Since a 1963 decision in *Sherbert v. Verner*, the Supreme Court has generally used a "compelling interest test" to resolve difficult cases.[26] Under this test, in order to justify interfering with religious practice the government must prove two things: (1) that it is doing so in the name of a compelling interest of the "highest order," and (2) that there is no other, less restrictive, means to achieve the same outcome.[27] If a law or policy cannot pass the test, the government cannot regulate the religious practice in question.

Sherbert v. Verner illustrates the compelling interest test in action.[28] A Seventh-Day Adventist named Adele Sherbert quit her factory job because it required her to work on Saturdays, which Adventists consider to be the Sabbath. When she applied for unemployment benefits from South Carolina, the state rejected her application because she had quit voluntarily and rejected other opportunities that also required work on Saturday. She disputed the decision, and the case went to the Supreme Court, which ruled 7–2 to require South Carolina to provide unemployment benefits to Sherbert. In its explanation, the Court charged South Carolina had failed the compelling interest test: it could not prove that refusing to accommodate Sherbert's religious practice was in the name of a "compelling state interest."[29] In a similar case in 1972, *Wisconsin v. Yoder*, the Court again applied the compelling interest test, this time to a Wisconsin law requiring school attendance after eighth grade. The Court decided that Amish students should be allowed to stay out of school, because "ensuring universal school attendance" was not a compelling state interest sufficient to override Amish religious expression.[30]

The Supreme Court has always decided what constitutes a "compelling" government interest on a case-by-case basis and has never precisely defined it. Some legal scholars argue that it "is obviously intended to be a higher interest than 'legitimate' or 'important,'" while others have described it as "'necessary' or 'crucial,' meaning more than an exercise of discretion or preference."[31] It is less clear whether free exercise can be restricted in order to secure a *different* fundamental right. The debate over this question is the most pressing challenge in the area of religious freedom today.

TESTING THE ESTABLISHMENT CLAUSE

The battle over when, where, how, and to what degree the government may support religion has been fought on many fronts. Public schools, which are government-run and therefore prohibited from explicitly promoting "religious beliefs or practices as part of the curriculum," are a common battleground.[32] Conflicts have included whether public school students may miss class to receive religious instruction elsewhere; whether it is constitutional for the words "under God" to appear in the Pledge of Allegiance; and whether it is constitutional to hold prayers in classrooms or during graduation ceremonies.[33]

Another frequent area of dispute concerns the display of religious symbols on public grounds. The Supreme Court, seeking to find the proper balance between non-establishment and the reasonable need to give religion room for public expression, has been inconsistent.[34] In two prominent cases, religious displays were ruled constitutional.[35] In a pair of similar cases, the displays were ruled unconstitutional.[36] In one particularly striking scenario, Justice Stephen Breyer voted on opposite sides of the issue on *the same day*. While these religious display cases did have some notable differences (which Breyer used to explain his apparent contradiction), legal scholars have criticized him for contributing to a broader trend of the Court blurring the line separating church and state.[37]

Other areas of government activity, such as the military and taxation, also present challenges. In the case of military service, the Supreme Court in 1965 broadly interpreted a statute requiring conscientious objectors to prove that their refusal to go to war was based on belief in a "Supreme Being" as not requiring proof of a specific religious belief.[38] In the case of taxation, when tax-exempt religious groups have violated the requirement that they abstain from electoral politics, the IRS has withdrawn their tax-exempt status.[39] In a less straightforward matter, the issue of whether religious organizations, particularly schools, may benefit from taxpayer-funded government programs has been an increasing area of controversy.[40]

DEBATING THE FREE EXERCISE CLAUSE

The debate over the Free Exercise Clause is equally complex. The central challenge is in deciding when certain forms of religious practice become unacceptable, requiring government regulation. For example, what happens if religious free exercise violates a law? Or, what happens when a practice that some citizens view as free exercise denies or imposes a burden on the rights of other citizens?

While such questions have long been decided by the "compelling interest test," the Supreme Court's ruling in the 1990 case *Employment Division v. Smith* complicated the situation by rejecting the need to apply the test. In that case, a Native American named Al Smith was fired from his job at a rehabilitation center for having ingested peyote, an illegal drug, during a religious ceremony. Smith argued that his dismissal—and the subsequent refusal of the state of Oregon to provide unemployment benefits—was an unconstitutional violation of his religious freedom.[41] Rather than applying the compelling interest test, the Court instead decided, according to Justice Antonin Scalia's majority opinion, that the test was too demanding because it risked granting too many exemptions for religious practice, which would encourage too many people to try to opt out of perfectly valid laws—leading, in Justice Scalia's view, to "anarchy."[42]

The Court not only ruled against Al Smith, but it also made it easier for governments to regulate religious practice in general. Now, the Court said the government only needed to apply the compelling interest test if a regulation *specifically* targeted a religious practice, or if it infringed upon "an additional constitutional right, such as free speech."[43] Because Oregon's law prohibiting the use of peyote was simply a public health measure, and not directed toward religion, it could not be subject to the compelling interest test.[44] But the debate was not over. The *Employment Division* ruling provoked a strong negative response from conservatives and liberals alike. Conservatives were concerned about the threat to religious liberty, while liberals criticized it as discrimination against a minority religious practice. As a result of this odd bipartisan consensus, Congress passed the Religious Freedom Restoration Act (RFRA) three years later.[45]

The RFRA reinstated the requirement to satisfy the compelling interest test for *all* laws or policies where religious exercise was burdened "even if the burden results from a rule of general applicability."[46] The Supreme Court struck back in 1997 in *City of Boerne v. Flores*, conceding that Congress was entitled to mandate the use of the compelling interest test in all cases concerning *federal* law, but could not force the states to do the same.[47]

CURRENT CONTROVERSIES OVER RELIGIOUS FREEDOM

More recently, concerted lobbying by the religious right, along with a conservative majority on the Supreme Court, is tilting the balance toward a preeminent status for religious free exercise over other rights. The role of the religious right as an organized part of modern U.S. politics began in the late-1970s;[48] since then, conservative evangelical Christians have become a powerful voting bloc in elections.[49] Although their mobilization stemmed generally from a belief that American society was becoming too secular, the matter came to a head in 1976 when the IRS revoked the tax-exempt status of a prominent evangelical institution, Bob Jones University in South Carolina, because of its policies allowing racial discrimination.[50] In 1979, a network of evangelical organizations was organized into "the political movement of the Religious Right."[51]

Subsequent decades saw increased activity from religious right organizations, particularly Protestant evangelical groups such as Jerry Falwell's Moral Majority.[52] Through the 1980s and 1990s, the functional merger between this network and the Republican Party increased.[53] Their primary power, in addition to fundraising and advertising, lay in voter mobilization, which often tipped elections to their preferred candidates.[54] The rise of the religious right also served to bridge the historical Protestant-Catholic divide, bringing together religious conservatives in their opposition to issues like abortion.[55] Although its relative influence has waxed and waned over the years, the religious right remains politically powerful today.[56]

At present, the movement is driven by a sense of the diminishing importance of organized religion in American public life.[57] In 1972, only 5 percent of Americans described themselves as "not affiliated" with any religion. By 2016, that number had risen to 23 percent, including 39 percent of people ages 18 to 29.[58] Court rulings and government regulations have reinforced the separation of church and state, creating fear on the religious right that religious expression is becoming unwelcome in American public life[59]—a fear often stoked and exaggerated by conservative media.[60]

The relationship between the religious right and the Republican Party intensified during the Trump administration. In recent years, the mission to promote conservative Christian values has begun to employ the tools of government, thereby coming into conflict with the Establishment Clause. President Trump's relationship with the religious right began with the 2016 election, in which White evangelical Christians helped deliver Trump his victory with a striking 81 percent of their vote.[61] They were such an important bloc of voters that, according to a study from the Association for the Sociology of Religion, "the single most important determinant of Trump support was whether voters expressed what the authors called 'Christian nationalism.'"[62] The Trump administration fulfilled many aspects of the religious right's agenda, such as:[63]

- appointing individuals into positions of power in his administration who are religious right leaders, including Betsy DeVos as Secretary of Education and Jerry Falwell Jr., an evangelical leader and son of the founder of the Moral Majority, as head of an education reform task force;[64]

- appointing judges with views in line with the religious right;[65]
- criticizing the Supreme Court's ruling that secured marriage equality for same-sex couples;[66]
- pledging to repeal the legislation that prevents tax-exempt nonprofit organizations from endorsing political candidates;[67]
- recognizing Jerusalem as the capital of Israel, a long-held goal of evangelical Christians;[68] and
- allowing Attorney General William Barr to use the Department of Justice to test the limits of the Establishment Clause.[69]

In this political environment, the free exercise of religion, especially by Christians, became preeminent over other constitutional rights and principles, which were effectively hijacked by the religious right.

FREE EXERCISE DISCRIMINATION

At the same time, discrimination against American Muslims escalated,[70] with a marked increase in Islamophobic, as well as anti-Semitic, hate crimes.[71]

An outside view of damaged Diyanet Mosque after an arson attack on the mosque in New Haven, Connecticut, on May 16, 2019. Photo by Atilgan Ozdil/Anadolu Agency/Getty Images.

Orthodox Jewish men walk past "Crown Heights Shmira Patrol" security vehicles in the wake of anti-Semitic attacks in the Brooklyn neighborhood of Crown Heights on February 27, 2019, in New York. Photo by ANGELA WEISS/AFP via Getty Images.

In 2019, the *Washington Post* reported a "spate of arsons and bombings that has plagued mosques across America."[72] Social media has become a vehicle for spreading extreme Islamophobic views,[73] and anti-Muslim activists and local governments have sought to prevent the construction of mosques or Islamic cemeteries.[74] Furthermore, there has also been extensive legislative discrimination against Muslim Americans. Since 2009, forty-three states have enacted statutes making the practice of any form of Islamic law ("Sharia") illegal, even for its common usage in interpersonal or community arbitration.[75]

Previous administrations of both parties made efforts to counter Islamophobia.[76] This was not the case for the Trump administration.[77] As a candidate, Donald Trump rhetorically conflated radical Islamist extremism with Islam in general, and he did not correct explicitly Islamophobic comments by his supporters. He also regularly repeated the false claim that he had personally witnessed Muslims cheering in New Jersey following the 9/11 attacks.[78] President Trump used his bully pulpit—and his Twitter account—to support Islamophobic rhetoric, as when he defended Fox News host Jeanine Pirro for asserting that Rep. Ilhan Omar (D-MN) is opposed to the U.S. Constitution because she wears a headscarf.[79]

The administration has gone beyond rhetoric, including an executive order creating a travel ban to the United States from thirteen predominantly Muslim countries. The ban, which the administration argued was necessary on national security grounds, survived several legal challenges, including in the Supreme Court.[80] In a 5–4 vote in *Trump v. Hawaii*, the Court chose not to apply the compelling interest test and accepted the government's contention "that the Proclamation was not based on anti-Muslim animus and was instead based on 'a sufficient national security justification.'"[81] This decision came despite the fact that the first version of the ban included an explicit preference for Christian refugees over Muslims, "even if the lives of both groups were equally in danger."[82] Civil rights organizations also documented anti-Muslim discrimination in law enforcement and elsewhere, including "infiltration and surveillance of Mosques and Muslim communities; government discrimination against Muslims; and discrimination against Muslims in public schools."[83]

These discriminatory practices against Muslims were based on a pernicious claim: that Islam is in fact *not* a religion, but instead a political ideology. This was not merely a fringe belief. Prominent former Trump administration officials—including Michael Flynn, Sebastian Gorka, and Stephen Bannon—espoused it,[84] and the notion came into play in attempts to suppress Sharia.[85] This discriminatory assertion sought to justify the suppression of free exercise for American Muslims under the false claim that Islam is not protected by the First Amendment at all.[86]

FREE EXERCISE VERSUS ESTABLISHMENT

Under pressure from the religious right, the prohibition against establishment of religion has increasingly been undermined. This has been noticeable in the debate over prayer in public schools. The Supreme Court has held that school-sponsored prayer violates the Establishment Clause, but students are permitted to pray privately on school grounds, so long as they do not pressure others to do so.[87] This is the delicate balance of free exercise and non-establishment in action. In several public comments, however, including the 2020 State of the Union Address, President Trump expressed support for prayer in public schools.[88] In one case, he threatened to withdraw federal funding from a school because it had restricted prayer.[89]

The debate about government aid to religious institutions has intensified. In *Zelman v. Simmons-Harris* (2002), the Supreme Court balanced the Establishment and Free Exercise Clauses in ruling when it is permissible for government assistance to benefit religious institutions. The Court held that the aid must be given indiscriminately to all citizens, and it is permissible for some citizens to then use the money for religious purposes.[90] In 2017, however, the Court held in *Trinity Lutheran Church of Columbia, Inc. v. Comer* that "[t]he exclusion of churches from an otherwise neutral and secular aid program violates the First Amendment's guarantee of free exercise of religion."[91]

The difference between the two rulings is significant. The 2002 case made it permissible for a neutral aid program to benefit religious institutions. *Trinity Lutheran*, on the other hand, said it was *impermissible* for a neutral aid program *not* to benefit religious institutions; they must be included. In her dissent, Justice Sonia Sotomayor described the ruling as "precisely the sort of direct connection between church and state that the Establishment Clause was intended to prevent."[92]

In June 2020, the Supreme Court's ruling on a similar case, *Espinoza v. Montana Department of Revenue*, further strengthened the Free Exercise Clause at the expense of the Establishment Clause.[93] In 2015, Montana created a state program that provided tax credits for individuals and businesses who donated to private, nonprofit scholarship organizations. However, owing to a clause in the state constitution prohibiting state support for religious institutions, the Montana Department of Revenue added a rule that the scholarships could not be used at religious schools.[94] After several parents challenged the rule, the Montana Supreme Court decided against them. When the case went to the U.S. Supreme Court, however, it ruled in favor of the parents.[95] In his 5–4 majority opinion, Chief Justice John Roberts Jr. employed the compelling interest test, arguing that Montana's interest in "creating greater separation of church and State than the Federal Constitution requires" is not compelling enough to justify restrictions on free exercise.[96] This ruling further blurred the line between church and state, cementing the notion that states are *required* to include religious entities in state aid programs[97]—a result difficult to distinguish from state support for religion.[98]

The Trump administration classified churches and other "faith-based organizations" as "businesses" in the COVID economic relief package.[99] The Paycheck Protection Program allowed taxpayer money to be used directly to pay the salaries of clergy. As prominent legal scholars have observed, this direct government funding of religious activity was unprecedented.[100]

FREE EXERCISE VERSUS EQUAL PROTECTION

In addition to its challenge to non-establishment, the expansive view of religious freedom effectively hijacks the right to equal protection and non-discrimination. This has been increasingly demonstrated in court cases pertaining to LGBTQ rights, employment rights, and women's reproductive rights.

The Supreme Court ruled in 2015 in *Obergefell v. Hodges* that equal protection covers same-sex marriage; however, rulings in other cases have denied LGBTQ rights in favor of religious freedom.[101] The most prominent example is *Masterpiece Cakeshop, Ltd. v. Colorado Civil Rights Commission*. In this case, the Supreme Court held that a Colorado baker's refusal to bake a wedding cake for a gay couple because of his religious objection to same-sex marriage was an element of his free exercise. Therefore, the ruling of the Colorado Civil Rights Commission to compel him to serve the couple was unconstitutional.[102] In other words, the baker's right to free exercise justified denying the gay couple's right to equal protection and non-discrimination.[103] Following this precedent, more cases are sure to come. As one commentator observed, "innkeepers, restaurant owners, and photographers are all using the free-exercise clause of the First Amendment to justify their refusal to serve gay customers."[104]

An additional area of conflict is employment and disability rights, particularly for employees of religious institutions. A 2012 case illustrates the growing pressure against claims of discrimination. After being diagnosed with narcolepsy, a teacher named Cheryl Perich was fired by her employer, an evangelical Lutheran school in Michigan. Perich argued that her firing violated her rights under the Americans with Disabilities Act. The Supreme Court, however, referring to a legal tradition of "ministerial exceptions," upheld the right of the religious school to make hiring and firing decisions as it wished, even if those decisions would otherwise have been considered discriminatory by a non-religious employer.[105]

In 2014, another employment-related case challenged women's reproductive rights. The right of a woman to choose when to bear a child is protected under the 1973 *Roe v. Wade* decision and the Due Process Clause of the

Fourteenth Amendment.[106] However, in *Burwell v. Hobby Lobby*, the Supreme Court held that a private company may deny contraceptive health coverage to their employees—coverage to which employees would "otherwise have been entitled" by the Affordable Care Act—based on the employer's religious beliefs.[107] In essence, the Court prioritized the free exercise of the employer over the employee's right to contraceptive health care.

In reaching its decision in *Hobby Lobby*, the Supreme Court employed the compelling interest test.[108] While conceding that a compelling interest—access to contraceptive care—was indeed at stake, the 5–4 majority opinion concluded that the second criterion of "least restrictive means" was not met, because there was another means to secure the compelling interest. The U.S. Department of Health and Human Services (HHS) had an alternative process to provide contraceptive care for employees of religious *nonprofit* corporations, and that process could also be used for the employees of religious, for-profit corporations like Hobby Lobby.[109]

The dissenting justices took issue with this reasoning. They warned that the majority opinion created a precedent under which commercial enterprises would now be able to "opt out of *any* law (saving only tax laws) they judge incompatible with their sincerely held religious beliefs."[110] The ruling risked opening the door for innumerable requests for exemptions. This point echoed Justice Scalia's earlier concern in *Employment Division v. Smith* about the potential "anarchic" danger of a proliferation of religious exceptions from the law.

The dissent also contended that the majority misused the "least restrictive method" criteria. It was incorrect to say the HHS system was a valid alternative for contraceptive care because forcing employees to figure out the HHS system shifts too much of a burden onto them: "No tradition, and no prior decision under RFRA, allows a religion-based exemption *when the accommodation would be harmful to others*—here, the very persons the contraceptive coverage requirement was designed to protect."[111] In other words, although Hobby Lobby's owners are entitled to their beliefs, it is unconstitutional for the expression of those beliefs to impose a burden on the lives, health, or rights of others. Indeed, as a group of law professors argued after the *Hobby Lobby* decision, the Supreme Court has historically held that the government may not "accommodate religious belief by lifting burdens on religious actors if that means shifting meaningful burdens to third parties."[112]

As things stand, the Supreme Court majority's expansive reading of the RFRA is now precedent, weakening women's reproductive rights in favor of the right of religious free exercise.

A BALANCING ACT

Whether religious free exercise is inherently more important than other constitutional rights is the core of this debate.

In general, the Supreme Court has indicated that it is not. It has done so by favoring—on a case-by-case basis—other compelling interests: public health (*Employment Division v. Smith*); national defense (*Gillette v. United States*); social security (*United States v. Lee*); and a "sound tax system" (*Hernandez v. Commissioner*).[113] These interests were considered to be sufficiently compelling to justify burdening free exercise.

The more difficult question is what happens when two rights collide. Whether it is a compelling government interest to *secure rights*—such as the right to equal treatment and non-discrimination, or women's reproductive and privacy rights—may be resolved by appealing to legal precedent.

The majority's rationale in *Hobby Lobby* created a seed of precedent for future argumentation that the protection of other constitutional rights is a compelling interest. The majority agreed that there was a compelling interest at stake in the assertion of a right of access to contraception. It referred to the compelling interest as "guaranteeing cost-free access to the challenged contraceptive methods."[114] If access to contraceptive care is a constitutional right, that would imply that constitutional rights are compelling interests.

Arguments about balance and burden-shifting may be convincing here as well. For example, in the 1985 case *Estate of Thornton v. Calder*, the Supreme Court struck down a Connecticut law allowing employees to refuse to work on their "Sabbath" day, arguing it violated the Establishment Clause by overly involving government in particular religious practices. The Court's reasoning seems applicable to cases where other rights are compelling interests: "The First Amendment . . . gives no one the right to insist that, in pursuit of their own interests, others must conform their conduct to his own religious necessities."[115] Following this line of reasoning, "conduct" could include actions like seeking contraceptive care or marrying the person whom one loves. Similarly,

Justice Ginsburg's observation in her *Hobby Lobby* dissent could be convincing: "No decision . . . allows a religion-based exemption when the accommodation would be harmful to others." What could be more "harmful" than an impingement on a core human right?[116]

DISPELLING HISTORICAL MYTHS

The debate over religious freedom is littered on both sides with appeals to history and the intentions of the Founders.[117] While there is room for argument on many interpretations, advocates for a greater balance in rights and responsibilities should seek to definitively put to bed at least three historical myths.

First, it is incorrect, as some modern religious conservatives claim, that "the concept of separation of church and state was actually invented in 1947 by an activist U.S. Supreme Court."[118] James Madison and Thomas Jefferson spent decades making the case for separation—and even the devout Puritan Roger Williams thought separation was necessary. Second, it is not true that just because "Judeo-Christian values" were influential in the nation's founding, Jewish Americans and their Christian counterparts have always been aligned, as some like to imply when attempting to justify Islamophobic discrimination. Jews were widely persecuted before, during, and after the formation of the republic.[119] And third, going even further back, it is a falsehood that the original settlers were champions of religious liberty: the Puritans claimed this right for themselves but denied it to others.

A fourth myth, that religious liberty was intended to predominate as a claim over other rights, touches on more complicated issues, but is also untrue. A central element of the Founders' political philosophy was their belief that religious diversity protects religious freedom. In the case of religious diversity, Madison argued that the "multiplicity of sects which pervades America . . . is the best and only security for religious liberty in any society. For where there is such a variety of sects, there cannot be a majority of any one sect to oppress and persecute the rest."[120] In Federalist Paper No. 10, Madison extended this view to politics, arguing that a diversity of political factions would prevent any of them from establishing tyrannical majority rule.[121] These views were then incorporated in the founding documents and are essential to pluralist democracy.

If the Founders were to apply this philosophy to the question of rights, what would they think? Almost certainly they would conclude that, as with religious sects and political factions, a plurality of rights should prevent any one right from gaining dominance over others. Seen through this lens, it is difficult to imagine that the architects of religious freedom would feel comfortable assigning free exercise of religion preeminence over all other rights. Further evidence of this claim can be found in Madison's arguments during the debate over the Virginia Declaration of Rights. Even at that early stage, Madison was conscious that the right to religious free exercise could not be preeminent in all circumstances: "all men are equally entitled to the free exercise of religion, according to the dictates of conscience, unpunished, and unrestrained by the magistrate, *unless* the preservation of equal liberty and the existence of the State are manifestly endangered."[122] Note the first exception: religious free exercise was not more important than "the preservation of equal liberty."

Today, the compelling interest test theoretically represents a tool to protect Madison's design. Indeed, the "preservation of equal liberty" is a compelling state interest that *could* be used to justify some burdening of religious freedom: equal liberty, for example, in being able to access needed health care, or in purchasing baked goods from fellow citizens without fear of discrimination.

SOLIDARITY AGAINST DISCRIMINATION

Responsible citizens can find ways to do their part against discrimination. There is precedent throughout American history for interfaith solidarity in the face of external pressures. During the Revolutionary War, the Founders compromised on the religious language used in the Declaration of Independence. Why? Because they recognized that, "to defeat Great Britain, they would need to put aside certain theological disagreements and seek language that would unite rather than divide."[123] More recently, in the wake of 9/11, President George W. Bush chose to defend Islam rather than scapegoat it.[124]

Today, interfaith partnerships to fight bigotry and discrimination—such as the Muslim-Jewish Advisory Council—capture a similar spirit. For example, Jewish groups such as the Anti-Defamation League have helped fight back against the anti-Sharia laws that have been implemented countrywide, recognizing that "such a flagrant attack on religious freedom would inevitably hurt them too," by weakening religious rights more generally.[125] In another case, the head of the Anti-Defamation League responded to President Trump's proposal to create a national Muslim registry by saying that he would register as a Muslim himself.[126] Finally, Republican Senator Orrin Hatch, a Mormon, defended the proposed construction of the Cordoba House mosque in New York City, understanding from his knowledge of Mormonism in American history when discrimination was at play.[127]

These examples of interfaith defense against bigotry and discrimination may chart the way to balance competing interests of religious freedom and equal protection, supporting a multiplicity of beliefs while recognizing the rights of others to follow their own beliefs.

Policy Recommendations

- **Guarantee Equality of Rights.** Confirm through federal legislation or executive order that all constitutional rights must be equally protected and no single constitutional right is privileged over other rights. The legislation or executive order should establish that there is a compelling interest in creating practical methods of providing for equal application of rights and not denying or unfairly burdening the exercise of a right when it comes into conflict with another right (e.g., religious freedom versus freedom from invidious discrimination).
- **Reestablish the Balance of Claims of Religious Freedom with Other Constitutional Rights.** Rescind provisions of Executive Order 13831 that unreasonably shift the burden of exercising constitutional rights to patients of faith-based health care providers; and restore Executive Order 11246 protection of LGBTQ employees of faith-based government contractors against employment discrimination resulting from employers' claims of religious freedom.

- **Protect the Free Exercise of Religion Equally for All Religions.** Make permanent President Biden's rescission of Executive Order 13769 banning travel from Muslim-majority countries and bar religious discrimination against Islam or any other religion and the free exercise of religious faith in the United States.
- **Encourage Interfaith Partnerships.** Encourage interfaith partnerships against religious discrimination, hate crimes, and discrimination by religious institutions against the exercise of other constitutional rights.

14

Crimes of Hate

On the morning of August 3, 2019, a twenty-one-year-old man walked into a crowded Walmart in El Paso, Texas, carrying a high-powered rifle. Many of the customers that day were Hispanic families, shopping for back-to-school deals. Without warning, the man suddenly opened fire, sending shoppers scrambling to hide, or flee, covered in blood, through the doors. When the chaos was over, twenty-two people were left dead, with another twenty-four wounded—a tragedy the Texas governor called "one of the most deadly days in the history of Texas."[1]

While the mass shooting initially seemed an act of senseless brutality, the perpetrator's motivation soon became clear. Earlier that day, according to the U.S. Department of Justice, he had uploaded a document to the internet labelled "An Inconvenient Truth," which explicitly justified the assault on racist grounds. "This attack is a response to the Hispanic invasion of Texas," it read. "They are the instigators, not me. I am simply defending my country from cultural and ethnic replacement brought on by the invasion."[2]

While the El Paso shooting stands out for its violence, it is just one of many recent hate crimes—offenses motivated by animus against individuals or groups because of their race, ethnicity, national origin, religion, sexual orientation, gender identity, or disability.[3] Data from the Federal Bureau of Investigation (FBI) shows that, after declining for almost a decade, the number of hate crimes shot up 17 percent in 2017 to 7,175 and continued to rise to 7,314 in 2019.[4] According to national civil rights groups, the FBI vastly undercounts these crimes, and even government estimates put the actual number much higher than the number reported by law enforcement agencies.

In March 2019, two men in Dallas used a dating app to lure several gay

Anti-hate protest, March 2021. Photo by Jason Leung via Unsplash.

men to locations before robbing them at gunpoint, sexually assaulting them, and covering them with urine and feces. In February 2020, a Louisiana man admitted to intentionally setting fire to three churches with predominantly African American congregations.[5] As the coronavirus epidemic intensified between January and May 2020, Asian Americans were subjected to countless threats and attacks, including being hit, stabbed, and having objects thrown at them, as well as verbal assaults including, "Go back to China!" and "Fucking Asians, motherfuckers. You brought this disease here," according to reports compiled by the Anti-Defamation League.

Premeditated attacks such as the El Paso shooting are a minority of hate crimes committed in the United States. Most of these crimes, according to experts, are not planned in advance and are committed by perpetrators "seeking thrills" by targeting victims with violence. They were fostered by escalating hate speech during the Trump presidency, and political discourse infected by rhetoric stoking animosity and inciting violence. Several academic studies have specifically tied inflammatory language by the former president and other officials to an increase in violent acts against individuals or groups based on their race, color, national origin, religion, gender, sexual orientation, or disability.[6]

Donald Trump has repeatedly made anti-immigrant statements—for example, calling Mexican immigrants "rapists" and "thugs" and warning of an "invasion of illegals," the same language used by the El Paso shooter.[7] In addition, the former president condoned White supremacist violence—for example, by saying there "were very fine people on both sides" of the White supremacist rally in Charlottesville that led to the death of a counter-protester.[8] After the outbreak of COVID in the United States, Trump and right-wing media repeatedly characterized the disease as the "China" or "Wuhan" virus,[9] or even "kung flu,"[10] despite specific warnings by the FBI of a rise in hate crimes against Asian Americans "based on the assumption that a portion of the U.S. public will associate COVID-19 with China and Asian American populations."[11]

While hate crime laws have only existed for the last fifty years, hate-motivated crimes have been committed since the founding of the United States. The persecution and destruction of indigenous people, the enslavement of Black people, the mass violence against and exclusion of Chinese people, the thousands of lynchings of African Americans, the terror sown by the Ku

Klux Klan, and the massacre of hundreds of Black residents of Tulsa, Oklahoma, in 1921 were among the many egregious examples of crimes of hate throughout U.S. history.

The use of the term "hate crime" in the United States emerged in the second half of the twentieth century during the Civil Rights Movement. The Department of Justice began prosecuting federal hate crimes cases after the enactment of the Civil Rights Act of 1968. The term *hate crime* refers to bias-motivated criminal conduct.[12] The variation in hate crimes laws and data collection policies at the state level has created disparities in protection against hate crimes, which leaves people vulnerable depending on where they live. Without uniform hate crime statutes and data collection, it is difficult to know the true nature and magnitude of the hate crime problem in the United States. In order to allocate resources and deter future crimes, law enforcement agencies need to understand the problem better.

DEFINING AND REPORTING HATE CRIMES

Hate crimes must be distinguished from hate speech—expressions of prejudice that do not involve violence, threats, or property damage. The First Amendment affords broad protection for speech, even when it is biased, offensive, or inflammatory, but hate speech that causes or is likely to result in violence is a crime.[13] To be classified as a hate crime in the Justice Department's National Crime Victimization Survey (NCVS), an act must involve an actual crime, such as assault, vandalism, or arson, along with at least one of three types of evidence: the offender used hate language, the offender left behind hate symbols, and/or the police identified the incident as a hate crime.[14]

Hate crimes carry enhanced penalties because of their broader societal impact compared to other kinds of crime. When a bias-motivated crime is committed, not only is the crime's immediate target victimized, but hate crimes also damage the target's family, community, and identity group and leave them victimized and vulnerable.[15]

Hate crimes reported to the FBI are broken down according to specific attributes, including the bias involved, the characteristics of victims and offenders (e.g., race, gender, religion, sexual orientation, disability), the location (e.g., residences or homes, schools or colleges, parking lots or garages), and the jurisdiction (e.g., federal, state, agency). Animus against the victim's race, color, national origin, religion, gender, sexual orientation, or disability can all be motivations for hate crimes.[16]

The FBI's Uniform Crime Reporting (UCR) program serves as the national repository for hate crimes along with other crime data. Since information is voluntarily collected and submitted by individual law enforcement agencies using widely varying local definitions of *hate crime*, many crimes are not reported or classified as hate crimes, resulting in major under-recording of hate crimes in the FBI database.

The Justice Department's NCVS, which relies upon a sampling of 95,000 households, has estimated that U.S. residents experienced an average of 250,000 hate crimes annually between 2004 and 2015. Over half of these, it found, were not reported to the police.[17] Victimized groups, such as African Americans or LGBTQ people, may be reluctant to report their victimization because of distrust, fear, or strained relationships with law enforcement. Victims may also fear retaliation from perpetrators and the potential for secondary victimization by police. Some may fear being stigmatized as a victim of a bias-motivated crime. Others may not speak English proficiently enough to report their victimization, or may worry about their immigration status.[18]

The nonprofit Southern Poverty Law Center (SPLC) has determined that only 14 percent of the nation's 15,588 state and local law enforcement agencies require the reporting of hate crimes. Most local agencies do not properly identify hate crimes, and only twelve states provide special training for officers to do so. In addition, acts of bias-motivated bullying in schools, workplaces, and public are not included in the FBI's hate crime analysis.

To ensure a more accurate count, some nongovernmental organizations have created hate crime trackers focused on victims of specific identity groups, such as Asian Americans and Pacific Islanders (AAPI), allowing them to report bias-motivated crimes themselves. After launching in March 2020, the group Stop AAPI Hate received over 1,700 cases of "bullying, harassment, hate speech, or violence" against Asian Americans and Pacific Islanders in just six weeks.[19] The ability to report such incidents anonymously to an organization from one's own identity group can make people feel more comfortable with reporting bias-motivated incidents, leading to a more accurate count.

The Council on American-Islamic Relations, for example, issued a report in 2018 documenting 1,664 hate crimes against Muslims, in contrast to the FBI's official count of 270.[20]

HISTORY OF HATE CRIMES IN THE UNITED STATES

There is a long legacy of bias-motivated criminal behavior in the United States. In the past, many of these actions were not treated as crimes or were condoned because they reflected the attitudes of dominant groups during the times in which they were committed.[21] Moreover, during these periods the U.S. and state governments were complicit in perpetrating hate crimes either by directly using state violence against racial and ethnic minorities or by denying legal redress to victims.

Government Protection of Slavery

The U.S. government was directly involved in the legitimization and perpetuation of race-based chattel enslavement, practiced in the United States from the early colonial days through the Civil War. During this time, the federal government allowed for the continuation of slavery and gave the enslavers disproportionate political power during the drafting of the Constitution, recognizing enslaved individuals as three-fifths of a person for state congressional apportionment purposes.[22] The U.S. government also made it extremely dangerous for enslaved people to attempt to escape by enacting the Fugitive Slave Acts, which authorized the capture and return of runaway enslaved people within the territory of the United States, even in states that had ended slavery.[23]

Genocidal Violence Against Native Americans

The United States government was responsible for the genocide of indigenous people in the name of "civilization" and "manifest destiny," including by authorizing or condoning over 1,500 wars and attacks on Native Americans. President Andrew Jackson pushed for the Indian Removal Bill of 1830, which led to the U.S. Army removing sixty thousand indigenous Americans from their ancestral lands over the next decade,[24] with thousands dying through forced marches in the removal process.[25] By the close of the Indian Wars in the late nineteenth century, fewer than 238,000 indigenous people remained of the estimated 5 to 15 million living in North America in the fifteenth century.[26]

The Ku Klux Klan and Lynching

The Ku Klux Klan (KKK) is one of the oldest and most notorious American hate groups, primarily targeting Blacks, but also attacking Jews, immigrants, LGBTQ people, and Catholics.[27] Founded during the Reconstruction era after the Civil War, the KKK intimidated African Americans from exercising their social, political, and economic rights through extrajudicial killings carried out by lynchings, tar-and-featherings, rapes, and other violent attacks.

The Equal Justice Initiative has documented that between the end of Reconstruction in 1877 and 1950, there were 4,084 lynchings in twelve states in the South[28] in a long-term campaign of terror and intimidation to maintain racial subordination and segregation. A recent study found historical continuity between such hate-motivated violence and contemporary hate crimes. In areas where lynching was prevalent before 1930, hate crimes targeting Blacks are today less likely to be reported by police or prosecuted.[29]

The KKK broadened its scope in the 1920s when it expanded its agenda to oppose and seek to block immigration, growing to an estimated 4 million members by 1925. The KKK experienced a resurgence in the 1950s and 1960s in support of preserving segregation and opposing civil rights, using bombings, murders, and other attacks to terrorize communities, including the killing of four young girls in a bombing of the 16th Street Baptist Church in Birmingham, Alabama, in 1963.[30] The Southern Poverty Law Center estimates that there are still between five thousand and eight thousand Klan members today.[31]

Anti-Chinese and Anti-Asian Bias and the Chinese Exclusion Act of 1882

Anti-Chinese sentiment and competition for jobs between Chinese immigrants and White Americans in the nineteenth century sparked racially motivated violence, as Chinese men often worked for lower wages than Whites. In the 1871 "Chinese Massacre," for example, a mob of approximately one hundred White men burned and pillaged Los Angeles's Chinatown, killing as many as twenty-eight Chinese citizens.[32]

Both federal and state governments sanctioned anti-Chinese discrimination at the state and federal level.[33] The Chinese Exclusion Act of 1882 became the first significant law restricting immigration into the United States, and the only law curtailing immigration for a specific nationality. Other laws followed, leading to Chinese immigration becoming illegal from 1902 to 1943, when China became a U.S. ally in World War II.[34]

Asian Americans have been targeted during times of political and economic unrest. During the Great Depression in 1929, a mob of hundreds of White men raided the Filipino community of Watsonville, California, beating and shooting people in an incident known as the Watsonville Riots. During World War II, 120,000 people of Japanese descent were arrested without due process and held in incarceration camps throughout the war.[35]

VICTIMS AND OFFENDERS

Despite its shortcomings, the FBI's Uniform Crime Reporting database is used by government, academics, and nonprofits to chart broad trends across recent hate crimes data. According to UCR statistics, the overall number of hate crimes increased from 6,121 in 2016 to a decade-high 7,175 in 2017—before rising another 2 percent to 7,314 in 2019.[36] In addition, there has been a trend away from crimes against property, such as vandalism, arson, and robbery, and toward crimes against individuals, such as intimidation, assault, murder, and rape.

Between 2017 and 2018 alone, hate-crime violence against individuals rose 11.8 percent to 4,571, a sixteen-year high that now accounts for 61 percent of all hate crimes, according to an analysis of FBI data by the Center for the Study of Hate and Extremism at California State University, San Bernardino.[37] The increase in hate crimes indicates a growing level of physical violence against vulnerable communities. The Center's director noted that "there has been a disturbing shift to hate crimes directed against people as opposed to property and these increases are seen almost across the board."[38]

In its analysis of hate crimes in 2019, the FBI reported that the majority (55.8 percent) were committed as a result of race/ethnicity/ancestry bias, followed by crimes committed on the basis of religion (19.9 percent) and sexual orientation (16.8 percent).[39] Among racially based hate crimes, 48.5 percent were victims of anti-Black bias, 15.7 percent were victims of anti-White bias, and 14.1 percent were victims of anti-Latinx bias.[40] Hate crimes against Latinx Americans have risen faster than crimes against other racial groups, causing some advocates to place the blame on anti-Latinx rhetoric from the Trump administration.[41] Of anti-religious hate crime victims, 60.2 percent were victims of anti-Jewish bias, 13.2 percent were victims of anti-Islamic bias, 3.8 percent were victims of anti-Catholic bias, and 3.8 percent were victims of other Christian bias. Of sexual orientation–based hate crimes, victims of anti-gay-male bias made up the majority of victims at 61.8 percent, followed by a mix of anti-lesbian, transgender, and bisexual bias.[42]

The FBI reported that of the victims for whom age data was available in 2019, 89 percent were adults, while 11 percent were juveniles.[43] Based on NCVS data from 2011 to 2015, the Justice Department reported that men and women had similar rates of hate crime victimization and that persons in households in the lowest income bracket ($24,999 or less) had the highest rate of victimization when compared to all other income categories.[44]

The FBI collected data in 2019 on more than six thousand hate crime offenders.[45] Of these, 52.5 percent were White, 23.9 percent were Black, 6.6 percent were individuals of multiple races, and 14.6 percent were unknown.[46] According to NCVS data, 43 percent of offenders were over the age of thirty, 17 percent were between eighteen and twenty-nine, and 15 percent were ages seventeen and under. The youth percentage may be underreported because bias incidents and hate crimes involving young people may be labeled as bullying and not recorded.

Hate crimes are more often committed by groups of offenders than non-hate crimes. While 63 percent of hate crime offenders acted alone, according to NCVS data[47] a higher percentage of violent hate crimes (30 percent) involved multiple offenders than violent non-hate crimes (17 percent). Hate crimes are also more likely to be committed by a stranger, with only 44 percent of offenders known to their victims, compared to 55 percent for non-hate crimes.

In a 1993 study still widely used by law enforcement, sociologists Jack McDevitt and Jack Levin delineated four bias motivation categories of offenders most likely to commit hate crimes.[48] While these categories sometimes blur and overlap, they are useful to understanding offender behavior. In McDevitt and Levin's first category, two-thirds of hate crimes are committed by people they characterize as "thrill-seeking" offenders who are looking for psychological excitement or acceptance by their peers. These offenders are typically not associated with an organized hate group, and over 90 percent do not know their victims.[49]

Attacks often involve desecration and vandalism as well as violence against persons.[50] In April 2020, for example, four teenage girls were arrested for hate crimes after they allegedly harassed an Asian woman on a New York City bus, calling her an expletive, accusing her of causing coronavirus, and hitting her on the head, causing an injury requiring stitches for the wound.[51] In another instance, police in Madison, Wisconsin, launched a hate crime investigation into an incident in which an eighteen-year-old Black teenager was attacked in her car at a red light while a Black Lives Matter protest was taking place nearby. A White man sprayed lighter fluid into the car window and set her on fire, causing her to be taken to the emergency room of a local hospital and treated for burns.[52]

The researchers' second category, "defensive" motivation, accounts for about one-fourth of hate crimes. These hate crime offenders typically see themselves as protectors of a perceived tangible asset or intangible right that they believe their targets are trying to "replace" and take away from them. They direct their attacks at victims who reflect the perceived intrusion, such as attacks on Latinx Americans because of a perceived threat to jobs. The third category, "retaliatory" attacks, make up about 8 percent of hate crimes. These offenders typically hear about a crime committed by members of a religious or racial group and take revenge by committing a hate crime against random members of that group, such as the crimes committed against Muslims after the 9/11 attacks or the 2015 San Bernardino terrorist attack.

A fourth category, "mission" hate crimes, make up about 1 percent of hate crimes. These offenders typically harbor an animus against groups whom they see as a threat to American culture, economy, and purity of racial heritage, and consider it their "right" to plan and carry out "replacement" attacks, with a high degree of premeditation and lethality. This is the most deadly type of offender, and many high-profile hate crimes come under this category,[53] including the El Paso Walmart shooter.

In another high-profile "mission" example, James Fields Jr. pleaded guilty in March 2019 to twenty-nine hate crimes charges in connection to the murder of Heather Heyer, an anti-racism activist, during the Unite the Right Rally in Charlottesville, Virginia, in 2017.[54] Before the attack, Fields posted inflammatory material on social media, including open support for the Holocaust, and called for violence against people of color.

Hate groups are on the rise in the United States. The SPLC tracked a 30 percent increase over two years in the number of active hate groups in the United States from 784 in 2014 to 1,020 in 2018. Propelled by a rise in extremism, the groups include White supremacists, neo-Nazis, and neo-Confederates.[55]

HATE CRIMES AND HATE SPEECH

The recent increase in hate crimes can be attributed in part to a rise in public hate speech, which normalizes animus against groups of people and creates a permissive context in which offenders feel free to express their hatred through violent acts. The surge in hate speech coincided in recent years with derogatory comments about racial and religious groups made by former President Donald Trump in campaign rallies, public events, and social media posts. Before, during, and after his presidency, Trump has made verbal attacks against Mexicans, Muslims, Jews, Blacks, and Native Americans.

The former president called for a ban on all Muslims entering the United States, claiming that Muslims inherently have a "hatred" for Americans. He repeatedly and falsely claimed that in New Jersey thousands of Muslims celebrated the 9/11 attacks.[56] He demanded that U.S. District Judge Gonzalo Curiel, born in Indiana to Mexican immigrant parents, recuse himself from hearing a case involving Trump University because of a "conflict of interest" inherent in Judge Curiel's "Mexican heritage."[57] He retweeted anti-Semitic and anti-Muslim messages.[58] In a 2019 speech, Trump used anti-Semitic stereotypes to characterize Jews as driven by money, and attacked liberal Jews for "disloyalty" to Israel.[59] He referred to Massachusetts Senator Elizabeth Warren as "Pocahontas," based on Senator Warren's claim of Native American lineage.[60] During Black Lives Matter protests in the wake of George Floyd's death, Trump tweeted, "When the looting starts, the shooting starts," quoting a police chief during the Civil Rights era who advocated violence against African Americans.[61]

During the Trump administration, other high-level officials also used hate speech. In the run-up to the 2016 election, White House senior policy adviser Stephen Miller promoted White nationalist literature, pushed racist immigration stories showing a supposed link between immigrants and rising crime—a claim that has been disproven—and obsessed over the loss of Confederate symbols in leaked emails to the conservative website Breitbart News.[62] Health and Human Services Assistant Secretary Michael Caputo made racist and derogatory comments about Chinese people. On March 12, 2020, Caputo tweeted that "millions of Chinese suck the blood out of rabid bats as an appetizer and eat the ass out of anteaters."[63]

Other public officials also made public hateful statements during the Trump presidency. Congressman Steve King (R-IA) was stripped of his committee assignments in 2019 after he questioned why White supremacy was bad: "White nationalist, White supremacist, Western civilization—how did that language become offensive?"[64] In 2018, Congressman King said that he did not want Somali Muslims working in meatpacking plants in Iowa: "I don't want people doing my pork that won't eat it, let alone hope I go to hell for eating pork chops."[65] In June 2020, King lost his congressional primary, widely interpreted as a condemnation of his remarks.[66] In 2019, Eric Porterfield, a West Virginia Republican lawmaker, used a homophobic slur and later defended himself by saying that the LGBTQ community is "a modern-day version of the Ku Klux Klan," referring to LGBTQ people as a "terrorist group."[67]

Research indicates that there often is a causal relationship between hate speech and hate crimes. A 2018 study by law professors at the University of Alabama and Loyola University found that the current political environment is associated with a statistically significant surge in reported hate crimes across the United States, even when controlling for alternative explanations. FBI data show that following President Trump's election there was an anomalous spike in hate crimes concentrated in counties where Trump had won by large margins. It was the second-largest uptick in hate crimes in the twenty-five years for which data are available, second only to the spike after 9/11.[68] A study conducted by the *Washington Post*, based on data collected by the Anti-Defamation League, showed that counties that hosted a Trump campaign rally in 2016 saw hate crime rates more than triple compared to counties that did not host a rally.[69]

Following the 2016 election, there was an increase in the number of reported cases of bias-motivated bullying in schools. In a 2019 survey of nearly five thousand twelve- to seventeen-year-olds, 52.3 percent of students said they had been bullied at school in the past thirty days, compared to 38.6 percent in 2016 (a 35 percent increase).[70] In Tennessee, a group of middle-schoolers linked arms, imitating the President's proposed border wall as they refused to let non-White students pass.[71] In Utah, two kindergartners told a classmate that President Trump would send him back to Mexico.[72] An online survey by the SPLC that included over ten thousand K–12 educators found that more than 2,500 "described specific incidents of bigotry and harassment that can be directly traced to election rhetoric." In 476 cases, offenders used the phrase "build the wall." In 672, they mentioned deportation.[73]

The act of being exposed to hateful or violent speech normalizes hate toward certain groups and may create a permissive environment where some feel empowered to commit actions motivated by prejudice. A 2019 New York University study found that cities with a higher incidence of a certain kind of racist tweets reported more actual hate crimes related to race, ethnicity, and national origin.[74] The research team analyzed the location and linguistic features of 532 million tweets published between 2011 and 2016. They trained a machine-learning model to identify and analyze two types of tweets: those that directly espouse discriminatory views and those that describe or comment upon discriminatory remarks or acts. The team found a rough correlation of each type of discriminatory tweet to the number of actual hate crimes reported during that period.

There was a surge in hate crimes against Asian Americans in response to the coronavirus. In California, a sixteen-year-old Asian American boy was physically assaulted by his classmates, who accused him of spreading the coronavirus.[75] In Texas, a Burmese American man and his two children, ages two and six, were stabbed by a man who said he believed they were "Chinese and infecting people with the coronavirus."[76]

Protester holds a "Stop Asian Hate" sign, 2021. Photo by Viviana Rishe via Unsplash.

Reports of aggression and acts of violence against Asian Americans and Pacific Islanders, as well as discrimination by business establishments, workplace discrimination, and harassment have been on the rise in the United States. The FBI had warned of this potential surge in anti-Asian hate crimes following reports about the origin of the coronavirus in Wuhan, China.[77]

Researchers at the Network Contagion Research Institute found that the coronavirus pandemic coincided with a surge in anti-Chinese sentiments.

The spike in verbal and physical assaults on people of Asian descent in the United States occurred during the time when President Trump repeatedly used inflammatory language about China. Trump's use of the terms "China virus," "Wuhan virus," and "kung flu" reinforced xenophobia and intolerance against Asian people.[78] The former president violated the World Health Organization's directive to avoid naming illnesses after locations to minimize stigma and blame toward a specific region or ethnic group for the emergence of an illness.[79] Following the initial surge of attacks, the president did nothing to direct a governmental response to protect people of Asian descent. The Department of Justice and the Centers for Disease Control and Prevention had worked to stop bias incidents and hate crimes following the SARS outbreak and the 9/11 terrorist attacks, but the Trump administration did not act to deter or punish the public targeting of Asians during the coronavirus crisis.[80]

The emergence of racist and violent attacks toward people of Asian descent was reminiscent of the discrimination and harassment faced by American Muslims, Arabs, and South Asians in the United States after 9/11, and the scapegoating of Japanese Americans after Pearl Harbor. Blaming racial or religious groups for the emergence of a public threat leads to an influx of hate crimes and normalization of discrimination.

HATE CRIME LAWS

Hate crime laws cover certain crimes committed on the basis of race, color, religion, national origin, sexual orientation, gender, gender identity, or disability. Federal law also criminalizes the threat of force or the use of force to intimidate people from practicing their constitutional and federally protected rights.

There are six separate federal hate crime laws.[81] These laws were passed under the general authority of Title I of the Civil Rights Act of 1968, which permits federal prosecution of anyone who "willfully injures, intimidates or interferes with, or attempts to injure, intimidate or interfere with . . . any person because of his race, color, religion or national origin" or because of the victim's attempt to engage in one of the six types of federally protected activities, such as attending school, patronizing a public place or facility, applying for employment, obtaining housing, acting as a juror in a state court, or voting.[82]

Federal hate crime laws have been enacted in response to horrific bias-motivated crimes. The Matthew Shepard and James Byrd Jr. Hate Crimes Prevention Act is named after Matthew Shepard, who was tortured and murdered in 1998 in Wyoming for being gay, and James Byrd, an African American man who was violently murdered by White supremacists in 1998 in Texas.[83] The murders and subsequent trials brought national and international attention to the prevalence of hate crimes in the United States and the need to strengthen U.S. anti-hate-crime law at both federal and state levels, including the urgency of making sexual orientation and gender identity protected classes.

The *Matthew Shepard and James Byrd, Jr. Hate Crimes Prevention Act of 2009* is the first statute allowing federal criminal prosecution of hate crimes motivated by the victim's actual or perceived sexual orientation or gender identity. The Act makes it a federal crime to willfully cause bodily injury, or attempt to do so using a dangerous weapon, because of the victim's actual or perceived race, color, religion, or national origin.[84]

The *Hate Crime Statistics Act of 1990* authorized the FBI UCR program to collect and analyze data from federal and state voluntarily participating police agencies to access the nature and scope of hate crimes. It also defined the criminal conduct that constituted a hate crime as an act that manifests evidence of prejudice based on the victim's actual or perceived race, ethnicity, national origin, religion, sexual orientation, or disability.[85]

The *Criminal Interference with Right to Fair Housing Act* makes it a crime to use or threaten to use force to interfere with housing rights because of the victim's race, color, religion, sex, disability, familial status, or national origin.[86]

The *Damage to Religious Property, Church Arson Prevention Act* prohibits the intentional defacement, damage, or destruction of religious property because of the religious nature of the property, or because of the race, color, or ethnic characteristics of the people associated with the property. The statute also criminalizes the intentional obstruction by force or threat of force of any person in the enjoyment of that person's free exercise of religious beliefs.[87]

The *Violent Interference with Federally Protected Rights Act* makes it a crime to use or threaten to use force to willfully interfere with a person's participation in a federally protected activity because of race, color, religion, or national origin.

The *Conspiracy Against Rights Act* makes it unlawful for two or more persons to conspire to injure, threaten, or intimidate a person in any state, territory, or district in the free exercise or enjoyment of any right or privilege secured to the individual by the U.S. Constitution or the laws of the United States.[88]

Although federal laws classify actions as hate crimes and mandate data collection on the occurrence of hate crimes, there are gaps in federal reporting. There is a wide disparity, for example, between the number of hate crimes reported by the FBI versus those reported by the Department of Justice's Bureau of Justice Statistics. Even considering that only half of hate crime victims report the crime, this does not explain the vast discrepancy between the relatively small number of hate crimes that the FBI reports each year in its "Hate Crime Statistics" report and the 250,000 estimated by the Bureau of Justice Statistics.[89] The 1988 Uniform Federal Crime Reporting Act requires federal agencies to submit crime data to the FBI, but many agencies do not. ProPublica reported in June 2017 that more than 120 federal agencies are not submitting crime data to the FBI.[90] For example, the Defense Department's Inspector General concluded in 2014: "DoD is not reporting criminal incident data to the Federal Bureau of Investigation for inclusion in the annual Uniform Crime Reports to the President, the Congress, State governments, and officials of localities and institutions participating in the Uniform Crime Report program."[91]

The federal government needs to ensure that all federal law enforcement agencies and state and local entities report hate crime data. Federal hate crime data is flawed and incomplete, due in part to the Department of Justice's reliance on voluntary reporting from state and local law enforcement to fulfill its obligation to report national hate crime data.[92]

Most states and U.S. territories have hate crime statutes that are enforced by state and local law enforcement. But hate crime laws in states and territories vary widely across jurisdictions, resulting in unequal protection from similar crimes in different jurisdictions. The federal government and forty-seven states—all but Arkansas, South Carolina, and Wyoming—have enacted hate crime laws that enhance penalties for the underlying crime.[93] These laws differ in significant ways. All cover bias based on race, ethnicity, or religion, but many do not include gender, disability, sexual orientation, or gender identity.

There are three areas where hate crime laws vary among state jurisdictions: bias motivations, penalty enhancements, and data collection. Different jurisdictions define hate crimes with different bias motivations. Laws in some jurisdictions increase the sentence for crimes motivated by identified factors. Forty-seven states and Washington, DC, have statutes with varying penalties for bias-motivated crimes. Some jurisdictions require collecting data on hate crimes, and others do not. Data collection is important because data provides better transparency into crimes that are occurring and helps states allocate support and resources to communities in greatest need.

Many law enforcement agencies do not properly train officers to address hate crimes. Only twelve states have laws requiring that officers be trained to identify and investigate hate crimes. Numerous police departments have misconceptions about handling hate crimes. According to ProPublica, several agencies believe it is up to prosecutors, not police, to deem an incident a hate crime.[94]

Thirty states and Washington, DC, have hate crime laws and require data collection on hate crimes. Eighteen states and territories have hate crime laws but do not require data collection: Alabama, Alaska, Colorado, Delaware, Kansas, Mississippi, Missouri, Montana, New Hampshire, North Carolina, North Dakota, Ohio, Puerto Rico, South Dakota, Tennessee, Vermont, West Virginia, and Wisconsin.[95]

The wide disparities among state hate crime laws, and disparities over whether hate crime data is collected, cause unequal protection from similar violent crimes in different jurisdictions and preclude the collection and maintenance of accurate national data regarding these attacks. Knowing the nature and magnitude of the hate crime problem is fundamental for resource allocation and crime deterrence. More important, targeted communities are much more likely to report crime and cooperate in investigations if they believe law enforcement authorities are ready and able to respond to hate violence.[96] For this reason, all states should have hate crime statutes that cover gender, disability, sexual orientation, and gender identity in addition to race, national origin, ethnicity, and religion, and data collection laws to ensure that offenders are being held accountable for their crimes against the victims and their communities.

Policy Recommendations

- **Strengthen Enforcement of Hate Crime Laws.** Increase the capacity and funding of Department of Justice enforcement of federal hate crime statutes covering race, ethnicity, religion, gender, LGBTQ, and disability hate crimes; strengthen the mandate of federal law enforcement agencies to investigate and prosecute hate crimes; and enact state hate crime statutes to cover all targeted categories.

- **Increase Hate Crime Data Collection.** Centralize hate crime data from federal, state, and local law enforcement agencies in the Department of Justice; train state and local law enforcement agencies to collect and report comprehensive hate crime data to the FBI; and require every state to collect and report hate crime data.

- **Provide Federal Resources for Reporting and Deterring Hate Crimes.** Increase funding for programs to encourage victims to report hate crimes to local law enforcement; provide federal support for programs to strengthen law enforcement trust and relationship with communities of color and immigrant communities; provide federal funding for states to establish hotlines for reporting hate crimes, training on data collection and reporting, and coordination among law enforcement agencies; and provide funding to support nongovernmental citizen mobilization programs to publicize and organize community responses, and deter hate crimes.

Part V

Privacy

15

Privacy, Personal Data, and Surveillance

Alyssa LeMay heard music. The eight-year-old wondered if it was her sister singing the playful notes of "Tiptoe Through the Tulips" in their shared bedroom of her Mississippi home. It wasn't. When Alyssa entered, the music abruptly stopped. An unrecognized voice began to speak, using racial epithets and challenging Alyssa to break the television in her room. The bizarre event was even more disturbing, since the voice told her that he was her "best friend" or "Santa Claus."[1]

The LeMay family does not know the culprit of this gross invasion of their daughter's bedroom, but they know the means by which the invasion occurred: two Ring cameras, supported by Amazon, which the family had bought weeks earlier. When Alyssa's mother reported the breach to Amazon, the company chided her for not using dual-factor identification to protect the security of the account. However, they provided no further information about how long the camera's feed may have been compromised, or the identity of the culprit.[2] The December 2019 incident wasn't unique; the *Washington Post* identified three such incidents across the country around the same time, in which internal security cameras and smart speakers were hacked to harass or threaten the occupants of a home.[3]

These incursions symbolize the threat to privacy in America. Recent decades have brought dramatic technological change that has shifted conceptions of what privacy entails and how it can be protected. The severity of privacy violations and their often-disturbing details have created a new area of common ground in public opinion about rights.

A poll by the Pew Research Center in June 2019 found that 81 percent of Americans were concerned about how companies were using their personal data; 66 percent were concerned about how the government was using their data. Less than 10 percent said they understood what was being done with the data.[4] In another Pew poll in November 2019, four out of five Americans felt the risks outweighed the benefits of personal data collection by companies, and three out of five shared that sentiment for government collection.[5] The consensus was bipartisan, with 83 percent of Democrats and 82 percent of Republicans favoring stronger data privacy protections. Clearly, privacy and control of personal information is an issue that cuts across demographic groups and provides a unique opportunity for reclaiming rights that have been hijacked by technology.[6]

PRIVACY: THE LOST HORIZON

How did we get to this point? Privacy has always been a precarious right because it lacks clear protection in the U.S. Constitution. Historically, privacy rights in the United States have been focused on protecting individuals from government overreach, but recent trends point to new threats by private companies. Privacy defenders must fight a two-front war, as increasing incursions are made by both private industry and government law enforcement.

The Fourth Amendment to the Constitution bars law enforcement agencies from searching a person's property without judicial authorization. Judicial precedent has long established that the government must not violate a person's "reasonable expectation of privacy." The collection and sale of personal data in the private sector, however, is almost completely unregulated. What little national legislative protection exists mostly predates the digital era. In the absence of digital regulation, ambitious corporations have seized on technological advances to collect, use, and sell personal data in ways that would have been previously unimaginable.

Enforcement of privacy regulations is inconsistent and decentralized. The Federal Trade Commission (FTC) is the principal regulator of the collection, sale, and storage of personal data by companies; however, only 5 percent of FTC employees are engaged in the agency's mission of "Privacy and Identity Protection."[7] Only three states have passed comprehensive privacy laws of their own, with another nineteen currently considering similar bills in their state legislatures.[8] The variance of state legislation further complicates the ability to effectively regulate the personal data market.

An analysis of data privacy in America must start with an acknowledgment of the enormous popularity and economic importance of the companies and organizations that collect personal data. The five most valuable technology companies in the world—Apple, Microsoft, Alphabet, Amazon, and Facebook—all collect and monetize data as part of their core business model.[9] Yet, despite negative reports, social media usage remains constant in the United States.[10] Google and its parent company, Alphabet, continue to hold a 92.26 percent market share of internet searches.[11] Americans clearly value these services and have integrated them into their lives.

Those seeking to avoid a privacy intrusion like the LeMays's nightmare scenario face opposition from two powerful fronts. Technology companies such as Amazon, Facebook, and Alphabet have a strong incentive to protect their data gained from customer surveillance, valuable for improving business operations and resale to other parties. It is in their interest to limit government regulation and conceal the extent to which their security measures have been circumvented or defeated. Government law enforcement agencies, on the other hand, see an opportunity to reduce crime through constant, invasive surveillance, in collaboration with private companies.

Americans are increasingly succumbing to a voyeuristic impulse to spy on neighbors and strangers. A survey of more than fifty Ring customers by the *Washington Post* found that in addition to security protection, most enjoyed using their cameras to watch non-criminal behavior. Respondents described spying on domestic workers and nannies, often without their knowledge, with one commenting, "I know maybe I should tell them but [then] they won't be as candid."[12]

The lack of oversight over industry data collection has led regulated government agencies to outsource to, or collaborate with, private companies. The National Security Agency and other intelligence agencies now use close connections with technology companies to access information and surveil individuals, at a level and scale that would have been technologically impossible only a few years ago. Immigration and law enforcement agencies increasingly use social media and internet data mining to gather information about individuals, which is fed to complex algorithms for threat assessments.[13] The municipal government of Washington, DC, offers a "private security camera incentive program" with its Office of Victim Services and Justice Grants. The program gives rebates of up to $500 for families who install security

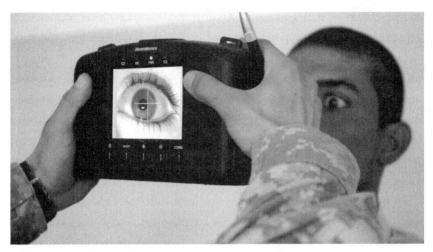

Biometric data collection. U.S. Army.

Facial recognition used on pedestrians on a New York street. Getty Images.

camera systems around their homes and give local police archival access to recordings.[14]

Personal data has emerged as a major determining feature of life in the twenty-first century. Credit scores determine people's ability to purchase a home or car. Social media algorithms create the connections that establish the growing hierarchy of social "influencers." In the post-pandemic economy, employment may be dictated by medical history, behavior in personal time off, and even genetic predispositions. As personal data has become our destiny, individuals have decreasing control over its collection and flow.

EMERGENCE OF THE PERSONAL DATA ECONOMY

The types of personal data collected by private companies fall into three categories:

Discrete data is obtained directly from consumers by companies with whom the customer has an ongoing relationship. Examples include phone number requests at a retail store counter or online fill-in-the-blank forms, as well as social media posts and other content directly and intentionally shared for publication. The definition of "ongoing relationship" is open to interpretation, but for the sake of clarity, it can be defined as direct contact between consumer and company within a year. This classification of data is the most straightforward. Consumers generally understand what data they are sharing, with whom, and for what purpose.

Behavioral data is gathered via acts that would traditionally be characterized as surveillance. The customer is not conscious of data transmission, even having previously acknowledged a data company's privacy policy. Examples include tracking cookies deployed by companies such as Facebook and Google, as well as recordings by smart speakers, security cameras, and cell phone location tracking data. Behavioral data is also increasingly collected in physical retail environments. Data analytics companies use facial recognition and other technologies to track purchases, movements, and even moods of shoppers within client stores.[15] Companies frequently engage in behavioral collection under concealed or misleading circumstances, despite the fact that the collection occurs when the customer and the company have an ongoing relationship.

Indefinite data is collected outside an ongoing relationship with the data subject. Examples include individuals' phone numbers and email addresses scraped from the web, or genome mapping from companies such as 23andMe retained for longer than one year. Also included in this category are data brokers that buy and sell information obtained from other sources.

Credit agencies were some of the first companies to collect and share indefinite data. Equifax dates to the nineteenth century and was joined by firms such as TransUnion and Experian in the twentieth century, when the credit data collection model saw significant growth. Over the years, indefinite data collection has been expanded by technological advances and changing business models. In a 2014 report on the data broker industry, the FTC outlined six primary functions of data brokerage companies that deal in individuals' information, beyond the original purpose of credit evaluation.[16]

These practices run counter to public opinion regarding "reasonable" data retention. Polling by Pew revealed that more than 50 percent of Americans believe it is not reasonable for most organizations to keep records of their personal activity for over one year. The only organizations excepted from that expectation were government agencies and credit card companies.[17] In practice, nearly every consumer-facing company now retains customer data for as long as possible.

COLLECTION, BUYING, AND SELLING OF BEHAVIORAL DATA

Metadata is defined by the National Information Standards Organization as "structured information that describes, explains, locates, or otherwise makes it easier to retrieve, use, or manage an information resource."[18] The collection and sale of metadata is largely regulation-free.

For example, investigative journalists have found it is surprisingly easy to purchase both the real-time and historic locations of consumer cell phones, information that is supposed to be available only to law enforcement agencies in criminal investigations.[19] In December 2019, the *New York Times*'s Privacy Project acquired metadata containing the locations of over 12 million phones from a private data brokerage company.[20] Using algorithms, it took the reporters only minutes to re-identify the supposedly anonymous data, and to specifically identify senior officials such as President Trump and members of his family through the cell phones of Secret Service agents. Telecom companies have pledged to tighten restrictions governing access to phone location data, but no regulatory enforcement compels compliance and the companies have not revealed the frequency or scale at which consumer location data is openly purchasable.[21]

One of the reasons that metadata has thus far eluded regulation is that the harm caused by its collection and dissemination is not always immediately clear. For example, when the computerized vacuum company iRobot began compiling the metadata records of its robots in customer homes, it seemed to be a harmless dataset that could enhance its business operations. However, iRobot was able to turn that information into a collection of blueprints of customers' homes. The company's CEO has acknowledged iRobot's intent to sell these diagrams to technology companies such as Google and Facebook without additional customer consent.[22] Metadata and behavioral data can provide companies with personal information that individual consumers cannot imagine or expect, and over which they have no control.

REDUCED DATA AUTONOMY

Janese Trimaldi thought she had put her past behind her. In July 2011, she was the victim of a domestic violence incident. She was arrested after her then-boyfriend asserted that she had grazed him with a knife. Trimaldi proved that the cut on her boyfriend was the result of an accidental scratch by fingernail, and charges against her were dropped. Months later, however, her mugshot appeared on a Florida-based mugshot aggregator, along with the dropped charges.[23]

The website is one of many that posts mugshots of arrested individuals, regardless of whether they are charged with or convicted of a crime. One such website, florida.arrests.org, posts the full legal name and mugshots of arrested individuals, sometimes within minutes of processing, and encourages users to label them with tags such as "Hotties," "Transgender," "Handicap," and "WTF."[24] Trimaldi had never been convicted of a crime, yet she still needed to pay a $30 fee to have her photographs removed from the website in question.

Shortly after her payment the images appeared on other sites, one of which demanded a $400 fee to remove them.

After the *New York Times* completed an investigative report that detailed the experiences of Trimaldi and other victims of being extorted by online mugshot aggregators, search engines such as Google worked to adjust their algorithm so that archived mugshots would be moved back in search results over time, and both MasterCard and PayPal refused to process payments to such sites.[25] Additionally, a number of newsrooms underwent a reevaluation of the use of mugshots in news coverage and by early 2020 decided to reduce usage to only truly newsworthy offenses.[26]

Trimaldi's story is representative of many online experiences. Data brokerage sites still sell or publish personal information, such as birthdays, email addresses, and physical addresses, while charging a premium for removal. The number of such sites and the unregulated nature of their business makes it expensive at best, or impossible at worst, for a person to control the personal information published about them. The unrestricted capability of data brokers to collect, aggregate, and transmit indefinite personal information makes independent consumer awareness and action nearly impossible.

There has been little attempt to map the data broker industry. One of the few exceptions is the establishment of a data broker registry by the state of Vermont. The 340 companies that have registered as of spring 2021 are a small sampling of a rapidly growing industry. In response to questions by the state registry, most companies indicated that there was no process in place to opt out of the collection, storage, and sale of their information; nor do they "permit a consumer to authorize a third party to perform the opt-out on the consumer's behalf."[27] Even when the opportunity to control a person's data is provided, the process is long and arduous. The Vermont registry compiles company opt-out policies that require phone calls, emails, or online forms to be filled out in order for a consumer to opt out. This puts an onus on the consumer to identify which companies have opt-out policies and then invest the time to contact them individually, with no guarantee their efforts will be successful.

The FTC has expressed concern about data brokers leaving "domestic violence victims, law enforcement officers, prosecutors or public officials" vulnerable to harassment, stalking, retaliation, or other harm.[28] A survey conducted by the National Network to End Domestic Violence (NNEDV) found that 13 percent of those surveyed had worked with a victim of "GPS tracking on a phone or other device." Ten percent reported first-hand experience with abusers "using online data to track or locate a victim."[29] A previous survey by NNEDV found that 36 percent of domestic violence victim service providers had encountered at least one incidence of offenders monitoring victims' activity by "gathering online data about the victim."[30]

DATA BREACHES

Data brokers and other organizations that collect and analyze personal data are often subject to data breaches. The cybersecurity analysis firm Risk Based Security identified nearly four thousand data breaches in 2020, resulting in the loss of more than 37 billion records. The most frequently breached sectors were health care, information, and finance.[31]

The digitization of personal data has made protection from data breaches increasingly challenging. Before the digital age, it would have been unthinkable for data thieves to move millions of paper pages without raising security concerns. Now such crimes can be completed within the blink of an eye. Verizon's 2020 Data Breach Investigations Report found that over 55 percent of breaches are conducted by organized crime.[32]

During one of the greatest recent data breaches, hackers stole the personal information of over 145 million Americans from Equifax in 2017. The records contained a combination of credit card numbers, driver's license numbers, social security numbers, dates of birth, phone numbers, and email addresses at a minimum. While the breach made headlines, it left consumers confused and disempowered. During Equifax's attempt to reach potential victims, official Equifax websites and social media profiles unknowingly directed victims to fake websites set up by hackers attempting to gather even more personal information.[33]

A 2018 report by the Government Accountability Office found that the Equifax data breach occurred because of poor cybersecurity practices.[34] Equifax utilized a server with out-of-date software, did not monitor its network-data inspection system, and stored the data in an unencrypted form.[35] The FTC settled a penalty proceeding with Equifax for $575 million, and the company's CEO at the time of the breach was permitted to resign while retaining bonuses worth more than $90 million.[36]

Although companies often enact simple solutions to close data breaches in the short-term, these are easily circumvented by future attackers. Josephine Wolff, a professor of cybersecurity policy at the Fletcher School at Tufts University, explains that companies rarely address large systemic risks. As a result, the opportunity to anticipate problems and develop new best practices to avoid data breaches is often missed.[37]

The first and only legislation designed to target data breaches is the Cybersecurity Information Sharing Act of 2015. The law encourages sharing of best practices in data management and cybersecurity,[38] and provides companies with legal protection when they establish cyber defenses and share cyber threat indicators with federal, state, and local governments.[39] The new law may incentivize better information-sharing and promulgation of best practices, but it also indemnifies companies from liability for negligent cyber defense of personal data.

Ultimately, the problem of data breaches and the resulting damage to the privacy of citizens will not be solved until the injury from these breaches becomes a liability for those directly involved in establishing and executing security practices. As it stands, when a company's data is stolen, it can still profit from the data it has retained, with the only loss being a slight reduction in the value of data due to duplication of data records by those who have stolen them. The consumer is faced with all the negative costs of losing control of their personal information.

THE DATA ECONOMY BUSINESS MODEL

The advent of large, scalable databases that collect personal and behavioral data has come under sharp criticism. In *The Age of Surveillance Capitalism*, Harvard Business School Professor Shoshana Zuboff compares companies and their privacy consent agreements to early conquistadors, who would read proclamations to indigenous populations in a language they did not understand prior to claiming their lands.[40] The CEO of leading video game publisher Epic Games described the current technological business environment as "businesses that profit from doing customers harm. . . . Facebook and Google have been leaders in this trend. They give you a service for free, and they make you pay for it in the form of currency that's dearer than money, the loss of privacy and loss of freedom."[41] Human rights experts argue that Facebook and Google's "surveillance-based business model forces people to make a Faustian bargain, whereby they are only able to enjoy their human rights online by submitting to a system predicated on human rights abuse."[42]

New state laws in California and Vermont have begun to address unaccountable monetization of personal data by enabling consumers to know what information is being collected about them, where it is being sold, and how they can opt out from that collection. However, both of these states narrowly define data brokers as companies who buy and sell an individual's personal data without a direct business relationship, a definition that misses the growth of the personal data marketplace beyond these data brokers. Consumer product companies of all kinds are increasingly adding personal data collection and sales to their business models; for example, Visa's sale of consumer data to banks was expected to grow by 20 percent in 2020.[43] These companies possess troves of consumer data that they have acquired at little or no cost and can reproduce for unlimited resale.

A right to privacy requires informed consent from an individual, including the content of the collected information and its future use. Data brokers act without any consumer awareness, and commercial companies who surreptitiously collect personal information for future profit are similarly taking advantage of consumer ignorance. Unlike traditional company activities focused on delivering the highest consumer satisfaction at the lowest price, monetizing data collection focuses on offering few services with the lowest consumer awareness possible. Thus, data companies have no business incentive, absent regulatory restrictions, to limit the collection of personal data or to invest in the protection of personal consumer data they have collected. As Zuboff concludes, "this new market form declares that serving the genuine needs of people is less lucrative, and therefore less important, than selling predictions of their behavior."[44]

GOVERNMENT SURVEILLANCE

Surveillance by government entities has long been a contentious issue in the United States. The Fourth Amendment and federal and state legislation provide some limits on law enforcement's ability to target individuals for electronic surveillance. Despite those protections, however, people in the United States have been subject to technological surveillance not only by government agencies, but also increasingly by their private contractors.

The Privacy Act of 1974 set the pre-technology standard for federal government collection, maintenance, and transmittal of personal data. It regulates "Personally Identifiable Information" (PII) within federal "agencies."[45] Today, technology has created new methods for private and public entities to observe and record personal activity and more legal ambiguity for law enforcement to circumvent civil liberties protections.

This has been especially true since the 9/11 terrorist attacks, in which public and political demands for security outweighed considerations of personal privacy and accelerated the practice of technological data collection.[46] As a result, internal checks on government surveillance are weak. For example, the Implementing Recommendations of the 9/11 Commission Act of 2007 resulted in the creation of an executive Privacy and Civil Liberties Oversight Board to provide oversight and advice for the "implementation of Executive Branch policies, procedures, regulations, and information-sharing practices relating to efforts to protect the nation from terrorism."[47] During the fourteen years of its existence, however, this small and obscure executive agency has had a quorum for only six years and has been fully staffed for only four. Its few actions and positions have been inconsequential and either ignored or disputed by the relevant federal agencies.

Three judicial decisions over the last half-century are central to the law of surveillance technology in the United States: *Katz v. the United States*, *Smith v. Maryland*, and *United States v. Graham*. These cases interpret in the context of changing technology the Fourth Amendment requirement that law enforcement obtain a search warrant to collect data through electronic surveillance.

- *Katz* was a 1967 case in which recordings by a physical device placed on a public phone were ruled to be inadmissible due to the lack of a search warrant and violation of the search and seizure protections of the Fourth Amendment.[48] This decision limits the use of a physical object to surveil a citizen and establishes the judicial standard of a "reasonable expectation of privacy."[49]

- *Smith* was a 1979 case in which law enforcement installed a "pen register" at a telephone company without a search warrant to log the phone numbers dialed by a suspect. The Supreme Court ruled that there was no "reasonable expectation of privacy" because the "petitioner voluntarily conveyed numerical information to the telephone company."[50]

- *Graham* was a 2016 case in which a U.S. District Court in Maryland held that electronic metadata (in this instance, historical location data) was not protected by the Fourth Amendment if it was collected and retained by a third party.[51] Thus, the court upheld the right of law enforcement to access metadata without a search warrant.

THIRD-PARTY CONTRACTORS

Intelligence and law enforcement agencies rely on private sector third-party contractors as a means of circumventing privacy law limiting government surveillance. "Third-party doctrine" established in cases such as *Smith* and *Graham* maintains that law enforcement agencies may access collected data about a person's activity from private third-party entities without a warrant.[52]

In 2004, Congress denied a funding request from the National Security Agency to implement a global artificial intelligence system called "Total Information Awareness" (TIA), citing a need to comply with the Foreign Intelligence Surveillance Act (FISA), which establishes a judicial warrant requirement for initiating domestic surveillance for intelligence purposes. An investigative report in 2006 by the *MIT Technology Review*, however, found that while TIA did not exist in name, the NSA had circumvented the congressional denial by executing a system of surveillance through partnerships with telecoms such as AT&T and other technology companies.[53]

One of the best-known facilitators of this practice is Palantir, a data-analysis company credited with helping the CIA identify the location of Osama Bin

Laden in 2011.[54] Palantir has recently expanded its operations to serve law enforcement; as a result, it bears an increasing resemblance to an intelligence agency that conducts international operations. Palantir software runs in many of the "fusion centers" furnished by the Department of Homeland Security and owned and operated by state and local law enforcement. These centers conduct data analysis and collection,[55] integrating data points from "suspicious activity reports, Automated License Plate Reader (ALPR) data, and unstructured data such as document repositories and emails."[56]

Local law enforcement agencies in municipalities across the country have begun using third-party software in crime prevention. Legal challenges have alleged that these algorithms can discriminate against protected groups.[57] In the absence of regulation, these programs and systems use variables that disproportionately identify members of racial, gender, religious, or other groups.

PERSONAL DATA-MINING, SOCIAL MEDIA, AND ARTIFICIAL INTELLIGENCE

Machine learning and algorithmic decision-making in the public sector represent a potential threat to the rule of law in a democracy. The U.S. legal system is built around standards that allow an understanding of the judgment process, whether through argumentation or written opinions. The lack of transparency of decisions made through artificial intelligence obscures this understanding, introducing opportunity for bias.

Facial recognition and biometric information databases are increasingly being compiled by law enforcement organizations, raising new concerns about the use of algorithmic searches on people who have not previously come into contact with law enforcement. The Georgetown Law Center Privacy Project notes, "We know very little about these systems," including their accuracy or "how any of these systems—local, state, or federal—affect racial and ethnic minorities." Twenty-one states and Washington, DC, now provide access to driver's license photos to the FBI and local law enforcement for algorithmic search.[58]

In 2017, Immigration and Customs Enforcement (ICE) undertook an "Extreme Vetting Initiative" to fund the internal creation of an artificial intelligence system capable of reviewing individuals' data scraped from the internet and provided by third-party contracts with data aggregators.[59] After public disclosure and outcry, the agency ultimately decided cost and privacy considerations made the project prohibitive. Instead, ICE outsourced the project to a private-sector third-party contractor to conduct similar behavioral vetting.[60] Meanwhile, Customs and Border Protection regularly reviews and mines the social media feeds and other internet activity of legal visitors within the country.[61]

Digital data brokering practices can exacerbate racial discrimination. A report by ProPublica in 2016 revealed that an algorithm developed in the private sector was being used by some state law enforcement agencies in making bail or sentencing recommendations. The algorithm substantially overestimated the recidivism risk of African American defendants.[62] These overestimates were based on police interactions, which are more common in communities of color, instead of criminal convictions, to predict the probability that a person would commit future crimes.

PRIVACY, PUBLIC HEALTH, AND SAFETY

The COVID pandemic brought attention to new tradeoffs between public health and privacy. The public has been generally supportive of measures to protect public health, but contact tracing and other provisions compromising individual privacy have been a point of skepticism. A 2020 *Washington Post*/University of Maryland Poll found that 82 percent of Americans were supportive of current public health restrictions or supportive of greater restriction, but only 41 percent of Americans would be willing to use a smart-phone-based contact tracing app. The least-trusted organizations for the handling of personal data were "tech companies like Apple and Google," followed by health insurance companies.[63] A similar Axios-Ipsos poll found that only half of Americans would participate in a "cell-phone-based contact tracing program." That number decreased significantly if the program was overseen by any organization other than "the CDC and public health officials."[64] Contact-tracing apps were available in nineteen states by the end of 2020, many using an app jointly designed by Google and Apple.[65] Adoption, however, was almost nonexistent, with most states at only 5 percent or less.[66]

Evidence indicates that public suspicions were warranted. North and South

Dakota were some of the first state governments to develop cell-phone-based contact tracing apps, contracting the work to app developer ProudCrowd free of charge. After completion, the app was vetted by state officials and Apple, and included a privacy policy that stated location data "will not be shared with anyone including government entities or third parties." An analysis by privacy company Jumbo, and follow-up reporting by the *Washington Post*, however, confirmed that some data from the app went directly to the location-marketing company Foursquare.[67] This failure highlights the dangers of rushing contact-tracing data products to market and the limits of privacy policies in the absence of regulation and penalties.

The civil rights of marginalized groups can come under the greatest threat from contact tracing. The disproportionate concentration of coronavirus cases among people of color and vulnerable populations could cause contact-tracing programs to result in increased surveillance of groups who have strong historical reasons to distrust government surveillance. Human rights experts express concern that "such tracking could open a dangerous new front in the surveillance and repression of marginalized groups."[68]

The potential privacy pitfalls of public health or public safety programs should not preclude their development or deployment but should result in a critical analysis by implementing policymakers. In the case of contact tracing apps, leading experts have raised questions about efficacy, privacy protections, and security, among other concerns.[69] These and additional concerns about the duration and conclusion of programs should be addressed prior to implementing any such initiatives.

WEAK REGULATORY ENVIRONMENT

A weak regulatory framework for data privacy has existed since the early 1970s, focused on government agencies and consumer reporting agencies. With the passage of time and the development of new technologies, however, the Fair Credit Reporting Act (FCRA) of 1970 and the Privacy Act of 1974 have become increasingly outdated. Following those early laws, Congress passed a patchwork of privacy protections for specific groups. The Children's Online Privacy Protection Act protects children under the age of thirteen. The Video Privacy Protection Act of 1988 protects "wrongful disclosure of video tape rentals" or similar audio-visual materials. The Health Insurance Portability and Accountability Act (HIPAA) of 1996 covers individually identifiable health information. The Gramm-Leach-Bliley Act of 1999 focuses on information directly tied to credit and financial institutions.[70]

Operating in this weak regulatory environment, private companies have capitalized on the narrow definitions of protected data with well-financed legal challenges. In the absence of broad, value-based legislation, privacy rights today are under serious threat.

Without comprehensive federal privacy legislation, states have been left to act. California has been one of the leading actors, most recently with the passage of the California Consumer Privacy Act.[71] Vermont has also enacted a data privacy law, the first state-level legislation to explicitly require the registration of data brokers and establish minimum security standards.[72] The California and Vermont laws could serve as models for other states. Currently, however, the limited jurisdiction of state attorneys general and the well-funded legal challenges by technology companies leave the efficacy of state legislation in question.

The few current federal protections are easily circumvented through loopholes, technological advances, and corporate secrecy. For example, Google has recently moved to gain access to health records, striking multiple deals for the sharing of medical records under a provision within HIPAA that allows the data to be shared if it is used "only to help the covered entity carry out its health-care functions."[73] In the financial sector, companies are developing nontraditional data aggregation methods to determine credit scores while eluding FCRA regulations.[74] Banks and financial technology companies such as Experian are currently lobbying to include more personal behavioral information into credit scores and decisions.[75]

Privacy Policies and Self-Regulation

There are no federal requirements for companies to post or explain their privacy policies. At the state level, the California Online Privacy Protection Act of 2003 created a requirement for online companies to post privacy policies on their home page.[76] Due to the high cost of companies' identifying California-based users, the legislation became a de facto requirement for almost all companies operating in the United States. Despite this legislation, however, a

2008 Carnegie Mellon study found that an effective reading of all the privacy policies that individuals are likely to encounter in a year would require thirty-one full workdays at a national opportunity cost of $781 billion.[77]

The California Consumer Privacy Act of 2018 (CCPA) provides some personal protection. CCPA requires companies to publish a description of a user's rights, categories of data the company has collected about consumers in the preceding twelve months, and categories of consumer data the company has sold or transmitted for a business purpose in the preceding twelve months. While the CCPA's protections are a step in the right direction, they do not prevent companies from obfuscating. The legislation requires websites to disclose "categories" of information collected, without specifically defining them. This creates the opportunity for companies to define categories in confusing and unclear ways. For instance, Google's privacy policy provides examples of the specific types of data the company collects. While some are straightforward, such as "terms you search for" and "videos you watch," others are less clear, such as "activity on third-party sites and apps that use our services."[78] Google's list of categories is not exhaustive, and the company often prefaces them with ambiguous statements, such as "the activity information we collect may include . . ."[79]

Obfuscation and ambiguity are critical factors in corporate efforts to circumvent regulation and consumer awareness. For example, Google's privacy policy states, "We never sell your *personal information* to anyone." The Electronic Frontier Foundation conducted an extensive evaluation of Google's treatment of personal data and found that statement incomplete at best and intentionally misleading at worst. Because no laws or regulations define "personal information" for private corporations, Google is free to provide its own definition. Google narrowly defines personal information as name, email address, and billing information. This allows it to obscure the fact that the company's Real Time Bidding (RTB) marketing platform sells a trove of other data, including granular location information, specific device identification numbers, and browsing history.[80]

Corporate legal departments frequently use privacy policies to preclude individuals from bringing lawsuits against companies for the mishandling or misuse of their information. This "private right to action" is partially reinstated by the CCPA, which gives individuals the right to bring a lawsuit against a company if their personal data was compromised as the result of a stolen data breach. If data was not stolen, however, but sold or shared with third parties, company privacy policies can still prevent individuals from filing lawsuits, even when data sharing is in direct contradiction of the practices outlined in the privacy policy.

As a result of these confusing policies, many Americans report that they have not felt "confident that [they] understood what would be done with [their] data" while interacting with companies in the prior month. Significant numbers report feeling impatient, discouraged, and confused while attempting to parse company privacy policies.[81]

Consent

No legislation defines informed consent for digital information disclosure, and thus there is no regulatory definition of consent in the nebulous world of digital data brokering. Organizations collecting data have benefited from a conception of legal consent that has not kept pace with digital technology. A 2019 survey of technology experts conducted by the Pew Research Center found that nearly half believed that use of technology will "mostly weaken core aspects of democracy in the next decade." This weakening process is a result of the power imbalance created by "citizens' lack of digital fluency."[82] The reality is even more bleak, as the rapid pace of data collection, artificial intelligence, and business needs preclude even the most sophisticated computer scientists from fully understanding the implications of sharing personal data. In such an environment, it is necessary to ask if informed consent of disclosure is even possible, and, if so, what determines it. In 2015, Pew Research found that 93 percent of Americans "believed it was important to have control of who can get information about you,"[83] one of a number of polls echoing this overwhelming public concern.[84]

The genetic testing company 23andMe has long marketed itself as focused on using customers' genetic data to provide personalized ancestry reports and health insights.[85] However, that business model is misleading. As customers paid to have their DNA analyzed, 23andMe was accumulating large amounts of genetic data to sell to research organizations and medical companies. While consumers tend to assume that their genetic information is protected by privacy protections, such as HIPAA, in practice, genetic testing companies

fall outside those regulations and frequently resell consumer genetic information.[86] In 2013, 23andMe board member Patrick Chung revealed that "[t]he
long game here is not to make money selling kits, although the kits are essential to get the base level data. Once you have the data, [23andMe] does actually
become the Google of personalized health care."[87]

Data collection corporations often present themselves as altruistic entities
while harvesting users' most sensitive data and putting it to work to create
financial value for themselves with little return for the individuals. In the
words of Shoshana Zuboff, we have been "harnessed to a market process in
which individuals are definitively cast as the means to others' market ends."[88]
This "bait and switch" strategy is increasingly prevalent within companies
that have business models based on the collection and sale of personal data,
collecting it for one stated purpose, while exploiting it for their own private
use. Can consumers consent to data sharing if they do not understand the way
in which their data will be used?

To collect customer data, companies rely on consumers' desire for expe-
dience. Most companies have created a system that requires customers to
"opt out" of data collection, aggregation, and sharing, an option codified by
Gramm-Leach-Bliley. However, such a process creates an extra burden for
users; research indicates that a shift to an "opt-in" system is the only way to
establish stronger customer consent and promote customer comprehension
of its privacy implications.[89] Another tactic companies use is overstating personal data collection requirements for the operation of consumer purchases.
Companies imply that they must have access to data in order to complete business operations, when in fact the data is extraneous or intended for purposes
beyond the service of the customer.

The Age of Surveillance Capitalism provides a chilling example of what the
combination of these practices can look like. In July 2017, iRobot released a
new version of its autonomous vacuum cleaner, Roomba, that can create a
digital map of the living space where it is used. In a conversation with Reuters,
iRobot's CEO Colin Angle revealed that the robots would create a new revenue
stream from selling the floorplans of customers' homes to Google, Amazon,
or Apple. Transmission of such data to the cloud required customers to "opt
in" to a data collection and sharing agreement. If they declined to do so, key

features such as the ability to start or pause a cleaning remotely are disabled. As Zuboff puts it, the proposal to the consumer for data collection purposes is "[b]end the knee or we will degrade your purchase."[90]

A critical concept for preventing companies from engaging in this deceptive behavior is "data minimization." The European Union's General Data Protection Regulation (GDPR) defines "data minimization" as allowing the collection of data that is "adequate, relevant and limited to what is necessary in relation to the purposes for which they are processed." The FTC endorsed this principle in a 2013 report, "The Internet of Things: Privacy and Security in a Connected World." In practice, however, data minimization is difficult to regulate or enforce. Even the GDPR allows companies to collect data "sufficient to properly fulfil [the company's] stated purpose,"[91] introducing ambiguity by allowing companies to decide what that purpose may be.

In this complex and convoluted privacy landscape, effective regulation must not only ensure consumers are aware of what they are giving up at the moment of collection, but that they also have rights to change their mind about data disclosure and use at a future date.

Private-sector data collection is principally regulated by the FTC. The FTC now consists of three bureaus—the Bureau of Competition, the Bureau of Consumer Protection, and the Bureau of Economic Affairs—with a total of approximately 1,100 full-time employees. For its Privacy and Identity Protection activities, the FTC had just fifty-two full-time employees in 2019, with a budget of only $9.9 million.[92] These miniscule resources hamper its ability to regulate the personal data market and surveillance by private actors.

In 2019, the FTC levied a $5 billion civil penalty against Facebook, describing the fine as a "paradigm shift."[93] Previously, the largest penalty paid by a technology company was $22.5 million by Google.[94] While the penalty is indeed one of the largest ever imposed by a federal agency on a private company, the judge in the case stated that the complaints against Facebook "call into question the adequacy of laws governing how technology companies that collect and monetize Americans' personal information must treat that information."[95] The fine was levied through a consent agreement that Facebook had previously signed with the FTC in 2011. Consent agreements have been the primary enforcement mechanism used by the government to penalize companies for violating the privacy agreements with customers they them-selves crafted; they require no admission of guilt or negligence, and they are mandated to expire in twenty years or less.

NEW REGULATORY MODELS

The European Union has begun to respond to the challenges of private entities that collect consumers' information. The EU's most sweeping regulation is the 2018 General Data Protection Regulation (GDPR), which allows for fines up to 4 percent of a company's worldwide revenue.[96] After several years of lack-luster enforcement, fines jumped significantly in 2020, with €272.5 million in total fines, including €50 million for Google in France—a 39 percent jump over the previous year and a half since the law went into effect.[97] Fines varied significantly by country, however, with nearly all of the fines from just five countries—Germany, Italy, France, the United Kingdom, and Spain.[98]

Multilateral organizations have been created to address the movement of personal data internationally, but with limited effect. The EU-U.S. Privacy Shield is a recognized set of guidelines for both the U.S. Chamber of Com-merce and the European Commission, ratified by the United States and the EU. Corporate participation with the organization, however, is voluntary and not a prerequisite to conducting international data transfers.[99] In July 2020, a European court struck down the shield because of the inadequacy of privacy protections in the United States, requiring U.S. companies to enter into sepa-rate security contracts to transfer money from Europe.[100]

Principles of transparency, personal agency, and accountability are the foundations upon which the right to privacy can be restored. Regulatory endorsement of these three values would be a key first step toward establish-ing a legal framework in which companies are accountable to the government and the government is accountable to its citizens. A broad consensus among the overwhelming majority of Americans who would like more to be done to protect their privacy can form a bipartisan basis for implementing regulations to protect personal information.

Policy Recommendations

- **Establish National Privacy Policies and Standards.** Require all government and private sector organizations and entities to state in clear and understandable terms what personal data they collect, how it is used, when and how it is disseminated, how long it will be retained, and what rights individuals have to change or opt out of collection or sharing, following their initial conscious consent.

- **Protect the Agency of Personal Data Subjects.** Enact federal legislation to require the subject's unconditional "conscious consent and opt-in" to any personal data that companies collect; prohibit indefinite personal data collection by companies with no relationship to targeted personal data subjects; establish a central data registry and a single process by which individuals can de-list information; and limit the collection and sale of specific forms of data, such as personal health and financial information.

- **Require Personal Data Security and Accountability.** Mandate strict standards for maintaining data security and provide remedies to data subjects for breaches of data security.

- **Create a Federal Privacy and Data Commission.** Establish the Federal Privacy and Data Commission, based on the regulatory model of the Securities Exchange Commission, with a sufficient budget and broad authority to promulgate and enforce privacy standards for personal data collection by government and private sector organizations and entities.

TOWARD EQUAL LIBERTY

Let's return to where we started. Most nations are rooted in the ancient belief that blood ties are what bind their people together. The United States is based on a different belief. As a nation of unparalleled racial, ethnic, religious, cultural, and political diversity, there is only one way for the United States to hold its people together—by reinforcing the rights that define their national and personal identities.

What are these rights? They include the right to vote; freedoms of speech, press, and religion; equal protection; equal opportunity; due process of law; rights of privacy; the right to fair resolution of disputes by an independent judiciary; and enforcement of rights by all levels of government. The government has a responsibility to protect these rights and institutions, and citizens have a responsibility to respect the rights of others and participate in the democratic process.

Rights fall into two categories, liberty and equality. The nation's founders believed that liberty and equality were mutually reinforcing. The first sentence of the Declaration of Independence proclaims that all people "are created equal, that they are endowed by their Creator with certain unalienable rights, that among these are life, liberty and the pursuit of happiness." Many people were excluded from the founding vision. Liberty left out enslaved people and offered nothing to the poor; equality excluded women and most non-White people.

Over the centuries liberty and equality have come into conflict over the role of government. Liberty addresses the legacy of tyranny and seeks to limit government. Equality addresses the legacy of slavery and the unequal starting points that people have in life, and seeks the help of government to address inequality. Liberty regards government as the enemy. Equality sees government as an ally.

Liberty protected American individualism during the building of the nation, but it promoted inequality. Equality promised that everyone would be given equal access to the fruits of liberty, but it expanded government.

In the Emancipation Proclamation, Abraham Lincoln sought to end the conflict by articulating a vision of equal liberty based on the nation's founding principle that all people are created equal. After Lincoln, hard-won expansions of rights were achieved—briefly during the post–Civil War Reconstruction period, more permanently in the movement for women's suffrage, for a time during the New Deal, and haltingly through the twentieth-century Civil Rights Movements. These victories were made possible by enlisting government in the promotion and enforcement of equal rights.

In response to these victories, political forces with an exclusionary vision hijacked the principles of equal liberty. This backlash produced the brutal Jim Crow era and the growth of vast inequality. Racial, gender, and religious discrimination, extremism, and violence were stimulated. Economic exploitation flourished in the anti-government environment.

Today democratic institutions again are under attack. Voting restrictions have been imposed to suppress voting by people of color and youth who support equal liberty. Press freedom, judicial independence, and law enforcement have come under extreme partisan pressure. Public discourse has been manipulated and degraded. Patterns of authoritarian governance have emerged, characterized by disregard of factual evidence and the rule of law. The assault on equal liberty has been magnified by technological changes in which powerful actors are now seemingly beyond the reach of any accountability to citizens and the government.

The chapters of this book demonstrate that Americans today across the political spectrum are well aware that their rights have been hijacked and are being denied. Eight out of ten Americans believe that rights are not secure. There is disagreement about the targets and causes of the attacks, but broad consensus that the system of rights in the United States is endangered.

Why are so many political leaders ignoring these views? Why are politicians leading the attack on equal liberty? The answer lies in a toxic disinformation landscape that has decimated public trust in virtually all institutions, and the reality that an exclusionary political movement with authoritarian leadership is sowing division and spreading lies to undermine democracy in the United States. Politicians are working against equal liberty by seeking to expand specific rights, like religious freedom or gun rights, at the expense of other rights, like nondiscrimination or public safety, that must be enforced if democracy is to survive.

The hijacking of rights is taking place at a time of accelerating political, economic, and cultural disruption. This has produced the conflicting results that are documented in this book. On the one hand, disruptive change has stimulated civic activism by new political movements working to protect rights. On the other hand, disruptive change has generated populist anger at elites and fear of "the other." Fear and anger have been manipulated by politicians seeking to aggrandize their power by provoking attacks on the rights of others.

Today's unprecedented COVID public health catastrophe has intensified this crisis of rights. "Social distancing" and "sheltering in place" directives have sharply limited freedom of movement. The pandemic's strain on health care, stress on the economy, widespread unemployment, disproportionate impact on people of color and the poor, coupled with acceleration of climate change and natural disasters, as well as structural changes in labor markets resulting from increased automation—have all called into question the basic rights of life, liberty, and the pursuit of happiness.

Americans care deeply about these rights and are searching for ways to reclaim them. Can the catastrophic events serve as a wake-up call for action? Can a public response to the crisis be channeled toward civic activism and political leadership that demands the renewal of rights for everyone? Can a rights-based democracy hold its own against authoritarian models that seek to destroy liberty or equality or both?

Preliminary answers to these questions can be found in the results of our national polls taken during the pandemic. The polls were conducted in July 2020 and May 2021 by the National Opinion Research Center at the University of Chicago using a nationwide sample of two thousand respondents representing all demographic groups and political perspectives in all the states. The results are both remarkable and counterintuitive.[1]

At a time when political trends seem to be driving Americans apart, there is evidence that the events of the past two years have brought them closer together. The COVID pandemic, economic hardship, racial reckoning, partisan division, and the attack on the U.S. Capitol all have stimulated political and social turmoil and a movement to undermine democracy. But these events have also been a cause for reflection for most people about what it means to be an American today, and the values that can hold the country together in a time of great disruption. In each area surveyed in this book, Americans not only regard rights as their core values; they have an expansive view of rights that includes economic as well and political and civil rights, and they endorse policy recommendations for reclaiming rights for everyone.

In the July 2020 poll, 71 percent reported that "Americans have more in common than many people think." By May 2021, that number had risen to 88 percent. In July 2020, 84 percent reported that "events in recent months have made me think differently about the role and responsibility of government to protect the rights of all Americans." By May 2021, 95 percent believed

Bipartisan majorities have an expansive view of rights, believing the following to be "essential" rights

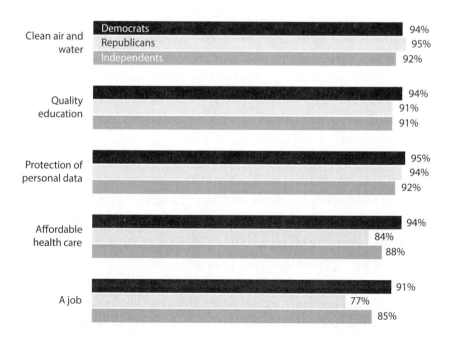

Percent of respondents who believe "Americans have more in common with each other than many people think"

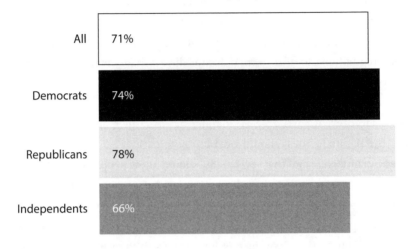

All	71%
Democrats	74%
Republicans	78%
Independents	66%

that "it is the responsibility of government to protect the lives, livelihoods and rights of all Americans."

The pandemic and the economic and racial crises have forced Americans to reflect on their responsibility to others. The pandemic has caused a bipartisan majority "to feel more positively toward Americans of different races from my own," including "African Americans, Native Americans, Asian Americans, and Latinx Americans." In July 2020, 85 percent reported that "recent events have made me think differently about the responsibility Americans have to our fellow citizens." By May 2021, 96 percent believed that "Americans have a responsibility to respect the rights of others." The willingness of majorities of the public to wear masks for public health protection was symbolic of the ways in which Americans began to think differently about their fellow citizens. Even when mask-wearing required sacrificing some of one's own rights to protect the rights of others, a majority continued to support public health restrictions.

The events of recent years have changed attitudes toward civil rights and the government's responsibility for protecting them. The May 2021 poll indicated that large bipartisan majorities now favor the policy recommendations we make in our chapter on voting rights that would strengthen the electoral process, encourage voting, and reduce voting restrictions, in sharp contrast to the campaign in Republican-led state legislatures to enact new voting restrictions and turn the management of elections over to partisan control. Our poll found that more than 80 percent (including two-thirds of Republicans) believe that "the U.S. Justice Department should review new state or local voting regulations to ensure they do not discriminate against voters based on race"; that "early voting should be equally available in every state"; and that "independent state commissions should determine the map of legislative districts to prevent partisan gerrymandering." A large majority also believes that "the [United States] should establish automatic voter registration of all American citizens"; and that "every state should allow people to vote by mail."

Police reform is another area where attitudes changed during the pandemic, with the spotlight on racial injustice after the police murder of George Floyd. Reforming police practices to protect citizen rights and promote public safety, in line with our policy recommendations, was favored by a bipartisan majority in the May 2021 poll. A majority agreed that "police should be accountable

Percent respondents who agree that the U.S. Justice Department should review new state or local voting regulations to ensure they do not discriminate against voters based on race

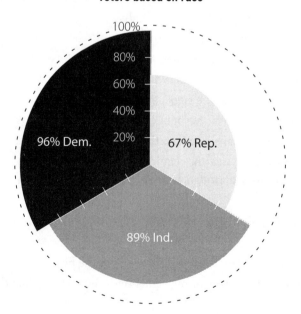

Participants voice perspectives on policing in the U.S.

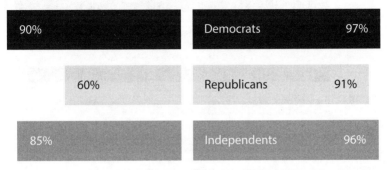

Believe Americans should have right to sue police officers for violations of civil rights	Believe police should be held accountable for violent or unlawful behavior	
90%	Democrats	97%
60%	Republicans	91%
85%	Independents	96%

for violent or unlawful behavior"; that "complaints about police misconduct should be submitted to an independent review board"; that "police departments should implement transparent guidelines on when and how to use force"; and that "Americans should have a right to sue police officers for violations of their civil rights."

The glaringly disparate impact of the pandemic and the economic crisis on people of color has moved large bipartisan majorities to support policy recommendations to strengthen civil rights protections against discrimination. Americans now favor reforms "to prevent hate crimes and punish people who commit them"; "to protect marginalized populations and communities from toxic and hazardous materials and other forms of environmental damage"; and "to strengthen the protection of people with disabilities against employment and workplace discrimination." A majority of Americans now agree that "Black people and some other racial minorities are often the targets of racism in law enforcement" and that "structural racism makes it difficult for racial minorities to get ahead."

Similar majorities (although fewer Republicans) believe that Americans should have a right of equal opportunity and access to "basic necessities of life," as described in our chapter on "Freedom from Want." The pandemic and the economic crisis stimulated support for government action to "protect the lives, livelihoods and rights of all Americans," including "universal access to health care," "more government support for public education," "more

Participants agree the pandemic has demonstrated the need for more government support of the following:

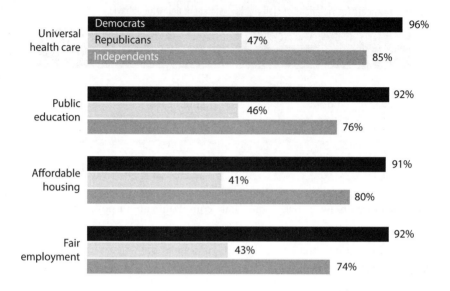

Universal health care — Democrats 96%, Republicans 47%, Independents 85%

Public education — 92%, 46%, 76%

Affordable housing — 91%, 41%, 80%

Fair employment — 92%, 43%, 74%

government support for fair employment," and "more government support for affordable housing."

Finally, consistent with our analysis and recommendations on data protection and disinformation, overwhelming bipartisan majorities of Americans agree that "social media companies should be required to protect the privacy of personal information"; that "there should be a law preventing social media companies from collecting and using personal data without the explicit consent of the data subjects"; that "disinformation is a threat to our democracy"; and that "social media companies should be required to prevent the spread of disinformation."

What are we to make of these strong expressions of public support for overcoming polarization and reinforcing rights? The polls show that Americans are searching for support from each other and from the government at a time of massive disruption, hoping to live their lives with dignity. They may disagree about how to achieve this but agree that the search is essential. They may disagree about the specific promises of liberty and equality but agree that these core values need to be reclaimed to hold Americans together. After decades of competition between liberty and equality, the polls show that Americans today want them to be reconciled.

Consistent with our policy recommendations, Americans want economic liberty to be regulated in order to reduce economic inequality. Majorities believe that "before America can be united we need to give equal opportunity to the 'haves' and the 'have nots'"; that "Americans should be guaranteed the opportunity to earn a living wage"; that "Americans should have a guaranteed paid sick time"; and that "the federal government should provide childcare support so that parents don't have to quit their jobs during a pandemic."

Beyond economic liberty, they want religious liberty to make room for the enforcement of nondiscrimination against women and LGBTQ people.

Americans want gun rights to be balanced with the government's responsibility to protect public safety by regulating the ownership and use of guns. A big majority agrees that the Second Amendment "should not keep government from regulating gun safety, ownership or use." They want the police to be accountable for violations of civil rights while at the same time protecting the public from crime, calling for "police departments to implement transparent guidelines overseen by the U.S. Justice Department on when and how to use force."

A majority wants the right of free speech not to block the regulation of campaign finance. They disagree with the Supreme Court's 2010 ruling that "political contributions and spending should not be regulated because they are a form of free speech," but they are divided on the question of whether "regulating social media platforms will infringe on free speech rights."

Above all, the polls show that large bipartisan majorities of Americans want more equality. A stunning 91 percent, including 86 percent of Republicans, agreed in the May 2021 poll that "the [United States] will not reach its full potential until all citizens—regardless of gender, race, religion, ethnicity, sexual orientation, disability, or economic status—are treated equally with respect." In addition to strengthening the laws against discrimination, Americans want to reduce economic inequality. They agree that "wealthy individuals, big corporations, and political action committees have too much influence in American politics." A large bipartisan majority would support a federal government plan requiring "investment in African American, Native

Participants who believe there should be increased legal protection against the following

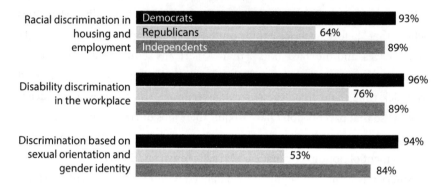

American and Latinx American communities that have been historically denied economic opportunity and equality as a result of federal policy."

Based on these national polling results supporting many of the policy recommendations in this book, a majority of Americans are seeking to reclaim the values of liberty and equality. Are the polls a harbinger of a new period of transformation like the one brought about by the Civil Rights Movement? Is it realistic to believe that with effective political leadership a diverse majority can overcome a divisive minority that has long been bent on blocking progress toward the full promise of liberty and equality for all Americans?

Time will tell. The polarization that characterizes American political life today is stimulated by destructive leaders like Donald Trump, their enablers in Congress, and their intransigent base of followers. This minority cannot win elections through the democratic process, so it is trying to impose its will on the majority by hijacking voting rights through anti-democratic tactics such as voter suppression, gerrymandering, and partisan control of election machinery. Meanwhile, the majority is seeking to reclaim rights by providing the basic necessities of life and reinforcing equal liberty for everyone. Polarized day-to-day politics belie an underlying consensus about the values described in this book that hold Americans together. The huge gap between public opinion and public policy is a result of the failure of government institutions, especially Congress, to reinforce the values of the majority.

This failure can be corrected through effective organizing and institutional reform. The battle for voting rights is at the heart of the struggle for equal liberty, and the new Civil Rights Movement must focus all its energy on winning it. The history of the earlier Civil Rights Movement shows the way. During the decade before the Voting Rights Act of 1965, despite continued massive resistance by many political leaders to civil rights progress, three out of four Americans had come to favor the abolition of poll taxes.[2] In 1963, as the resistance intensified before the historic congressional debate over voting rights, 86 percent of Americans registered approval of "the new law to give Negroes an equal right to vote," and 76 percent favored sending federal officials into states with a history of voting discrimination to make sure that all citizens had the opportunity to register and vote.[3] This overwhelming public support for voting rights was the result of years of intensive organizing and struggle by the Civil Rights Movement.

The recalcitrant minority that opposed federal voting rights enforcement in the 1960s was roughly the same proportion of the electorate as today's obdurate opposition. In both cases the minority is disproportionately represented by congressional leaders who are out of step with the majority—die-hard Democratic segregationists in the 1960s, and die-hard opponents of equal liberty today. In today's struggle for rights, there is no substitute for a modern civil rights movement that can work to build public opinion, demand effective leadership, create a political majority, and overcome resistance in order to reclaim the promise of rights for everyone. John Lewis pointed the way during the 1965 March to Selma that symbolized the struggle for equal liberty: "Freedom is not a state; it is an act. It is not some enchanted garden perched high on a distant plateau where we can finally sit down and rest. Freedom is the continuous action we all must take, and each generation must do its part to create an even more fair, more just society."[4]

ACKNOWLEDGMENTS

Holding Together is the product of a major two-year study of the condition of rights in the United States and the attitudes of Americans toward their rights and responsibilities conducted at the Harvard Kennedy School's Carr Center for Human Rights Policy. The study, "Reimagining Rights and Responsibilities in the United States," was directed by John Shattuck, Carr Center Senior Fellow, former U.S. Assistant Secretary of State for Democracy, Human Rights and Labor, and the lead author of *Holding Together*. Important contributions to the study and the book were made by national public opinion polls administered in July 2020 and May 2021 by the National Opinion Research Center at the University of Chicago. The polling questions were informed by three town hall meetings organized for the Carr Center by John Della Volpe of the Harvard Kennedy School's Institute of Politics in March and April 2020 in Phoenix, Arizona; Detroit, Michigan; and Atlanta, Georgia.

Research for the study was overseen by a faculty committee chaired by Carr Center Faculty Director Mathias Risse with major participation by Executive Director Sushma Raman, both of whom are co-authors of *Holding Together*. Michael Blanding contributed excellent editorial and drafting assistance. Ellen Hume gave helpful support and advice. The outstanding team of researchers included Kathleen Addison, Amita Arudpragasam, Sam Barrak, Diego Garcia Blum, Kadija Diallo, Anne Dietterich, Daniel A. Estupinan, Philip Hamilton, Aimee Hwang, Christie Lawrence, Malcolm Rogge, Ben Rutledge, Rahaf Safi, Katie Stenclik, Cathy Sun, Toby Voght, Colin Wall, and Katherine Williams. Special thanks goes to Kadija Diallo, Daniel Estupinan, Katie Stenclik, and Katherine Williams for their extended commitment to the project. The project benefited from the public affairs and media expertise of Jim Smith, Alexandra Gilliard, Ralph Ranalli, and Moira Notarstefano. Alexandra Geller provided superb online and imagery guidance. Steady logistical assistance was supplied by Laryssa Da Silveira and Sarah Peck.

Distinguished rights scholars and experts generously gave their guidance and advice. We are especially grateful to Martha Minow for her insightful and inspiring foreword, and for her thoughtful comments on early drafts of several chapters. We thank Tim McCarthy for his excellent chapter on LGBTQ rights. We also acknowledge the extensive contributions of Gloria Ayee, Archon Fung, Alan Jenkins, and Kathryn Sikkink. Helpful comments on specific topics were provided by Danielle Allen, Jacqueline Bhabha, Eric Blumenson, John Bowers, William Clark, Martha Davis, Nancy Gertner, Nancy Gibbs, Patricia Graham, Alex Keyssar, Tim McCarthy, Michael Meltsner, John Ruggie, Ani B. Satz, Jessica Shattuck, Michael Stein, Jonathan Zittrain, Shoshana Zuboff, and Ethan Zuckerman. Experts and advocates in civil rights, civil liberties, and international human rights contributed comments in more than two dozen seminars, outreach sessions, and consultations. They included Lecia Brooks, Denise Bell, Rob Berchinski, Sofia Costas, Jamil Dakwar, Nicholas Espiritu, Richard Fabian, Catherine Flowers, Deb Flower, Linda Susan Dakin-Grimm, Wade Henderson, Margaret Huang, Nicole Austin-Hillery, Peggy Koenig, Tyler Lewis, Michael Lieberman, Catherine Bettinger-Lopez, Elisa Massimino, Roger-Mark De Souza, Chirag Mehta, Wade McMullen, Alberto Mora, Irene Monroe, Mark Munger, Alison Leal-Parker, Sarah Paoletti, Sarah Repucci, Russell Reed, Carol Rose, Jonathan Ryan, Bill Schulz, Minor Sinclair, Robert Silverman, Alexandra Schmitt, JoAnn Kamuf Ward, LaShawn Warren, and Corrine Yu.

Generous financial support was provided by Vin Ryan and the Schooner Foundation, with the assistance of Julia Pettengill; by Peggy Koenig; and by an additional major donor who wishes to remain anonymous.

NOTES

Introduction: The Struggle for Rights
Research contributed by Christie Lawrence and drafting by Gloria Ayee.

1. "Americans' Attitudes Toward Civil Rights, Voting, Role of Government Find More Common Ground Since Pandemic," National Opinion Research Center at the University of Chicago and Carr Center for Human Rights Policy at the Harvard Kennedy School, July 20, 2021, https://carrcenter.hks.harvard.edu/reimagining-rights-responsibilities-2021-poll.

2. "National Research Finds Bipartisan Support for Expansive View of Rights," National Opinion Research Center at the University of Chicago and Carr Center for Human Rights Policy at the Harvard Kennedy School, September 15, 2020, https://carrcenter.hks.harvard.edu/reimagining-rights-responsibilities-united-states.

3. Eric Foner, *The Second Founding: How the Civil War and Reconstruction Remade the Constitution* (New York: W.W. Norton & Company, 2019).

4. Frank Edwards, Hedwig Lee, and Michael Esposito, "Risk of Being Killed by Police Use of Force in the United States by Age, Race–Ethnicity, and Sex," *Proceedings of the National Academy of Sciences* 116, no. 34 (August 2019): 16793–16798. There is a debate about whether "White" should be capitalized when used in relation to "Black" or other racial designations when these are capitalized. See Kwame Anthony Appiah, "The Case for Capitalizing the *B* in Black," *The Atlantic*, June 18, 2020. Recognizing that both "White" and "Black" as racial designations include a similarly wide diversity of people, we have chosen to capitalize both terms.

5. Larry Buchanan, Quoctrung Bui, and Jugal K. Patel, "Black Lives Matter May Be the Largest Movement in U.S. History," *New York Times*, July 3, 2020.

Part I: The Democratic Process

1. Voting Rights Battleground
Research and drafting contributed by Aimee Hwang.

1. Sam Levine, "Trump Says Republicans Would 'Never' Be Elected Again If It Was Easier to Vote," *The Guardian*, March 30, 2020.

2. Grace Panetta, Olivia Reaney, and Talia Lakritz, "The 19th Amendment Passed 100 Years Ago Today. The Evolution of American Voting Rights in 244 Years Shows How Far We've Come—and How Far We Still Have to Go," Business Insider, August 18, 2020.

3. Carol Anderson, *One Person, No Vote: How Voter Suppression Is Destroying Our Democracy* (New York: Bloomsbury Publishing, 2018).

4. "Historical Reported Voting Rates," U.S. Census Bureau, October 7, 2019, www.census.gov/library/visualizations/time-series/demo/voting-historical-time-series.html.

5. William H. Frey, "Census Shows Pervasive Decline in 2016 Minority Vote Turnout," Brookings Institution, May 18, 2017, www.brookings.edu/blog/the-avenue/2017/05/18/census-shows-pervasive-decline-in-2016-minority-voter-turnout.

6. U.S. Census Bureau, "Historical Reported Voting Rates."

7. Frey, "Census Shows Pervasive Decline."

8. Rashawn Ray and Mark Whitlock, "Setting the Record Straight on Black Voter Turnout," Brookings Institution, September 12, 2019, www.brookings.edu/blog/how-we-rise/2019/09/12 /setting-the-record-straight-on-black-voter-turnout.

9. Shelby County v. Holder, 570 U.S. 529 (2013).

10. "Grandfather clauses" provided that only those citizens who had the right to vote before 1870 or their descendants would be exempt from the literacy, property, or tax requirements for voting. See Anderson, *One Person, No Vote.*

11. Steven Levitsky and Daniel Ziblatt, *How Democracies Die* (New York: Crown, 2018), 92.

12. History, "Voting Rights Act of 1965," November 9, 2009, www.history.com/topics/black -history/voting-rights-act; "Section 4 of the Voting Rights Act," U.S. Department of Justice, May 5, 2020, www.justice.gov/crt/section-4-voting-rights-act.

13. Panetta, Reaney, and Lakritz, "The 19th Amendment Passed 100 Years Ago Today."

14. Anabelle Timsit, "2020's Record Voter Turnout in the U.S. Is Still Lower Than Many Other Countries," Quartz, November 9, 2020; see also Drew DeSilver, "U.S. Trails Most Developed Countries in Voter Turnout," Pew Research Center, November 3, 2020, www.pewresearch.org /fact-tank/2018/05/21/u-s-voter-turnout-trails-most-developed-countries.

15. William H. Frey, "How Young Americans Are Set to Change the U.S. Forever," BBC, July 17, 2017.

16. Jonathan Vespa, Lauren Medina, and David M. Armstrong, "Demographic Turning Points for the United States: Population Projections for 2020 to 2060," Current Population Reports, P25-1144, U.S. Census Bureau, February 2020, www.census.gov/content/dam/Census/library /publications/2020/demo/p25-1144.pdf.

17. Monica Duffy Toft, "White Right? How Demographics Is Changing U.S. Politics," The Conversation, January 7, 2019, https://theconversation.com/white-right-how-demographics-is -changing-us-politics-107872.

18. Toft, "White Right?"

19. Jamelle Bouie, "The Democrats' Demographic Dreams," *American Prospect*, June 14, 2012.

20. J. Baxter Oliphant, "6 Facts About Democrats in 2019," Pew Research Center, June 26, 2019, www.pewresearch.org/fact-tank/2019/06/26/facts-about-democrats.

21. Brennan Center for Justice, "New Voting Restrictions in America," November 19, 2019, www.brennancenter.org/our-work/research-reports/new-voting-restrictions-america.

22. "2016 Presidential Election Results," *New York Times*, August 9, 2017.

23. Brennan Center for Justice, "New Voting Restrictions in America."

24. For example, a 2017 North Dakota law requiring voters to show a form of identification that includes a residential address made it difficult for many Native Americans living on reservations to vote, since many did not have residential street addresses. The law was partially altered after being challenged in federal court; see Brennan Center for Justice, "New Voting Restrictions in America."

25. Zachary Roth, "Lawsuit: 'Exact Match' System Negatively Impacts Georgia's Minority Voters," NBC News, September 14, 2016.

26. Turnout dropped by a higher rate than in the United States as a whole. See "Historical

Reported Voting Rates: Table A-5a. Reported Voting for Total and Citizen Voting-Age Population by State: Presidential Elections 1972 to 2016," U.S. Census Bureau, October 7, 2019, www .census.gov/data/tables/time-series/demo/voting-and-registration/voting-historical-time -series.html.

27. Philip Bump, "17,000 Wisconsinites in Two Counties Likely Didn't Vote in 2016 Because of the State's Voter ID Law," *Washington Post*, September 26, 2017.

28. Shelby County v. Holder.

29. Brennan Center for Justice, "The Effects of *Shelby County v. Holder*," August 6, 2018, www .brennancenter.org/our-work/policy-solutions/effects-shelby-county-v-holder.

30. Kevin Morris, "Voter Purge Rates Remain High, Analysis Finds," Brennan Center for Justice, August 21, 2019, www.brennancenter.org/our-work/analysis-opinion/voter-purge-rates -remain-high-analysis-finds.

31. Andy Sullivan, "Southern U.S. States Have Closed 1,200 Polling Places in Recent Years: Rights Group," Reuters, September 10, 2019.

32. Aaron Blake, "Trump and Kobach Say Illegal Votes May Have Given Clinton the Popular Vote. The Math Disagrees," *Washington Post*, July 19, 2017.

33. Ryan Struyk and Lauren Peale, "Fact-Checking Trump's Repeated Unsubstantiated Claim of Widespread Voter Fraud," ABC News, May 11, 2017.

34. Tal Kopan and Ariane de Vogue, "New Lawsuits Cite Trump Comments, Tweets to Challenge Voting Panel," CNN Politics, July 11, 2017.

35. Lorraine C. Minnite, "The Politics of Voter Fraud," Project Vote, March 5, 2007, www .projectvote.org/wp-content/uploads/2007/03/Politics_of_Voter_Fraud_Final.pdf.

36. Christal Hayes, "This Is Why Republicans Are Claiming Voter Fraud in Florida and Arizona," *USA Today*, November 9, 2018.

37. German Lopez, "The Florida Voter Fraud Allegations, Explained," Vox, November 12, 2018.

38. Hayes, "This Is Why."

39. Jessica Boehm, "Despite Rampant Claims, There Is No Evidence of Voter Fraud in Arizona," *Arizona Republic*, November 12, 2018; Lauren Gambino, "Kyrsten Sinema Wins Arizona Senate Race in Breakthrough for Democrats," *The Guardian*, November 12, 2018.

40. Miles Parks, "Skeptics Urge Kentucky Governor to Show Proof of Voter Fraud Claims," MPR News, November 10, 2019, www.mprnews.org/story/2019/11/10/npr-skeptics-urge -kentucky-governor-to-show-proof-of-voter-fraud-claims.

41. Campbell Robertson, "In Kentucky, a Governor Who Picked Fights Loses a Big One," *New York Times*, November 15, 2019.

42. The Heritage Foundation, "A Sampling of Recent Election Fraud Cases from Across the United States," May 2021, www.heritage.org/voterfraud.

43. Douglas Keith, Myrna Pérez, and Christopher Famighetti, "Noncitizen Voting: The Missing Millions," Brennan Center for Justice, May 5, 2017, www.brennancenter.org/our-work /research-reports/noncitizen-voting-missing-millions.

44. Michael Tackett and Michael Wines, "Trump Disbands Commission on Voter Fraud," *New York Times*, January 3, 2018; Christopher Ingraham, "Trump's Voter Commission Is Now Facing at Least 7 Federal Lawsuits," *Washington Post*, July 18, 2017.

45. "What's remarkable about the documents," said Matthew Dunlop, a Democratic former

member of the commission, "is what's not in there, and what's not in there is any substantiated evidence of voter misconduct at any scale. In fact, one of the troubling things about the documents that we saw was that before we were even really meeting, commission staff were working on a framework of a report. And several sections of the report talk about voter fraud, and those sections are completely blank. They didn't insert any information whatsoever. So that's why we've been saying that, even though the idea was to investigate voter fraud, it is pretty clear that the purpose of the commission was to actually affirm and validate the president's claims whether or not we had any evidence of any such voter misconduct"; see Matthew Dunlap, "Member of Disbanded Trump Voter Fraud Commission Speaks Out," interview by Don Gonyea, NPR, August 4, 2018; "PACEI Docs Page," Maine Secretary of State, n.d., http://paceidocs.sosonline .org.

46. David Cottrell, Michael C. Herron, and Sean J. Westwood, "An Exploration of Donald Trump's Allegations of Massive Voter Fraud in the 2016 General Election," *Electoral Studies* 51 (February 2018): 124. https://doi.org/10.1016/j.electstud.2017.09.002.

47. Cottrell, Herron, and Westwood, "An Exploration," 138.

48. Anderson, *One Person, No Vote*, 29.

49. Heather Cox Richardson, "'Voter Fraud' Is a Myth That Helps Republicans Win, Even When Their Policies Aren't Popular," *Boston Globe*, October 23, 2018; Thomas B. Edsall, "'Ballot Security' Effects Calculated," *Washington Post*, October 25, 1986.

50. Elise Viebeck, Amy Gardner, and Michael Scherer, "Trump, GOP Challenge Efforts to Make Voting Easier Amid Coronavirus Pandemic," *Washington Post*, April 4, 2020.

51. Hope Yen, "AP FACT CHECK: Trump Misleads on Mail Ballots, Virus Vaccine," AP News, August 8, 2020.

52. National Conference of State Legislatures, "Voter Identification Requirements | Voter ID Laws," August 25, 2020, www.ncsl.org/research/elections-and-campaigns/voter-id.aspx.

53. Brennan Center for Justice, "New Voting Restrictions in America."

54. Tennessee Secretary of State, "What ID Is Required When Voting?" https://sos.tn.gov /products/elections/what-id-required-when-voting.

55. Diana Kasdan, "State Restrictions on Voter Registration Drives," Brennan Center for Justice, November 30, 2012, www.brennancenter.org/publication/state-restrictions-voter-regi stration-drives.

56. Reid Wilson, "Republicans Target Voter Registration Drives with New State Laws," The Hill, April 28, 2019.

57. Jonathan Mattise and Elaina Sauber, "Federal Judge Blocks Tennessee Voter Registration Law, Citing Harm to 'Constitutional Rights,'" *Tennessean*, September 12, 2019.

58. Wilson, "Republicans Target Voter Registration Drives."

59. Mattise and Sauber, "Federal Judge Blocks Tennessee Voter Registration Law."

60. Lizette Alvarez, "Judge to Block Changes in Florida Voter Registration," *New York Times*, August 29, 2012.

61. Florida Congress, Senate, *Election Administration*, SB 90, 2021 sess., introduced in Senate February 3, 2021, https://flsenate.gov/Session/Bill/2021/90.

62. Garrett Epps, "What Does the Constitution Actually Say About Voting Rights?" *The Atlantic*, August 19, 2013.

63. Eugene Volokh, "Why Has the Supreme Court Held That Felons Lack the Constitutional Right to Vote?" *Washington Post*, April 29, 2015.

83. Nick Corasanti and Reid J. Epstein, "What Georgia's Voting Law Really Does," *New York Times*, April 2, 2021.

84. Ethan DeWitt, "What You Need to Know About New Hampshire's New Voter Residency Law," *Concord Monitor*, July 16, 2018, www.concordmonitor.com/Capital-Beat-Five-questions -about-the-internet-sales-tax-bill-18814866.

85. Michael Wines, "The Student Vote Is Surging. So Are Efforts to Suppress It," *New York Times*, October 24, 2019.

86. Kerry Sheridan, "Early Voting on Campus Boosts Youth, Minority Turnout, but Battle Brews over Parking," WUSF, August 15, 2019, https://wusfnews.wusf.usf.edu/politics/2019-08 -15/early-voting-on-campus-boosts-youth-minority-turnout-but-battle-brews-over-parking.

87. Nancy Thomas et al., "Democracy Counts: A Report on U.S. College and University Student Voting," Institute for Democracy and Higher Education, Tufts University, 2017, https://idhe .tufts.edu/sites/default/files/NSLVE%20Report%202012-2016-092117%5B3%5D.pdf.

88. Christopher Ingraham, "What Is Gerrymandering and Why Is It Problematic?" *Washington Post*, June 24, 2019.

89. Ballotpedia, "Historical Partisan Composition of State Legislatures: Election Breakdowns: 2012 Elections," https://ballotpedia.org/Historical_partisan_composition_of_state_legislatures #2012_Elections; "Election Statistics: 1920 to Present," History, Art, & Archives, U.S. House of Representatives, https://history.house.gov/Institution/Election-Statistics/Election-Statistics.

90. Ingraham, "What Is Gerrymandering?"

91. Wilfred Codrington, "The Electoral College's Racist Origins," *The Atlantic*, November 17, 2019.

92. Jens Manuel Krogstad, Luis Noe-Bustamente, and Antonio Flores, "Historic Highs in 2018 Voter Turnout Extended Across Racial and Ethnic Groups," Pew Research Center, May 1, 2019, www.pewresearch.org/fact-tank/2019/05/01/historic-highs-in-2018-voter-turnout-extended -across-racial-and-ethnic-groups.

93. Drew DeSilver, "Turnout Soared in 2020 as Nearly Two-Thirds of Eligible U.S. Voters Cast Ballots for President," Pew Research Center, January 28, 2021, www.pewresearch.org/fact-tank /2021/01/28/turnout-soared-in-2020-as-nearly-two-thirds-of-eligible-u-s-voters-cast-ballots -for-president.

94. U.S. Congress, House, *For the People Act of 2019*, HR 1, 116th Cong., 1st sess., introduced in House January 3, 2019, www.congress.gov/bill/116th-congress/house-bill/1/text; U.S. Congress, House, *For the People Act of 2021*, HR 1, 117th Cong., 1st sess., introduced in House January 4, 2021, www.congress.gov/bill/117th-congress/house-bill/1/text.

95. Brennan Center for Justice, "Automatic Voter Registration," www.brennancenter.org /issues/ensure-every-american-can-vote/voting-reform/automatic-voter-registration.

96. "History of AVR & Implementation Dates," Brennan Center for Justice, December 22, 2020, www.brennancenter.org/analysis/history-avr-implementation-dates; "Automatic Voter Registration," National Conference of State Legislatures, February 8, 2021, www.ncsl.org /research/elections-and-campaigns/automatic-voter-registration.aspx; "Automatic Voter Registration," Ballotpedia, https://ballotpedia.org/Automatic_voter_registration.

97. Nicholas Casey, "Ohio Was Set to Purge 235,000 Voters. It Was Wrong About 20 Percent," *New York Times*, October 14, 2019.

98. Morgan McLeod, "Expanding the Vote: Two Decades of Felony Disenfranchisement Laws," Sentencing Project, October 17, 2018, www.sentencingproject.org/publications/expanding-vote

64. Emily Bazelon, "Will Florida's Ex-Felons Finally Regain the Right to Vote?" *New Yo Times*, September 26, 2018.

65. Nicholas Nehamas, "More Than a Million Convicted Felons in Florida Won Their Voti Rights Back. Now What?" *Miami Herald*, November 8, 2018.

66. Patricia Mazzei, "Florida Law Restricting Felon Voting Is Unconstitutional, Judge Rule *New York Times*, May 24, 2020.

67. Nina Totenberg, "Supreme Court Deals Major Blow to Felons' Right to Vote in Florid; NPR, July 17, 2020; Gary Fineout, "Federal Appeals Court Considers Whether to Uphold Flori Felon Voting Law," Politico, August 18, 2020.

68. Jason Noble, "Iowa Supreme Court Upholds Ban on Felons Voting," *Des Moines Registe June 30, 2016.

69. Office of the Governor of Iowa, "Gov. Reynolds Signs Executive Order to Restore Votin Rights of Felons Who Have Completed Their Sentence," August 5, 2020, https://governor.iow .gov/press-release/gov-reynolds-signs-executive-order-to-restore-voting-rights-of-felons-wh -have.

70. South Dakota Secretary of State, "Elections & Voting," https://sdsos.gov/elections-votin /voting/register-to-vote/felony-convictions.aspx.

71. National Conference of State Legislatures, "Felon Voting Rights," April 12, 2021, wwv .ncsl.org/research/elections-and-campaigns/felon-voting-rights.aspx.

72. Myrna Pérez, "Voter Purges," Brennan Center for Justice, September 30, 2008, www .brennancenter.org/our-work/research-reports/voter-purges.

73. U.S. Department of Justice, "About the National Voter Registration Act," May 21, 2019, www.justice.gov/crt/about-national-voter-registration-act.

74. Kevin Morris, Myrna Pérez, Jonathan Brater, and Christopher Deluzio, "Purges: A Grow- ing Threat to the Right to Vote," Brennan Center for Justice, July 20, 2018, www.brennancenter .org/our-work/research-reports/purges-growing-threat-right-vote.

75. Christopher Ingraham, "This Anti-Voter-Fraud Program Gets It Wrong over 99 Percent of the Time. The GOP Wants to Take It Nationwide," *Washington Post*, July 20, 2017.

76. Peggy Lowe, "Kansas Voter Tracking System Championed by Former SOS Kris Kobach Is 'Dead,'" KCUR, December 10, 2019, www.kcur.org/politics-elections-and-government/2019-12 -10/kansas-voter-tracking-system-championed-by-former-sos-kris-kobach-is-dead.

77. Trevor Brown, "In Latest Purge, Nearly 90,000 Inactive Voters Removed from Rolls," *Oklahoma Watch*, October 28, 2019, https://oklahomawatch.org/2019/04/22/nearly-90000 -inactive-oklahomans-removed-from-voter-rolls.

78. Morris, "Voter Purge Rates Remain High."

79. Ben Nadler, "Voting Rights Become a Flashpoint in Georgia Governor's Race," AP News, October 9, 2018.

80. Ted Enamorado, "Georgia's 'Exact Match' Law Could Potentially Harm Many Eligible Voters," *Washington Post*, October 20, 2018.

81. Brennan Center for Justice, "New Voting Restrictions in America"; Jackie Bor- chardt, "Ohio House Passes Bills to Change Absentee Ballot Rules, Eliminate Six Days of Early Voting," Cleveland, January 12, 2019, www.cleveland.com/open/index.ssf/2014/02 /ohio_house_passes_bills_to_cha.html.

82. The Leadership Conference Education Fund, "The Great Poll Closure," November 2016, http://civilrightsdocs.info/pdf/reports/2016/poll-closure-report-web.pdf.

-two-decades-felony-disenfranchisement-reforms; for the state of disenfranchisement laws as of May 2021, see "Disenfranchisement Laws," Brennan Center for Justice, www.brennancenter.org /issues/ensure-every-american-can-vote/voting-rights-restoration/disenfranchisement-laws.

99. National Conference of State Legislatures, "Online Voter Registration," April 6, 2021, www.ncsl.org/research/elections-and-campaigns/electronic-or-online-voter-registration.aspx.

100. National Conference of State Legislatures, "State Laws Governing Early Voting," October 22, 2020, www.ncsl.org/research/elections-and-campaigns/early-voting-in-state-elections .aspx; Rebecca Klar, "Virginia Governor Signs Legislation Dropping Voting Restrictions," The Hill, April 13, 2020; "States That Expanded Voting Since the 2012 Election," Brennan Center for Justice, May 9, 2016, www.brennancenter.org/sites/default/files/legal-work /Expansive_Appendix_Post-2012.pdf; "Voting Laws Roundup 2013," Brennan Center for Justice, December 19, 2013, www.brennancenter.org/analysis/election-2013-voting-laws-roundup #expansive.

101. National Conference of State Legislatures, "Voting Outside the Polling Place: Absentee, All-Mail and Other Voting at Home Options," September 24, 2020, www.ncsl.org/research /elections-and-campaigns/absentee-and-early-voting.aspx.

102. National Conference of State Legislatures, "Voting Outside the Polling Place."

103. National Conference of State Legislatures, "Same Day Voter Registration," May 7, 2021, www.ncsl.org/research/elections-and-campaigns/same-day-registration.aspx.

104. National Conference of State Legislatures, "Preregistration for Young Voters," February 12, 2019, www.ncsl.org/research/elections-and-campaigns/preregistration-for-young-voters .aspx.

105. FairVote, "Details About Ranked Choice Voting," www.fairvote.org/rcv.

2. The Corrupting Influence of Money in Politics
Research and drafting contributed by Katherine Williams.

1. Richard Cowan, "'Stay Out of Politics,' Republican Leader McConnell Tells U.S. CEOs, Warns of 'Consequences,'" Reuters, April 5, 2021.

2. Office of Senator Mitch McConnell, "McConnell: Corporations Shouldn't Fall for Absurd Disinformation on Voting Laws," April 5, 2021, https://www.mcconnell.senate.gov/public/index .cfm/pressreleases?ID=54AB06DF-4E02-4991-BC94-6D980FE85925.

3. Jon Skolnik, "I'm Not Talking About Political Contribution": McConnell Adds Important Caveat to Corporate Threat," Salon, April 6, 2021.

4. James Walker, "Mitch McConnell Reminded of Citizens United Backing After Warning to CEOs," Newsweek, April 6, 2021.

5. Shane Goldmacher, "Dozen Megadonors Gave $3.4 Billion, One in Every 13 Dollars, Since 2009," New York Times, April 20, 2021.

6. OpenSecrets.org and Followthemoney.org, "Unprecedented Donations Poured into 2020 State and Federal Races," November 19, 2020.

7. OpenSecrets, "Total Cost of Election (1998–2020)," https://www.opensecrets.org/elections -overview/cost-of-election.

8. Max Galka, "How 2016 Compares to 56 Years of Presidential Campaign Spending," Huff-Post, November 7, 2016.

9. OpenSecrets, "Did Money Win?"

10. Maggie Koerth, "How Money Affects Elections," FiveThirtyEight, September 10, 2018.

11. Peter Overby, "Beyond Quid Pro Quo: What Counts as Political Corruption," NPR, May 4, 2015.

12. Lawrence Lessig, *Republic, Lost: How Money Corrupts Congress—and a Plan to Stop It* (New York: Twelve, 2011).

13. Lawrence Lessig and Ilya Shapiro, "How Much Does Money Matter for Political Campaigns?" CNBC, November 6, 2020.

14. Gabriela Schulte, "Poll: 57 Percent of Voters Say U.S. Political System Works Only for Insiders with Money & Power," The Hill, March 31, 2020.

15. Megan Brenan, "Americans Most Satisfied with Nation's Military, Security," Gallup, January 28, 2019.

16. Soo Rin Kim, "Just 12 Megadonors Accounted for 7.5 Percent of Political Giving over Past Decade, Says Report," ABC News, April 20, 2021.

17. Sheely Edwards, "Bipartisan Poll Finds Voters Want Stronger Enforcement of Campaign Finance Laws, Increased Transparency in Elections," Campaign Legal Center, November 18, 2019.

18. Unless indicated otherwise, information on historic regulations of campaign finance may be found in OpenSecrets, "Money-in-Politics Timeline," October 15, 2019; more information on the role of court cases in shaping money in politics may be found in OpenSecrets, "Grant to Trump: How Court Cases Influenced Campaign Finance," October 6, 2017.

19. Federal Election Commission, "1971 FECA and Amendment Legislative History."

20. *Buckley v. Valeo*, 424 U.S. 1 (1976).

21. OpenSecrets, "Money-in-Politics Timeline."

22. See FEC v. Mass. Cit. for Life, 479 U.S. 238 (1986); Austin v. Mich. Chamber of Comm., 494 U.S. 652 (1990). While the Supreme Court decisions only reference—but do not define—the term *general treasury funds*, these funds typically refer to all of the assets of an organization that are not allocated to specific efforts or costs, but rather to funding the "necessary, usual, ordinary running and incidental expenses of an organization"; see, for example, Washington State Legislature, WAC 390-05-510, October 25, 2019.

23. "Big Labor Grows New Muscle," *Wall Street Journal*, August 1, 2017.

24. "Campaign Finance—Special Report," *Washington Post*, 1998.

25. "Clinton Ok'd Using Lincoln Bedroom for Contributors," CNN, February 25, 1997; see also Margarate Ebrahim, "Fat Cat Hotel," *Center for Public Integrity Newsletter* 2, no. 5 (August 1996).

26. "Lincoln Bedroom Guests Gave DNC at Least $5.2 Million," CNN, February 24, 1997.

27. Roberto Suro, "Campaign Fund Probe Winds Down," *Washington Post*, May 30, 1999.

28. "Buying Time 2000: Political Parties and Soft Money," Brennan Center for Justice, October 30, 2000; see also OpenSecrets, "Soft Money Backgrounder," www.opensecrets.org/parties /softsource.php.

29. Internal Revenue Service, Internal Revenue Code, I.IRC 527, Political Organizations; U.S. Code, Title 26, section 304.

30. Drew DeSilver and Patrick van Kessel, "As More Money Flows into Campaigns, Americans Worry About Its Influence," Pew Research Center, December 7, 2015.

31. U.S. Congress, House, *Bipartisan Campaign Reform Act of 2002*, HR 2356, 107th Congress, passed in March 20, 2002.

32. For a study of the impacts of this provision, see Kristina Gale et al., "Elections: Effects of the Stand by Your Ad Provision on Attitudes About Candidates and Campaigns," *Presidential Studies Quarterly* 35, no. 4 (2005): 771–783.

33. "Campaign Finance Law Quick Reference for Reporters," Federal Election Commission, December 2, 2019.

34. McConnell v. Federal Election Commission, 540 U.S. 93 (2003).

35. "Total Outside Spending by Election Cycle, Excluding Party Committees," OpenSecrets, https://www.opensecrets.org/outsidespending/cycle_tots.php.

36. Bob Biersack, "Outside Spending: The Big Picture (So Far)," OpenSecrets, June 11, 2012. Biersack notes that the role of electioneering communications could have dropped in elections after 2010 due to the ruling in *FEC v. SpeechNow.org v. FEC*, which eliminated restrictions on the types of funds that can be used for independent expenditures. He contends that this change could have reduced the appeal of the electioneering communications due to their "less direct" targeting of voters and the legal uncertainty on disclosure requirements for donors.

37. Open Secrets, "Money-in-Politics Timeline."

38. Arizona Free Enterprise Club's Freedom Club PAC et al., v. Bennett, et al; McComish et al., v. Bennett, et al., 564 U.S. 721 (2011); and United States, Court of Appeals for the D.C. Circuit, EMILY'S List v. FEC, Docket no. 08-5422, December 18, 2009.

39. EMILY'S List v. FEC.

40. Tim Lau, "Citizens United Explained," Brennan Center for Justice, December 12, 2019.

41. Citizens United v. Federal Election Commission, 558 U.S. 310 (2010) (Stevens, J., dissenting).

42. SpeechNow.Org v. FEC, No. 08-5223 (D.C. Cir. 2010).

43. Building on its decision in *Citizens United*, the court ruled in *Speechnow.org v. FEC* that outside groups could accept unlimited contributions from both individual donors and corporations, provided that these groups do not directly contribute to candidates; see Robert Maguire, "Dark Money, Super Pac Spending Surges Ahead of 2018 Midterms," OpenSecrets, August 25, 2017.

44. "Outside Spending by Group," OpenSecrets.

45. McCutcheon v. Federal Election Commission, 572 U.S. 185 (2014).

46. Federal Election Commission, "McCutcheon et al., v. FEC: Case Summary," December 5, 2019.

47. Ian Vandewalker, "The 2018 Small Donor Boom Was Drowned Out by Big Donors, Thanks to Citizens United," Brennan Center for Justice, January 10, 2020.

48. Spencer MacColl, "Super PAC Registrations Accelerate, Favor Conservatives," OpenSecrets, June 17, 2011.

49. According to the Federal Election Commission, super PACs cannot spend money "in concert or cooperation with, or at the request or suggestion of, a candidate, the candidate's campaign or a political party." See MacColl, "Super PAC Registrations."

50. "What Is a PAC?" OpenSecrets; "Super PACs," Open Secrets.

51. Daniel I. Weiner, "Citizens United Five Years Later," Brennan Center for Justice, January 15, 2015.

52. Karl Evers-Hillstrom, "The Most Generous Megadonors of the 2020 Cycle—So Far," OpenSecrets, April 22, 2019.

53. Braden Goyette, "Cheat Sheet: How Super PACs Work, and Why They're So Controversial," *New York Daily News*, January 13, 2012.

54. Frank Bass, "'Dark Money' Groups More Likely to Sponsor Attack Ads," MapLight, August 17, 2016.

55. See, for example, Kathy Lohr, "Romney, Gingrich Spar over Negative Super PAC Ads," NPR, December 21, 2011.

56. Howard Homonoff, "2020 Political Ad Spending Exploded: Did It Work?" *Forbes*, December 8, 2020.

57. Ari Levy et al., "Why Political Campaigns Are Flooding Facebook with Ad Dollars," NBC News, October 9, 2020.

58. Brian Fung, "Facebook Allowed Hundreds of Misleading Super PAC Ads, Activist Group Finds," CNN, September 23, 2020.

59. Evers-Hillstrom, "The Most Generous Megadonors."

60. Paul Blumenthal, "McCutcheon v. FEC's Other Threat: Case Could Super-Size Joint Fundraising Committees," *HuffPost*, October 7, 2013.

61. Libby Watson, "How Political Megadonors Can Give Almost $500,000 with a Single Check," Sunlight Foundation, June 1, 2016.

62. Watson, "How Political Megadonors Can Give."

63. Blumenthal, "McCutcheon v. FEC's Other Threat."

64. OpenSecrets, "Dark Money Basics," November 7, 2019.

65. OpenSecrets, "Dark Money Process," November 7, 2019.

66. Open Secrets, "Dark Money Process."

67. Anna Massoglia and Ilma Hasan, "'Dark Money' Overshadows 2020 Election Political Ad Spending," OpenSecrets, May 19, 2020.

68. Anna Massoglia, "'Dark Money' Groups Find New Ways to Hide Donors in 2020 Election," OpenSecrets, October 30, 2020.

69. Open Secrets, "Dark Money Basics."

70. "Public Financing of Campaigns Overview," National Conference of State Legislatures, February 2019.

71. U.S. Senator Sheldon Whitehouse of Rhode Island, "Whitehouse Introduces Disclose Act to Restore Americans' Trust in Democracy," April 11, 2019.

72. Wendy Weiser and Alicia Bannon, "Democracy: An Election Agenda for Candidates, Activists, and Legislators," Brennan Center for Justice, May 4, 2018.

73. In addition to its own challenges, these issues also apply to the IRS and its capacity for regulating 501(c)(4) in particular; for example, see Benjamin Martinez, "Nearly 10,000 501c4s Failed to Meet Reporting Rules, Says U.S. Treasury," *Nonprofit Quarterly*, January 14, 2020.

74. Weiser and Bannon, "Democracy."

75. Brennan Center for Justice, "Reform Money in Politics," November 7, 2019.

76. Brennan Center for Justice, "Public Campaign Financing," November 7, 2019.

77. Brennan Center for Justice, "Reform Money in Politics."

78. Brennan Center for Justice, "Annotated Guide to the For the People Act of 2021," March 18, 2021.

79. Common Cause, "Citizens United & Amending the U.S. Constitution."

80. U.S. Representative Ted Deutch, Press Release, "Bipartisan Constitutional Amendment to Overturn Citizens United Introduced," January 21, 2021.

81. U.S. Congress, Senate, *Democracy for All*, 116th Congress, 1st session, Senate Joint Resolution.

3. Civic Education: "A Republic, If You Can Keep It"
Research and drafting contributed by Aimee Hwang.

1. On average, roughly 2,916 youth ages zero to nineteen each year had reported causes of death involving firearms during this period. These data exclude deaths from terrorism involving firearms and war operations involving firearm discharge. See "Underlying Cause of Death, 1999–2019," Centers for Disease Control and Prevention, http://wonder.cdc.gov/controller /datarequest/D76.

2. "Table B-6. Poverty Status of People by Age, Race, and Hispanic Origin: 1959 to 2019," U.S. Census Bureau, September 2020, www.census.gov/data/tables/2020/demo/income-poverty/p60 -270.html.

3. Richard R. Beeman, "Perspectives on the Constitution: A Republic, If You Can Keep It," National Constitution Center, http://constitutioncenter.org/learn/educational-resources /historical-documents/perspectives-on-the-constitution-a-republic-if-you-can-keep-it.

4. "Amid Pandemic and Protests, Civics Survey Finds Americans Know More of Their Rights," Annenberg Public Policy Center, University of Pennsylvania, September 14, 2020, www .annenbergpublicpolicycenter.org/pandemic-protests-2020-civics-survey-americans-know -much-more-about-their-rights.

5. FairVote, "Voter Turnout," https://www.fairvote.org/voter_turnout%20-%20voter_turn out_101.

6. Lee Rainie and Andrew Perrin, "Key Findings About Americans' Declining Trust in Government and Each Other," Pew Research Center, July 22, 2019, www.pewresearch.org/fact-tank /2019/07/22/key-findings-about-americans-declining-trust-in-government-and-each-other.

7. Steve Inskeep, "Timeline: What Trump Told Supporters for Months Before They Attacked," NPR, February 8, 2021.

8. Liz Cheney, Twitter Post, May 3, 2021, 10:27 AM. https://twitter.com/Liz_Cheney/status /1389225154639695881?ref_src=twsrc%5Etfw%22%3EMay%203%2C%202021.

9. Emily Chen et al., "COVID-19 Misinformation and the 2020 U.S. Presidential Election," *Misinformation Review*, March 3, 2021, www.misinforeview.hks.harvard.edu/article/covid-19 -misinformation-and-the-2020-u-s-presidential-election.

10. "Civic Education," *Stanford Encyclopedia of Philosophy*, last modified August 31, 2018, plato.stanford.edu/entries/civic-education.

11. Michael Hansen, Elizabeth Levesque, Jon Valant, and Diana Quintero, *The 2018 Brown Center Report on American Education: How Well Are American Students Learning?* (Brown Center on Education Policy, Brookings Institution, June 2018), www.brookings.edu/wp-content /uploads/2018/06/2018-Brown-Center-Report-on-American-Education_FINAL1.pdf.

12. Jonathan Gould (ed.), *Guardian of Democracy: The Civic Mission of Schools* (Rep. Philadelphia: The Leonore Annenberg Institute for Civics of the Annenberg Public Policy Center

at the University of Pennsylvania and the Campaign for the Civic Mission of Schools, 2011), 11.

13. Gould, *Guardian of Democracy*, 16.

14. Gould, *Guardian of Democracy*.

15. Thomas Jefferson, letter to Richard Price, January 8, 1789, Library of Congress, www.loc .gov/exhibits/jefferson/60.html.

16. Benjamin Franklin, *Works of the Late Dr. Benjamin Franklin: Consisting of Memoirs of His Early Life Written by Himself; Together with a Collection of His Essays, Humorous, Moral, and Literary. Chiefly in the Manner of the Spectator* (London: Forgotten Books, 2018), 264, forgot-tenbooks.com/en/books/WorksoftheLateDrBenjaminFranklin_10779519.

17. George Washington, "Eighth Annual Address to Congress," *The American Presidency Project*, University of California, Santa Barbara, www.presidency.ucsb.edu/documents/eighth -annual-address-congress.

18. Kathleen Hall Jamieson, "The Challenges Facing Civic Education," *Dædalus* 142, no. 2 (Spring 2013): 65–83, www.amacad.org/publication/challenges-facing-civic-education.

19. Paulette Patterson Dilworth, "Competing Conceptions of Citizenship Education: Thomas Jesse Jones and Carter G. Woodson," *International Journal of Social Education* 18, no. 2 (2003–4): 4, eric.ed.gov/?id=EJ718715.

20. Diane Ravitch and Joseph P. Viteritti, "Introduction," in *Making Good Citizens: Education and Civil Society*, eds. Diane Ravitch and Joseph P. Viteritti (New Haven, CT: Yale University Press, 2001), 6.

21. Jamieson, "The Challenges," 68.

22. Gould, *Guardian of Democracy*, 12.

23. Jamieson, "The Challenges," 67.

24. Gould, *Guardian of Democracy*, 12.

25. Ravitch and Viteritti, *Making Good Citizens*, 5.

26. Kristina Rizga, "Why Teaching Civics in America's Classrooms Must Be a Trump-Era Priority," *Mother Jones*, January/February 2017, www.motherjones.com/politics/2017/02/civics -education-trump-bullying.

27. David Klein, "A Brief History of American K-12 Mathematics Education in the 20th Century," in *Mathematical Cognition*, ed. James Royner (Charlotte, NC: Information Age Publishing, 2003), www.csun.edu/~vcmth00m/AHistory.html; "Recommendations" in *A Nation at Risk: The Imperative for Educational Reform*, National Commission on Excellence in Education (Washington, DC: U.S. Department of Education, 1983), www2.ed.gov/pubs/NatAtRisk /recomm.html.

28. John F. Kennedy, *A Nation of Immigrants*, 60th anniversary edition (New York: Harper-Collins, 1964; New York: HarperCollins, 2018).

29. Gould, *Guardian of Democracy*, 4.

30. Hansen et al., *The 2018 Brown Center Report on American Education*, 4, 12, 32.

31. Martin West, "Testing, Learning, and Teaching: The Effects of Test-Based Accountability on Student Achievement and Instructional Time in Core Academic Subjects," in *Beyond the Basics: Achieving a Liberal Education for All Children*, eds. Chester E. Finn Jr. and Diane Ravitch (Washington, DC: Thomas B. Fordham Institute, 2007), 51–52, http://fordhaminstitute.org /national/research/beyond-basics-achieving-liberal-education-all-children.

32. Gould, *Guardian of Democracy*, 27.

33. National Center for Education Statistics, "2014 Civics Assessment," *The Nation's Report Card*, www.nationsreportcard.gov/hgc_2014/ - civics/scores.

34. Kei Kawashima-Ginsberg, "Do Discussion, Debate, and Simulations Boost NAEP Civics Performance?" Center for Information & Research on Civic Learning & Engagement (CIRCLE), Tufts University, April 2013, circle.tufts.edu/sites/default/files/2020-01/discussion_debate_naep_2013.pdf.

35. Gould, *Guardian of Democracy*, 26–27.

36. Sarah Shapiro and Catherine Brown, "The State of Civics Education," Center for American Progress, February 21, 2018, www.americanprogress.org/issues/education-k-12/reports/2018/02/21/446857/state-civics-education.

37. Shapiro and Brown, "The State of Civics Education."

38. U.S. Department of Education, "Fiscal Year 2011 Budget Summary–February 1, 2010," last modified February 1, 2010, www2.ed.gov/about/overview/budget/budget11/summary/edlite-section4.html.

39. Jenny Montgomery, "Federal Budget Cuts Lead to Uncertainty for State's Student Civic Programs," Indiana Lawyer, April 15, 2011, www.theindianalawyer.com/articles/26170-federal-budget-cuts-lead-to-uncertainty-for-states-student-civic-programs.

40. Lee White, "Working Toward the Restoration of Federal Funding for History, Civics, and Social Studies Education," Perspectives on History, American Historical Association, March 1, 2015, www.historians.org/publications-and-directories/perspectives-on-history/march-2015/working-toward-the-restoration-of-federal-funding-for-history-civics-and-social-studies-education.

41. Alyson Klein, "House GOP Looks to Slash Education Spending," Education Week, February 12, 2011, www.edweek.org/policy-politics/house-gop-looks-to-slash-education-spending/2011/02.

42. U.S. Congress, Senate, *Every Student Succeeds Act*, S 1177, 114th Cong., introduced in Senate April 30, 2015, www.congress.gov/bill/114th-congress/senate-bill/1177/text.

43. Elizabeth Whitehouse and Abbey Bowe, "Federal Education Policy Opens Door to Civic Engagement," *Capitol Ideas* 4 (July/August 2017): 18–19, issuu.com/csg.publications/docs/ci_jul_aug_2017_website.

44. Jan Brennan, "ESSA: Mapping Opportunities for Civic Education," *Education Trends*, Education Commission of the States, April 2017, www.ecs.org/wp-content/uploads/ESSA-Mapping-opportunities-for-civic-education.pdf; Scott Warren and Dana Harris, "DeVos, Invest in the Future of Our Democracy by Focusing on Civics," The Hill, October 31, 2017.

45. Warren and Harris, "DeVos, Invest."

46. Kimberly Adams, "What Federal Funding for Civics Reveals About American Political Discourse," Marketplace, November 6, 2019, www.marketplace.org/2019/11/06/what-federal-funding-for-civics-reveals-about-american-political-discourse.

47. U.S. Department of Education, "Fiscal Year 2019 Budget: Summary and Background Information," 51–52, www2.ed.gov/about/overview/budget/budget19/summary/19summary.pdf.

48. Kei Kawashima-Ginsberg and Felicia Sullivan, "Study: 60 Percent of Rural Millennials Lack Access to a Political Life," Conversation, March 26, 2017, theconversation.com/study-60-percent-of-rural-millennials-lack-access-to-a-political-life-74513; Matthew N. Atwell, John

Bridgerland, and Peter Levine, "Civic Deserts: America's Civic Health Challenge," National Conference on Citizenship, 2017, www.ncoc.org/wp-content/uploads/2017/10/2017CHIUpdate -FINAL-small.pdf.

49. RAND Corporation, "Countering Truth Decay," www.rand.org/research/projects/truth -decay.html.

50. Pulitzer Center, "The 1619 Project Curriculum," pulitzercenter.org/lesson-plan-grouping /1619-project-curriculum.

51. Jake Silverstein, "Why We Published the 1619 Project," *New York Times Magazine*, December 20, 2019.

52. Adam Serwer, "The Fight over the 1619 Project Is Not About the Facts," *The Atlantic*, December 23, 2019; Nikole Hannah-Jones, "Our Democracy's Founding Ideals Were False When They Were Written. Black Americans Have Fought to Make Them True," *New York Times Magazine*, August 14, 2019.

53. Serwer, "The Fight."

54. Carole Levine, "Republicans in 5 States Seek to Keep 1619 Project Curriculum out of Schools," *Nonprofit Quarterly*, February 15, 2021, nonprofitquarterly.org/republicans-in -5-states-seek-to-keep-1619-project-curriculum-out-of-schools.

55. Jamieson, "The Challenges," 66.

56. Robert Lerner, Althea K. Nagai, and Stanley Rothman, *Molding the Good Citizen: The Politics of High School History Texts* (Westport, CT: Praeger Publishers, 1995), 70.

57. Kate Shuster, "Teaching Hard History," Southern Poverty Law Center, January 31, 2018, www.splcenter.org/20180131/teaching-hard-history.

58. Jamieson, "The Challenges," 66, 75, 77.

59. Ravitch and Viteritti, *Making Good Citizens*, 6.

60. Peter Levine and Kei Kawashima-Ginsberg, "Teaching Civics in a Time of Partisan Polarization," *Social Education* 77, no. 4 (September 2013): 216, www.socialstudies.org/system/files /publications/articles/se_7704215.pdf.

61. Kate Thayer, "Teachers Leave Political Views at Schoolhouse Gate," *Chicago Tribune*, November 6, 2016, www.chicagotribune.com/news/ct-teachers-politics-met-20161104-story .html.

62. Valerie Strauss, "Teachers Are Told Not to Get 'Political' in the Classroom. What Does That Actually Mean?" *Washington Post*, January 17, 2019.

63. Diana C. Mutz, *Hearing the Other Side: Deliberative Versus Participatory Democracy* (Cambridge, UK: Cambridge University Press, 2006); Patricia G. Avery, "Can Tolerance Be Taught?" in *Social Studies Today: Research and Practice*, ed. Walter C. Parker (New York: Routledge, 2009), 235–243.

64. Jennifer Bachner, "From Classroom to Voting Booth: The Effect of High School Civic Education on Turnout," 2010, www.semanticscholar.org/paper/From-Classroom-to-Voting -Booth%3A-The-Eect-of-High-on-Bachner/c91611001590e55b68a99fdaf8faf62835528a2b.

65. Alex Vandermaas-Peeler, "American Democracy in Crisis: Civic Engagement, Young Adult Activism, and the 2018 Midterm Elections," Public Religion Research Institute, October 11, 2018, www.prri.org/research/american-democracy-in-crisis-civic-engagement-young-adult-act ivism-and-the-2018-midterm-elections.

66. Tufts Now, "Youth Vote Up Significantly in 2020; Young People of Color Pivotal," Novem-

ber 19, 2020, now.tufts.edu/news-releases/youth-vote-significantly-2020-young-people-color
-pivotal.

67. March for Our Lives, "Mission & Story," marchforourlives.com/mission-story.

68. Sherri Kolade, "Clean Water Activist Little Miss Flint Raises Almost $500K for Communities," *Michigan Chronicle*, April 20, 2021, michiganchronicle.com/2021/04/20/clean-water
-activist-little-miss-flint-raises-almost-500k-for-communities.

69. "Civics Secures Democracy Act Proposes Grants to Support Civics Education," interview by Steve Inskeep, *Morning Edition*, NPR, April 14, 2021, www.npr.org/2021/04/14/987099824
/civics-secures-democracy-act-proposes-grants-to-support-civics-education.

70. Andrew Ujifusa, "Biden Administration Cites 1619 Project as Inspiration in History Grant Proposal," Education Week, April 19, 2021, www.edweek.org/teaching-learning/biden
-administration-cites-1619-project-as-inspiration-in-history-grant-proposal/2021/04.

71. "Executive Order 13985 of January 20, 2021, Advancing Racial Equity and Support for Underserved Communities Through the Federal Government," *Federal Register* 86, no. 14 (January 25, 2021): 7009–7013, www.federalregister.gov/documents/2021/01/25/2021-01753
/advancing-racial-equity-and-support-for-underserved-communities-through-the-federal
-government.

72. Gould, *Guardian of Democracy*, 6–7.

73. "Overview of Strategies and Recommendations," *Our Common Purpose: Reinventing American Democracy for the 21st Century* (Cambridge, MA: American Academy of Arts and Sciences, 2020), www.amacad.org/ourcommonpurpose/report/section/3.

Part II: Equal Protection of Law

4. Bending the Arc Toward Racial Justice
Research and drafting contributed by Kadijatou Diallo.

1. Martin Luther King Jr., "Remaining Awake Through a Great Revolution." Speech given at the National Cathedral, March 31, 1968.

2. "March on Washington for Jobs and Freedom," Martin Luther King, Jr. Research and Education Institute at Stanford University, kinginstitute.stanford.edu/encyclopedia/march
-washington-jobs-and-freedom; "March on Washington for Jobs and Freedom," National Park Service, updated August 4, 2020, www.nps.gov/articles/march-on-washington.htm.

3. "March on Washington."

4. Ourdocuments.gov, "Civil Rights Act 1964," www.ourdocuments.gov/doc.php?flash
=false&doc=97.

5. Otis S. Johnson, "Two Worlds: A Historical Perspective on the Dichotomous Relations Between Police and Black and White Communities," *Human Rights Magazine* 42, no. 1 (2017).

6. "The Civil Rights Movement and the Second Reconstruction, 1946–1968," United States House of Representatives, history.house.gov/Exhibitions-and-Publications/BAIC/Historical
-Essays/Keeping-the-Faith/Civil-Rights-Movement.

7. Alia Chughtai, "Know Their Names: Black People Killed by Police in the U.S.," Al-Jazeera, 2020.

8. Frank Edwards et al., "Risk of Being Killed by Police Use of Force in the United States by Age, Race–Ethnicity, and Sex," *Proceedings of the National Academy of Sciences* 116, no. 34 (2019): 16793–16798.

9. Shytierra Gaston, "Enforcing Race: A Neighborhood-Level Explanation of Black–White Differences in Drug Arrests," *Crime & Delinquency* 65, no. 4 (2019): 499–526.

10. Chughtai, "Know Their Names."

11. George L. Kelling and James Q. Wilson, "Broken Windows," *The Atlantic*, March 1982.

12. "The Civil Rights Implications of 'Broken Windows' Policing in NYC and General NYPD Accountability to the Public," New York Advisory Committee to the U.S. Commission on Civil Rights, March 2018, www.usccr.gov/pubs/2018/03-22-NYSAC.pdf.

13. Emily Badger, "The Lasting Effects of Stop-and-Frisk in Bloomberg's New York," *New York Times*, March 2, 2020.

14. Andrew Bacher-Hicks and Elijah de la Campa, "Social Costs of Proactive Policing: The Impact of NYC's Stop and Frisk Program on Educational Attainment," *Harvard Kennedy School Working Paper*, February 2020, https://drive.google.com/file/d/1sSxhfmDY3N1VAN5X wyRObE65tmAZzhTj/view.

15. Jennifer Eberhardt et al., "Seeing Black: Race, Crime, and Visual Processing," *Journal of Personality and Social Psychology* 87, no. 6 (2004): 876–893.

16. Ashley Nellis, "The Color of Justice: Racial and Ethnic Disparity in State Prisons," The Sentencing Project, June 14, 2016, www.sentencingproject. org/publications/color-of-justice-ra cial-and-ethnic-disparity-in-state-prisons.

17. Devon W. Carbado, "From Stopping Black People to Killing Black People: The Fourth Amendment Pathways to Police Violence," *California Law Review* 105 (2017): 125.

18. Shelley S. Hyland, "Body-Worn Cameras in Law Enforcement Agencies, 2016," Bureau of Justice Statistics, November 2018, www.bjs.gov/content/ pub/pdf/bwclea16.pdf.

19. Mike Males, "Who Are Police Killing?" Center on Juvenile and Criminal Justice, August 24, 2014, www.cjcj.org/news/8113.

20. Jon Marcus, "Bringing Native American Stories to a National Audience," *Nieman Reports*, February 11, 2016, http://niemanreports.org/articles/ bringing-native-american-storie s-to-a-national-audience.

21. Stephanie Woodard, "The Police Killings No One Is Talking About," In These Times, October 17, 2016, inthesetimes.com/features/native_ american_police_killings_native_lives_matter. html.

22. Jennifer Bronson and Ann Carson, "Prisoners in 2017," U.S. Department of Justice, Bureau of Justice Statistics, April 2019, https://bjs.ojp.gov/content/pub/pdf/p17.pdf.

23. Aaron Gottlieb and Karen Flynn, "The Legacy of Slavery and Mass Incarceration: Evidence from Felony Case Outcomes," *Social Science Review* (March 2021).

24. NAACP, "Criminal Justice Fact Sheet," 2020, www.naacp.org/criminal- justice-fact-sheet.

25. National Academy of Sciences, *The Growth of Incarceration in the United States: Exploring Causes and Consequences* (2014), chapter 4.

26. Nellis, "The Color of Justice."

27. Nellis, "The Color of Justice."

28. Jawjeong Wu, "Racial/Ethnic Discrimination and Prosecution: A Meta-Analysis," *Criminal Justice and Behavior* 43, no. 4 (2016): 437–458.

29. Nellis, "The Color of Justice."

30. Kim M. Blankenship et al., "Mass Incarceration, Race Inequality, and Health: Expanding Concepts and Assessing Impacts on Well-Being," *Social Science & Medicine* 215 (2018): 45–52.

31. The National Education Association defines the school-to-prison pipeline as encompassing "the policies and practices that are directly and indirectly pushing students of color out of school and on a pathway to prison, including, but not limited to: harsh school discipline policies that overuse suspension and expulsion, increased policing and surveillance that creates prison-like environments in schools, overreliance on referrals to law enforcement and the juvenile justice system, and an alienating and punitive high-stakes testing-driven academic environment"; see "Discipline and the School-to-Prison Pipeline," National Education Association, 2016, ra .nea.org/business-item/2016-pol-e01-2.

32. In the broader criminal justice framework, zero-tolerance policies and policing, in particular, refer to "the style of policing generally associated with the full and complete enforcement of all criminal violations, from minor infractions (such as disorderly conduct or public loitering) to major crimes (such as robbery and burglary)."

33. Daniel J. Losen and Russel J. Skiba, "Suspended Education: Urban Middle Schools in Crisis," Southern Poverty Law Center, 2010.

34. Libby Nelson and Dara Lind, "The School to Prison Pipeline, Explained," Justice Policy Institute, February 24, 2015, www.justicepolicy.org/ news/8775.

35. Erin M. Hickey, "Zero Tolerance for Policies Depriving Children of Education: Comment on Zero Tolerance Policies," Children's Legal Rights Journal 24, no. 4 (2004): 18–25.

36. U.S. Department of Education Office for Civil Rights, "Civil Rights Data Collection Data Snapshot: School Discipline," March 2014, ed.gov/about/offices/list/ocr/docs/crdc-discipline -snapshot.pdf.

37. Annie E. Casey Foundation, "Youth Incarceration Rates in the United States," February 26, 2013, www.aecf.org/resources/youth-incarceration- in-the-united-states/#findings-and-stats.

38. Nelson and Lind, "The School to Prison Pipeline."

39. Denisa R. Superville, "Most Principals Have No Say in Choosing Police for Their Schools," Education Week, December 11, 2019, www.edweek.org/ew/articles/2019/12/11/most -principals-have-no-say-in-choosing.html.

40. Nathan James and Gail McCallion, "School Resource Officers: Law Enforcement Officers in Schools," Congressional Research Service, June 26, 2013, fas.org/sgp/crs/misc/R43126 .pdf.

41. Eva Ruth Moravec, "Teen Shot by Northside Officer Identified," My San Antonio, January 4, 2011, www.mysanantonio.com/news/education/article/Teen-shot-by-Northside-officer -identified-813859.php.

42. Eliott C. McLaughlin, "Texas Student Tased by Police Exits Coma, Enters Rehabilitation, Attorney Says," CNN, February 3, 2014.

43. Connie Leonard, "LMPD Officer Accused of Assaulting Students," Wave 3 News, February 4, 2015, www.wave3.com/story/28018314/lmpd-officer-accused-of-student-assault/?autosta rt=true.

44. Addie C. Rolnick and Neelum Arya, "A Tangled Web of Justice: American Indian and Alaska Native Youth in Federal, State, and Tribal Justice Systems," University of Nevada Boyd School of Law Scholarly Works, 2008, scholars.law.unlv.edu/cgi/viewcontent.cgi?article=2005&c ontext=facpub.

45. Wendy Sawyer, "Youth Confinement: The Whole Pie 2019," Prison Policy Initiative, December 19, 2019, www.prisonpolicy.org/reports/youth2019.html.

46. Rolnick and Arya, "A Tangled Web of Justice."

47. Centers for Disease Control and Prevention, "Effects on Violence of Laws and Policies

Facilitating the Transfer of Youth from the Juvenile to the Adult Justice System," November 30, 2007, www.cdc.gov/mmwr/pdf/rr/rr5609.pdf.

48. Amy Hillier, "Redlining in Philadelphia," in *Past Time, Past Place: GIS for History*, ed. Anne Kelly Knowles (Redlands, CA: ESRI Press, 2002), 79–92, www2.oberlin.edu/octet/HowTo /GIS/Tutorial/PastTime,PastPlaceCh6.pdf.

49. Ourdocuments.gov, "Servicemen's Readjustment Act 1944," www.ourdocuments.gov/doc .php?flash=- false&doc=76.

50. History, "G.I. Bill," May 27, 2010, www.history.com/topics/world-war-ii/gi-bill.

51. Terry Gross, "A 'Forgotten History' of How the U.S. Government Segregated America," NPR, May 3, 2017.

52. Daniel Aaronson et al., "The Effects of the 1930s HOLC 'Redlining' Map," *Federal Reserve Bank of Chicago Working Paper Series*, February 2019, ideas.repec.org/p/fip/fedhwp/wp-2017-12 .html.

53. Judson Murchie and Jindong Pang, "Rental Housing Discrimination Across Protected Classes: Evidence from a Randomized Experiment," *Regional Science and Urban Economics* 73 (2018): 170–179.

54. Margery A. Turner et al., "Housing Discrimination Against Racial and Ethnic Minorities 2012," Department of Housing and Urban Development, June 2013, www.huduser.gov/portal /Publications/pdf/HUD-514_HDS2012.pdf.

55. Matthew Kredell, "Sociologist Reports Only Minor Progress in Racial Equality over Last 40 Years," USC Sol Price Center for Social Innovation, February 27, 2015, priceschool.usc.edu /sociologist-reports-only-minor-progress-in-racial-equality-over-last-40-years.

56. Brian Smedley and Rachel A. Davis, "The Effects of Housing Discrimination on Health Can Reverberate for Decades," The Hill, August 27, 2019.

57. Kriston McIntosh et al., "Examining the Black-White Wealth Gap," Brookings, February 27, 2020, www.brookings.edu/blog/up-front/2020/02/27/examining-the-black-white-wealth -gap.

58. Richard Rothstein, *The Color of Law: A Forgotten History of How Our Government Segregated America* (New York: Liveright, 2017).

59. Nancy Pindus et al., "Housing Needs of American Indians and Alaska Natives in Tribal Areas: A Report from the Assessment of American Indian, Alaska Native, and Native Hawaiian Housing Needs," Department of Housing and Urban Development, January 2017, www.huduser .gov/ portal/sites/default/files/pdf/HNAIHousingNeeds.pdf.

60. Ourdocuments.gov, "Transcript of Brown v. Board of Education (1954)," www .ourdocuments.gov/doc.php?flash=-false&doc=87&page=transcript

61. Thirteen, "Southern Manifesto on Integration (March 12, 1956)," www.thirteen.org/wnet /supremecourt/rights/sources_document2.html.

62. "Nonwhite School Districts Get $23 Billion Less Than White Districts Despite Serving the Same Number of Students," EdBuild, February 2019, edbuild.org/content/23-billion.

63. Linda Darling-Hammond, "Unequal Opportunity: Race and Education," Brookings Institution, March 1, 1998.

64. Ivan Moreno, "U.S. Charter Schools Put Growing Numbers in Racial Isolation," AP News, December 3, 2017.

65. "Affirmative Action," Legal Information Institute, www.law.cornell.edu/wex/affirma tive_action.

66. "Bakke Decision," *Encyclopedia Britannica*, www.britannica.com/event/Bakke-decision.

67. Legal Information Institute, "Affirmative Action."

68. "Students for Fair Admission (SFFA) v. Harvard," Lawyers' Committee for Civil Rights Under Law, lawyerscommittee.org/students-for-fair-admissions-sffa-v-harvard.

69. Scott M. Bortot, "Once a Training Ground for Black Leaders, Unions Still Attract African-American Workers," ShareAmerica, February 4, 2015, share.america.gov/labor-unions-played -key-role-in-civil-rights.

70. Department of Labor, "Executive Order 11246–Equal Employment Opportunity."

71. Bureau of Labor Statistics, "Labor Force Characteristics by Race and Ethnicity, 2018," October 2019.

72. Lincoln Quillian et al., "Hiring Discrimination Against Black Americans Hasn't Declined in 25 Years," *Harvard Business Review*, October 11, 2017.

73. Marianne Bertrand and Sendhil Mullainathan, "Discrimination in the Job Market in the United States," Abdul Latif Jameel Poverty Action Lab (J-PAL), www.povertyactionlab.org /evaluation/discrimination-job-market-united-states.

74. Equal Employment Opportunity Commission, "Race-Based Charges (Charges Filed with EEOC) FY 1997–FY 2019," www.eeoc.gov/eeoc/statistics/enforcement/race.cfm.

75. Maryam Jameel and Joe Yerardi, "Workplace Discrimination Is Illegal. But Our Data Shows It's Still a Huge Problem," Vox, February 28, 2019.

76. Fidan Ana Kurtulus, "The Impact of Eliminating Affirmative Action on Minority and Female Employment: A Natural Experiment Approach Using State-Level Affirmative Action Laws and EEO-4 Data," *Harvard Kennedy School Working Paper Series*, October 30, 2013, gap .hks.harvard.edu/impact-eliminating-affirmative-action-minority-and-female-employment -natural-experiment-approach.

77. Black Lives Matter, "Herstory," blacklivesmatter.com/herstory.

78. Centers for Disease Control and Prevention, "Health Equity Considerations & Racial & Ethnic Minority Groups," July 24, 2020.

79. Louis Casiano, "Coronavirus: Who Are Considered 'Essential' Workers?" Fox News, March 23, 2020.

80. Centers for Disease Control and Prevention, "Health Equity Considerations."

81. Megan Wallace et al., "COVID-19 in Correctional and Detention Facilities—United States, February–April 2020," Centers for Disease Control and Prevention, May 15, 2020.

82. The Legal Aid Society, "COVID-19 Infection Tracking in NYC Jails," www.legalaidnyc.org /covid-19-infection-tracking-in-nyc-jails.

83. City of New York Correction Department, "NYC Department of Correction at a Glance: Information for the First 6 Months of FY 2020 (July–December)," www1.nyc.gov/assets/doc /downloads/press-release/DOC_At_Glance_6_Months_FY2020.pdf.

84. Nick Charles, "Race Rises to the Forefront for Activists in the Coronavirus Pandemic," NBC News, April 10, 2020.

85. "Racial Toll of Coronavirus Grows Even Starker as More Data Emerges," *Tampa Bay Times*, April 18, 2020, www. tampabay.com/news/health/2020/04/18/racial-toll-of-coronavirus -grows-even-starker-as-more-data-emerges.

86. Centers for Disease Control and Prevention, "Risk for COVID-19 Infection, Hospitalization, and Death by Race/Ethnicity," April 23, 2021.

87. Indian Health Services, "Indian Health Disparities," October 2019.

88. Indian Health Services, "About IHS," www.ihs.gov/aboutihs.

89. Kenzi Abou-Sabe et al., "Coronavirus Batters the Navajo Nation, and It's About to Get Worse," NBC News, April 20, 2020.

90. Centers for Disease Control and Prevention, "Health Equity Considerations."

91. Biden–Harris Campaign, "The Biden Plan for Strengthening America's Commitment to Justice," joebiden.com/justice.

92. The White House, "Fact Sheet: President Biden to Take Action to Advance Racial Equity and Support Underserved Communities," January 26, 2021, www.whitehouse.gov/briefing-room/statements-releases/2021/01/26/fact-sheet-president-biden-to-take-action-to-advance-racial-equity-and-support-underserved-communities.

93. David Leonhardt and Ian Prasad Philbrick, "One Year Later," *New York Times*, May 25, 2021.

94. "Attorney General Merrick B. Garland Announces Investigation of the City of Minneapolis, Minnesota, and the Minneapolis Police Department," Department of Justice, April 21, 2021, www.justice.gov/opa/pr/attorney-general-merrick-b-garland-announces-investigation-city-minneapolis-minnesota-and.

95. Tracy Jan, "Ben Carson's HUD Dials Back Investigations into Housing Discrimination," *Washington Post*, December 24, 2018.

96. Natalie Moore, "Federal Housing Agency Seeks to Raise the Bar in Discrimination Cases," NPR, October 16, 2019.

97. Texas Department of Housing and Community Affairs v. Inclusive Communities Project, 576 U.S. 519 (2015).

98. The White House, "Memorandum on Redressing Our Nation's and the Federal Government's History of Discriminatory Housing Practices and Policies," January 26, 2021, www.whitehouse.gov/briefing-room/presidential-actions/2021/01/26/memorandum-on-redressing-our-nations-and-the-federal-governments-history-of-discriminatory-housing-practices-and-policies/.

99. Federal Register, "HUD's Implementation of the Fair Housing Act's Disparate Impact Standard," August 19, 2019, www.federalregister.gov/documents/2019/08/19/2019-17542/huds-implementation-of-the-fair-housing-acts-disparate-impact-standard.

100. Department of Housing and Urban Development, "Fact Sheet: Housing Provisions in the American Rescue Plan Act of 2021," www.hud.gov/sites/dfiles/Main/documents/Factsheet_Housing_Provisions_American_Rescue_Plan_Act-2021.pdf.

101. The White House, "Fact Sheet: The American Jobs Plan," March 31, 2021, www.whitehouse.gov/briefing-room/statements-releases/2021/03/31/fact-sheet-the-american-jobs-plan.

102. Katy O'Donnell, "How Biden Hopes to Fix the Thorniest Problem in Housing," Politico, April 10, 2021.

103. Matt Barnum, "Asked Whether She Is Using Crisis to Support Private School Choice, DeVos Says 'Yes, Absolutely,'" Chalkbeat, May 20, 2020, www.chalkbeat.org/2020/5/20/21265527/devos-using-coronavirus-to-boost-private-schools-says-yes-absolutely.

104. Betsy Klein, "Biden Announces $81 Billion for Schools as Part of COVID-19 Relief Law," CNN, March 24, 2021.

105. The White House, "Fact Sheet: The American Families Plan," April 28, 2021, www

.whitehouse.gov/briefing-room/statements-releases/2021/04/28/fact-sheet-the-american
-families-plan/.

106. Brooke Auxier and Colleen McClain, "Americans Think Social Media Can Help Build
Movements, but Can Also Be a Distraction," Pew Research Center, September 9, 2020.

107. "Critical Race Theory," Encyclopedia Britannica, April 2, 2021, www.britannica.com
/topic/critical-race-theory.

5. The Ongoing Struggle for Women's Rights
Research and drafting contributed by Katie Stenclik.

1. Madison Feller, "Watch Kamala Harris Make Her First Speech as Vice President," *Elle*,
January 21, 2021.

2. Center for American Women and Politics, Rutgers University Eagleton Institute of Politics, "Milestones for Women in American Politics," https://cawp.rutgers.edu/facts/milestones
-for-women.

3. Alexander Burns et al., "Who's Running for President in 2020?" *New York Times*,
April 8, 2020, www.nytimes.com/interactive/2019/us/politics/2020-presidential-candidates
.html.

4. Kelly Dittmar, "Why Scaling Up Women's Political Representation Matters," *Gender Watch 2018*, November 16, 2018, www.genderwatch2018.org/scaling-womens-political
-representation-matters.

5. Legal Momentum, "Women and Poverty in America," www.legalmomentum.org/women
-and-poverty-america; Robin Bleiweis, "Quick Facts About the Gender Wage Gap," Center for
American Progress, March 24, 2020, www.americanprogress.org/issues/women/reports/2020
/03/24/482141/quick-facts-gender-wage-gap.

6. Ravneet Kaur and Suneela Garg. "Addressing Domestic Violence Against Women: An
Unfinished Agenda," *Indian Journal of Community Medicine* 33, no. 2 (April 2008): 73–76, https:
//doi.org/10.4103/0970-0218.40871.

7. Annenberg Public Policy Center, University of Pennsylvania, "Women's Rights," www
.annenbergclassroom.org/resource/womens-rights.

8. Catherine Allgor, "Coverture: The Word You Probably Don't Know but Should," National
Women's History Museum, September 4, 2014, www.womenshistory.org/articles/coverture
-word-you-probably-dont-know-should.

9. Claudia Zaher, "When a Woman's Marital Status Determined Her Legal Status: A Research
Guide on the Common Law Doctrine of Coverture," *Law Library Journal* 94, no. 3 (June 2002):
459–486.

10. Madison Pauly, "It's 2019, and States Are Still Making Exceptions for Spousal Rape,"
Mother Jones, November 21, 2019, www.motherjones.com/crime-justice/2019/11/deval-patrick
-spousal-rape-laws.

11. History, "Women's Suffrage," October 29, 2009, www.history.com/topics/womens-history
/the-fight-for-womens-suffrage.

12. Brent Staples, "When the Suffrage Movement Sold Out to White Supremacy," *New York
Times*, February 2, 2019; see "Race and Voting," Constitutional Rights Foundation, www.crf-usa
.org/brown-v-board-50th-anniversary/race-and-voting.html.

13. U.S. Congress, House, *Equal Pay Act of 1963*, www.eeoc.gov/statutes/equal-pay-act-1963.

14. U.S. Congress, House, *Title VII of the Civil Rights Act of 1964*, www.eeoc.gov/statutes/title-vii-civil-rights-act-1964.

15. "Title X Program Funding History," Office of Population Affairs, U.S. Department of Health & Human Services, www.hhs.gov/opa/title-x-family-planning/about-title-x-grants/funding-history/index.html.

16. U.S. Congress, House, *Title IX of the Education Amendments of 1972*, www.justice.gov/crt/title-ix-education-amendments-1972.

17. Legal Information Institute, Cornell Law School, "Equal Employment Opportunity Commission," www.law.cornell.edu/wex/equal_employment_opportunity_commission.

18. U.S. Equal Employment Opportunity Commission, "Pregnancy Discrimination," www.eeoc.gov/pregnancy-discrimination.

19. U.S. Department of Labor, "Family and Medical Leave (FMLA)," www.dol.gov/general/topic/benefits-leave/fmla.

20. Emily S. Rueb and Niraj Chokshi, "The Violence Against Women Act Is Turning 25. Here's How It Has Ignited Debate," *New York Times*, April 4, 2019.

21. United States, Congress, House, United States Code Title 20, section 1092, Legal Information Institute, Cornell Law School, www.law.cornell.edu/uscode/text/20/1092.

22. "Affordable Care Act (ACA)," HealthCare.gov, U.S. Centers for Medicare & Medicaid Services, www.healthcare.gov/glossary/affordable-care-act; and Healthcare.gov, U.S. Centers for Medicare & Medicaid Services, "Health Coverage Rights and Protections," www.healthcare.gov/health-care-law-protections.

23. Meritor Savings Bank v. Vinson, 477 U.S. 57 (1986), and Oncale v. Sundowner Offshore Services, Inc., 523 U.S. 75 (1998).

24. "A Summary of Actions Taken by the United States Supreme Court on a Variety of Matters," *New York Times*, November 8, 1975.

25. General Elec. Co. v. Gilbert, 429 U.S. 125 (1976).

26. "Roe v. Wade," *Legal Information Institute*, Cornell Law School.

27. Planned Parenthood of Southeastern PA. v. Casey, 505 U.S. 833 (1992).

28. Planned Parenthood of Southeastern PA. v. Casey.

29. Planned Parenthood of Southeastern PA. v. Casey.

30. Meaghan Winter, "Roe v. Wade Was Lost in 1992," Slate, March 27, 2016.

31. Planned Parenthood of Southeastern PA. v. Casey.

32. Gonzalez v. Carhart (2007) and Gonzales v. Planned Parenthood Federation of America, Inc. (2007).

33. Kelly Cooke and Heidi Guetschow, "Gonzales v. Planned Parenthood Federation of America, Inc.," Legal Information Institute, Cornell Law School.

34. Whole Woman's Health v. Hellerstedt, 579 U.S. 136 (2016).

35. Harris v. McRae, 448 U.S. 297 (1980); Anna North, "Lack of Medicaid Coverage Blocked 29 Percent of Abortion Seekers from Getting the Procedure, Study Says," Vox, June 20, 2019.

36. Webster v. Reproductive Health Services, 492 U.S.490 (1989).

37. Rust v. Sullivan, 500 U.S. 173 (1991).

38. Amanda Marcotte, "It Wasn't Abortion That Formed the Religious Right. It Was Support for Segregation," *Slate*, May 29, 2014.

39. Randall Balmer, "The Real Origins of the Religious Right," Politico, May 27, 2014.

40. Michele McKeegan, "The Politics of Abortion: A Historical Perspective," *Women's Health Issues* 3, no. 3 (September 1, 1993): 127–131.

41. Clyde Haberman, "Religion and Right-Wing Politics: How Evangelicals Reshaped Elections," *New York Times*, October 28, 2018.

42. Paul Butler, "The Rightwing Takeover of the U.S. Court System Will Transform America," *The Guardian*, December 12, 2017.

43. Bleiweis, "Quick Facts."

44. National Women's Law Center, "The Wage Gap: The Who, How, Why, and What to Do," September 2019.

45. Kristen Schilt and Matthew Wiswall, "Before and After: Gender Transitions, Human Capital, and Workplace Experiences," *The B.E. Journal of Economic Analysis & Policy* 8, no. 1 (September 11, 2008).

46. Claudia Goldin, "How to Achieve Gender Equality," *Milken Institute Review* (Q3 July 2015): 24–33.

47. Kim Parker and Cary Funk, "42 Percent of U.S. Working Women Have Faced Gender Discrimination on the Job," Pew Research Center, December 14, 2017.

48. Bleiweis, "Quick Facts."

49. Gus Wezerek and Kristen R. Ghodsee, "Women's Unpaid Labor Is Worth $10,900,000,000,000," *New York Times*, March 5, 2020.

50. Nikki Graf et al., "The Narrowing, but Persistent, Gender Gap in Pay," Pew Research Center, March 22, 2019.

51. Lindsay Oncken, "Policy Recommendation: Paid Family Leave," New America, https://www.newamerica.org/in-depth/care-report/policy-recommendation-paid-family-leave/.

52. World Policy Analysis Center, "Is Paid Leave Available to Mothers and Fathers of Infants?" https://www.worldpolicycenter.org/policies/is-paid-leave-available-to-mothers-and-fathers-of-infants/is-paid-leave-available-for-both-parents-of-infants.

53. Bipartisan Policy Center, "State Paid Family Leave Laws Across the U.S.," November 18, 2019.

54. American Civil Liberties Union, "In Historic Decision on Digital Bias, EEOC Finds Employers Violated Federal Law When They Excluded Women and Older Workers from Facebook Job Ads," September 25, 2019.

55. Ted Mann, "White House Won't Require Firms to Report Pay by Gender, Race," *Wall Street Journal*, August 29, 2017.

56. Courtney Connley, "President Biden Says Closing Gender Pay Gap Is 'a Moral Imperative' as House Passes Paycheck Fairness Act," CNBC, April 16, 2021.

57. Sophie Quinton, "Unions, States Confront Trump Home Care Worker Rule," Pew Charitable Trusts, May 28, 2019.

58. Campbell Robertson and Robert Gebeloff, "How Millions of Women Became the Most Essential Workers in America," *New York Times*, April 18, 2020.

59. Rasheed Malik and Taryn Morrissey, "The COVID-19 Pandemic Is Forcing Millennial Mothers Out of the Workforce," Center for American Progress, August 12, 2020.

60. National Women's Law Center, "How the American Rescue Plan Provides Critical Relief to Women and Families," March 24, 2021.

61. Legal Momentum, "Women and Poverty in America."

62. Gretchen Livingston, "About One-Third of U.S. Children Are Living with an Unmarried Parent," Pew Research Center, April 27, 2018.

63. Kathryn Cronquist, "Characteristics of Supplemental Nutrition Assistance Program Households: Fiscal Year 2018," Food and Nutrition Service Office of Policy Support, U.S. Department of Agriculture, November 2019.

64. Executive Order 13828 of April 10, 2018, *Reducing Poverty in America by Promoting Opportunity and Economic Mobility.*

65. Maria Godoy, "Judge Blocks Rule That Would Have Kicked 700,000 People Off SNAP," NPR, March 14, 2020.

66. Laura Reiley, "Biden Administration Reverses Trump Decision, Will Provide $1 Billion a Month More in Emergency Food Assistance," *Washington Post*, April 2, 2021.

67. National Women's Law Center, "How the American Rescue Plan Provides Critical Relief to Women and Families," March 24, 2021.

68. Last name omitted from the original source for privacy purposes.

69. Esther Honig, "For Women in Rural Kansas, a Longer Drive Can Mean Less Health Care," KCUR 89.3, February 26, 2016.

70. Usha Ranji et al., "Women's Coverage, Access, and Affordability: Key Findings from the 2017 Kaiser Women's Health Survey," Kaiser Family Foundation, March 13, 2018.

71. Sarah Houssayni and Kari Nilsen, "Transgender Competent Provider: Identifying Transgender Health Needs, Health Disparities, and Health Coverage," *Kansas Journal of Medicine* 11, no. 1 (February 28, 2018): 15–19.

72. Austin Frakt, "Bad Medicine: The Harm That Comes from Racism," *New York Times*, July 8, 2020.

73. Committee on Health Care for Underserved Women, "Health Disparities in Rural Women," *American College of Obstetricians and Gynecologists* no. 586 (February 2014).

74. Office of Population Affairs, "Title X Program Funding History."

75. Meilan Solly, "CDC Says More Than Half of the U.S.' Pregnancy-Related Deaths Are Preventable," *Smithsonian Magazine*, May 9, 2019.

76. Roni Caryn Rabin, "Huge Racial Disparities Found in Deaths Linked to Pregnancy," *New York Times*, May 7, 2019.

77. U.S. Congress, House, *Preventing Maternal Deaths Act*, HR 1318, 115th Cong., introduced in House March 2, 2017.

78. U.S. Centers for Medicare and Medicaid Services, "Affordable Care Act (ACA)."

79. Sarah Heath, "How the ACA Improved Women's Health, Patient Access to Care," Patient Engagement HIT, March 4, 2020.

80. Nora V. Becker and Daniel Polsky, "Women Saw Large Decrease in Out-of-Pocket Spending for Contraceptives After ACA Mandate Removed Cost Sharing," *Health Affairs* 34, no. 7 (July 1, 2015): 1204–1211.

81. Anna Bernstein and Kelly Jones, "The Economic Effects of Contraceptive Access: A Review of the Evidence," Institute for Women's Policy Research, September 26, 2019.

82. Jacoba Urist, "Social and Economic Benefits of Reliable Contraception," *The Atlantic*, July 2, 2014.

83. Burwell v. Hobby Lobby Stores, Inc., 573 U.S. 682 (2014).

84. U.S. Department of Health and Human Services, "Religious Exemptions and Accommodations for Coverage of Certain Preventive Services Under the Affordable Care Act," *Federal Register* 83, no. 221 (November 5, 2020): 57536–57590.

85. "Fact Sheet: Final Rules on Religious and Moral Exemptions and Accommodation for Coverage of Certain Preventive Services Under the Affordable Care Act," U.S. Department of Health & Human Services, November 7, 2018.

86. Jenny Samuels, "Joe Biden's Next Move on the Contraceptive Mandate," OnLabor, April 21, 2021.

87. Laurie Sobel et al., "New Title X Regulations: Implications for Women and Family Planning Providers," Kaiser Family Foundation, March 8, 2019.

88. Margaret Talbot, "How the Trump Administration Is Stigmatizing Abortion," *The New Yorker*, August 24, 2019.

89. *We Are Planned Parenthood: Annual Report 2018–2019*, Planned Parenthood, https://www.plannedparenthood.org/uploads/filer_public/2e/da/2eda3f50-82aa-4ddb-acce-c2854c4ea80b/2018-2019_annual_report.pdf.

90. Pam Belluck, "Planned Parenthood Refuses Federal Funds over Abortion Restrictions," *New York Times*, August 19, 2019.

91. Anna North, "How a Beloved Clinic for Low-Income Women Is Fighting to Stay Alive in the Trump Era," Vox, November 22, 2019.

92. Joyce Friedan, "Biden Administration Will Rescind Trump-Era Title X 'Gag Rule,'" MedPage Today, March 23, 2021.

93. National Women's Law Center, "How the American Rescue Plan Provides Critical Relief to Women and Families," March 24, 2021.

94. "U.S. Public Continues to Favor Legal Abortion, Oppose Overturning Roe v. Wade," Pew Research Center, August 29, 2019.

95. "State Policy Trends 2020: Reproductive Health and Rights in a Year Like No Other," Guttmacher Institute, December 15, 2020 (updated February 3, 2021).

96. Rebecca B. Reingold and Lawrence O. Gostin, "State Abortion Restrictions and the New Supreme Court: Women's Access to Reproductive Health Services," *JAMA* 322, no. 1 (July 2, 2019): 21–22.

97. Elizabeth Nash et al., "State Policy Trends 2019: A Wave of Abortion Bans, but Some States Are Fighting Back," Guttmacher Institute, December 6, 2019.

98. Reingold and Gostin, "State Abortion Restrictions."

99. Hodes & Nauser, MDs, P.A. v. Schmidt (2019).

100. Elizabeth Skerry, "Let HUD Give Survivors of Domestic Violence Fewer Protections from Housing Discrimination? Not in This House!" National Women's Law Center, October 31, 2019.

101. Centers for Disease Control and Prevention, U.S. Department of Health and Human Services, "Preventing Intimate Partner Violence," October 3, 2019.

102. National Domestic Violence Hotline, "Why Do People Stay in Abusive Relationships?"

103. Pennsylvania Coalition Against Rape (PCAR), "Oppression & Sexual Violence," March 1, 2020.

104. Natalie J. Sokoloff and Ida Dupont, "Domestic Violence at the Intersections of Race, Class, and Gender," *Violence Against Women* 11, no. 1 (January 1, 2005): 38–64.

105. National Network to End Domestic Violence, "Immigration Policy."

106. Office for Victims of Crime, U.S. Department of Justice, "Intimate Partner Violence," 2018.

107. Based on data from Sharon G. Smith et al., "The National Intimate Partner and Sexual Violence Survey: 2010–2012 State Report," National Center for Injury Prevention and Control, Centers for Disease Control and Prevention, April 2017.

108. American Psychological Association, "Intimate Partner Violence: Facts and Resources."

109. National Organization for Women, "Intimate Partner Violence: Undocumented and Immigrant Women," June 2017.

110. National Coalition Against Domestic Violence, "Domestic Violence and the LGBTQ Community," June 6, 2018.

111. Corinne Peek-Asa et al., "Rural Disparity in Domestic Violence Prevalence and Access to Resources," *Journal of Women's Health* 20, no. 11 (November 11, 2011): 1743–1749.

112. Rachel L. Snyder, "The Particular Cruelty of Domestic Violence," *The Atlantic*, May 8, 2019.

113. Jennifer A. Bennice and Patricia A. Resick, "Marital Rape: History, Research, and Practice," *Trauma, Violence, & Abuse* 4, no. 3 (July 2003): 228–246.

114. Pauly, "It's 2019, and States Are Still."

115. Rueb and Chokshi, "The Violence Against Women Act."

116. National Women's History Alliance, "Timeline of Legal History of Women in the United States," https://nationalwomenshistoryalliance.org/resources/womens-rights-movement/detailed-timeline.

117. American Bar Association, "Violence Against Women Act Reauthorization Threatened," May 16, 2019.

118. Rueb and Chokshi, "The Violence Against Women Act."

119. Giffords Law Center to Prevent Gun Violence, "Domestic Violence & Firearms," March 6, 2020.

120. Sherly G. Stolberg, "Why the NRA Opposes New Domestic Abuse Legislation," *New York Times*, April 1, 2019.

121. Susan Davis, "House Renews Violence Against Women Act, but Senate Hurdles Remain," NPR, March 17, 2021.

122. David Cantor et al., *Report on the AAU Campus Climate Survey on Sexual Assault and Misconduct*, Association of American Universities, January 17, 2020.

123. Office for Civil Rights, U.S. Department of Education, "Title IX and Sex Discrimination," April 2015.

124. U.S. Congress, House, United States Code, Title 20, section 1092, *Legal Information Institute*, Cornell Law School.

125. United States, Department of Education, Office of Postsecondary Education, Violence Against Women Act, *Federal Register* 79, no. 202 (October 20, 2014): 62751–62790.

126. Know Your IX, "Why Schools Handle Sexual Violence Reports," https://www.knowyourix.org/issues/schools-handle-sexual-violence-reports/#:~:text=Title%20IX%20requires%20schools%20to%20combat%20sex%20discrimination%20in%20education.&text=To%20make%20sure%20that%20all,to%20reports%20of%20sexual%20violence.

127. Center for Public Integrity, "Sexual Assault on Campus: A Frustrating Search for Justice,"

2010, https://cloudfront-files-1.publicintegrity.org/documents/pdfs/Sexual%20Assault%20on%20Campus.pdf.

128. Victoria Yuen and Osub Ahmed, "4 Ways Secretary DeVos' Proposed Title IX Rule Will Fail Survivors of Campus Sexual Assault," Center for American Progress, November 16, 2018.

129. R. Shep Melnick, "Analyzing the Department of Education's Final Title IX Rules on Sexual Misconduct," Brookings Institution, June 11, 2020.

130. Office for Civil Rights, U.S. Department of Education, "Summary of Major Provisions of the Department of Education's Title IX Final Rule."

131. Katie Rogers and Erica Green, "Biden Will Revisit Trump Rules on Campus Sexual Assault," *New York Times*, March 8, 2021.

132. Alice Paul Institute, Equal Rights Amendment, "Frequently Asked Questions."

133. Patrick J. Lyons et al., "Why the Equal Rights Amendment Is Back," *New York Times,* January 15, 2020.

134. Eleanor Mueller and Alice Miranda Ollstein, "How the Debate over the ERA Became a Fight over Abortion," Politico, February 11, 2020.

135. Mueller and Ollstein, "Debate over the ERA," and Lyons et al., "Why the Equal Rights Amendment Is Back."

136. Debbie Elliott, "Alabama, Louisiana, and South Dakota Sue to Block Equal Rights Amendment," NPR, December 19, 2019.

137. Julie G. Brufke, "House Passes Bill Paving Way for ERA Ratification," The Hill, February 13, 2020.

138. "Senate Push for Equal Rights Amendment Won't End Court Fight," Bloomberg Law, January 22, 2021.

139. Meridith McGraw and Adam Kelsey, "Everything You Need to Know About the Women's March," ABC News, January 20, 2017.

140. Anna Watts, "Full Coverage: Harvey Weinstein Is Found Guilty of Rape," *New York Times*, July 14, 2020.

141. Anna North, "The #MeToo Movement and Its Evolution, Explained," Vox, October 9, 2018.

142. Andrea Johnson et al., "2020 Progress Update: MeToo Reforms in the States," National Women's Law Center, September 2020.

6. Living Queer History: The Fight for LGBTQ Rights

Research and drafting contributed by Sam Barrak and Diego Garcia Blum.

1. Language matters when it comes to LGBTQ history and identity, politics and policy, rights, and the like. Though it's beyond the scope of this chapter to trace this complex history, it's worth noting that identity categories related to gender and sexuality have changed dramatically over time. Even the most common modern lexicon and taxonomy—lesbian, gay, bisexual, transgender, and queer—"LGBTQ" or "LGBTQ+"—is hotly debated and contested, both inside the United States and globally. For instance, "queer" itself—embraced far more frequently among younger generations than older ones—means different things to different people, and sometimes "Q" implies "questioning" or "queer and questioning." The category of "transgender" or "trans*" has its own history, including, at different times, people who were referred to (or referred to themselves) as "transsexual," "transvestites," "genderqueer," "non-binary," and other terms of

designation and self-identification. Early gay and lesbian activists referred to their organizations as "homophile," whereas members of the Stonewall generation talked of "gay liberation," "gay power," "women-identified woman," and the like. In the last generation or so, "equality" and "rights"—as opposed to "liberation" and "power"—have gained real currency in the larger LGBTQ movement and community. Debates about whether and how to include "intersex" and "asexual" individuals in "LGBTQ" are still ongoing. As you can imagine, these debates and differences with respect to language and identity have profound implications for rights-based advocacy and policy. That said, we mostly use "LGBTQ" in this chapter.

2. See Margot Canaday, *The Straight State: Sexuality and Citizenship in Twentieth Century America* (Princeton, NJ: Princeton University Press, 2009); John D'Emilio, *Sexual Politics, Sexual Communities: The Making of a Homosexual Minority in the United States, 1940–1970* (Chicago: Chicago University Press, 1998); Eric Cervini, *The Deviant's War: The Homosexual vs. The United States of America* (New York: Farrar, Straus and Giroux, 2020).

3. Timothy P. McCarthy, "Rethinking Progress," TEDx Talk, 2015; see also Timothy P. McCarthy, *Stonewall's Children: Living Queer History in an Age of Liberation, Loss, and Love* (New York: New Press, 2020).

4. See Alfred C. Kinsey, *Sexual Behavior in the Human Male* (St. Louis, MO: Elsevier Health Sciences Division, 1948), and Alfred C. Kinsey et al., *Sexual Behavior in the Human Female* (St. Louis, MO: Elsevier Health Sciences Division, 1953).

5. The NYC-based Quaker Emergency Committee's Readjustment Center, a community center founded in 1945 to provide counseling and legal aid to young people arrested on charges of homosexuality, is widely believed to be the first formal LGBTQ organization in the United States.

6. We may well now be entering a fourth generation, which we refer to as the "Trans* Generation."

7. Lucien Truscott, "Gay Power Comes to Sheridan Square," in *The Stonewall Riots: A Documentary History*, ed. Marc Stein (New York: NYU Press, 2020), 138–143. Note the language of "pride," "power," "liberation" (as opposed to "equality" or "rights") and the emphasis on resistance and rebellion (as opposed to "riot").

8. Timothy P. McCarthy, "Reclaiming Stonewall," *The Nation*, June 25, 2019.

9. Martin Duberman, *Stonewall: The Definitive History of the LGBTQ Rights Uprising That Changed America* (New York: Plume Penguin Random House, 2019).

10. Larry Kramer, "1,112 and Counting," *New York Native*, March 1983. A giant of the movement, Kramer passed away on May 27, 2020, just as we were finishing the draft of this chapter. May he rest in power.

11. When the virus was first reported, medical experts, journalists, and others referred to it as "GRIDS" (Gay-Related Immune Deficiency Syndrome); in 1982, *AIDS* became the official term of designation.

12. For more on HIV/AIDS statistics, see the Centers for Disease Control and Prevention (CDC), "HIV Statistics Overview," www.cdc.gov/hiv/statistics/overview/index.html; "HIV/AIDS: Snapshots of an Epidemic," The Foundation for AIDS Research (amfAR), www.amfar.org/thirty-years-of-hiv/aids-snapshots-of-an-epidemic; "Global HIV & AIDS Statistics—2020 Fact Sheet," UNAIDS, www.unaids.org/en/resources/fact-sheet.

13. Randy Shilts, *And the Band Played On* (New York, 1987).

14. "Jerry Falwell, Polarizing Preacher, Merged Religion, Politics, Dies at 73," *Seattle Times*, May 16, 2007.

15. "ONE Magazine," ONE Archives at the USC Libraries, University of Southern California, January 1, 1970, one.usc.edu/archive-location/one-magazine.

16. Lillian Faderman, *The Gay Revolution: The Story of the Struggle* (New York: Simon & Schuster, 2015), 91–97.

17. American Civil Liberties Union, "History of Sodomy Laws and the Strategy That Led Up to Today's Decision," www.aclu.org/other/history-sodomy-laws-and-strategy-led-todays-decision.

18. Bowers v. Hardwick (1986).

19. Faderman, *The Gay Revolution*, 546; American Civil Liberties Union, "History of Sodomy Laws."

20. Faderman, *The Gay Revolution*, 551.

21. Baker v. Nelson (1971).

22. History, "Gay Marriage," June 9, 2017, www.history.com/topics/gay-rights/gay-marriage.

23. Baeher v. Lewin (1993).

24. Richard Wolf, "Timeline: Same-Sex Marriage Through the Years," *USA Today*, June 26, 2015, www.usatoday.com/story/news/politics/2015/06/24/same-sex-marriage-timeline/29173703.

25. Goodridge v. Department of Public Health (2003).

26. Obergefell v. Hodges (2015).

27. Shannon Minter, "Sodomy and Public Morality Offenses Under U.S. Immigration Law: Penalizing Lesbian and Gay Identity," *Cornell International Law Journal* 26, no. 3 (1993).

28. Janet M. Calvo, "U.S. v. Windsor's Impact on Immigration Law," *CUNY Law Review* 17, no. 19 (September 2013), www.cunylawreview.org/prof-janet-calvo-on-u-s-v-windsors-impact-on-immigration-law.

29. Timothy Stewart-Winter, "Queer Law and Order: Sex, Criminality, and Policing in the Late Twentieth-Century United States," *Journal of American History* 102, no. 1 (June 2015): 61–72, https://doi.org/10.1093/jahist/jav283.

30. George Chauncey, "The Forgotten History of Gay Entrapment," *The Atlantic*, June 26, 2019.

31. German Lopez, "Police Used to Raid Gay Bars. Now They March in Pride & Parades," Vox, June 14, 2017.

32. Federal funding for HIV/AIDS has increased from a few thousand dollars in 1982 to $34.8 billion in 2019 (Kaiser Family Foundation, "U.S. Federal Funding for HIV/AIDS: Trends over Time," March 5, 2019, www.kff.org/hivaids/fact-sheet/u-s-federal-funding-for-hivaids-trends-over-time).

33. Nurith Aizenman, "How to Demand a Medical Breakthrough: Lessons from the AIDS Fight," NPR, February 9, 2019.

34. Ryan White HIV/AIDS Program, U.S. Health Resources and Services Administration, "Ryan White HIV/AIDS Program Legislation," February 2019, https://hab.hrsa.gov/about-ryan-white-hivaids-program/ryan-white-hivaids-program-legislation.

35. Centers for Disease Control and Prevention, "Newly Diagnosed with HIV," February 10, 2020, www.cdc.gov/hiv/basics/livingwithhiv/newly-diagnosed.html.

36. U.S. Department of Health and Human Services, Office of Infectious Disease and HIV/AIDS Policy, "Overview of Ending the HIV Epidemic: A Plan for America," HIV.gov, May 8, 2020, www.hiv.gov/federal-response/ending-the-hiv-epidemic/overview.

37. *The Advocate*, "Biden Seeks $267 Million Increase in HIV Prevention Funds," April 14, 2021.

38. Victory Institute, "Out for America," December 9, 2019, http://outforamerica.org.

39. Faderman, *The Gay Revolution*, 256.

40. Victory Fund, "California 'Harvey Milk Day' Proclamation Gets History Wrong," May 23, 2011, http://victoryfund.org/california-harvey-milk-day-proclamation-gets-history-wrong.

41. Victory Institute, "Presidential Appointments Initiative," http://victoryinstitute.org /programs/presidential-appointments-initiative.

42. Anagha Srikanth, "Trump Names the First Openly Gay Person to a Cabinet-Level Position," The Hill, February 21, 2020, www.thehill.com/changing-america/respect/diversity -inclusion/484026-trump-names-the-first-openly-gay-person-to-a.

43. Human Rights Campaign, "HRC Story: About Us," www.hrc.org/hrc-story.

44. Samantha Schmidt, John Wagner, and Teo Armus, "Biden Selects Transgender Doctor Rachel Levine as Assistant Health Secretary," *Washington Post*, January 19, 2021.

45. Faderman, *The Gay Revolution*, 466–467.

46. Freedom for All Americans, "LGBTQ Americans Aren't Fully Protected from Discrimination in 29 States," www.freedomforallamericans.org/states.

47. Human Rights Campaign, "The Equality Act," www.hrc.org/resources/the-equality-act.

48. U.S. Department of Justice, "The Matthew Shepard and James Byrd, Jr., Hate Crimes Prevention Act of 2009," October 18, 2018, www.justice.gov/crt/matthew-shepard-and-james-byrd -jr-hate-crimes-prevention-act-2009-0.

49. Katharine S. Milar, "The Myth Buster," *Monitor on Psychology* 42, no. 2 (February 2011): 24, www.apa.org/monitor/2011/02/myth-buster; Dani Heffernan, "The APA Removes 'Gender Identity Disorder' from Updated Mental Health Guide," GLAAD, December 3, 2012, www.glaad .org/blog/apa-removes-gender-identity-disorder-updated-mental-health-guide .

50. Movement Advancement Project, "Conversion 'Therapy' Laws," www.lgbtmap.org /equality-maps/conversion_therapy.

51. Jonah E. Bromwich, "How U.S. Military Policy on Transgender Personnel Changed Under Obama," *New York Times*, July 26, 2017, www.nytimes.com/2017/07/26/us/politics/trans -military-trump-timeline.html.

52. Dan De Luce and Shannon Pettypiece, "Biden Admin Scraps Trump's Restrictions on Transgender Troops," NBC News, March 31, 2021.

53. "Calif. Senate Passes Bill to Teach Gay History," CBS News, April 14, 2011.

54. Sarah Schwartz, "Four States Now Require Schools to Teach LGBT History," Education Week, August 12, 2019, http://blogs.edweek.org/teachers/teaching_now/2019/08/four_states _now_require_schools_to_teach_lgbt_history.html.

55. Human Rights Campaign, "The Equality Act," www.hrc.org/resources/the-equality-act.

56. Movement Advancement Project, "Snapshot: LGBTQ Equality by State," www.lgbtmap .org/equality-maps. Note: A state's "policy tally" counts the number of laws and policies within the state that help drive equality for LGBTQ people. The major categories of laws covered by the policy tally include: relationship and parental recognition, nondiscrimination, religious exemptions, LGBTQ youth, health care, criminal justice, and identity documents.

57. Movement Advancement Project, "Conversion 'Therapy' Laws."

58. American Civil Liberties Union, "Weakened ENDA Means Less Protection for Everyone,"

www.aclu.org/other/weakened-enda-means-less-protection-everyone; Liz Meyer, "Human Rights Campaign Responds to ENDA Concerns," *Seattle Gay News*, www.sgn.org/sgnnews35_42/mobile/page3.cfm.

59. The Williams Institute, UCLA School of Law, "LGBT People in the U.S. Not Protected by State Non-Discrimination Statutes," April 2020, https://williamsinstitute.law.ucla.edu/publications/lgbt-nondiscrimination-statutes.

60. Daniel Cox et al., "Majority of Americans Oppose Transgender Bathroom Restrictions," PPRI, March 10, 2017, www.prri.org/research/lgbt-transgender-bathroom-discrimination-religious-liberty/#page-section-1.

61. Lucas Acosta, "1 Year Ago: Trump Opposes the Equality Act," Human Rights Campaign, May 14, 2020, www.hrc.org/blog/1-year-ago-trump-opposes-the-equality-act.

62. Daniella Diaz and Annie Grayer, "House Passes Equality Act Aimed at Ending Discrimination Based on Sexual Orientation and Gender Identity," CNN, March 16, 2021.

63. Alexa Ura, "Bathroom Fears Flush Houston Discrimination Ordinance," *Texas Tribune*, November 3, 2015, www.texastribune.org/2015/11/03/houston-anti-discrimination-ordinance-early-voting.

64. Brian S. Barnett et al., "The Transgender Bathroom Debate at the Intersection of Politics, Law, Ethics, and Science," *Journal of the American Academy of Psychiatry and the Law Online* 46, no. 2 (June 2018): 232–241, https://doi.org/10.29158/JAAPL.003761-18.

65. Ballotpedia, "Massachusetts Question 3, Gender Identity Anti-discrimination Veto Referendum," 2018, https://ballotpedia.org/Massachusetts_Question_3,_Gender_Identity_Anti-Discrimination_Veto_Referendum_(2018).

66. Amira Hasenbush et al., "Gender Identity Nondiscrimination Laws in Public Accommodations: A Review of Evidence Regarding Safety and Privacy in Public Restrooms, Locker Rooms, and Changing Rooms," *Sexuality Research and Social Policy* 16 (March 2019): 70–83, https://doi.org/10.1007/s13178-018-0335-z.

67. Gabriel R. Murchison et al., "School Restroom and Locker Room Restrictions and Sexual Assault Risk Among Transgender Youth," *Pediatrics* 143, no. 6 (June 2019), https://doi.org/10.1542/peds.2018-2902.

68. National Center for Transgender Equality, *The Report of the 2015 U.S. Transgender Survey*, December 2016, https://transequality.org/sites/default/files/docs/usts/USTS-Executive-Summary-Dec17.pdf.

69. Cox et al., "Majority of Americans Oppose."

70. Erwin Chemerinsky, "Not a Masterpiece: The Supreme Court's Decision in Masterpiece Cakeshop v. Colorado Civil Rights Commission," *Human Rights Magazine* 43, no. 4 (October 2018), www.americanbar.org/groups/crsj/publications/human_rights_magazine_home/the-ongoing-challenge-to-define-free-speech/not-a-masterpiece.

71. Cox et al., "Majority of Americans Oppose."

72. Movement Advancement Project, "Discrimination Laws," www.lgbtmap.org/equality-maps/non_discrimination_laws.

73. Pride at Work, "Workplace Discrimination," www.prideatwork.org/issues/workplace-discrimination.

74. U.S. Department of Justice, Office of Public Affairs, "Attorney General Holder Directs Department to Include Gender Identity Under Sex Discrimination Employment Claims," December 18, 2014, www.justice.gov/opa/pr/attorney-general-holder-directs-department-include-gender-identity-under-sex-discrimination.

75. U.S. Department of Justice, Office of the Attorney General. "Memorandum: Revised Treatment of Transgender Employment Discrimination Claims Under Title VII of the Civil Rights Act of 1964," October 4, 2017, www.justice.gov/ag/page/file/1006981/download.

76. Kirsten Berg and Moiz Syed, "Under Trump, LGBTQ Progress Is Being Reversed in Plain Sight," ProPublica, November 22, 2019, https://projects.propublica.org/graphics/lgbtq-rights-rollback.

77. Berg and Syed, "Under Trump, LGBTQ."

78. Centers for Disease Control and Prevention, Youth Risk Behavior Survey (2016).

79. Laura Kann et al., "Sexual Identity, Sex of Sexual Contacts, and Health-Risk Behaviors Among Students in Grades 9–12," *Morbidity and Mortality Weekly Report Surveillance Summaries* 65, no. 9 (2016).

80. The Trevor Project, "Research Brief: Data on Transgender Youth," February 22, 2019, www.thetrevorproject.org/2019/02/22/research-brief-data-on-transgender-youth.

81. Joseph G. Kosciw et al., *The 2017 National School Climate Survey: The Experiences of Lesbian, Gay, Bisexual, Transgender, and Queer Youth in Our Nation's Schools*, GLSEN, 2018, http://live-glsen-website.pantheonsite.io/sites/default/files/2019-10/GLSEN-2017-National-School-Climate-Survey-NSCS-Full-Report.pdf.

82. The Trevor Project, "About Conversion Therapy," www.thetrevorproject.org/get-involved/trevor-advocacy/50-bills-50-states/about-conversion-therapy.

83. The Trevor Project, "Landmark Study Finds 39 Percent of LGBTQ Youth and More Than Half of Transgender and Non-Binary Youth Report Having Seriously Considered Suicide in the Past Twelve Months," June 11, 2019, www.thetrevorproject.org/trvr_press/landmark-study-finds-39-percent-of-lgbtq-youth-and-more-than-half-of-transgender-and-non-binary-youth-report-having-seriously-considered-suicide-in-the-past-twelve-months; Peter Goldblum et al., "The Relationship Between Gender-Based Victimization and Suicide Attempts in Transgender People," *Professional Psychology: Research and Practice* 43, no. 5 (October 2012): 468–475, https://doi.org/10.1037/a0029605; Kosciw et al., *The 2017 National School Climate Survey*.

84. For a map of the current landscape of LGBTQ inclusive curriculum across the United States, see Noble Ingram, "The State of LGBTQ Curriculum: Tide Is Turning as Some States Opt for Inclusion, Others Lift Outright Restrictions," The 74, June 11, 2019, www.the74million.org/the-state-of-lgbtq-curriculum-tide-is-turning-as-some-states-opt-for-inclusion-others-lift-outright-restrictions.

85. Movement Advancement Project, "Conversion 'Therapy' Laws"; National Center for Transgender Equality, "FAQ on the Withdrawal of Federal Guidance on Transgender Students," February 21, 2017, https://transequality.org/issues/resources/faq-on-the-withdrawal-of-federal-guidance-on-transgender-students.

86. Cory Turner and Anya Kamenetz, "The Education Department Says It Won't Act On Transgender Student Bathroom Access," NPR, February 12, 2018.

87. Timothy C.J. Blanchard, "Letter to Attorneys Mizerak, Monastersky, Murphy, Yoder, and Zelman," United States Department of Education, May 15, 2020, www.adfmedia.org/files/SouleDOEImpendingEnforcementLetter.pdf.

88. Christine Fernando, "'It Gave Us Hope': Biden Tells Transgender Youth He's on Their Side. Advocates Say That's Huge for the Community," *USA Today*, April 29, 2021.

89. Molly Sprayregen, "226 Bills Target LGBTQ Americans This Year. One Organization Is

Behind a Lot of Them," LGBTQ Nation, February 18, 2020, www.lgbtqnation.com/2020/02/226
-bills-target-lgbtq-americans-year-one-organization-behind-lot.

90. Tim Fitzsimons, "Puberty Blockers Linked to Lower Suicide Risk for Transgender People,"
NBC News, January 24, 2020, www.nbcnews.com/feature/nbc-out/puberty-blockers-linked
-lower-suicide-risk-transgender-people-n1122101

91. Jo Yurcaba, "'State of Crisis': Advocates Warn of 'Unprecedented' Wave of Anti-LGBTQ
Bills," NBC News, April 25, 2021.

92. National LGBT Health Education, "Providing Inclusive Services and Care for LGBT
People," www.lgbthealtheducation.org/wp-content/uploads/Providing-Inclusive-Services-and
-Care-for-LGBT-People.pdf

93. Ryan Thoreson, "You Don't Want Second Best," Human Rights Campaign, July 23, 2018,
www.hrw.org/report/2018/07/23/you-dont-want-second-best/anti-lgbt-discrimination-us
-health-care.

94. U.S. Centers for Medicare and Medicaid Services, Office of the Secretary, "Proposed Rule:
Nondiscrimination in Health and Health Education Programs or Activities," *Federal Register*,
June 14, 2019, www.federalregister.gov/documents/2019/06/14/2019-11512/nondiscrimination
-in-health-and-health-education-programs-or-activities.

95. Tim Fitzsimons, "Nearly 1 in 5 Hate Crimes Motivated by Anti-LGBTQ Bias, FBI Finds,"
NBC News, November 12, 2019.

96. LGBT Bar, "Gay and Trans Panic Defenses Resolution," February 2014, https://lgbtbar.org
/wp-content/uploads/2014/02/Gay-and-Trans-Panic-Defenses-Resolution.pdf.

97. Movement Advancement Project, "Panic Defense Bans," www.lgbtmap.org/equality-maps
/panic_defense_bans.

98. Lambda Legal, Transgender Rights Toolkit, "Transgender Incarcerated People in Crisis,"
www.lambdalegal.org/sites/default/files/transgender_booklet_-_incarcerated.pdf.

99. Sadie Dingfelder, "Psychologist Testifies on the Risks of Solitary Confinement," *Monitor in
Psychology* 43, no. 9 (October 2012), www.apa.org/monitor/2012/10/solitary

100. Annette Brömdal et al., "Whole-Incarceration-Setting Approaches to Supporting and
Upholding the Rights and Health of Incarcerated Transgender People," *International Journal of
Transgenderism* 20, no. 4 (2019): 341–350, DOI: 10.1080/15532739.2019.1651684.

101. U.S. Department of Justice, Federal Bureau of Prisons, "Transgender Offender Manual,"
May 11, 2018, www.bop.gov/policy/progstat/5200-04-cn-1.pdf.

102. Human Rights Campaign, "The Crisis at the Border Is an LGBTQ Issue. Here's Why,"
November 30, 2018, www.hrc.org/blog/the-crisis-at-the-border-is-an-lgbtq-issue-heres-why;
Brooke Sopelsa, "Trump's Immigration Restrictions Could Be LGBTQ 'Death Sentence,'" NBC
News, January 30, 2017.

103. Movement Advancement Project, "Data Collection," www.lgbtmap.org/equality-maps
/data_collection.

104. National LGBTQ Task Force, "Why Data Collection Matters to LGBT People," www
.thetaskforce.org/why-data-collection-matters-to-lgbt-people.

105. Movement Advancement Project, "Identity Document Laws and Policies," www.lgbtmap
.org/equality-maps/identity_document_laws/name_change.

106. Michaé Pulido and Arli Christian, "Who's the Expert on My Gender? The Importance of
Self-Attestation," National Center for Transgender Equality, March 16, 2018, https://medium

.com/transequalitynow/whos-the-expert-on-my-gender-the-importance-of-self-attestation
-d03ab60a4a37.

107. Hansi Lo Wang, "Census Bureau Caught in Political Mess over LGBT Data," NPR, July 18, 2017.

108. Berg and Syed, "Under Trump, LGBTQ."

7. Rights of Individuals with Disabilities
Research and drafting contributed by Katie Stenclik.

1. U.S. Department of Health & Human Services, Centers for Disease Control and Prevention, "Disability Impacts All of U.S.," September 9, 2019.

2. Lewis Kraus et al., "2017 Disability Statistics Annual Report," Institute on Disability, University of New Hampshire, January 2018.

3. Ani B. Satz, "Disability, Vulnerability, and the Limits of Antidiscrimination," *Washington Law Review* 83, no. 513 (2008), https://digitalcommons.law.uw.edu/wlr/vol83/iss4/6.

4. Ani B. Satz, "Overcoming Fragmentation in Disability and Health Law," *Emory Law Journal* 68, no. 277 (2010), https://scholarlycommons.law.emory.edu/elj/vol60/iss2/2.

5. *Wharton Business Daily*, "The ADA at 25: Important Gains, but Gaps Remain," August 7, 2015.

6. Kristen Bialik, "7 Facts About Americans with Disabilities," Pew Research Center, July 27, 2017; see also Kraus et al., "2017 Disability Statistics Annual Report."

7. Andy Jones, "Biden Administration Undoes Key Trump Regulations Affecting People with Disabilities," Special Needs Answers, February 17, 2021, https://specialneedsanswers.com/biden -administration-undoes-key-trump-regulations-affecting-people-with-disabilities-18163.

8. Sarah Kim, "As Someone with a Disability, Biden's Inclusion of 'Disability' in His Victory Speech Was Monumental," *Business Insider*, November 16, 2020.

9. Biden-Harris Campaign, "The Biden Plan for Full Participation and Equality for People with Disabilities."

10. ADA National Network, "What Is the Definition of Disability Under the ADA?" https:// adata.org/faq/what-definition-disability-under-ada.

11. Society for Human Resource Management, "Does the Americans with Disabilities Act (ADA) Provide a List of Conditions That Are Covered Under the Act?" November 5, 2019.

12. ADA National Network, "What Does a 'Record of' a Disability Mean?" https://adata.org /faq/what-does-record-disability-mean.

13. Risa M. Mish, "'Regarded as Disabled' Claims Under the ADA: Safety Net or Catch-All?" *University of Pennsylvania Journal of Labor and Employment Law* 1, no. 1 (1998): 159–175.

14. Robert L. Burgdorf Jr., "Why I Wrote the Americans with Disabilities Act," *Washington Post*, July 24, 2015.

15. Legal Information Institute, Cornell Law School, "Buck v. Bell, Superintendent of State Colony Epileptics and Feeble Minded," https://www.law.cornell.edu/supremecourt/text/274/200.

16. Anti-Defamation League, "A Brief History of the Disability Rights Movement," 2018.

17. U.S. Department of Justice, "A Guide to Disability Rights Laws," February 2018.

18. David Pettinicchio, "Why Disabled Americans Remain Second-Class Citizens," *Washington Post*, July 23, 2019.

19. U.S. Department of Justice, "Civil Rights of Institutionalized Persons," August 6, 2015.

20. ADA National Network, "What Is the Americans with Disabilities Act (ADA)?" https://adata.org/learn-about-ada.

21. Burgdorf Jr., "Why I Wrote the ADA."

22. Nancy Lee Jones, "The Americans with Disabilities Act: Supreme Court Decisions," Congressional Research Service, October 14, 2008.

23. Olmstead v. L.C., 527 U.S. 581 (1999).

24. Olmstead Rights, "*Olmstead v. L.C.*: History and Current Status."

25. Georgetown Law Library, "A Brief History of Civil Rights in the United States: ADA Amendments Act of 2008," https://guides.ll.georgetown.edu/c.php?g=592919&p=4230126.

26. George Washington Graduate School of Education & Human Development, "ADA Amendments Passed and Has Become Law," May 26, 2021.

27. Lawrence P. Postol, "Temporary Disabilities—No Need to Worry About the ADA, Right? Think Again," *Employment Law Lookout*, February 6, 2014, https://www.laborandemploymentlawcounsel.com/2014/02/temporary-disabilities-no-need-to-worry-about-the-ada-right-think-again/.

28. Summers v. Altarum Institute, Corp. (2014).

29. Rosalind S. Helderman, "Senate Rejects Treaty to Protect Disabled Around the World," *Washington Post*, December 4, 2012.

30. Glenn Kessler, "Donald Trump's Revisionist History of Mocking a Disabled Reporter," *Washington Post*, August 2, 2016.

31. Jaime Ducharme, "The Paralympics Fire Back After Trump Calls Them 'Tough to Watch,'" *Time*, April 28, 2018.

32. David Nakamura and John Wagner, "Trump Mocks 16-Year-Old Greta Thunberg a Day After She Is Named Time's Person of the Year," *Washington Post*, December 12, 2019.

33. National Disability Navigator Resource Collaborative, "CHRIL Article Examines Health Care Coverage and Costs for People with Disabilities," January 11, 2018.

34. World Health Organization, "Disability and Health," December 1, 2020.

35. Elizabeth Pendo and Lisa Iezzoni, "The Role of Law and Policy in Achieving Healthy People's Disability and Health Goals," Saint Louis U. Legal Studies Research Paper No. 2020-11, https://ssrn.com/abstract=3614800

36. National Council on Disability, *The Impact of the Affordable Care Act on People with Disabilities: A 2015 Status Report* (Washington, DC: National Council on Disability, 2016), 9.

37. Margot Sanger-Katz, "G.O.P. Health Plan Is Really a Rollback of Medicaid," *New York Times*, June 21, 2017; Abigail Abrams, "'Our Lives Are at Stake:' How Donald Trump Inadvertently Sparked a New Disability Rights Movement," *Time*, February 26, 2018.

38. Erica Reaves and MaryBeth Musumeci, "Medicaid and Long-Term Services and Supports: A Primer," Kaiser Family Foundation, December 15, 2015.

39. Reaves and Musumeci, "Medicaid and Long-Term Services and Supports."

40. Kaiser Family Foundation, "A Guide to the Supreme Court's Decision on the ACA's Medicaid Expansion," August 2012.

41. Kaiser Family Foundation, "Status of State Medicaid Expansion Decisions: Interactive Map," October 1, 2012.

42. Kaiser Family Foundation, "Medicaid Financial Eligibility for Seniors and People with Disabilities: Findings from a 50-State Survey," June 14, 2019.

43. Center on Budget and Policy Priorities, "Taking Away Medicaid for Not Meeting Work Requirements Harms People with Disabilities," March 10, 2020.

44. In other words, anyone who has a disability and does not receive SSI or SSDI would likely need to adhere to the new work requirements, should their state implement them; see Robyn Powell, "Despite Republican Claims, Medicaid Work Requirements Would Hurt People with Disabilities," Rewire News Group, January 12, 2018.

45. Powell, "Despite Republican Claims."

46. Center on Budget and Policy Priorities, "Taking Away Medicaid."

47. Rachel Roubein, "Biden Administration Begins Throwing Out Medicaid Work Rules," Politico, March 17, 2021.

48. Chelsea Cirruzzo, "Long COVID Sufferers Are Seeking Disability Benefits. Will They Change the System?" U.S. News & World Report, April 15, 2021.

49. Trenton Straube, "$90K Settlement in HIV Discrimination Case Against Sheriff's Office," POZ, April 23, 2020.

50. "Sheriff Sued for HIV Discrimination," POZ, October 25, 2017.

51. Nico Lang, "Ex-Cop Gets $90,000 Settlement in HIV Employment Discrimination Suit," NBC News, April 24, 2020.

52. U.S. Department of Justice, Information and Technical Assistance on the Americans with Disabilities Act, Employment (Title I), https://www.ada.gov/ta-pubs-pg2.htm.

53. Institute on Disability, University of New Hampshire, "2019 Annual Report on People with Disabilities in America," 2020.

54. U.S. Bureau of Labor Statistics, "Persons with a Disability: Labor Force Characteristics —2019," February 26, 2020,

55. Aimee Picchi, "Americans with Disabilities Still Can't Land Jobs," CBS News, July 26, 2017.

56. Geri Stengel, "Working from Home Opens the Door to Employing People with Disabilities," Forbes, April 20, 2020.

57. U.S. Equal Employment Opportunity Commission, "Work at Home/Telework as a Reasonable Accommodation," www.eeoc.gov/laws/guidance/work-hometelework-reasonable-accommodation.

58. Rakesh Kochhar and Jeffrey S. Passel, "Telework May Save U.S. Jobs in COVID-19 Downturn, Especially Among College Graduates," Pew Research Center, May 6, 2020.

59. Katherine Guyot and Isabel V. Sawhill, "Telecommuting Will Likely Continue Long After the Pandemic," Up Front, Brookings Institution, April 6, 2020.

60. Monica Anderson and Andrew Perrin, "Disabled Americans Are Less Likely to Use Technology," Fact Tank, Pew Research Center, April 7, 2017.

61. Maryland Department of Budget and Management, "Maryland State Government Employment and Job Seekers with Disabilities."

62. Caroline Cournoyer, "How States Are Helping People with Disabilities Break into Government Jobs," Governing, June 7, 2018.

63. U.S. Department of Education, "Thirty-Five Years of Progress in Educating Children

with Disabilities Through IDEA," November 2010, https://www2.ed.gov/about/offices/list/osers/idea35/history/idea-35-history.pdf.

64. U.S. Department of Justice, "A Guide to Disability Rights Laws," February 2020. https://www.ada.gov/cguide.htm.

65. GovTrack, "S6 (94th): Education for All Handicapped Children Act," May 21, 2019, https://www.govtrack.us/congress/bills/94/s6/summary.

66. U.S. Department of Education, "About IDEA."

67. U.S. Department of Education, "Individuals with Disabilities Education Act: Statute and Regulations."

68. Emin Gharibian, "Individualized Education Plans (IEP) vs. 504 Plans: What's the Difference Between Them?" *Verdugo Psychological Associates*.

69. U.S. Department of Education, "Sec. 300.320 Definition of Individualized Education Program," July 12, 2017.

70. U.S. Department of Education, "Protecting Students with Disabilities."

71. Kyrie E. Dragoo, "The Individuals with Disabilities Education Act (IDEA) Funding: A Primer," Congressional Research Service, August 29, 2019.

72. Margaret M. Wakelin, "Challenging Disparities in Special Education: Moving Parents from Disempowered Team Members to Ardent Advocates," *Northwestern Journal of Law & Social Policy* 3, no. 2 (2008).

73. National Center for Education Statistics, "Students with Disabilities," May 2021.

74. Disability Rights Education and Defense Fund, "School-to-Prison Pipeline."

75. Institute on Disability, "2019 Annual Report."

76. U.S. Department of Education, "Improving Regulation and Regulatory Reform," October 5, 2017.

77. Vijay Das, "Trump Is Waging a War on People with Disabilities," Al Jazeera, November 3, 2018.

78. Moriah Balingit, "DeVos Rescinds 72 Guidance Documents Outlining Rights for Disabled Students," *Washington Post*, October 21, 2017.

79. Kenny Fries, "How We Can Make the World a Better Place for Immigrants with Disabilities," *Quartz*, April 19, 2019.

80. U.S. Citizenship and Immigration Services, "Public Charge," https://www.uscis.gov/green-card/green-card-processes-and-procedures/public-charge; and National Conference of State Legislatures, "Immigration and Public Charge," November 6, 2020.

81. Kaiser Family Foundation, "Changes to 'Public Charge' Inadmissibility Rule: Implications for Health and Health Coverage," August 12, 2019.

82. Disability Rights Education and Defense Fund, "How Trump's Public Charge Changes Hurt People with Disabilities," August 14, 2019.

83. Cara Schulte, "Trump Administration to Deport Sick Children, People with Disabilities," Human Rights Watch, August 30, 2019.

84. Jeff Gammage and Jesenia De Moya Correa, "Immigrant Families with Severely Ill or Disabled Children Now Face Deportation by Trump Administration," *Philadelphia Inquirer*, September 13, 2019.

85. Schulte, "Trump Administration to Deport."

86. Gammage and De Moya Correa, "Immigrant Families."

87. Camilo Montoya-Galvez, "Administration Reinstates Protections from Deportation for Sick Immigrants After Massive Uproar," CBS News, September 20, 2019.

88. Office of Equal Opportunity and Inclusion, U.S. Citizenship and Immigration Services, "Access and Accommodations for Individuals with Disabilities: Plan for Improving Access to USCIS Public-Facing Programs and Activities," October 2018.

89. Statista, "Poverty Rate Among People with and Without Disabilities in the U.S. from 2008 to 2019," www.statista.com/statistics/979003/disability-poverty-rate-us/#:~:text=According%20 to%20the%20data%2C%20in,disabilities%20were%20living%20in%20poverty.

90. Loren Berlin, "Using Housing to Fight Discrimination Against People with Disabilities," Next50, Urban Institute, April 24, 2019.

91. American Association of People with Disabilities and The Leadership Conference Education Fund, "Equity in Transportation for People with Disabilities."

92. National Aging and Disability Transportation Center, "New National Poll: Inability to Drive, Lack of Transportation Options Are Major Concerns for Older Adults, People with Disabilities and Caregivers," December 7, 2018.

93. U.S. Social Security Administration, "Benefits for People with Disabilities."

94. Elaine Waxman and Nathan Joo, "How Households with Seniors and Adults with Disabilities Are Affected by Restricting Broad-Based Categorical Eligibility for SNAP," Urban Institute, September 2019, www.urban.org/sites/default/files/publication/101028/how_house holds_with_seniors_and_adults_with_disabilities_are_affected_by_restricting_broad -based_categorical_eligibility_for_snap_0.pdf.

95. Steven Carlson et al., "SNAP Provides Needed Food Assistance to Millions of People with Disabilities," Center on Budget and Policy Priorities, June 14, 2017.

96. Michael H. Schill and Samantha Friedman, "The Fair Housing Amendments Act of 1988: The First Decade," *Cityscape: A Journal of Policy Development and Research* 4, no. 3 (1999): 57–78; Joy Hammel et al., "Rental Housing Access & Discrimination Experienced by People with Multiple Disabilities: Study of Rental Housing Discrimination on the Basis of Mental Disabilities," U.S. Department of Housing and Urban Development, August 2017.

97. Benefits.gov, "Section 811 Supportive Housing for Persons with Disabilities," https://www .benefits.gov/benefit/5892.

98. American Association of People with Disabilities and the Leadership Conference Education Fund, "Equity in Transportation for People with Disabilities."

99. Pettinicchio, "Why Disabled Americans Remain."

100. Ruth Igielnik, "A Political Profile of Disabled Americans," Pew Research Center, September 22, 2016.

101. American Association of People with Disabilities, "Statistics & Data."

102. Lisa Schur et al., "Disability, Voter Turnout, and Voting Difficulties in the 2012 Elections," Research Alliance for Accessible Voting, July 18, 2013.

103. Rutgers School of Management and Labor Relations, "Report: Voter Turnout Surges Among People with Disabilities," July 10, 2019.

104. Rutgers School of Management and Labor Relations, "New Data: 17.7 Million Americans with Disabilities Voted in 2020, a Significant Increase over 2016," July 7, 2021.

105. Government Accountability Office, "Voters with Disabilities: Observations on Polling Place Accessibility and Related Federal Guidance," October 2017.

106. Rutgers, "Report: Voter Turnout Surges."

107. Government Accountability Office, "Voters with Disabilities."

108. U.S. Department of Justice, "The Americans with Disabilities Act and Other Federal Laws Protecting the Rights of Voters with Disabilities," September 2014.

109. Legal Information Institute, Cornell Law School, "Voting Rights Act, 52 U.S. Code § 10508. Voting Assistance for Blind, Disabled or Illiterate Persons," December 10, 2020.

110. United States Congress, House, HR 5762, Voting Accessibility for the Elderly and Handicapped Act, June 20, 1984.

111. U.S. Department of Justice, "The Americans with Disabilities Act."

112. Help America Vote Act of 2002, Pub. L. 107-252.

113. Government Accountability Office, "Voters with Disabilities."

114. National Conference of State Legislatures, "Voter Identification Requirements: Voter ID Laws," August 25, 2020.

115. Sarah R. Kamens et al., "Voting Rights for Persons with Serious Mental Illnesses in the U.S," *Psychiatric Rehabilitation Journal* 42, no. 2 (2019): 197–200.

116. Abrams, "Our Lives Are at Stake."

117. Matt Cohen, "Report: More Than 1600 Polling Places Have Closed Since the Supreme Court Gutted the Voting Rights Act," *Mother Jones*, September 10, 2019.

8. Economic Inequality and the Freedom from Want

Research and drafting contributed by Daniel Estupinan and Ben Rutledge.

1. Franklin D. Roosevelt, "Acceptance Speech for the Re-nomination for the Presidency," Philadelphia, Pennsylvania, June 27, 1936.

2. Franklin D. Roosevelt, "State of the Union," Washington, DC, January 6, 1941.

3. Dwight D. Eisenhower, "Remarks to the United Negro College Fund," Washington, DC, May 19, 1953.

4. See Danielle S. Allen, *Our Declaration: A Reading of the Declaration of Independence in Defense of Equality* (New York: Liveright, 2014), 107.

5. See Eric Foner, *The Second Founding: How the Civil War and Reconstruction Remade the Constitution* (New York: W.W. Norton & Company, 2019).

6. Daron Acemoglu and James A. Robinson, *The Narrow Corridor: States, Societies, and the Fate of Liberty* (New York: Penguin Press, 2019).

7. Franklin D. Roosevelt, "Fireside Chat 28: On the State of the Union," Washington, DC, January 11, 1944.

8. UN General Assembly, "Universal Declaration of Human Rights," December 10, 1948.

9. See generally Amartya Sen, *Development as Freedom* (New York: Anchor Books, 1999).

10. Monica Hake et al., "The Impact of the Coronavirus on Local Food Insecurity," Feeding America, May 19, 2020.

11. See Amartya Sen, "The Ends and Means of Sustainability," *Journal of Human Development and Capabilities* 14, no. 1 (February 1, 2013): 6–20.

12. Roosevelt, "Fireside Chat 28."

13. Kathleen S. Swendiman, *Health Care: Constitutional Rights and Legislative Powers*, Congressional Research Service, April 5, 2010.

14. Aaron van Dorn et al., "COVID-19 Exacerbating Inequalities in the U.S.," *The Lancet* 395, no. 10232, April 18, 2020.

15. Sarah Kliff, "Under Trump, the Number of Uninsured Americans Has Gone Up by 7 Million," Vox, January 23, 2019.

16. U.S. Centers for Medicare and Medicaid Services, "National Health Expenditure Data: Historical," https://www.cms.gov/Research-Statistics-Data-and-Systems/Statistics-Trends-and -Reports/NationalHealthExpendData/NationalHealthAccountsHistorical.

17. Jonathan Gruber, "Program Report: Health Care," *NBER The Reporter*, no. 4, December 2019.

18. Theda Skocpol, "The Rise and Resounding Demise of the Clinton Plan," *Health Affairs* 14, no. 1 (1995).

19. Margot Sanger-Katz and Quoctrung Bui, "The Impact of Obamacare, in Four Maps," *New York Times*, October 31, 2016; Steve Benen, "U.S. Uninsured Rate Climbs in First Two Years of Trump's Presidency," MSNBC, January 23, 2019.

20. See "Top 7 Fiscal Charts from 2016," Peter G. Peterson Foundation, December 23, 2016.

21. Uptin Saiidi, "U.S. Life Expectancy Has Been Declining. Here's Why," CNBC, July 9, 2019.

22. Centers for Disease Control and Prevention, "Health Equity Considerations and Racial and Ethnic Minority Groups," 2020.

23. Samantha Artiga and Kendal Orgera, "Key Facts on Health and Health Care by Race and Ethnicity," KFF, November 12, 2019.

24. Centers for Disease Control and Prevention, "Health Equity Considerations."

25. Aviva Aron-Dine and Matt Broaddus, "Latest Republican ACA Repeal Plan Would Have Similar Harmful Impacts on Coverage and Health as All the Others," Center on Budget and Policy Priorities, June 20, 2018.

26. Kimberly Amadeo, "Donald Trump's Health Care Policies," The Balance, December 20, 2019.

27. Matthew Fielder, "How Did the ACA's Individual Mandate Affect Insurance Coverage?" USC-Brookings Schaeffer Initiative for Health Policy, May 2018.

28. Amadeo, "Donald Trump's Health Care Policies."

29. Kliff, "Under Trump, the Number of Uninsured Americans."

30. Thomas Jefferson, Letter to Charles Yancey, January 6, 1816, Jefferson Papers, Founders Online, National Archives.

31. Northwest Ordinance, Art. III, July 13, 1787, The Avalon Project, Yale Law School Library.

32. Brown v. Board of Education of Topeka, 347 U.S. 483 (1954).

33. Brown v. Board of Education of Topeka.

34. Roslin Growe and Paula S. Montgomery, "Educational Equity in America: Is Education the Great Equalizer?" *The Professional Educator* 25, no. 2 (2003): 23–29.

35. Kriston Mcintosh et al., "Examining the Black-White Wealth Gap," Brookings Institution, February 27, 2020.

36. See Cory Turner et al., "Why America's Schools Have a Money Problem," NPR, April 18, 2016.

37. Edward Graham, "A Nation at Risk Turns 30: Where Did It Take Us?" *NEA Today*, April 25, 2013.

38. Thomas S. Dee et al., "The Impact of No Child Left Behind on Students, Teachers, and Schools," *Brookings Papers on Economic Activity* (2010): 149–207.

39. National Center for Education Statistics, "High School Graduation Rates."

40. See Jonathan Rabinovitz, "Local Education Inequities Across U.S. Revealed in New Stanford Data," Stanford Graduate School of Education, April 29, 2016.

41. James P. Steyer, "COVID-19 Is a Wake-Up Call to Close the Digital Divide," The Hill, April 16, 2020.

42. Franklin D. Roosevelt, "Second Inaugural Address," Washington, DC, January 20, 1937.

43. U.S. Department of Housing and Urban Development, "The Federal Housing Administration (FHA)."

44. Raquel Rolnik, "Report of the Special Rapporteur on Adequate Housing as a Component of the Right to an Adequate Standard of Living, and on the Right to Non-discrimination in This Context, Addendum 4," UN Human Rights Council, 2010.

45. Khristopher J. Brooks, "Redlining's Legacy: Maps Are Gone, but the Problem Hasn't Disappeared," CBS News, June 12, 2020.

46. Tristia Bauman et al., "Housing Not Handcuffs 2019: Ending the Criminalization of Homelessness in U.S. Cities," National Law Center on Homelessness & Poverty, December 2019.

47. See Danyelle Solomon et al., "Systemic Inequality: Displacement, Exclusion, and Segregation," Center for American Progress, August 7, 2019; Richard Rothstein, *The Color of Law: A Forgotten History of How Our Government Segregated America* (New York: Liveright, 2017); Kimberly Quick and Richard D. Kahlenberg, "Attacking the Black–White Opportunity Gap That Comes from Residential Segregation," The Century Foundation, June 25, 2019; Neil J. Smelser et al., "Residential Segregation and Neighborhood Conditions in U.S. Metropolitan Areas," in *America Becoming: Racial Trends and Their Consequences* (Washington, DC: National Academies Press, 2001).

48. "The Housing Crisis Is Worse than You Think," *In These Times*, July 23, 2019.

49. Samuel Stebbins, "Poverty Level: These Are the Cities in Each State Hit the Hardest by Extreme Poverty," *USA Today*, December 2, 2020.

50. National Low Income Housing Coalition, "The Gap, A Shortage of New Homes," March 2019.

51. "NLIHC Releases 'Out of Reach 2019': National Housing Wage Is Nearly $23 Per Hour for a Modest Two-Bedroom Rental," National Low Income Housing Coalition, June 24, 2019.

52. National Low Income Housing Coalition, "The Gap."

53. Douglas Rice, "Chart Book: Cuts in Federal Assistance Have Exacerbated Families' Struggles to Afford Housing," Center on Budget and Policy Priorities, April 12, 2016.

54. Sarah Holder, "Minimum Wage Still Can't Pay for a Two-Bedroom Apartment Anywhere," Bloomberg CityLab, June 19, 2019.

55. National Low Income Housing Coalition, "The Gap."

56. National Alliance to End Homelessness, "State of Homelessness: 2020 Edition."

57. Connecticut Coalition to End Homelessness, "Methods for Creating a Racially Equitable System."

58. Theodore Roosevelt, "Seventh Annual Message to the Senate and House of Representatives," The American Presidency Project, December 3, 1907.

59. United States Congress, "The National Environmental Policy Act of 1969."

60. United States, Congress, House, United States Code, Title 42, section 4331, Legal Information Institute, Cornell University Law School.

61. Paul Krugman, "Trumpism Is Bad for Business," *New York Times*, September 5, 2019.

62. U.S. Environmental Protection Agency, "EPA History."

63. Laignee Barron, "Here's What the EPA's Website Looks like After a Year of Climate Change Censorship," *Time*, March 1, 2018.

64. Arthur Nelson, "Donald Trump Taking Steps to Abolish Environmental Protection Agency," *The Guardian*, February 1, 2017.

65. Miranda Green, "Trump Proposes Slashing EPA Budget by 31 Percent," The Hill, March 11, 2019.

66. Nadja Popovich et al., "The Trump Administration Rolled Back More Than 100 Environmental Rules. Here's the Full List," *New York Times*, January 20, 2021.

67. American Lung Association, "Disparities in the Impact of Air Pollution."

68. Niv Elis, "U.S. Debt Surpasses $23 Trillion for First Time," The Hill, November 1, 2019.

69. "Briefing Book: How Did the Tax Cuts and Jobs Act Change Personal Taxes?" Tax Policy Center, Urban Institute and Brookings Institution.

70. "Briefing Book: How Did the TCJA Affect the Federal Budget Outlook?" Tax Policy Center, Urban Institute and Brookings Institution.

71. William G. Gale and Aaron Krupkin, "How Big Is the Problem of Tax Evasion?" Brookings Institution, April 9, 2019.

72. Aaron Lorenzo, "IRS Chief Says Some $1 Trillion in Taxes Going Uncollected Annually," Politico, April 13, 2021.

73. See Justin Fox, "Critics of Stock Buybacks Will Outlast Coronavirus," *Bloomberg*, April 1, 2020; Michael Sainato, "Retail Workers at Amazon and Whole Foods Coordinate Sick-Out to Protest Covid-19 Conditions," *The Guardian*, May 1, 2020.

74. Peter Whoriskey, "U.S. Companies Cut Thousands of Workers While Continuing to Reward Shareholders During Pandemic," *Washington Post*, May 5, 2020.

75. Drew Desilver, "As Coronavirus Spreads, Which U.S. Workers Have Paid Sick Leave—and Which Don't," Pew Research Center, March 12, 2020.

76. Gabriel Zucman, "Taxing Multinational Corporations in the 21st Century," Economics for Inclusive Prosperity, February 2019.

77. On Boeing's "shareholder-first culture," see Dan Catchpole, "Boeing's Long Descent," *Fortune*, February 2020; see also "Why Boeing's Shares Have Not Fallen Further After the 737 Max Crashes," *The Economist*, April 7, 2019.

78. David Kiron et al., "The Innovation Bottom Line," *MIT Sloan Management Review* 54, no. 3 (2013).

79. Matthew Desmond, "Americans Want to Believe Jobs Are the Solution to Poverty. They're Not," *New York Times*, September 11, 2018.

80. U.S. Bureau of Labor Statistics, "BLS Reports: A Profile of the Working Poor, 2016," July 2018.

81. The working poor are defined by the U.S. Census Bureau as people who spent at least twenty-seven weeks in the labor force (that is, working or looking for work) but whose incomes still fell below the poverty level.

82. Silvia Amaro, "OECD Backs Biden's Plan to Raise the Minimum Wage," CNBC, April 16, 2021.

83. Oxfam America, "Few Rewards," 2019.

84. Emmanuel Saez and Gabriel Zucman, "Wealth Inequality in the United States Since 1913: Evidence from Capitalized Income Tax Data," *Quarterly Journal of Economics* 131, no. 2 (May 2016): 519–578.

85. Anton Korinek, "Labor in the Age of Automation and Artificial Intelligence," Economics for Inclusive Prosperity, February 2019.

86. AFL-CIO, "AFL-CIO Commission on the Future of Work and Unions," September 13, 2019.

87. Eli Rosenberg, "Workers Are Fired Up. But Union Participation Is Still on the Decline, New Statistics Show," *Washington Post*, January 23, 2020.

88. U.S. Bureau of Labor Statistics, "Union Members Summary," Economics News Release, January 22, 2020.

89. Atul Gawande, "Why Americans Are Dying from Despair," *New Yorker*, March 16, 2020.

90. In *Industrializing English Law,* Ron Harris notes that the turnpike trusts and river improvement corporations of early eighteenth-century England were considered to be "branches of local government." See Ron Harris, *Industrializing English Law: Entrepreneurship and Business Organization, 1720–1844* (Cambridge, UK: Cambridge University Press, 2000), 171.

91. William T. Allen, "Our Schizophrenic Conception of the Business Corporation," *Cardozo Law Review* 14, no. 2 (2012): 271.

92. Milton Friedman, "The Social Responsibility of Business Is to Increase Its Profits," *New York Times Magazine*, September 13, 1970.

93. David Hauck et al., "Two Decades of Debate: The Controversy over U.S. Companies in South Africa," Investor Responsibility Research Center, 1983.

94. Robert E. Edgar, *Sanctioning Apartheid* (Trenton, NJ: Africa World Press, 1990).

95. Danny Hakim, "On Wall St., More Investors Push Social Goals," *New York Times,* February 11, 2001.

96. "Statement on the Purpose of a Corporation," Business Roundtable, 2019.

97. U.S. Security and Exchange Commission, "Recommendations of the Investor Advisory Committee—Human Capital Management Disclosure," March 28, 2019; the committee stated that "[a]s the U.S. transitions from being an economy based almost entirely on industrial production to one that is becoming increasingly based on technology and service, it becomes more and more relevant for our corporate disclosure system to evolve and include disclosure regarding intangible assets, such as intellectual property and human capital [employees]."

98. Colin Mayer, *Prosperity: Better Business Makes the Greater Good* (Oxford: Oxford University Press, 2019), 227.

99. Milton Friedman, *Capitalism and Freedom* (Chicago: University of Chicago Press, 1962).

Part III: Due Process of Law

9. Giving Justice Its Due
Research and drafting contributed by Rahaf Safi.

1. Jacob Kang-Brown and Jasmine Heiss, "People in Jail and Prison in 2020," Vera Institute of Justice, January 2021.

2. Don Stemen, "The Prison Paradox: More Incarceration Will Not Make Us Safer," Vera Institute of Justice, July 2017.

3. Cameron Kimble and Ames Grawert, "Between 2007 and 2017, 34 States Reduced Crime and Incarceration in Tandem," Brennan Center for Justice, August 6, 2019.

4. Nicole D. Porter, "Top Trends in State Criminal Justice Reform, 2019," The Sentencing Project, January 17, 2020.

5. Jeff Adachi, "Police Militarization and the War on Citizens," *ABA Human Rights Magazine* 2, no. 1 (February 1, 2017).

6. "How America's Police Became So Heavily Armed," *The Economist*, May 18, 2015.

7. "How America's Police Became So Heavily Armed."

8. Radley Balko, "21 More Studies Showcasing Racial Disparities in the Criminal Justice System," *Washington Post*, April 9, 2019.

9. Executive Office of the President of the United States, "Economic Perspectives on Incarceration and the Criminal Justice System," April 2016.

10. Susan Stellin, "Is the 'War on Drugs' Over? Arrest Statistics Say No," *New York Times*, November 5, 2019.

11. John Gramlich, "Four-in-Ten U.S. Drug Arrests in 2018 Were for Marijuana Offenses—Mostly Possession," Pew Research Center, January 22, 2020.

12. Christopher Dunn and Michelle Shames, "Stop-and-Frisk in the de Blasio Era," New York Civil Liberties Union, March 2019.

13. Emma Pierson et al., "A Large Scale Analysis of Racial Disparities in Police Stops Across the United States," *Nature Human Behaviour* 4 (May 4, 2020): 736–745.

14. Ben Poston and Cindy Chang, "LAPD Searches Blacks and Whites More. But They're Less Likely to Have Contraband Than Whites," *Los Angeles Times*, October 8, 2019.

15. Fred Dews and Betsy Broaddus, "Charts of the Week: Criminal Justice Disparities," Brookings Institution, August 9, 2019.

16. Vivian Ho, "'Outdated, Unsafe, and Unfair': Coronavirus Renews Battle over California's Bail System," *The Guardian*, April 29, 2020.

17. Zhen Zeng, "Jail Inmates in 2017," U.S. Department of Justice, Bureau of Justice Statistics, April 2019.

18. Liu Patrick et al., "The Economics of Bail and Pretrial Detention," The Hamilton Project, Brookings Institution, December 2018.

19. Vera Institute for Justice, "The State of Bail," January 10, 2017; P.R. Lockhart, "Thousands of Americans Are Jailed Before Trial. A New Report Shows the Lasting Impact," Vox, May 7, 2019.

20. Megan T. Stevenson, "Distortion of Justice: How the Inability to Pay Bail Affects Case Outcomes," *Journal of Law, Economics, and Organization* 34, no. 4 (November 2018): 511–542.

21. Patrick et al., "The Economics of Bail"; The Criminal Justice Policy Program at Harvard Law School, "Moving Beyond Money: A Primer on Bail Reform," October 2016; Bryan Covert, "America Is Waking Up to the Injustice of Cash Bail," *The Nation*, October 19, 2017.

22. Balko, "21 More Studies."

23. Vanessa Romo, "California Becomes First State to End Cash Bail After 40-Year Fight," NPR, August 28, 2018.

24. Patrick McGreevy, "Prop. 25, Which Would Have Abolished California's Cash Bail System, Is Rejected by Voters," *Los Angeles Times*, November 4, 2020.

25. Jon Schuppe, "Jails Are Releasing Inmates Because of Coronavirus. New York Just Took a Step to Lock More People Up," NBC News, April 8, 2020.

26. Executive Office of the President of the United States, "Economic Perspectives."

27. Patrick et al., "The Economics of Bail."

28. Matthew Van Meter, "One Judge Makes the Case for Judgment," *The Atlantic*, February 25, 2016.

29. John Villasenor and Virginia Foggo, "Algorithms and Sentencing: What Does Due Process Require?" Brookings Institution, March 21, 2019.

30. United States Supreme Court, Petition for Writ of Certiorari, *Eric Loomis v. State of Wisconsin*.

31. Bernard E. Harcourt, "Risk as Proxy for Race," *University of Chicago Public Law Working Paper No. 323*, September 16, 2010.

32. John Gramlich, "Only 2 Percent of Federal Criminal Defendants Go to Trial, and Most Who Do Are Found Guilty," Pew Research Center, June 11, 2019.

33. Gretchen Gavett, "The Problem with Pleas," *PBS Frontline*, October 31, 2011.

34. William H. Pryor et al., "An Overview of Mandatory Minimum Penalties in the Federal Criminal Justice System," U.S. Sentencing Commission, July 2017.

35. Criminal Justice Policy Foundation, "Mandatory Minimums and Sentencing Reform."

36. Death Penalty Information Center, "State by State."

37. Death Penalty Information Center, "Botched Executions."

38. American Civil Liberties Union, "The Case Against the Death Penalty," 2012.

39. Samuel R. Gross et al., "Rate of False Conviction of Criminal Defendants Who Are Sentenced to Death," *PNAS* 111, no. 20 (May 20, 2014): 7230–7235.

40. Death Penalty Information Center, "Innocence."

41. Peter Collins et al., "An Analysis of the Economic Cost of Seeking the Death Penalty in Washington State," Seattle University School of Law, January 1, 2015.

42. Kelly Phillips Erb, "Considering the Death Penalty: Your Tax Dollars at Work," *Forbes*, May 1, 2014.

43. Govtrack.com, United States Congress, House, Violent Crime and Drug Enforcement Improvements Act of 1982, 97th Congress, House Resolution 6497.

44. Lesile Maitland, "Reagan Offers Bill to Tighten Rules on Criminal Defendants," *New York Times*, September 14, 1982.

45. United States, Congress, Senate, *Crime Control Act of 1990*, S 3266 101st Cong.

46. Lauren-Brooke Eisen and Inimai M. Chettiar, "The Complex History of the Controversial 1994 Crime Bill," Brennan Center for Justice, April 14, 2016.

47. Tara O'Neill Hayes, "The Economic Costs of the Criminal Justice System," *American Action Forum*, July 16, 2020.

48. Nicole Lewis and Beatrix Lockwood, "How Families Cope with Hidden Costs of the Incarceration for the Holidays," *New York Times*, December 20, 2019.

49. Eisen and Chettiar, "The Complex History."

50. Alfred Blumstein and Joel Wallman, eds., *The Crime Drop in America* (Cambridge: Cambridge University Press, 2005).

51. The Pew Charitable Trusts, "Factors Contributing to Crime Decline," September 11, 2014.

52. John Gramlich, "America's Incarceration Rate Is at a Two-Decade Low," Pew Research Center, May 2, 2018; Thomas Baker, "Most Americans Support Rehabilitation Compared to 'Tough on Crime' Policies," LSE U.S. Centre.

53. Prison Fellowship, "Our Founder, Chuck Colson."

54. Steven M. Teles and David Dagan, "Conservatives and Criminal Justice," National Affairs, 2016.

55. The White House, "Fact Sheet: President Bush Signs Second Chance Act of 2007," April 9, 2008.

56. Debbie Elliott and Walter Ray Watson, "After Inmate Deaths, Mississippi Faces Pressure to Reform Its Prisons," NPR, April 20, 2020.

57. Jeff Pegues, "Investigation Finds Alabama Prison Conditions Are 'Unconstitutional,'" CBS News, May 15, 2019.

58. Ian Simpson et al., "Gang Dispute Sparks Deadliest U.S. Prison Riot in 25 Years: Official," Reuters, April 16, 2018.

59. Laignee Barron, "Here's Why Inmates in the U.S. Prison System Have Launched a Nation-wide Strike," *Time*, August 22, 2018.

60. Luis Gomez, "For $1 an Hour, Inmates Fight California Fires. 'Slave Labor' or Self-Improvement," *San Diego Union Tribune*, October 20, 2017.

61. Peter Baker and Erica Goode, "Critics of Solitary Confinement Are Buoyed as Obama Embraces Their Cause," *New York Times,* July 21, 2015.

62. Erica Goode, "Solitary Confinement: Punished for Life," *New York Times*, August 3, 2015.

63. Troy Closson, "New York Will End Long-Term Solitary Confinement in Prisons and Jails," *New York Times*, April 24, 2021.

64. The Marshall Project, "A State-by-State Look at Coronavirus in Prisons."

65. "Prisons Have Been Overwhelmed by the Virus," *New York Times*, May 24, 2020.

66. Rebecca Griesbach and Libby Seline, "Granted Parole or Awaiting Trial, Inmates Died of Covid-19 Behind Bars," *New York Times*, May 6, 2021.

67. Prison Policy Initiative, "The Most Significant Criminal Justice Policy Changes from the COVID-19 Pandemic," May 8, 2021.

68. Executive Office of the President of the United States, "Economic Perspectives."

69. Amanda Agan and Sonja B. Starr, "The Effect of Criminal Records on Access to Employment," *American Economic Review: Papers & Proceedings* 107, no. 5 (2017): 560–564.

70. The Brennan Center for Justice, "Criminal Disenfranchisement Laws Across the United States," December 18, 2019.

71. Chris Uggen et al., "Locked Out 2020: Estimates of People Denied Voting Rights Due to a Felony Conviction," The Sentencing Project, October 30, 2020.

72. Office of Juvenile Justice and Delinquency Prevention Statistical Briefing Book, U.S. Department of Justice, "Law Enforcement and Juvenile Crime."

73. Easy Access to the Census of Juveniles in Residential Placement, National Center for Juvenile Justice.

74. Executive Office of the President of the United States, "Economic Perspectives on Incarceration and the Criminal Justice System," April 2016.

75. Katie Rose Quandt, "Why Does the U.S. Sentence Children to Life in Prison?" *JSTOR Daily*, January 31, 2018.

76. Malcolm Ritter, "Experts Link Teen Brains' Immaturity, Juvenile Crime," ABC News, December 3, 2007.

77. Jeremy Travis et al., *The Growth of Incarceration in the United States: Exploring Causes and Consequences* (Washington, DC: National Academies Press, 2014).

78. Vincent M. Southerland and Jody Kent Lavy, "Why Are We Sentencing Children to Life in Prison Without Parole?" *Newsweek*, August 10, 2017.

79. Josh Rovner, "Juvenile Life Without Parole: An Overview," The Sentencing Project, February 25, 2020.

80. Nina Totenberg, "Supreme Court Rejects Restrictions on Life Without Parole for Juveniles," NPR, April 22, 2021.

81. American Civil Liberties Union, "ACLU Fact Sheet on the Juvenile Justice System."

82. Sally Q. Yates, "Memorandum for the Acting Director Federal Bureau of Prisons," U.S. Department of Justice, August 18, 2016

83. Office of the Inspector General, U.S. Department of Justice, "Review of the Bureau of Prisons Monitoring of Contract Prisons," August 2016.

84. Sally Q. Yates, "Phasing Out Our Use of Private Prisons," Office of Public Affairs, Department of Justice Archives, August 18, 2016.

85. Kara Gotsch and Vinay Basti, "Capitalizing on Mass Incarceration: U.S. Growth in Private Prisons," The Sentencing Project, August 2, 2018.

86. Bryce Covert, "How Private Prison Companies Could Get Around a Federal Ban," *American Prospect*, June 28, 2019.

87. Char Adams, "Biden's Order Terminates Federal Private Prison Contracts. Here's What That Means," NBC News, January 27, 2021.

88. Eric Markowitz, "Making Profits on the Captive Prison Market," *New Yorker*, September 4, 2016.

89. Nicolas Fandos, "Senate Passes Bipartisan Criminal Justice Bill," *New York Times*, December 18, 2018.

90. Van Jones and Jessica Jackson, "10 Reasons to Celebrate the First Step Act," CNN, December 21, 2018.

91. Ames Grawert, "What Is the First Step Act—and What's Happening with It?" Expert Policy Brief, Brennan Center for Justice Reform, June 23, 2020.

92. Committee on the Judiciary, "Durbin, Grassley Introduce Bipartisan Legislation to Advance the First Step Act's Goals," March 26, 2021.

93. Justice Action Network, "Accomplishments."

94. Nicole Porter, "Top Trends in State Criminal Justice Reform, 2020," The Sentencing Project, January 2021.

95. Jacob Denney and Adam Gelb, "National Prison Rate Continues to Decline Amid Sentencing, Re-entry Reforms," The Pew Charitable Trusts, January 16, 2018.

96. Jerry Madden, "Prisons, Probation, and Parole Reforms—the Texas Model," The Hill, December 9, 2018.

97. Tim Walz and Mike Parson, "Criminal Justice Reform Shouldn't Just Focus on People Behind Bars. Here's How We Can Improve the Lives of Millions More," *Time*, October 15, 2019.

98. Dana Shoenberg, "How State Reform Efforts Are Transforming Juvenile Justice," The Pew Charitable Trusts, November 26, 2019.

99. Daniel Nichanian, "How States Transformed Criminal Justice in 2020, and How They Fell Short," *The Appeal*, December 18, 2020; Porter, "Top Trends in State Criminal Justice Reform, 2020."

10. Building Bridges, Not Walls: Refugees and Asylum-Seekers
Research and drafting contributed by Cathy Sun and Philip Hamilton.

1. "A Brief History of Civil Rights in the United States," Georgetown Law Library, April 12, 2021, guides.ll.georgetown.edu/c.php?g=592919&p=4171684.

2. Georgetown Law Library, "A Brief History."

3. History, "U.S. Immigration Before 1965," April 20, 2021, www.history.com/topics /immigration/u-s-immigration-before-1965; Mae Ngai, "This Is How Immigration Reform Happened 50 Years Ago. It Can Happen Again," *The Nation*, October 2, 2015.

4. Erika Lee, "Trump's Xenophobia Is an American Tradition—But It Doesn't Have to Be," *Washington Post*, November 26, 2019.

5. History, "U.S. Immigration Timeline," April 20, 2021, www.history.com/topics /immigration/immigration-united-states-timeline; "HR 40, Naturalization Bill, March 4, 1790," U.S. Capitol Visitor Center, www.visitthecapitol.gov/exhibitions/artifact/h-r-40-naturalization -bill-march-4-1790.

6. History, "U.S. Immigration Timeline."

7. History, "Chinese Exclusion Act," September 13, 2019, www.history.com/topics /immigration/chinese-exclusion-act-1882.

8. History, "U.S. Immigration Timeline."

9. U.S. Congress, House, *An Act in Amendment to the Various Acts Relative to Immigration and the Importation of Aliens Under Contract or Agreement to Perform Labor*, 51st Cong., 2nd sess., adopted March 3, 1891, www.loc.gov/law/help/statutes-at-large/51st-congress/session-2 /c51s2ch551.pdf.

10. History, "U.S. Immigration Timeline."

11. History, "U.S. Immigration Timeline"; "Immigration Act of 1917 Bans Asians, Other Non-White People from Entering U.S.," Equal Justice Initiative, calendar.eji.org/racial-injustice/feb /5.

12. History, "U.S. Immigration Timeline."

13. United States Holocaust Memorial Museum, "How Many Refugees Came to the United States from 1933–1945?" Americans and the Holocaust, exhibitions.ushmm.org/americans-and -the-holocaust/how-many-refugees-came-to-the-united-states-from-1933-1945.

14. "Chapter 1: The Nation's Immigration Laws, 1920 to Today," Pew Research Center, September 28, 2015, www.pewresearch.org/hispanic/2015/09/28/chapter-1-the-nations-immigration -laws-1920-to-today.

15. Muzaffar Chishti, Faye Hipsman, and Isabel Ball, "Fifty Years On, the 1965 Immigration and Nationality Act Continues to Reshape the United States," Migration Information Source, October 15, 2015, www.migrationpolicy.org/article/fifty-years-1965-immigration-and -nationality-act-continues-reshape-united-states.

16. Migration Policy Institute, "U.S. Annual Refugee Resettlement Ceilings and Number of Refugees Admitted, 1980–Present," www.migrationpolicy.org/programs/data-hub/charts/us -annual-refugee-resettlement-ceilings-and-number-refugees-admitted-united.

17. Pew Research Center, "Chapter 2: Immigration's Impact on Past and Future U.S. Population Change," September 28, 2015, www.pewresearch.org/hispanic/2015/09/28/chapter-2-immigrations-impact-on-past-and-future-u-s-population-change.

18. "Zadvydas v. Davis (99-7791)," Legal Information Institute, Cornell University Law School, www.law.cornell.edu/supct/html/99-7791.ZS.html.

19. United Nations High Commissioner for Refugees (UNHCR), "The 1951 Refugee Convention," www.unhcr.org/en-us/1951-refugee-convention.html.

20. United Nations High Commissioner for Refugees (UNHCR), "States Parties, Including Reservations and Declarations, to the 1967 Protocol Relating to the Status of Refugees," September 2019, www.unhcr.org/en-us/5d9ed66a4.

21. UNHCR, "Convention and Protocol Relating to the Status of Refugees."

22. United Nations High Commissioner for Refugees (UNHCR), "Handbook and Guidelines on Procedures and Criteria for Determining Refugee Status Under the 1951 Convention and the 1967 Protocol Relating to the Status of Refugees," December 2011, www.refworld.org/pdfid/4f33c8d92.pdf.

23. U.S. Citizenship and Immigration Services, "Refugees and Asylum," November 12, 2015, www.uscis.gov/humanitarian/refugees-and-asylum.

24. UNHCR, "Convention and Protocol Relating to the Status of Refugees."

25. UNHCR, "States Parties."

26. U.S. Constitution, art. 6, cl. 2.

27. UNHCR, "Convention and Protocol Relating to the Status of Refugees."

28. "Chae Chan Ping v. United States," Legal Information Institute, Cornell University Law School, www.law.cornell.edu/supremecourt/text/130/581; "Nishimura Ekiu v. United States, 142 U.S. 651 (1892)," Justia, supreme.justia.com/cases/federal/us/142/651.

29. "Kaoru Yamataya v. Fisher," FindLaw, caselaw.findlaw.com/us-supreme-court/189/86.html.

30. Legal Information Institute, "Zadvydas v. Davis (99-7791)."

31. FindLaw, "Kaoru Yamataya v. Fisher."

32. FindLaw, "Kaoru Yamataya v. Fisher."

33. "U.S. Reports: Reno v. Flores, 507 U.S. 292 (1993)," Library of Congress, www.loc.gov/item/usrep507292.

34. Library of Congress, "U.S. Reports: Reno v. Flores."

35. Philip G. Schrag et al., *Refugee Roulette: Disparities in Asylum Adjudication and Proposals for Reform* (New York: NYU Press 2009); Daniel Kanstroom, *Deportation Nation: Outsiders in American History* (Cambridge, MA: Harvard University Press 2010).

36. Legal Information Institute, "Zadvydas v. Davis (99-7791)."

37. Legal Information Institute, "Zadvydas v. Davis (99-7791)."

38. Amelia Cheatham, "Central America's Turbulent Northern Triangle," Council on Foreign Relations, last modified October 1, 2019, www.cfr.org/backgrounder/central-americas-turbulent-northern-triangle.

39. Michael Shifter, "Countering Criminal Violence in Central America," Council Special Report no. 64, Council on Foreign Relations, April 2012, www.cfr.org/sites/default/files/pdf/2012/03/Criminal_Violence_CSR64.pdf.

40. "Monroe Doctrine," *Encyclopaedia Brittanica*, March 17, 2021, www.britannica.com /event/Monroe-Doctrine.

41. Amelia Cheatham, Claire Felter, and Zachary Laub, "How the U.S. Patrols Its Borders," Council on Foreign Relations, last modified April 12, 2021, www.cfr.org/backgrounder/how-us -patrols-its-borders.

42. Nick Corasaniti, "A Look at Trump's Immigration Plan, Then and Now," *New York Times*, August 31, 2016; Katie Reilly, "Here Are All the Times Donald Trump Insulted Mexico," *Time*, August 31, 2016.

43. Immigration Policy Tracking Project, "Trump-Era Asylum Restrictions," immpoli-cytracking.org/analyses/compilation-principal-trump-era-asylum-restrictions/; Immigration Policy Tracking Project, "Major Biden Administration Actions," immpolicytracking.org /analyses/summary-biden-administration-actions.

44. U.S. President, Proclamation, "Addressing Mass Migration Through the Southern Border of the United States, Proclamation 9880 of May 8, 2019," *Federal Register* 84, no. 92 (May 13, 2019): 21229, www.govinfo.gov/content/pkg/FR-2019-05-13/pdf/2019-09992.pdf; American Civil Liberties Union (ACLU), "East Bay Sanctuary Covenant v. Trump—Complaint," November 9, 2018, www.aclu.org/legal-document/east-bay-sanctuary-covenant-v-trump-complaint.

45. ACLU, "East Bay Sanctuary Covenant v. Trump—Complaint."

46. East Bay Sanctuary Covenant v. Trump, 950 F.3d 1242 (9th Cir. 2020).

47. U.S. Department of Homeland Security and U.S. Department of Justice, Executive Office for Immigration Review, Rule, "Asylum Eligibility and Procedural Modifications," *Federal Register* 84, no. 136 (July 16, 2019): 33829, www.govinfo.gov/content/pkg/FR-2019-07-16/pdf/2019 -15246.pdf.

48. Cheatham, "Central America's Turbulent Northern Triangle"; Doctors Without Borders, "Escaping Violence into Danger—No Way Out for Central American Migrants," February 11, 2020, www.msf.org/escaping-violence-danger-no-way-out-central-american-migrants-mexico.

49. Susan Gzesh, "'Safe Third Country' Agreements with Mexico and Guatemala Would Be Unlawful," Just Security, July 15, 2019, www.justsecurity.org/64918/safe-third-country -agreements-with-mexico-and-guatemala-would-be-unlawful.

50. Hamed Aleaziz, "The Trump Administration Is Scrambling to Make Its 'Safe Third Country' Asylum Deal with Guatemala a Reality, a Memo Shows," BuzzFeed News, July 30, 2019, www.buzzfeednews.com/article/hamedaleaziz/safe-third-country-asylum-deal-guatemala -obstacles-memo; Colleen Long and Astrid Galvan, "U.S., El Salvador Sign Asylum Deal, Details to Be Worked Out," Associated Press, September 20, 2019; Michelle Hackman and Juan Montes, "U.S. Asylum Pact with Honduras Cements Trump Administration's Regional Strategy," *Wall Street Journal*, September 25, 2019.

51. Human Rights First, "Is Guatemala Safe for Refugees and Asylum Seekers?" July 1, 2019, www.humanrightsfirst.org/resource/guatemala-safe-refugees-and-asylum-seekers.

52. U.S. Department of Homeland Security, "Joint Statement Between the U.S. Government and the Government of El Salvador," September 20, 2019, www.dhs.gov/news/2019/09/20/joint -statement-between-us-government-and-government-el-salvador.

53. U.S. Department of State, "El Salvador Travel Advisory," travel.state.gov/content/travel/en /traveladvisories/traveladvisories/el-salvador-travel-advisory.html.

54. James Fredrick, "'Metering' at the Border," interview by Sarah McCammon, *Weekend Edition Saturday*, NPR, June 29, 2019.

55. Muzaffar Chishti and Jessica Bolter, "Interlocking Set of Trump Administration Policies at

the U.S.-Mexico Border Bars Virtually All from Asylum," Migration Information Source, February 27, 2020, www.migrationpolicy.org/article/interlocking-set-policies-us-mexico-border-bars-virtually-all-asylum.

56. Human Rights Watch, "'Like I'm Drowning': Children and Families Sent to Harm by the U.S. 'Remain in Mexico' Program," January 6, 2021, www.hrw.org/report/2021/01/06/im-drowning/children-and-families-sent-harm-us-remain-mexico-program.

57. Innovation Law Lab v. Chad Wolf, no. 19-15716 (9th Cir. 2020), Politico.

58. Human Rights Watch, "'Like I'm Drowning.'"

59. Camilo Montoya-Galvez, "'Leave Me in a Cell': The Desperate Pleas of Asylum Seekers Inside El Paso's Immigration Court," CBS News, August 11, 2019.

60. Women's Refugee Commission, "Separation of Families via the 'Migrant Protection Protocols,'" August 16, 2019, www.womensrefugeecommission.org/research-resources/separation-of-families-via-the-migrant-protection-protocols.

61. Human Rights Watch, "'Like I'm Drowning.'"

62. U.S. Department of Homeland Security, "DHS Statement on the Suspension of New Enrollments in the Migrant Protection Protocols Program," January 20, 2021, www.dhs.gov/news/2021/01/20/dhs-statement-suspension-new-enrollments-migrant-protection-protocols-program; "The Biden Plan for Securing Our Values as a Nation of Immigrants," Biden–Harris Campaign, joebiden.com/immigration.

63. Olafimihan Oshin and Rafael Bernal, "Biden Formally Ends Trump-Era 'Remain in Mexico' Immigration Program," The Hill, June 1, 2021.

64. Brian Naylor and Tamara Keith, "Kamala Harris Tells Guatemalans Not to Migrate to the United States," NPR, June 7, 2021.

65. Naylor and Keith, "Kamala Harris."

66. Zolan Kanno-Youngs, "In Guatemala, Harris Tells Undocumented to Stay Away from U.S. Border," New York Times, June 7, 2021; Cindy Carcamo and Andrea Castillo, "'Do Not Come': Kamala Harris' Three Words to Guatemalans Stir Debate and Backlash," Los Angeles Times, June 9, 2021.

67. Geoffrey Jones and Marcelo Bucheli, "The Octopus and the Generals: The United Fruit Company in Guatemala," Harvard Business School Case 805-146, last modified January 2021, www.hbs.edu/faculty/Pages/item.aspx?num=32372; "Taking Stock of Trump's Legacy in Latin America," Washington Office on Latin America, accessed May 28, 2021, www.wola.org/analysis/taking-stock-trump-legacy-latin-america.

68. "Family Separation Under the Trump Administration—a Timeline," Southern Poverty Law Center, June 17, 2020, www.splcenter.org/news/2020/06/17/family-separation-under-trump-administration-timeline.

69. Associated Press, "More Than 5400 Children Split at Border, According to New Count," NBC News, Oct 25, 2019.

70. Meagan Flynn, "Detained Migrant Children Got No Toothbrush, No Soap, No Sleep. It's No Problem, Government Argues," Washington Post, June 21, 2019; Dan Barry et al., "Cleaning Toilets, Following Rules: A Migrant Child's Days in Detention," New York Times, July 14, 2018.

71. Olga Khazan, "Separating Kids from Their Families Can Permanently Damage Their Brains," The Atlantic, June 22, 2018.

72. Matthew Haag, "Thousands of Immigrant Children Said They Were Sexually Abused in U.S. Detention Centers, Report Says," New York Times, February 27, 2019.

73. Executive Office of the President, Presidential Document, "Affording Congress an Opportunity to Address Family Separation, Executive Order 13841 of June 20, 2018," *Federal Register* 83, no. 122 (July 25, 2018): 29435, www.govinfo.gov/content/pkg/FR-2018-06-25/pdf/2018-13696.pdf.

74. Nicole Narea, "The Trump Administration Just Admitted That It Separated an Additional 1,500 Immigrant Families," Vox, October 25, 2019.

75. Ginger Thompson, "Families Are Still Being Separated at the Border, Months After 'Zero Tolerance' Was Reversed," ProPublica, November 27, 2018.

76. Associated Press, "More Than 5400 Children Split"; Jacob Soboroff and Julia Ainsley, "Trump Administration Identifies at Least 1,700 Additional Children It May Have Separated," NBC News, May 18, 2019.

77. Mona Chalabi, "How Many Migrant Children Are Detained in U.S. Custody?" *The Guardian*, December 22, 2018.

78. Suzanne Gamboa, "'Race Against the Clock': Lawyers Work to Track Down Migrant Children Separated from Parents," NBC News, June 26, 2018.

79. Hamed Aleaziz, "ICE Is Detaining Thousands of Immigrants Who Have Passed a Test Showing Fear of Persecution or Torture," BuzzFeed News, August 15, 2019.

80. "Removal Without Recourse: The Growth of Summary Deportations from the United States," American Immigration Council, May 2014, www.americanimmigrationcouncil.org/sites/default/files/research/removal_without_recourse.pdf; American Immigration Council, "A Primer on Expedited Removal," July 22, 2019, www.americanimmigrationcouncil.org/research/primer-expedited-removal.

81. American Immigration Council, "Summary of Executive Order 'Border Security and Immigration Enforcement Improvements," February 27, 2017, www.americanimmigrationcouncil.org/research/border-security-and-immigration-enforcement-improvements-executive-order.

82. U.S. Department of Homeland Security, Office of the Secretary, "Designating Aliens for Expedited Removal," *Federal Register* 84, no. 141 (July 23, 2019): 35409, www.govinfo.gov/content/pkg/FR-2019-07-23/pdf/2019-15710.pdf.

83. American Immigration Council, "Summary of Executive Order."

84. Chishti and Bolter, "Interlocking Set of Trump Administration Policies"; Tanvi Misra and Camila DeChalus, "DHS Expands Programs That Fast-Track Asylum Process," Roll Call, February 26, 2020, www.rollcall.com/2020/02/26/dhs-expands-asylum-programs-that-fast-track-deportations.

85. American Bar Association, "Recent White House and Executive Agency Immigration Pronouncements," February 3, 2021, www.americanbar.org/groups/public_interest/immigration/immigration-updates/recent-white-house-and-executive-agency-immigration-pronouncemen.

86. American Immigration Council, "A Guide to Title 42 Expulsions at the Border," March 2021, www.americanimmigrationcouncil.org/sites/default/files/research/title_42_expulsions_at_the_border.pdf.

87. Human Rights Watch, "Q&A: U.S. Title 42 Policy to Expel Migrants at the Border," April 8, 2021, www.hrw.org/news/2021/04/08/qa-us-title-42-policy-expel-migrants-border#.

88. American Immigration Council, "A Guide to Title 42 Expulsions."

89. Molly O'Toole, "U.S. Border Closure Cracks Under Pressure from Lawsuits, Advocates and the Easing Pandemic," *Los Angeles Times*, May 17, 2021.

90. UNHCR, "Convention and Protocol Relating to the Status of Refugees."

91. U.S. Citizenship and Immigration Services, "Questions and Answers: Credible Fear Screening," July 15, 2015, www.uscis.gov/humanitarian/refugees-and-asylum/asylum/questions -and-answers-credible-fear-screening.

92. "USCIS Executive Summary of Changes to the Credible Fear Lesson Plan," AILA doc. no. 17022438, American Immigration Lawyers Association, February 13, 2017, www.aila.org /infonet/uscis-executive-summary-of-changes-to-the-credible.

93. Tal Kopan, "Impact of Sessions' Asylum Move Already Felt at Border," CNN, July 14, 2018.

94. Amanda Holpuch, "Asylum: 90 Percent of Claims Fall at First Hurdle After U.S. Process Change, Lawsuit Alleges," *The Guardian*, November 13, 2019.

95. "AG Garland Vacates Asylum Precedents That Harmed Victims of Violence," *American Immigration Lawyers Association*, June 16, 2021, www.aila.org/advo-media/press-releases/2021 /ag-garland-vacates-asylum-precedents.

96. Sushma Raman, "On Immigration, 'Building Back Better' Isn't Enough," *Foreign Policy*, April 8, 2021, foreignpolicy.com/2021/04/08/immigration-biden-trump-comprehensive -reform.

97. Ingrid Eagly and Steven Shafer, "Access to Counsel in Immigration Court," American Immigration Council, September 2016, www.americanimmigrationcouncil.org/sites/default /files/research/access_to_counsel_in_immigration_court.pdf.

98. *Prima facie* eligibility for asylum means that the asylum-seeker has demonstrated that they have sufficient evidence to support a finding that they are eligible for asylum. "Prima Facie," Legal Information Institute, Cornell Law School, accessed June 2, 2021.

99. Eleanor Acer, "Sessions Decision Undermines Fairness in Asylum System," Human Rights First, March 8, 2018, www.humanrightsfirst.org/press-release/sessions-decision-undermines -fairness-asylum-system.

100. Eagly and Shafer, "Access to Counsel in Immigration Court"; Nikhil Sonnad, "The Real Language Barrier Between Migrant Children and the Americans Detaining Them," *Quartz*, June 23, 2018, qz.com/1312256/many-migrant-children-arriving-in-the-us-dont-speak -spanish.

101. John D. Montgomery, "Cost of Counsel in Immigration: Economic Analysis of Proposal Providing Public Counsel to Indigent Persons Subject to Immigration Removal Proceedings," NERA Economic Consulting, May 28, 2014, www.nera.com/content/dam/nera/publications /archive2/NERA_Immigration_Report_5.28.2014.pdf.

102. "Empty Benches: Underfunding of Immigration Courts Undermines Justice," American Immigration Council, June 17, 2016, www.americanimmigrationcouncil.org/research/empty -benches-underfunding-immigration-courts-undermines-justice.

103. Quinn Owen, "Immigration Court Backlogs Compound as Shutdown Enters Fourth Week," ABC News, January 14, 2019, abcnews.go.com/Politics/immigration-court-backlogs -compound-shutdown-enters-fourth-week/story?id=60232074.

104. American Immigration Council, "Empty Benches."

105. Tal Kopan, "Justice Department Rolls Out Case Quotas for Immigration Judges," CNN, April 2, 2018.

106. "The State of the Immigration Courts: Trump Leaves Biden 1.3 Million Case Backlog in Immigration Courts," Transactional Records Access Clearinghouse (TRAC), Syracuse University, January 19, 2021, trac.syr.edu/immigration/reports/637.

107. "Immigration Courts: Actions Needed to Reduce Case Backlog and Address Long-standing Management and Operational Challenges," GAO-17-438, U.S. Government Account-ability Office, June 2017, www.gao.gov/assets/gao-17-438.pdf.

108. "Executive Office of Immigration Review: FY 2020 Budget Request at a Glance," Depart-ment of Justice, accessed June 27, 2021.

109. "IRS Budget & Workforce," Internal Revenue Service, last updated June 24, 2021, www.irs.gov/statistics/irs-budget-and-workforce.

110. "New Documents Reveal Immigration Judge Hiring Plan Designed to Stack the Courts, Prioritize Politics over Justice," AILA doc. no. 20050441, American Immigration Lawyers Asso-ciation, May 4, 2020, www.aila.org/advo-media/press-releases/2020/new-documents-reveal-immigration-judge-hiring-plan.

111. "Why U.S. Immigration Judges Are Leaving the Bench in Record Numbers," *The World*, July 20, 2020, www.pri.org/stories/2020-07-20/why-us-immigration-judges-are-leaving-bench-record-numbers; Molly Hennessy-Fiske, "Immigration Judges Are Quitting or Retiring Early Because of Trump," *Los Angeles Times*, January 27, 2020; "More Immigration Judges Leaving the Bench," TRAC, Syracuse University, July 13, 2020, trac.syr.edu/immigration/reports/617.

112. "CBP Through the Years," U.S. Customs and Border Protection, last modified May 5, 2021, www.cbp.gov/about/history.

113. A.C. Thompson, "Over 200 Allegations of Abuse of Migrant Children; 1 Case of Home-land Security Disciplining Someone," ProPublica, May 31, 2019, www.propublica.org/article/over-200-allegations-of-abuse-of-migrant-children-1-case-of-homeland-security-disciplining-someone.

114. Guillermo Cantor and Walter Ewing, "Still No Action Taken: Complaints Against Border Patrol Agents Continue to Go Unanswered," American Immigration Council, August 2, 2017, www.americanimmigrationcouncil.org/research/still-no-action-taken-complaints-against-border-patrol-agents-continue-go-unanswered.

115. Ken Klippenstein, "Exclusive: Customs and Border Protection Gains an Extra Layer of Secrecy," *The Nation*, February 4, 2020.

116. Jacob Soboroff and Julia Ainsley, "Migrant Kids in Overcrowded Arizona Border Station Allege Sex Assault, Retaliation from U.S. Agents," NBC News, July 9, 2019, www.nbcnews.com/politics/immigration/migrant-kids-overcrowded-arizona-border-station-allege-sex-assault-retaliation-n1027886.

117. Alene Tchekmedyian, "Authorities Arrest Customs and Border Protection Officer Sus-pected of Selling Guns Without License," *Los Angeles Times*, February 6, 2019, www.latimes.com/local/lanow/la-me-ln-cbp-officer-selling-guns-20190206-story.html.

118. Tim Dickinson, "'Guats,' 'Tonks' and 'Subhuman Shit': The Shocking Texts of a Border Patrol Agent," *Rolling Stone*, June 13, 2019.

119. Michael D. Shear and Zolan Kanno-Youngs, "Trump Slashes Refugee Cap to 18,000, Cur-tailing U.S. Role as Haven," *New York Times*, September 26.

120. Christopher Ingraham, "The Incredible Shrinking Refugee Cap, in One Chart," *Washing-ton Post*, September 26, 2017.

121. Kira Monin, Jeanne Batalova, and Tianjian Lai, "Refugees and Asylees in the United States," Migration Information Source, May 13, 2021, www.migrationpolicy.org/article/refugees-and-asylees-united-states-2021.

122. "Statement by President Joe Biden on Refugee Admissions," Briefing Room, The White House, May 3, 2021, www.whitehouse.gov/briefing-room/statements-releases/2021/05/03/sta

tement-by-president-joe-biden-on-refugee-admissions/; Executive Office of the President, Presidential Document, "Emergency Presidential Determination on Refugee Admissions for Fiscal Year 2021, Presidential Determination No. 2021-06 of May 3, 2021," *Federal Register* 86, no. 87 (May 7, 2021): 24475, www.govinfo.gov/content/pkg/FR-2021-05-07/pdf/2021-09861.pdf.

123. Charles Kamasaki, "U.S. Immigration Policy: A Classic, Unappreciated Example of Structural Racism," Brookings Institution, March 26, 2021, www.brookings.edu/blog/how-we-rise/2021/03/26/us-immigration-policy-a-classic-unappreciated-example-of-structural-racism.

124. History, "U.S. Immigration Timeline"; U.S. Capitol Visitor Center, "HR 40."

125. Karla McKanders, "Immigration and Blackness: What's Race Got to Do with It?" American Bar Association, May 16, 2019, www.americanbar.org/groups/crsj/publications/human_rights_magazine_home/black-to-the-future/immigration-and-blackness.

126. Kica Matos and Nana Gyamfi, "Centering Black Voices in the Struggle for Immigrant Rights," Vera Institute of Justice, September 9, 2020, www.vera.org/blog/centering-black-voices-in-the-struggle-for-immigrant-rights.

127. Clyde Haberman, "For Private Prisons, Detaining Immigrants Is Big Business," *New York Times*, October 1, 2018.

128. Stef W. Kight, "How Companies Profit from Immigrant Detention," Axios, June 8, 2019, www.axios.com/private-prisons-immigrant-detention-8e5b3317-8ecf-476c-b915-25330852e66f.html.

129. Emily Kassie, "Detained: How the U.S. Built the World's Largest Immigrant Detention System," *The Guardian*, September 24, 2019.

130. Rebecca Plevin, "ICE Signs Long-Term Contracts Worth Billions for Private Detention Centers, Dodging New State Law," *Desert Sun*, December 22, 2019, www.desertsun.com/story/news/2019/12/20/ice-signs-long-term-contracts-private-detention-centers-two-weeks-ahead-state-law/2713910001.

131. Human Rights Watch, "U.S.: New Report Shines Spotlight on Abuses and Growth in Immigrant Detention Under Trump," April 30, 2020, www.hrw.org/news/2020/04/30/us-new-report-shines-spotlight-abuses-and-growth-immigrant-detention-under-trump.

132. Eunice Hyunhye Cho et al., "Justice-Free Zones: U.S. Immigration Detention Under the Trump Administration," ACLU, Human Rights Watch, and National Immigrant Justice Center, April 2020, www.hrw.org/sites/default/files/supporting_resources/justice_free_zones_immigrant_detention.pdf.

133. U.S. Immigration and Customs Enforcement, "Detainee Deaths—Oct. 2003 through Jun. 5, 2017," ice.gov/doclib/foia/reports/detaineedeaths-2003-2017.pdf; CoreCivic, "Eloy Detention Center," www.corecivic.com/facilities/eloy-detention-center.

134. Victoria Bekiempis, "More Immigrant Women Say They Were Abused by ICE Gynecologist," *The Guardian*, December 22, 2020.

135. Bekiempis, "More Immigrant Women."

136. Biden–Harris Campaign, "The Biden Plan."

137. Executive Office of the President, Presidential Document, "Reforming Our Incarceration System to Eliminate the Use of Privately Operated Criminal Detention Facilities, Executive Order 14006 of January 26, 2021," *Federal Register* 86, no. 18 (January 29, 2021): 7483, www.govinfo.gov/content/pkg/FR-2021-01-29/pdf/2021-02070.pdf.

138. Monique O. Madan and Alex Roarty, "Will Biden Officials Renew ICE Contract with GEO Group? It's Not off the Table," *Herald-Mail Media*, April 30, 2021, www.heraldmailmedia.com

/story/news/2021/04/30/will-biden-officials-renew-ice-contract-with-geo-group-its-not-off-the
-table/43785995.

139. "Palantir Valued at $20 Billion in Choppy Stock Exchange Debut," Reuters, September 30, 2020, www.reuters.com/article/us-palantir-ipo/palantir-valued-at-20-billion-in-choppy-stock
-exchange-debut-idUSKBN26L3DR.

140. Sam Biddle and Ryan Devereaux, "Peter Thiel's Palantir Was Used to Bust Relatives of Migrant Children, New Documents Show," Intercept, May 2, 2019, theintercept.com/2019/05
/02/peter-thiels-palantir-was-used-to-bust-hundreds-of-relatives-of-migrant-children-new
-documents-show.

141. Ryan Devereaux, "Documents Detail ICE Campaign to Prosecute Migrant Parents as Smugglers," Intercept, April 29, 2019, theintercept.com/2019/04/29/ice-documents-prosecute
-migrant-parents-smugglers.

142. Biddle and Devereaux, "Peter Thiel's Palantir."

143. April Glaser, "Palantir Said It Had Nothing to Do with ICE Deportations. New Documents Seem to Tell a Different Story," *Slate*, May 2, 2019.

144. Devereaux, "Documents Detail ICE Campaign."

145. "Fact Sheet: President Biden Sends Immigration Bill to Congress as Part of His Commitment to Modernize Our Immigration System," Briefing Room, the White House, January 20, 2021, www.whitehouse.gov/briefing-room/statements-releases/2021/01/20/fact-sheet-president
-biden-sends-immigration-bill-to-congress-as-part-of-his-commitment-to-modernize-our
-immigration-system.

146. Shirin Ghaffary, "The 'Smarter' Wall: How Drones, Sensors, and AI Are Patrolling the Border," Vox, February 7, 2020, www.vox.com/recode/2019/5/16/18511583/smart-border-wall
-drones-sensors-ai.

147. Ghaffary, "The 'Smarter' Wall"; "Border Security Technologies," ACLU, accessed May 28, 2021, www.aclu.org/other/border-security-technologies; Evan Greer, "More Border Surveillance Tech Could Be Worse for Human Rights Than a Wall," *Washington Post*, February 13, 2019.

148. Thomas Franco, "Will Biden's 'Smart Borders' Be Any Different from Trump's?" Open-Democracy, March 30, 2021, www.opendemocracy.net/en/pandemic-border/will-bidens-smart
-borders-be-any-different-from-trumps.

149. Priscilla Alvarez and Geneva Sands, "Exclusive: DHS to Start DNA Testing to Establish Family Relationships on the Border," CNN, May 1, 2019, www.cnn.com/2019/04/30/politics
/homeland-security-dna-testing-immigration/index.html.

150. Megan Kauffman, "Rapid DNA Testing at the Border: Protecting the Children," *Immigration and Human Rights Law Review*, University of Cincinnati, May 1, 2020, lawblogs.uc.edu
/ihrlr/2020/05/01/rapid-dna-testing-at-the-border-protecting-the-children/; Nicole Narea, "The U.S. Is Expanding Its Collection of DNA from Immigrant Detainees for a Federal Criminal Database," Vox, March 6, 2020, www.vox.com/policy-and-politics/2019/10/3/20895459/dna-test
-immigrant-detention-criminal-database.

151. Electronic Frontier Foundation, "EFF Sues DHS to Obtain Information About the Agency's Use of Rapid DNA Testing on Migrant Families at the Border," November 12, 2019, www
.eff.org/press/releases/eff-sues-dhs-obtain-information-about-agencys-use-rapid-dna-testing
-migrant-families.

152. Electronic Frontier Foundation, "ICE's Rapid DNA Testing on Migrants at the Border Is Yet Another Iteration of Family Separation," August 2, 2019, www.eff.org/deeplinks/2019/08
/ices-rapid-dna-testing-migrants-border-yet-another-iteration-family-separation.

11. Gun Rights and Public Safety
Research and drafting contributed by Anne Dietterich.

1. Oliver Laughland and Lois Beckett, "March for Our Lives: Thousands Join Anti-gun Protests Around the World," *The Guardian*, March 25, 2018.

2. Katie Peters, "7 Ways America Has Changed Since the March for Our Lives," *Giffords*, March 20, 2019.

3. Catie Edmondson, "House Passes First Major Gun Control Law in Decades," *New York Times*, February 27, 2019.

4. John Bowden, "2 in 3 Support Stricter Gun Control Laws: Poll," The Hill, April 14, 2021, and Pew Research Center, "Amid a Series of Mass Shootings in the U.S., Gun Policy Remains Deeply Divisive," 2021.

5. Brady Campaign to Prevent Gun Violence, "Key Stats," https://www.bradyunited.org/key-statistics.

6. Alvin Chang, "Every Mass Shooting in the U.S.—A Visual Database," *The Guardian*, https://www.theguardian.com/us-news/ng-interactive/2021/may/27/us-mass-shootings-database.

7. Federal Bureau of Investigation, "Quarterly Uniform Crime Report," March 21, 2021.

8. Julia P. Schleimer et al., "Firearm Purchasing and Firearm Violence in the First Months of the Coronavirus Pandemic in the United States," *MedRxiv*, July 2020.

9. Rob Arthur and Jeff Asher, "What Drove the Historically Large Murder Spike in 2020?" Intercept, February 21, 2021.

10. Martin Kaste, "Did Record Gun Sales Cause a Spike in Gun Crime? Researchers Say It's Complicated," NPR, March 3, 2021.

11. Associated Press, "U.S. Has Been Wracked with Several Mass Shootings in 2021," April 16, 2021.

12. Christopher Ingraham, "There Are More Guns Than People in the United States, According to a New Study of Global Firearm Ownership," *Washington Post*, June 19, 2018.

13. World Population Review, "Gun Ownership by Country 2020."

14. Chris Cillizza, "8 Charts That Explain America's Gun Culture," CNN, October 3, 2017.

15. Kim Parker et al., "America's Complex Relationship with Guns: An In-Depth Look at the Attitudes and Experiences of U.S. Adults."

16. John Gramlich and Katherine Schaeffer, "7 Facts About Guns in the U.S.," Pew Research Center, October 22, 2019.

17. Rashawn Ray and Rebecca Shankman, "How COVID-19 Is Changing the Gun Debate," Brookings, June 17, 2020.

18. Giffords Law Center, "Gun Violence Statistics."

19. Gramlich and Schaeffer, "7 Facts About Guns."

20. Giffords Law Center, "Gun Violence Statistics."

21. Erin Grinshteyn and David Hemenway, "Violent Death Rates in the U.S. Compared to Those of the Other High-Income Countries, 2015," *Nursing and Health Professions Faculty Research and Publications*, 2019, 130.

22. Giffords Law Center, "Gun Violence Statistics."

23. Andrew Anglemyer et al., "The Accessibility of Firearms and Risk for Suicide and Homicide

Victimization Among Household Members: A Systematic Review and Meta-Analysis," *Annals of Internal Medicine* 160, no. 2 (2014): 101–110.

24. National Institute of Mental Health, "Suicide."

25. Tony Hicks, "Why Suicides Have Decreased During the COVID-19 Pandemic," Healthline, April 12, 2021.

26. Samantha Raphelson, "How Often Do People Use Guns in Self-Defense?" NPR, April 13, 2018.

27. Giffords Law Center, "Gun Violence Statistics."

28. Daniel Lathrop and Anna Flagg, "Killings of Black Men by Whites Are Far More Likely to Be Ruled 'Justifiable,'" Marshall Project, August 14, 2017.

29. J.C. Campbell et al., "Risk Factors for Femicide in Abusive Relationships: Results from a Multisite Case Control Study," *American Journal of Public Health* 93, no. 7 (2003): 1089–1097.

30. Giffords Law Center, "Gun Violence Statistics."

31. Ron Elving, "The NRA Wasn't Always Against Gun Restrictions," NPR, October 10, 2017.

32. Elving, "The NRA Wasn't Always," and Ann Gerhart and Chris Alcantara, "How the NRA Transformed from Marksmen to Lobbyists," *Washington Post*, May 29, 2018.

33. Jeff Suess, "NRA: 'Revolt at Cincinnati' Molded National Rifle Association," *Cincinnati Enquirer*, March 8, 2018.

34. Joel Achenbach et al., "How NRA's True Believers Converted a Marksmanship Group into a Mighty Gun Lobby," *Washington Post*, January 12, 2013.

35. Legal Information Institute, Cornell Law School, "Bearing Arms: Second Amendment."

36. Carl T. Bogus, "The Hidden History of the Second Amendment," *UC Davis Law Review* 31, 309 (1998).

37. Legal Information Institute, "Bearing Arms."

38. United States v. Miller, 317 U.S. 369 (1943).

39. Eugene Volokh, "Supreme Court Cases on the Right to Keep and Bear Arms," UCLA Law School.

40. Adam Liptak, "A Liberal Case for Gun Rights Sways Judiciary," *New York Times*, May 6, 2007.

41. District of Columbia v. Heller, 554 U.S. 570 (2008).

42. Alison Frankel, "Second Amendment Does Not Apply to Assault Weapons," Reuters, February 22, 2017.

43. Volokh, "Supreme Court Cases."

44. Scott Neuman and Nina Totenberg, "Supreme Court to Take Up 1st Major Gun Rights Case in More Than a Decade," NPR, April 26, 2021.

45. John K. Roman, "Race, Justifiable Homicide, and Stand Your Ground Laws: Analysis of FBI Supplementary Homicide Report Data," Urban Institute, July 2013.

46. Leila N. Sadat and Madaline George, "The U.S. Gun Violence Crisis: Human Rights Perspectives and Remedies," *Washington University in St. Louis Legal Studies Research Paper No. 19-01-11*, 2019.

47. DeShaney v. Winnebago Cty. DSS, 489 U.S. 189 (1989).

48. United States v. Miller.

49. Navegar, Inc. v. United States, 986 F. Supp. 650 (D.D.C. 1997).

50. U.S. Department of Justice, "Navegar v. United States—Opposition," July 2000.

51. Vivian S. Chu, "Federal Assault Weapons Ban: Legal Issues," Congressional Research Service, February 14, 2013.

52. Chu, "Federal Assault Weapons Ban."

53. Nicole Wetsman, "After a 20-Year Drought, U.S. Lawmakers Fund Gun Violence Research," *The Verge*, December 19, 2019.

54. Annie Karni, "With Gun Control Measures Stalled in Congress, Biden Announces Actions Against Gun Violence," *New York Times*, April 8, 2021.

55. Catie Edmondson, "House Passes Gun Control Bills to Strengthen Background Checks," *New York Times*, March 12, 2021.

56. John Rosenthal, "Restrictions Work, Says Man Who Brought Massachusetts Gun Deaths to Record Low," *The Guardian*, April 24, 2021.

57. Giffords Law Center, "Gun Violence Statistics."

58. Permit to purchase: CT, HI, IA, MD, MA, MI, NE, NJ, NC, RI; license to own: IL, MA, NY; registration: DC; safety certificate: CA, WA.

59. Universal background checks: WA, OR, CA, CO, MA, NY, CT, RI, DE, IL, HI, NJ; partial background checks: NE, IA, MI, NC, PA, MD.

60. Domestic violence regulations: AL, CA, CO, CT, DE, DC, HI, IL, IN, IA, KS, LA, MA, ME, MD, MN, NE, NV, NJ, NM, NY, OR, PA, RI, SC, SD, TE, TX, UT, VT, WA, WV.

61. Amanda Taub, "A New Covid-19 Crisis: Domestic Abuse Rises Worldwide," *New York Times*, April 14, 2020.

62. May-issue: CA, CT, DE, DC, HI, MD, MA, NJ, NY; shall-issue: AL, AR, CO, FL, GA, IL, IN, IA, LA, MI, MN, MT, NE, NV, NM, NC, OH, OR, PA, RI, SC, TN, TX, UT, VA, WA, WI; unrestricted: AK, AZ, ID, KS, KY, ME, MS, MO, NH, ND, OK, SD, VT, WV, WY; no open carry: CA, DC, FL, IL, NY, SC; permitted open carry: AL, CT, GA, HI, IN, IA, MD, MA, MN, MO, NJ, ND, OK, PA, RI, TN, TX, UT, VA, WA.

63. Bump stock regulations: FL, VT, DE, HI, MD, WA, DC, NV.

64. States with age limit of twenty-one (for at least some types of guns): CA, CT, DE, DC, FL, HI, IL, IA, MD, MA, NE, NJ, NY, OH, RI, VT, WA.

65. Matt Vasilogambros, "Red Flag Laws Spur Debate over Due Process," Pew Charitable Trusts, September 4, 2019; Priyanka Boghani, "'Red Flag' Laws Allow Guns to Be Taken from 'Dangerous' People," PBS, August 7, 2019.

66. All states have provisions for removal of guns in response to domestic violence; otherwise, the following states have additional Extreme Risk Protective Order (ERPO) petitions: CA, CO, DE, DC, HI, IL, MD, MA, NV, NJ, NY, OR, WA, FL, RI, VT.

67. Gramlich and Schaeffer, "7 Facts About Guns"; Giffords Law Center, "Gun Violence Statistics."

68. Giffords Law Center, "Gun Violence Statistics."

69. Giffords Law Center, "City Rights in an Era of Preemption: A State-by-State Analysis," February 16, 2017.

Part IV: Speech, Media, and Belief

12. Speech, Lies, and Insurrection
Research and drafting contributed by Kathleen Addison.

1. William Davies, "The Age of Post-Truth Politics," *New York Times,* August 24, 2016.

2. Lucia Graves, "How Trump Weaponized 'Fake News' for His Own Political Ends," *Pacific Standard,* February 26, 2018, https://psmag.com/social-justice/how-trump-weaponized-fake-news-for-his-own-political-ends.

3. Andrew S. Ross and Damian J. Rivers. "Discursive Deflection: Accusation of 'Fake News' and the Spread of Mis- and Disinformation in the Tweets of President Trump," *Social Media + Society* 4, no. 2 (May 18, 2018), https://journals.sagepub.com/doi/10.1177/2056305118776010.

4. Emily Stewart, "Trump Calls Media the 'True Enemy of the People' the Same Day a Bomb Is Sent to CNN," Vox, October 29, 2018.

5. Admitted by President Trump, according to Judy Woodruff of PBS NewsHour: "Lesley Stahl: Trump Said He Bashes Press to 'Demean' and 'Discredit' Them," CBS News, May 23, 2018.

6. Donald Trump, Twitter post, https://twitter.com/realDonaldTrump/status/1168499357 131427840; Janice Williams, "Donald Trump Says His 'Real Opponent' in 2020 Election Is the 'Fake News Media,' Not Democrats," *Newsweek*, September 2, 2019.

7. Knight Foundation, "American Views: Trust, Media and Democracy," January 16, 2018, https://knightfoundation.org/reports/american-views-trust-media-and-democracy.

8. "Donald Trump," Politifact, the Poynter Institute, www.politifact.com/personalities /donald-trump.

9. James P. Pfiffner, "The Lies of Donald Trump: A Taxonomy," SSRN, September 17, 2018, http://dx.doi.org/10.2139/ssrn.3286278.

10. Pfiffner, "The Lies of Donald Trump," 14.

11. Michael Schudson, "The Fall, Rise, and Fall of Media Trust," *Columbia Journalism Review,* 2019.

12. Megan Brenan, "Americans' Trust in Mass Media Edges Down to 41%," Gallup, September 26, 2019, https://news.gallup.com/poll/267047/americans-trust-mass-media-edges-down .aspx.

13. Galen Stocking, Elizabeth Grieco, and Jeffrey Gottfried, "Partisans Are Divided on Whether They Associate the News Media or Trump with 'Made-Up' News," Pew Research Center, June 5, 2019, www.pewresearch.org/fact-tank/2019/06/05/partisans-are-divided-on -whether-they-associate-the-news-media-or-trump-with-made-up-news.

14. Schudson, "The Fall, Rise, and Fall."

15. In 2019, *The Washington Post* added ten investigative journalists in what it called a "major expansion of its investigative journalism"; see Rob Williams, "'The Washington Post' Adds 10 Investigative Journalists," *Washington Post*, June 21, 2019, www.mediapost.com/publications /article/337333/the-washington-post-adds-10-investigative-journa.html.

16. Mark Schapiro, "The Story of the Ukraine Scandal Begins with Documents Dumped in a River," *Mother Jones*, March/April 2020, www.motherjones.com/politics/2020/02/ukraine -impeachment-trump-journalism-yanukovych.

17. "Political Polarization in the American Public," Pew Research Center, June 12, 2014, www .people-press.org/2014/06/12/section-1-growing-ideological-consistency.

18. Richard Pérez-Peña, "After Protests, I.M.F. Chief Withdraws as Smith College's Commencement Speaker," *New York Times*, May 12, 2014, www.nytimes.com/2014/05/13/us/after-protests-imf-chief-withdraws-as-smith-colleges-commencement-speaker.html?_r=0.

19. Peter Beinart, "A Violent Attack on Free Speech at Middlebury," *The Atlantic*, March 6, 2017.

20. Maleeha Syed, "Middlebury College Cancels Talk with Conservative Speaker for Safety Purposes," *Burlington Free Press*, April 17, 2019, www.burlingtonfreepress.com/story/news/local/2019/04/17/campus-free-speech-middlebury-college-charles-murray-european-parliament-ryszard-legutko/3494450002.

21. Caroline Simon, "Free Speech Isn't Free: It's Costing College Campuses Millions," *Forbes*, November 20, 2017.

22. "George Floyd: What Happened in the Final Moments of His Life," BBC News, July 16, 2020.

23. Philip Bump, "Timeline: The Clearing of Lafayette Square," *Washington Post*, June 5, 2020.

24. Sergio Olmos, "Federal Agents Unleash Militarized Crackdown on Portland," *New York Times*, July 17, 2020.

25. Emma Kerr, "Should Students Be Expelled for Posting Racist Videos?" *The Chronicle of Higher Education*, January 26, 2018.

26. Vera Eidelman and Sarah Hinger, "Some Schools Need a Lesson on Students' Free Speech Rights," American Civil Liberties Union, September 18, 2018, www.aclu.org/blog/free-speech/student-speech-and-privacy/some-schools-need-lesson-students-free-speech-rights.

27. L. Paige Whitaker, *The Whistleblower Protection Act: An Overview*, Congressional Research Service, March 12, 2007, https://fas.org/sgp/crs/natsec/RL33918.pdf.

28. Jan Wolfe, "Explainer: Is It Illegal for Trump or Congress to Name the Impeachment Whistleblower?" Reuters, November 7, 2019.

29. Maggie Haberman and Michael S. Schmidt. "Trump Has Considered Firing Intelligence Community Inspector General," *New York Times*, November 12, 2019.

30. Kyle Cheney, Natasha Bertrand, and Meridith Mcgraw, "Impeachment Witnesses Ousted amid Fears of Trump Revenge Campaign." Politico, February 7, 2020.

31. John Hudson, "Does Thomas Drake Owe the Media His Freedom?" *The Atlantic*, June 10, 2011.

32. Greg Myre, "Once Reserved for Spies, Espionage Act Now Used Against Suspected Leakers," NPR, June 28, 2017.

33. Peter Sterne, "Obama Used the Espionage Act to Put a Record Number of Reporters' Sources in Jail, and Trump Could Be Even Worse," Freedom of the Press Foundation, June 21, 2017, https://freedom.press/news/obama-used-espionage-act-put-record-number-reporters-sources-jail-and-trump-could-be-even-worse.

34. Elizabeth Goitein, "The U.S. Says Julian Assange 'Is No Journalist.' Here's Why That Shouldn't Matter," *Washington Post*, May 25, 2019.

35. "Julian Assange's Indictment Aims at the Heart of the First Amendment," *New York Times*, May 23, 2019.

36. Elisa Shearer, "Social Media Outpaces Print Newspapers in the U.S. as a News Source," Pew Research Center, December 10, 2018, www.pewresearch.org/fact-tank/2018/12/10/social-media-outpaces-print-newspapers-in-the-u-s-as-a-news-source.

37. Elisa Shearer and Jeffrey Gottfried, "News Use Across Social Media Platforms 2017," Pew Research Center, September 7, 2017; Katherine Schaeffer, "U.S. Has Changed in Key Ways in the Past Decade, from Tech Use to Demographics," Pew Research Center, December 20, 2019.

38. Mercedes Bunz, "Most Journalists Use Social Media Such as Twitter and Facebook as a Source," *The Guardian*, February 15, 2010.

39. Henry Farrell, "Blame FOX, Not Facebook for Fake News," *Washington Post*, November 6, 2018.

40. Monica Anderson et al., "Public Attitudes Toward Political Engagement on Social Media," Pew Research Center, July 11, 2018.

41. The specific actions listed in the survey were "(1) taken part in a group that shares an interest in an issue/cause (34 percent), (2) encouraged others to take action on issues important to them (32 percent), (3) looked up information on local protests/rallies (19 percent), (4) changed profile picture to show support for a cause (18 percent), and (5) used hashtags related to a political/social issue (14 percent)."

42. A.J. Willingham, "Slacktivism Is Over. The #Neveragain Movement Is About What's Next," CNN, March 25, 2018.

43. March for Our Lives, "Mission and Story," https://marchforourlives.com/mission-story; "March for Our Lives Highlights: Students Protesting Guns Say 'Enough Is Enough,'" *New York Times*, March 24, 2018, www.nytimes.com/2018/03/24/us/march-for-our-lives.html.

44. Malcolm Gladwell and Clay Shirky, "From Innovation to Revolution: Do Social Media Make Protests Possible?" *Foreign Affairs* 90, no. 2 (March 2011): 153–154, http://search.proquest.com.ezp-prod1.hul.harvard.edu/docview/853657631?accountid=11311.

45. Philip N. Howard and Muzammil M. Hussain, "The Upheavals in Egypt and Tunisia: The Role of Digital Media." *Journal of Democracy* 22, no. 3 (2011): 35–48, doi:10.1353/jod.2011.0041.

46. Paul S. N. Lee et al., "Social Media and Umbrella Movement: Insurgent Public Sphere in Formation," *Chinese Journal of Communication* 8, no. 4 (2015): 356–375, https://doi.org/10.1080/17544750.2015.1088874.

47. Monica Anderson et al., "Activism in the Social Media Age," Pew Research Center, July 11, 2018, www.pewresearch.org/internet/2018/07/11/public-attitudes-toward-political-engagement-on-social-media.

48. Laura W. Murphy et al., "Facebook's Civil Rights Audit," Facebook, July 8, 2018, https://about.fb.com/wp-content/uploads/2020/07/Civil-Rights-Audit-Final-Report.pdf.

49. Donald J. Trump, Facebook post, May 29, 2020, www.facebook.com/DonaldTrump/posts/10164767134275725www.facebook.com/DonaldTrump/posts/10164767134275725.

50. Murphy, "Facebook's Civil Rights Audit."

51. Shearer, "Social Media Outpaces Print."

52. Electronic Frontier Foundation, "Section 230 of the Communications Decency Act," www.eff.org/issues/cda230.

53. Alina Selyukh, "Section 230: A Key Legal Shield for Facebook, Google Is About To Change," NPR, March 21, 2018.

54. Joshua A. Geltzer, "The President and Congress Are Thinking of Changing This Important Internet Law," *Slate*, February 25, 2019.

55. Ted Cruz, "Sen. Ted Cruz: Facebook Has Been Censoring or Suppressing Conservative Speech for Years," Fox News, April 11, 2018; Taylor Hatmaker, "Nancy Pelosi Warns Tech Companies That Section 230 Is 'in Jeopardy,'" *TechCrunch*, April 12, 2019, techcrunch.com/2019/04/12/nancy-pelosi-section-230.

56. Online Censorship, "Offline-Online," www.onlinecensorship.org/content/infographics.

57. Elliot Harmon, "Changing Section 230 Would Strengthen the Biggest Tech Companies," *New York Times*, October 16, 2019.

58. Facebook for Business, "How News Feed Works," www.facebook.com/help/publisher /718033381901819; Twitter Help Center, "About Your Twitter Timeline," https://help.twitter.com /en/using-twitter/twitter-timeline.

59. Gregory Eady et al., "How Many People Live in Political Bubbles on Social Media? Evidence from Linked Survey and Twitter Data," *SAGE Open* 9, no. 1 (2019), https://doi.org/10.1177 /2158244019832705.

60. Seth Flaxman, Sharad Goel, and Justin M. Rao, "Filter Bubbles, Echo Chambers, and Online News Consumption," *Public Opinion Quarterly* 80, no. S1 (2016): 298–320, https://doi .org/10.1093/poq/nfw006.

61. Kristen Bialik, "14 Percent of Americans Have Changed Their Mind About an Issue Because of Something They Saw on Social Media," Pew Research Center, August 15, 2018.

62. Eytan Bakshy et al., "Exposure to Diverse Information on Facebook," Facebook Research, May 7, 2015, https://research.fb.com/blog/2015/05/exposure-to-diverse-information-on-face book-2.

63. J. Bettina, "Confirmation Bias," *Encyclopedia Britannica*, www.britannica.com/science /confirmation-bias.

64. Nick Clegg, "Facebook, Elections and Political Speech," Facebook, September 24, 2019, https://newsroom.fb.com/news/2019/09/elections-and-political-speech.

65. Donie O'Sullivan, "He's Running for Governor to Run False Ads on Facebook. Now Facebook Is Stopping Him," CNN Business, October 30, 2019.

66. Cecilia Kang and Thomas Kaplan, "Warren Dares Facebook with Intentionally False Political Ad," *New York Times*, October 12, 2019.

67. Jack Dorsey, Twitter thread, 4:05pm, October 30, 2019.

68. Emily Stewart, "Twitter Chose to Ban Political Ads. But Pressuring Facebook to Do the Same Could Backfire," Vox, November 5, 2019.

69. Shannon C. McGregor, "Why Twitter's Ban on Political Ads Isn't as Good as It Sounds," *Guardian*, November 4, 2019.

70. Charlie Savage, "Trump Can't Block Critics from His Twitter Account, Appeals Court Rules," *New York Times*, July 9, 2019.

71. United States, Court of Appeals for the Second Circuit, Knight First Amendment Institute, et. al v. Donald J. Trump et al., Docket no. 18-1691-cv, 9 July 2019. https://int.nyt.com/data /documenthelper/1365-trump-twitter-second-circuit-r/c0f4e0701b087dab9b43/optimized/full .pdf#page=1.

72. Queenie Wong, "Trump vs. Twitter," CNET, June 2, 2020, www.cnet.com/news/trump-vs -twitter-heres-what-you-need-to-know-about-the-free-speech-showdown/.

73. Twitter, "Permanent Suspension of @realDonaldTrump," January 8, 2021, https://blog .twitter.com/en_us/topics/company/2020/suspension.html.

74. Hannah Denham, "These Are the Platforms That Have Banned Trump and His Allies," *Washington Post*, January 14, 2021.

75. Facebook, "Oversight Board," https://oversightboard.com/meet-the-board/.

76. Shannon Bond, "Facebook Ban on Donald Trump Will Hold, Social Network's Oversight Board Rules," NPR, May 5, 2021.

77. Elaine Fahey, "Trump's Facebook Ban Upheld—but the Future of the Oversight Board Is in Doubt," *Conversation*, May 6, 2021, https://theconversation.com/trumps-facebook-ban-upheld-but-the-future-of-the-oversight-board-is-in-doubt-160395.

78. Shoshana Zuboff, *The Age of Surveillance Capitalism: The Fight for a Human Future at the New Frontier of Power* (New York: Public Affairs, 2019.)

79. Ethan Zuckerman, "Building a More Honest Internet," *Columbia Journalism Review*, 2019, www.cjr.org/special_report/building-honest-internet-public-interest.php.

80. Jonathan Zittrain, "Facebook Could Decide an Election Without Anyone Ever Finding Out," *The New Republic*, June 1, 2014.

81. Tim Hwang, "Dealing with Disinformation: Evaluating the Case for CDA 230 Amendment," SSRN, December 17, 2017, http://dx.doi.org/10.2139/ssrn.3089442.

82. Aja Romano, "A New Law Intended to Curb Sex Trafficking Threatens the Future of the Internet as We Know It," Vox, July 2, 2018.

83. Hwang, "Dealing with Disinformation."

84. Mark Zuckerberg, "A Blueprint for Content Governance and Enforcement," Facebook, November 15, 2018, www.facebook.com/notes/mark-zuckerberg/a-blueprint-for-content-governance-and-enforcement/10156443129621634/?hc_location=ufi.

85. Amy Mitchell et al., "Many Americans Say Made-Up News Is a Critical Problem That Needs to Be Fixed," Pew Research Center, June 5, 2019, www.journalism.org/2019/06/05/political-leaders-activists-viewed-as-prolific-creators-of-made-up-news-journalists-seen-as-the-ones-to-fix-it.

86. Amy Mitchell et al., "Distinguishing Between Factual and Opinion Statements in the News," Pew Research Center, June 18, 2018, www.journalism.org/2018/06/18/distinguishing-between-factual-and-opinion-statements-in-the-news.

87. Lee Raine et al., "Trust and Distrust in America," Pew Research Center, July 22, 2019, www.people-press.org/2019/07/22/trust-and-distrust-in-america.

88. Alfonso Gutiérrez-Martín and Kathleen Tyner, "Media Education, Media Literacy and Digital Competence," *Comunicar* 19, no. 38 (2012): 31–39, https://doi.org/10.3916/C38-2012-02-03.

13. Religious Freedom and Civil Rights
Research and drafting contributed by Colin Wall.

1. Dave Roos, "What's the Difference Between Puritans and Pilgrims?" *History*, July 31, 2019; Steven Waldman, *Sacred Liberty: America's Long, Bloody, and Ongoing Struggle for Religious Freedom* (New York: HarperCollins, 2019), 13; and Steven Waldman, *Founding Faith: How Our Founding Fathers Forged a Radical New Approach to Religious Liberty* (New York: Penguin Random House, 2009), 7.

2. Waldman, *Founding Faith*, 9.

3. Charles C. Haynes, "History of Religious Liberty in America," Freedom Forum Institute, December 26, 2002; Waldman, *Sacred Liberty*, 18.

4. The historical evidence indicates Madison was also inspired by his own spiritual journey and by the influence of Enlightenment thinkers like David Hume and John Locke; Waldman, *Sacred Liberty*, 26–27.

5. Waldman, *Sacred Liberty*, 26–27, 30, and National Archives, "The Virginia Declaration of Rights," June 12, 1776.

6. Waldman, *Founding Faith*, 115.

7. James Madison, "Memorial and Remonstrance Against Religious Assessments."

8. Waldman, *Founding Faith*, 130.

9. Waldman, *Founding Faith*, 144–151.

10. National Archives, "The Constitution of the United States: A Transcription," 1789.

11. The amendment had passed in the House; Waldman, *Founding Faith*, 150–151.

12. History, "Freedom of Religion," August 21, 2018

13. Sometimes, even those who converted to Christianity were prevented from practicing freely. Peter Gottschalk, "Hate Crimes Associated with Both Islamophobia and Anti-Semitism Have a Long History in America's Past," *Conversation*, June 3, 2019, https://theconversation .com/hate-crimes-associated-with-both-islamophobia-and-anti-semitism-have-a-long-history -in-americas-past-116255.

14. Haynes, "History of Religious Liberty in America"; "Know-Nothing Party," *Encyclopedia Brittanica*, March 22, 2007.

15. Church of Jesus Christ of Latter-Day Saints, "Extermination Order," December 27, 2020.

16. Gottschalk, "Hate Crimes," and David Grubin, "The Jewish Americans," PBS.

17. Gottschalk, "Hate Crimes."

18. Ryan Anningson, "Before Americans Turned to Buddhism for Life Hacks, They Treated It Like a Dangerous Cult," Quartz, March 15, 2018.

19. "The Bill of Rights: A Transcription," National Archives, 1789, updated October 28, 2020.

20. Waldman, *Founding Faith*, 130.

21. In 1953, Earl Warren became Chief Justice of the Court, triggering a "constitutional revolution" based on two core notions: "The first was the idea of a living constitution: a constitution that evolves according to changing values and circumstances. The second was marked by the reemergence of the discourse of rights as a dominant constitutional mode." This new iteration of the Court was increasingly willing to hear cases on core rights like free exercise. Morton J. Horowitz, "The Warren Court and the Pursuit of Justice," *Washington and Lee Law Review* 50, no. 1 (Winter 1993).

22. Waldman, *Sacred Liberty*, 199, and Haynes, "History of Religious Liberty."

23. "Your Right to Religious Freedom," ACLU, December 2020.

24. Waldman, *Sacred Liberty*, 207.

25. Haynes, "History of Religious Liberty."

26. Waldman, *Sacred Liberty*, 209.

27. Haynes, "History of Religious Liberty"; Bette Novit Evans, "Religious Freedom vs. Compelling State Interests," Kripke Center for the Study of Religion and Society, Spring 1998. For fundamental rights, the burden of proof of constitutionality shifts to the lawmakers, as opposed to the party challenging the law. This is similar to the legal concept of "strict scrutiny"; "Strict Scrutiny," Legal Information Institute, Cornell Law School.

28. Kathleen P. Kelly, "Abandoning the Compelling Interest Test in Free Exercise Cases," *Catholic University Law Review* 40, no. 4 (Summer 1991).

29. Sherbert v. Verner, 374 U.S. 398 (1963).

30. Wisconsin v. Yoder, 406 U.S. 205 (1972).

31. Ronald Steiner, "Compelling State Interest," The First Amendment Encyclopedia, Middle Tennessee State University, 2009.

32. American Civil Liberties Union, "Your Right to Religious Freedom."

33. Zorach v. Clauson, 343 U.S. 306 (1952), and Kalpana Jain, "How the Religious Right Shaped American Politics: 6 Essential Reads," *Conversation*, December 21, 2017. In 1954, President Eisenhower signed a bill adding the words "under God" to the Pledge of Allegiance. This has been challenged multiple times but never ruled unconstitutional. Scott Bomboy, "The History of Legal Challenges to the Pledge of Allegiance," *National Constitution Center*, June 14, 2019. However, in *Lee v. Weisman* (1992), the Court ruled that it was unconstitutional to have clergy offer prayers at official public school ceremonies; Lee v. Weisman, 505 U.S. 577 (1992).

34. *Sacred Liberty* provides an account of the history of Supreme Court "tinkering" in trying to find the right balance; Waldman, *Sacred Liberty*, 205–208.

35. Geoff McGovern, "Lynch v. Donnelly (1984)," *The First Amendment Encyclopedia*, Middle Tennessee State University, 2009. In *Van Orden v. Perry*, the Supreme Court declared that religious displays in the Texas State Capital declared were constitutional. "Van Orden v. Perry," Oyez.

36. In *County of Allegheny v. American Civil Liberties Union, Greater Pittsburgh Chapter*, the Supreme Court ruled that religious displays outside Allegheny courthouse and city council buildings were unconstitutional. "County of Allegheny v. American Civil Liberties Union, Greater Pittsburgh Chapter," Oyez; and in *McCreary County v. American Civil Liberties Union of Kentucky*, the Supreme Court declared that religious displays in Kentucky courthouses were unconstitutional. "McCreary County v. American Civil Liberties Union of Ky," Oyez.

37. Tyson Radley O'Connell, "How Did the Ten Commandments End Up on Both Sides of the Wall of Separation Between Church and State?: The Contradicting Opinions of *Van Orden v. Perry* and *McCreary v. ACLU*," *Montana Law Review* 6, no. 1 (Winter 2008).

38. "United States v. Seeger," Oyez, www.oyez.org/cases/1964/50.

39. Whitney Untiedt, "Lighting the Way: The Johnson Amendment Stands Strong Against Dark Money in Politics," *Emory Corporate Governance and Accountability Review* 6, no. 1 (2019); and, Brendan Fischer, "Destroying the Johnson Amendment: How Allowing Charities to Spend on Politics Would Flood the Swamp That President Trump Promised to Drain," Campaign Legal Center.

40. Nelson Tebbe et al., "The Quiet Demise of the Separation of Church and State," *New York Times*, June 8, 2020.

41. "Employment Division v. Smith," Oyez.

42. Waldman, *Sacred Liberty*, 211. While it may seem contradictory for Justice Scalia to rule against religious freedom, given his conservative reputation, there is an explanation stemming from another aspect of his judicial philosophy: he believed that the courts should not be the ones to decide how to protect religious freedom—that was a job for legislatures. It would be an overreach, in his view, for the Court to carve out exceptions from an otherwise benign, generally applicable law. Amul R. Thaper, "Smith, Scalia, and Originalism," *Catholic University Law Review* 68, no. 4 (Fall 2019).

43. Haynes, "History of Religious Liberty."

44. This is also called a law of "general effect."

45. The Senate voted 97–3 to pass the law. Waldman, *Sacred Liberty*, 212.

46. "H.R. 1308," Congress.gov.

47. "City of Boerne v. Flores," Oyez.

48. Although they could trace their spiritual ancestry back to America's original evangelicals during "The Great Awakening." Waldman, *Sacred Liberty*, 21–22.

49. Clyde Haberman, "Religion and Right-Wing Politics: How Evangelicals Reshaped Elections," *New York Times*, October 28, 2018; Michael J. McVicar, "The Religious Right in America," *Oxford Research Encyclopedia*; and Waldman, *Sacred Liberty*, 233.

50. More specifically, banning interracial dating. The IRS was simply enacting the DC District Court ruling in the 1973 case of *Green v. Connally*; Richard Flory, "Revisiting the Legacy of Jerry Falwell Sr. in Trump's America," *Conversation*, July 10, 2017; and Randall Balmer, "The Real Origins of the Religious Right," Politico, May 27, 2014.

51. McVicar, "The Religious Right." "Jerry Falwell's Moral Majority, Tim LaHaye's Council for National Policy, Beverly LaHaye's Concerned Women for America, and Ed McAteer's Religious Roundtable."

52. Haberman, "Religion and Right-Wing Politics."

53. Mason Adams, "Flashback 1990: George H.W. Bush Delivers Liberty University Commencement Speech," Roanoke, July 13, 2012.

54. "[I]n party primaries, local elections, and national congressional mid-term elections where voter turnout and razor-thin margins decided outcomes, the organs of the Religious Right could prove decisive." McVicar, "The Religious Right."

55. As Waldman notes, this is consistent with a trend throughout American history: "whenever the majority has been on the verge of losing control it has shape-shifted, reassembling in order to maintain its dominant size. Whereas Protestant denominations warred with each other in the eighteenth century, they coalesced as a Protestant majority when combatting Catholics in the nineteenth century. In the twentieth century, they invited in Catholics and even Jews to become a Judeo-Christian majority." Waldman, *Sacred Liberty*, 233–237.

56. Jeremy Leaming, "The Religious Right," *The First Amendment Encyclopedia*, Middle Tennessee State University, 2009. There was some overlap with the Tea Party movement as well, but it was an imperfect alignment. "The Tea Party and Religion," Pew Research Center, February 23, 2011.

57. A feeling that "the country they know is slipping away—if not already lost." Haberman, "Religion and Right-Wing Politics."

58. Waldman, *Sacred Liberty*, 241–242. Even among believers, the share of White evangelical Protestants has dropped from 23 percent in 2006 to 17 percent just eleven years later.

59. For a list of such rulings/regulations, see Waldman, *Sacred Liberty*, 241.

60. Waldman, *Sacred Liberty*, 243–244. "Many of the instances in which modern Christians claim victimhood are 'accommodation' cases, which is to say that they're being harmed only incidentally, as a by-product of some secular law that wasn't targeting them. We have to come to think of this new kind of religious freedom as the moral equivalent of earlier claims against overt oppression." Ibid., 254.

61. Peter Wehner, "The Deepening Crisis in Evangelical Christianity," *The Atlantic*, July 5, 2019; and Josh Hafner, "Meet the Evangelicals Who Prophesied a Trump Win," *USA Today*, November 10, 2016.

62. "The voters who supported him most strongly responded affirmatively to all of these statements: 'The federal government should declare the United States a Christian nation.' 'The federal government should advocate Christian values. . . . The federal government should allow prayer in public schools.'" Andrew L. Whitehead et al., "Make America Christian Again: Christian

Nationalism and Voting for Donald Trump in the 2016 Presidential Election," *Sociology of Religion* 79, no. 2 (2018): 147–171, and Waldman, *Sacred Liberty*, 246–247.

63. Kara Bettis, "Who Are the Evangelicals?: Frances FitzGerald Studied American History to Explain," *Religion Unplugged*, February 15, 2019.

64. Flory, "Revisiting the Legacy." Masha Gessen, "Mike Pompeo's Faith-Based Attempt to Narrowly Redefine Human Rights," *New Yorker*, July 10, 2019.

65. Linda Greenhouse, "Religious Crusaders at the Supreme Court's Gates," *New York Times*, September 12, 2019; Russell Wheeler, "Judicial Appointments in Trump's First Three Years: Myths and Realities," Brookings, January 28, 2020; Carl Hulse, "Trump and Senate Republicans Celebrate Making the Courts More Conservative," *New York Times*, November 6, 2019; Colby Itkowitz, "1 in Every 4 Circuit Court Judges Is Now a Trump Appointee," *Washington Post*, December 21, 2019; and Susanna Luthi, "How Trump Is Filling the Liberal 9th Circuit with Conservatives," Politico, December 22, 2019.

66. Rachel B. Tiven, "If Abortion Rights Fall, LGBT Rights Are Next," *Washington Post*, February 22, 2017.

67. Michael Gryboski, "Congress Fails to Repeal Johnson Amendment in Tax Bill," *Christian Post*, December 18, 2017. The House tried to include a repeal of the Amendment in the 2017 tax bill, but the Senate parliamentarian ultimately took it out before it could become law.

68. Jain, "How the Religious Right."

69. Katherine Stewart and Caroline Fredrickson, "Bill Barr Thinks America Is Going to Hell," *New York Times*, December 29, 2019. For example, "[t]he U.S. Department of Justice has thrown its support behind a small group of Maine parents who have filed a federal lawsuit seeking reimbursement for their children's religious school tuition"; Anderson, J. Craig, "Justice Department Backs Parents Suing Maine over Tuition for Religious Schools," *Portland Press Herald*, June 11, 2019; Jeffrey Toobin, "William Barr's Wild Misreading of the First Amendment," *New Yorker*, October 17, 2019. ("Barr portrays these efforts as the free exercise of religion when, in fact, they are the establishment of religion"); and Catherine M. Odell, "Notre Dame Adjunct Rebuts Barr's Contentious Talk on Religious Freedom," *National Catholic Reporter*, November 22, 2019.

70. For a longer account of the cultural shift, see Peter Beinart, "When Conservatives Oppose 'Religious Freedom,'" *The Atlantic*, April 11, 2017.

71. Recent years have seen an increase in anti-Semitic and Islamophobic hate crimes. Gottschalk, "Hate Crimes."

72. Asma Uddin, "The Baffling Argument That Has Become Mainstream Under Trump: 'Islam Is Not a Religion,'" *Washington Post*, March 19, 2019.

73. Waldman, *Sacred Liberty*, 290–291.

74. Waldman, *Sacred Liberty*, 273–275. Local governments often denied permits to Muslims even as they granted them to Christian churches. The most famous case was the Cordoba House, an Islamic center that was planned to be built in New York City—near the former site of the World Trade Center—before intense opposition and harassment of the Imam leading the project caused it to be effectively canceled; Waldman, *Sacred Liberty*, 284–285.

75. Uddin, "The Baffling Argument." Tennessee passed a bill that created a *15-year* prison sentence for "anyone who helped a 'Sharia organization,'" which was defined as two or more people acting to 'support' Sharia"; Waldman, *Sacred Liberty*, 275–280.

76. "'Islam Is Peace' Says President," White House Archives, September 17, 2001, and, Erik Ortiz, "President Obama Asks All Americans to Fight Islamophobia During First Mosque Visit," *NBC News*, February 3, 2016.

77. Waldman, *Sacred Liberty*, 311–312; and Peter Beinart, "The Denationalization of American Muslims," *The Atlantic*, March 19, 2017.

78. Waldman, *Sacred Liberty*, 292–293.

79. Uddin, "The Baffling Argument."

80. Zolan Kanno-Youngs, "Trump Administration Adds Six Countries to Travel Ban," *New York Times*, February 3, 2020; Saba Hamedy, "Everything You Need to Know About the Travel Ban: A Timeline," CNN, June 26, 2018; and "Timeline of the Muslim Ban," ACLU of Washington.

81. "Trump v. Hawaii," Oyez.

82. Waldman, *Sacred Liberty*, 296; and Laurie Goldstein, "Christian Leaders Denounce Trump's Plan to Favor Christian Refugees," *New York Times*, January 29, 2017. His comments as a candidate were explicit. In December 2015, he called for a "total and complete shutdown of Muslims entering the United States until our country's representatives can figure out what is going on"; Jenna Johnson and Abigail Hauslohner, "'I Think Islam Hates Us': A Timeline of Trump's Comments About Islam and Muslims," *Washington Post*, May 20, 2017. In July 2016, "Trump explained that Muslim refugees were 'trying to take over our children and convince them how wonderful ISIS is and how wonderful Islam is.'" Waldman, *Sacred Liberty*, 293.

83. "Protecting the Religious Freedom of Muslims," ACLU.

84. "I don't see Islam as a religion. I see it as a political ideology . . . it will mask itself as a religion globally because, especially in the west, especially in the United States, because it can hide behind and protect itself behind what we call freedom of religion"; Uddin, "The Baffling Argument."

85. Waldman, *Sacred Liberty*, 279.

86. Similar claims were made in the past about previous minority faiths, including Mormons, Catholics, and Native Americans. Waldman *Sacred Liberty*, 271.

87. Franco Ordonez, "Trump Defends School Prayer. Critics Say He's Got It All Wrong," NPR, January 16, 2020.

88. Ordonez, "Trump Defends School Prayer"; Valerie Strauss, "In State of the Union, Trump Makes Clear His Aversion to Public Schools," *Washington Post*, February 5, 2020.

89. Ordonez, "Trump Defends School Prayer."

90. "Zelman v. Simmons-Harris," Oyez.

91. "Trinity Lutheran Church of Columbia, Inc. v. Comer," Oyez.

92. "Trinity Lutheran," Emphasis added. Justice Ruth Bader Ginsburg joined the dissent.

93. "Espinoza v. Montana Department of Revenue," SCOTUS Blog.

94. "Espinoza v. Montana Department of Revenue," Oyez.

95. Robert Barnes, "Supreme Court Says States That Subsidized Private Education Must Include Religious Schools," *New York Times*, June 30, 2020.

96. Espinoza v. Montana Department of Revenue, No. 18-1195 (2020).

97. Barnes, "Supreme Court Says States."

98. Linda Greenhouse, "The Supreme Court's Collapsing Center on Religion," *New York Times*, January 30, 2020.

99. Tom Gjelten, "Another Break from the Past: Government Will Help Churches Pay Pastor Salaries," *All Things Considered* on NPR, April 6, 2020.

100. Tebbe et al., "The Quiet Demise."

101. "Obergefell v. Hodges," *Legal Information Institute*, Cornell Law School; and Tiven, "If Abortion Rights Fall."

102. "Masterpiece Cakeshop, Ltd. v. Colorado Civil Rights Commission," Oyez. Although they tried to provide some nuance: "Though the court ruled in favor of the business owner, the majority said it did so because the Colorado government showed clear anti-religious bias when handling the case. Justice Anthony Kennedy, who wrote the majority opinion, made clear that religious beliefs do not justify discrimination against LGBTQ individuals. . . . 'Our society has come to the recognition that gay persons and gay couples cannot be treated as social outcasts or as inferior in dignity and worth. For that reason the laws and the Constitution can, and in some instances must, protect them in the exercise of their civil rights.'" Alexia Fernández Campbell, "Trump's Plan to Let Employers Discriminate Against LGBTQ Workers, Explained," Vox, August 16, 2019.

103. There is legislation currently held up in Congress that would "add sexual orientation and gender identity as protected characteristics to existing civil rights law, including the Civil Rights Act." Guthrie Graves-Fitzsimmons, "No Conflict Between True Religious Liberty and LGBTQ Rights," The Hill, February 27, 2020. It has passed the House and been received in the Senate. United States Congress, House of Representatives, *The Equality Act*, 116th Congress, 1st session, House Resolution 5, passed May 20, 2019.

104. Toobin, "William Barr's Wild Misreading." For example, *Fulton v. City of Philadelphia*. See "Fulton v. City of Philadelphia, Pennsylvania," *SCOTUS Blog*; and Adam Liptak, "Supreme Court to Hear Case on Gay Rights and Foster Care," *New York Times*, February 24, 2020.

105. "Hosanna-Tabor Evangelical Lutheran Church and School v. EEOC," Oyez.

106. "Roe v. Wade," Oyez.

107. Burwell v. Hobby Lobby Stores, Inc.

108. Another important point: the RFRA was designed, in the wake of Al Smith's peyote case, to protect religious *minorities*. Appealing to it to protect a Christian corporation would therefore seem a stretch. Steven Waldman, *Sacred Liberty*, 253.

109. Burwell v. Hobby Lobby Stores, Inc.; the fact that the party to the case was a corporation, and not an individual, did not change the majority's reasoning. Essentially, they argued that because a corporation is composed of individuals with legitimate religious beliefs, the corporation itself can also be said to have protected religious beliefs. Justice Ginsburg, in her dissent, rejected this view.

110. Burwell v. Hobby Lobby Stores, Inc., emphasis added.

111. Burwell v. Hobby Lobby Stores, Inc., emphasis added. In other words, it is simply unfair to force Hobby Lobby's female employees to jump though the bureaucratic hoops of joining the HHS program—particularly as at least some would inevitably not manage to do so, and their health would suffer as a result.

112. Katherine Franke et al., "Letter to Representative Ed DeLaney, Indiana House of Representatives, Regarding the Religious Freedom Restoration Act," Columbia University Law, February 27, 2015.

113. Kathleen P. Kelly, "Abandoning the Compelling Interest Test in Free Exercise Cases," *Catholic University Law Review* 40, no. 4 (Summer 1991): 947–949.

114. Burwell v. Hobby Lobby.

115. Estate of Thornton v. Caldor, Inc., 472 U.S. 703 (1985).

116. Burwell v. Hobby Lobby.

117. Of course, the Founders disagreed constantly among themselves, and to say there was a unified view among them is false. Waldman, *Sacred Liberty*, 39. Furthermore, the final language of the First Amendment was a compromise and—because of the dominance of concerns about states' rights during the debate—it passed "even though there was no consensus about the philosophical matter of how separate church should be from state." Waldman, *Founding Faith*, 157–158. Finally, even individual Founding Fathers occasionally contradicted themselves on this topic, or found their viewpoint changing over time. Waldman, *Founding Faith*.

118. Waldman, *Sacred Liberty*, 46. Madison wrote: "Every new & successful example therefore of a perfect separation between ecclesiastical and civil matters is of importance. . . . And I have no doubt that every new example, will succeed, as every past one has done, in shewing that *religion & Govt. will both exist in greater purity, the less they are mixed together.*" Waldman, *Sacred Liberty*, 201–202. Emphasis added.

119. Waldman, *Founding Faith*, 17.

120. "Over the decades, a virtuous cycle developed. Religious liberty allowed for more sects, and those minority faiths demanded more freedom. Thanks to that forward motion, government's role changed from promoting religion to promoting religious freedom"; Waldman, *Founding Faith*, 138.

121. James Madison, "Federalist Papers No. 10 (1787)," Bill of Rights Institute.

122. Irving Brant, *James Madison: The Virginia Revolutionist*, Bobbs-Merrill (1941), 246, emphasis added, and Waldman, *Founding Faith*, 114.

123. Waldman, *Founding Faith*, 91.

124. White House Archives, "'Islam Is Peace.'"

125. Waldman, *Sacred Liberty*, 280.

126. Waldman, *Sacred Liberty*, 297.

127. Ray Gustini, "Utah Republican Stands Up for NYC 'Mosque,'" *The Atlantic*, August 31, 2010.

14. Crimes of Hate
Research and drafting contributed by Aimee Hwang.

1. Simon Romero et al., "Massacre at a Crowded Walmart in Texas Leaves 20 Dead," *New York Times*, August 3, 2019; "El Paso Walmart Shooting by Cielo Vista Mall: What We Know About the Number of Victims, the Suspect," *USA Today*, August 5, 2019; Heather Murphy, "El Paso Shooting Suspect Indicted on Capital Murder Charge," *New York Times*, September 12, 2019.

2. U.S. Department of Justice, "Hate Crimes Case Examples," 2020.

3. U.S. Department of Justice, "Learn About Hate Crimes."

4. Niall McCarthy, "U.S. Hate Crimes Remain at Heightened Levels," Statista, November 13, 2019; Federal Bureau of Investigation, "FBI Releases 2019 Hate Crime Statistics," November 16, 2020, https://www.fbi.gov/news/pressrel/press-releases/fbi-releases-2019-hate-crime-statistics.

5. U.S. Department of Justice, "Hate Crimes Case Examples."

6. Micheal Kunzelman and Astrid Galvan, "Trump Words Linked to More Hate Crime? Some Experts Think So," AP News, August 7, 2019.

7. Eugene Scott, "Trump's Most Insulting—and Violent—Language Is Often Reserved for Immigrants," *Washington Post*, October 2, 2019.

8. "Full Text: Trump's Comments on White Supremacists, 'Alt-Left' in Charlottesville," Politico, August 15, 2017.

9. Allyson Chiu, "Trump Has No Qualms About Calling Coronavirus the 'Chinese Virus.' That's a Dangerous Attitude, Experts Say," *Washington Post,* March 20, 2020.

10. David Nakamura, "With 'Kung Flu,' Trump Sparks Backlash over Racist Language—and a Rallying Cry for Supporters," *Washington Post,* June 24, 2020.

11. Josh Margolin, "FBI Warns of Potential Surge in Hate Crimes Against Asian Americans Amid Coronavirus," ABC News, March 27, 2020.

12. Valerie Jenness, "Hate Crimes," in *The Oxford Handbook of Crime and Public Policy*, ed. by Micheal Tonry (Oxford: Oxford University Press, 2012).

13. The FBI's "Learn About Hate Crimes" states, "Under the First Amendment of the U.S. Constitution, people cannot be prosecuted simply for their beliefs. People may be offended or upset about beliefs that are untrue or based upon false stereotypes, but it is not a crime to express offensive beliefs, or to join with others who share such views. However, the First Amendment does not protect against committing a crime, just because the conduct is rooted in philosophical beliefs." See U.S. Department of Justice, "Learn About Hate Crimes."

14. Madeline Masucci and Lynn Langton, "Hate Crime Victimization, 2004–2015," Bureau of Justice Statistics, U.S. Department of Justice, June 2017.

15. U.S. Department of Justice, "Learn About Hate Crimes."

16. Federal Bureau of Investigation, "Hate Crime Statistics."

17. Masucci and Langton, "Hate Crime Victimization, 2004–2015."

18. Frank S. Pezzella, "Hate Crime Statutes: A Public Policy and Law Enforcement Dilemma," Springer, 2017.

19. Cynthia Choi, "In Six Weeks, STOP AAPI HATE Receives over 1700 Incident Reports of Verbal Harassment, Shunning and Physical Assaults," *Chinese for Affirmative Action,* May 20, 2020.

20. Adeel Hassan, "Hate-Crime Violence Hits 16-Year High, F.B.I. Reports," *New York Times,* November 12, 2019.

21. Pezzella, "Hate Crime Statutes."

22. Steven Philbrick, "Understanding the Three-Fifths Compromise," Constitutional Accountability Center, September 16, 2018.

23. History, "Fugitive Slave Acts," February 11, 2020.

24. Fixico, "When Native Americans Were Slaughtered in the Name of 'Civilization,'" History, August 16, 2019.

25. History, "Trail of Tears," July 7, 2020.

26. Fixico, "When Native Americans Were Slaughtered."

27. Southern Poverty Law Center, "Ku Klux Klan."

28. Equal Justice Initiative, "Lynching in America: Confronting the Legacy of Racial Terror," 2017.

29. Ryan D. King et al., "Contemporary Hate Crimes, Law Enforcement, and the Legacy of Racial Violence," *American Sociological Review* 74, no. 2 (April 2009): 291–315.

30. National Park Service, "16th Street Baptist Church Bombing (1963)," March 23, 2016.

31. Southern Poverty Law Center, "Ku Klux Klan," 2020.

32. Iris Chang, "The Chinese in America: A Narrative History," Viking, 2003.

33. History, "Chinese Exclusion Act," September 13, 2019.

34. Fong Yue Ting v. United States, 149 U.S. 698 (1893).

35. Andrew R. Chow, "Violence Against Asian Americans Is on the Rise—But It's Part of a Long History," *Time*, May 20, 2020.

36. McCarthy, "U.S. Hate Crimes Remain"; Federal Bureau of Investigation, "FBI Releases 2019."

37. Brian Levin and Lisa Nakashima, "Report to the Nation: Illustrated Almanac," Center for the Study of Hate and Extremism, 2019.

38. Jaweed Kaleem, "Latinos and Transgender People See Big Increases in Hate Crimes, FBI Reports," *Los Angeles Times*, November 12, 2019.

39. Federal Bureau of Investigation, "Incidents and Offenses," 2019 Hate Crime Statistics, https://ucr.fbi.gov/hate-crime/2019/topic-pages/incidents-and-offenses.

40. Federal Bureau of Investigation, "Victims," 2019 Hate Crime Statistics, https://ucr.fbi.gov /hate-crime/2019/topic-pages/victims.

41. Hassan, "Hate-Crime Violence."

42. Federal Bureau of Investigation, "Victims."

43. Federal Bureau of Investigation, "Victims."

44. Masucci and Langton, "Hate Crime Victimization, 2004–2015."

45. In the UCR Program, the term *known offender* does not imply that the suspect's identity is known; rather, the term indicates some aspect of the suspect was identified, thus distinguishing the suspect from an unknown offender. Law enforcement agencies specify the number of offenders and when possible, the race, ethnicity, and age of the offender or offenders as a group.

46. Federal Bureau of Investigation, "Offenders," 2019 Hate Crime Statistics, https://ucr.fbi .gov/hate-crime/2019/topic-pages/offenders.

47. Masucci and Langton, "Hate Crime Victimization, 2004–2015."

48. Pezzella, "Hate Crime Statutes"; Jack Levin and Jack McDevitt, "Hate Crimes," *The Encyclopedia of Peace, Violence, and Conflict*, 2008.

49. Swathi Shanmugasundaram, "Hate Crimes, Explained," Southern Poverty Law Center, April 15, 2018.

50. "Bias Crime Offenders," *Responding to Hate Crimes: A Multidisciplinary Curriculum*, National Center for Hate Crime Prevention.

51. Scottie Andrew and Taylor Romine, "Teens Charged with Hate Crimes for Attacking a Woman on a Bus and Saying She Caused Coronavirus, NYPD Says," CNN, April 6, 2020.

52. "Hate Crime Probe Underway After Black Woman Says She Was Burned by Lighter Fluid and Flame Thrown by White Man," CBS News, June 26, 2020.

53. U.S. Department of Justice, "Hate Crimes Case Examples."

54. Sasha Ingber, "Neo-Nazi James Fields Gets 2nd Life Sentence for Charlottesville Attack," NPR, July 15, 2019.

55. Chris Woodyard, "Hate Group Count Hits 20-Year High Amid Rise in White Supremacy, Report Says," *USA Today*, February 20, 2019.

56. Patrick Healy and Michael Barbaro, "Donald Trump Calls for Barring Muslims from Entering U.S.," *New York Times*, December 7, 2015.

57. Brent Kendall, "Trump Says Judge's Mexican Heritage Presents 'Absolute Conflict,'" *Wall Street Journal*, June 3, 2016.

58. Sarah Wildman and Jen Kirby, "Trump Retweeted Anti-Muslim Propaganda Videos from a British Hate Group," Vox, November 30, 2017.

59. Bess Levin, "Trump Goes Full Anti-Semite in Room Full of Jewish People," *Vanity Fair*, December 9, 2019.

60. Julie Hirchfeld Davis, "Trump Mocks Warren as 'Pocahontas' at Navajo Veterans' Event," *New York Times*, November 27, 2017.

61. Barbara Sprunt, "The History Behind 'When the Looting Starts, the Shooting Starts,'" NPR, May 29, 2020.

62. Michael Edison Hayden, "Stephen Miller's Affinity for White Nationalism Revealed in Leaked Emails," Southern Poverty Law Center, November 12, 2019.

63. Andrew Kaczynski et al., "New HHS Spokesman Made Racist Comments About Chinese People in Now-Deleted Tweets," CNN, April 23, 2020.

64. Trip Gabriel et al., "Steve King Removed from Committee Assignments over White Supremacy Remark," *New York Times*, January 14, 2019.

65. Kyle Cheney, "Steve King Singles Out Somali Muslims over Pork," Politico, June 22, 2018.

66. Trip Gabriel, "Steve King, House Republican with a History of Racist Remarks, Loses Primary," *New York Times*, June 3, 2020.

67. Kristin Lam, "West Virginia Lawmaker Called to Resign After Comparing LGBTQ People to the Ku Klux Klan," *USA Today*, February 13, 2019.

68. Griffin Sims Edwards and Stephen Rushin, "The Effect of President Trump's Election on Hate Crimes," SSRN, January 14, 2018.

69. Ayal Feinberg et al., "Counties That Hosted a 2016 Trump Rally Saw a 226 Percent Increase in Hate Crimes," *Washington Post*, March 22, 2019.

70. Justin W. Patchin, "School Bullying Rates Increase by 35 Percent from 2016 to 2019," Cyberbullying Research Center, May 29, 2019.

71. Amelia Ferrell Knisely, "Racist Incidents Are Occurring in Williamson Schools. Is the District Doing Enough?" *The Tennessean*, March 8, 2019.

72. Marjorie Cortez, "Trump Presidency Worrisome to Immigrants, Refugees," *Deseret News*, November 9, 2016.

73. "After Election Day the Trump Effect: The Impact of the 2016 Presidential Election on Our Nation's Schools," Southern Poverty Law Center, 2016.

74. "Hate Speech on Twitter Predicts Frequency of Real-Life Hate Crimes," *New York University*, June 24, 2019.

75. Christina Capatides, "Bullies Attack Asian American Teen at School, Accusing Him of Having Coronavirus," CBS News, February 14, 2020.

76. CBS7, "FBI Calling Stabbing at Midland Sam's a Hate Crime," March 30, 2020.

77. Margolin, "FBI Warns of Potential Surge."

78. Chiu, "Trump Has No Qualms."

79. Seashia Vang, "Trump Adds to Asian-Americans' Fears," Human Rights Watch, April 1, 2020.

80. Alexia Fernández Campbell and Alex Ellerbeck, "Federal Agencies Are Doing Little About the Rise in Anti-Asian Hate," NBC News, April 16, 2020.

81. U.S. Department of Justice, "Hate Crime Laws," March 7, 2019.

82. United States Congress, House, United States Code Title 18, section 245, *Legal Information Institute*, Cornell University Law School.

83. Eliott C. McLaughlin, "There Are Two Names on the Federal Hate Crimes Law. One Is Matthew Shepard. The Other Is James Byrd Jr.," CNN, April 25, 2019.

84. U.S. Department of Justice, "Hate Crime Statistics 2010," November 2011.

85. U.S. Department of Justice, "Hate Crime Laws."

86. U.S. Department of Justice, "Criminal Interference with Fair Housing Rights," December 7, 2015.

87. "Damage to Religious Property," U.S. Department of Justice, August 6, 2015.

88. United States Congress, Code Title 18, section 245.

89. Shanmugasundaram, "Hate Crimes, Explained."

90. A.C. Thompson and Ken Schwencke, "More Than 100 Federal Agencies Fail to Report Hate Crimes to the FBI's National Database," ProPublica, June 22, 2017.

91. U.S. Department of Defense Office of Inspector General, "Evaluation of the Defense Criminal Investigative Organizations' Defense Incident-Based Reporting System Reporting and Reporting Accuracy," October 29, 2014.

92. Brennan Center for Justice, "State Hate Crimes Statutes."

93. Shanmugasundaram, "Hate Crimes, Explained."

94. Ken Schwencke, "Why America Fails at Gathering Hate Crime Statistics," ProPublica, December 4, 2017.

95. U.S. Department of Justice, "Laws and Policies."

96. Anti-Defamation League, "ADL Hate Crime Map."

Part V: Privacy

15. Privacy, Personal Data, and Surveillance
Research and drafting contributed by Toby Voght.

1. Allyson Chiu, "She Installed a Ring Camera in Her Children's Room for 'Peace of Mind.' A Hacker Accessed It and Harassed Her 8-Year-Old Daughter," *Washington Post*, December 12, 2019.

2. Rachel DeSantis, "Families Are Suing Ring over Hacked Home Security Cameras: 'It Was from a Horror Film,'" Yahoo, January 31, 2020.

3. Chiu, "She Installed a Ring Camera."

4. Brooke Auxier, "How Americans See Digital Privacy Issues amid the COVID-19 Outbreak," Pew Research Center, May 4, 2020.

5. Brooke Auxier et al., "Americans and Privacy: Concerned, Confused and Feeling Lack of Control over Their Personal Information," Pew Research Center, November 15, 2019.

6. Sam Sabin, "Most Voters Say Congress Should Make Privacy Legislation a Priority Next Year," Morning Consult, December 18, 2019.

7. Federal Trade Commission, "Fiscal Year 2021 Congressional Budget Justification," February 10, 2020.

8. Noordyke, "U.S. State Comprehensive Privacy Law Comparison," International Association of Privacy Professionals, July 6, 2020.

9. As of May 17, 2021, the values of these companies are: Apple $2.1 trillion, Microsoft $1.8 trillion, Alphabet $1.5 trillion, Amazon $1.6 trillion, and Facebook $0.9 trillion.

10. Edison Research, "The Infinite Dial 2019," March 6, 2019.

11. Statcounter, "Search Engine Market Share Worldwide, Dec 2019–Dec 2020."

12. Quoted from the comments section of Chiu, "She Installed a Ring Camera."

13. U.S. President, Executive Order, "Enhancing Public Safety in the Interior of the United States," January 25, 2017, *Federal Register* 82, no. 8799.

14. Office of Victim Services and Justice Grants, "Private Security Camera Rebate Program FAQs."

15. Today, "New Technology Allows Retailers to Track Customers' Every Move," February 21, 2020.

16. The categories are direct marketing, online marketing, marketing analytics, identity verification, fraud detection, and people searching. Federal Trade Commission, "Data Brokers: A Call for Transparency and Accountability," May 2014.

17. Mary Madden and Lee Rainie, "Americans' Views About Data Collection and Security," Pew Research Center, May 20, 2015.

18. National Information Standards Organization Press, "NISO Offers Public Free Primer on Metadata," 2004.

19. Zach Whittaker, "Despite Promises to Stop, U.S. Cell Carriers Are Still Selling Your Real-Time Phone Location Data," *TechCrunch*, January 9, 2019.

20. Stuart A. Thompson and Charlie Warzel, "Twelve Million Phones, One Dataset, Zero Privacy," *New York Times*, December 19, 2019.

21. Karl Bode, "In Letters to Senate, Wireless Carriers Downplay Their Latest Location Data Scandal," Vice, April 18, 2019.

22. Jan Wolfe, "Roomba Vacuum Maker iRobot Betting Big on the 'Smart' Home," Reuters, July 24, 2017; Melissa Wen, "iRobot Shares Surge on Strong Sales of Roomba Vacuum Cleaners," Reuters, July 26, 2017.

23. David Segal, "Mugged by a Mug Shot Online," *New York Times*, October 5, 2013.

24. Florida Arrests, "Most Recent Florida Bookings."

25. Segal, "Mugged by a Mug Shot Online."

26. Lulu Garcia-Navarro, "Some Newsrooms Are Rethinking Their Approach to Publishing Mugshots," *Weekend Edition Sunday* on NPR, February 16, 2020.

27. V.S.A. § 2446, Vermont State Legislature.

28. Federal Trade Commission, "Data Brokers."

29. National Network to End Domestic Violence, "Tech Abuse: Information from the Field," September 14, 2018.

30. National Network to End Domestic Violence, "A Glimpse from the Field: How Abusers Are Misusing Technology," February 17, 2015.

31. Risk Based Security, "Data Breach Quick View Report: 2020 Year End Report," January 2021.

32. Verizon, "2020 Data Breach Investigations Report," 2020.

33. Maggie Astor, "Someone Made a Fake Equifax Site. Then Equifax Linked to It," *New York Times*, September 20, 2017.

34. Government Accountability Office, "Actions Taken by Equifax and Federal Agencies in Response to the 2017 Breach," August 30, 2018.

35. Glenn Fleishman, "Equifax Data Breach, One Year Later: Obvious Errors and No Real Changes, New Report Says," *Fortune*, September 7, 2018.

36. Jen Wieczner, "Equifax CEO Richard Smith Who Oversaw Breach to Collect $90 Million," *Fortune*, September 26, 2017.

37. Josephine Wolff, *You'll See This Message When It Is Too Late: The Legal and Economic Aftermath of Cybersecurity Breaches* (Cambridge, MA: MIT Press, 2018).

38. United States Congress, Senate, The Cybersecurity Information Sharing Act of 2015, Congress, 114th Congress, 1st Sess., Senate Resolution 754, passed October 27, 2015.

39. Cybersecurity Information Sharing Act, section 106.

40. Shoshana Zuboff, *The Age of Surveillance Capitalism* (New York: PublicAffairs, 2019).

41. Gene Park, "Facebook, Google 'Profit from Doing Customers Harm,' Says Epic Games CEO Tim Sweeney," *Washington Post*, February 12, 2020.

42. Amnesty International, "Surveillance Giants: How the Business Model of Google and Facebook Threatens Human Rights," November 21, 2019.

43. Visa projects revenue of $3.5 billion from such sales, which represents 14 percent of their total revenue in that period. "Visa Sees Data Sales Driving $3.5 Billion in Consulting Revenue," *Bloomberg News*, February 11, 2020.

44. Zuboff, *Surveillance Capitalism*.

45. United States Code, 5 USC §552a—Records Maintained on Individuals, *Legal Information Institute*, Cornell Law School.

46. Zuboff, *Surveillance Capitalism*, 113–114.

47. U.S. Privacy and Civil Liberties Oversight Board, *"About."*

48. Wayne R. LaFave, *Search & Seizure: A Treatise on the Fourth Amendment*, 2nd ed. (Eagan, MN: West Publishing Company, 1987).

49. This physical standard was recently upheld by the *United States v. Jones* decision, which eliminated evidence collected by placing a physical GPS tracker on a suspect's car. Jason Medinger, "Post-*Jones*: How District Courts Are Answering the Myriad Questions Raised by the Supreme Court's Decision in *United States v. Jones*," *University of Baltimore Law Review* 42, no. 3, 2013; the "reasonable expectation of privacy" legal standard is credited to U.S. Supreme Court Justice John Marshall Harlan in his concurring opinion.

50. Smith v. Maryland, 1979.

51. Jeremy Derman, "Constitutional Law—Maryland District Court Finds Government's Acquisition of Historical Cell Site Data Immune from Fourth Amendment—*United States v. Graham*," *Suffolk University Law Review* 46, no. 1 (2013).

52. *"United States v. Graham*: Fourth Circuit Holds That Government Acquisition of Historical Cell-Site Location Information Is Not a Search," *Harvard Law Review* 130, no. 4 (February 2017), https://harvardlawreview.org/2017/02/united-states-v-graham.

53. Mark Williams Pontin, "The Total Information Awareness Project Lives On," *MIT Technology Review*, April 26, 2006.

54. Andy Greenberg, "How a 'Deviant' Philosopher Built Palantir, a CIA-Funded Data-Mining Juggernaut," *Forbes*, August 14, 2013.

55. Electronic Frontier Foundation, "Surveillance Tech in San Diego County, California"; U.S. Department of Homeland Security, "Fusion Centers," September 19, 2019.

56. Caroline Haskins, "Revealed: This Is Palantir's Top Secret User Manual for Cops," Vice, July 12, 2019; Palantir, "Law Enforcement."

57. Dave Collins, "Should Police Use Computers to Predict Crimes and Criminals?" Associated Press, July 5, 2018.

58. Only the state of Arizona has affirmatively denied the use of facial recognition in its law enforcement departments, after ending the practice in 2013.

59. McKenzie Funk, "How ICE Picks Its Targets in the Surveillance Age," *New York Times*, October 2, 2019.

60. Drew Harwell and Nick Miroff, "ICE Just Abandoned Its Dream of 'Extreme Vetting' Software That Could Predict Whether a Foreign Visitor Would Become a Terrorist," *Washington Post*, May 17, 2018.

61. Electronic Frontier Foundation, "NSA Spying."

62. Julia Angwin et al., "Machine Bias," ProPublica, May 23, 2016.

63. "Washington Post–University of Maryland National Poll, April 21–26, 2020," *Washington Post*, May 21, 2020.

64. Margaret Talev, "Axios-Ipsos Coronavirus Index Week 9: Americans Hate Contact Tracing," Axios, May 12, 2020.

65. Mia Sato, "Contact Tracing Apps Now Cover Nearly Half of America. It's Not Too Late to Use One," *MIT Technology Review*, December 14, 2020.

66. Alejandro de la Garza, "Contact Tracing Apps Were Big Tech's Best Idea for Fighting COVID-19. Why Haven't They Helped?" *Time*, November 10, 2020.

67. Geoffrey A. Fowler, "One of the First Contact-Tracing Apps Violates Its Own Privacy Policy," *Washington Post*, May 21, 2020.

68. Amos Toh and Deborah Brown, "How Digital Contact Tracing for COVID-19 Could Worsen Inequality," Human Rights Watch, June 4, 2020.

69. Ramesh Raskar et al., "Apps Gone Rogue: Maintaining Personal Privacy in an Epidemic," arXiv, Cornell University, March 19, 2020; Editorial Board, "Show Evidence That Apps for COVID-19 Contact-Tracing Are Secure and Effective," *Nature*, April 29, 2020.

70. Sarah Hodges, "Examining the Gramm-Leach-Bliley Act's Opt-Out Method for Protecting Consumer Data Privacy Rights on the Internet," *Information & Communications Technology Law* 22, no. 1 (2013).

71. Odia Kagan, "CCPA Amendment Adds Data Broker Registration," Fox Rothschild, September 18, 2019.

72. Vermont Office of the Attorney General, "Guidance on Vermont's Act 171 of 2018: Data Broker Regulation," December 11, 2018.

73. Rob Copeland and Sarah E. Needleman, "Google's 'Project Nightingale' Triggers Federal Inquiry," *Wall Street Journal*, November 12, 2019.

74. "Non-traditional credit" is a wide-ranging term that can involve all sorts of personal data. Some examples are rent payment history, child support/alimony payments, utilities, and tuition. Amy Dobson, "Non-Traditional Credit Options for Mortgage Applicants," *Forbes*, September 14, 2018.

75. Experian, "State of Alternative Credit Data," May 2019.

76. The privacy policy must identify the categories of personally identifiable information the operator collects; identify the categories of third parties with whom the operator may share such personally identifiable information; describe the information review and change request process—if such a process exists, disclose whether third parties may collect consumer data directly from the website; disclose the response to "do-not-track" signals; describe the process of notification of change; and identify the effective date of the privacy policy.

77. Alecia M. McDonald and Lorrie Faith Cranor, "The Cost of Reading Privacy Policies," *I/S: A Journal of Law and Policy for the Information Society*, 2009.

78. The two large sections are "Things you create or provide to [Google]" and "Information [Google] collects as you use [Google's] services." These would fall into discrete and behavioral data categorizations. The subsections of information collected by Google are "Your apps, browsers and devices," "Your activity," and "Your location information." "We want you to understand the types of information we collect as you use our services"; Google, "Privacy & Terms."

79. Google, "How Our Business Works," https://about.google/intl/ALL_us/how-our-business-works.

80. Bennett Cypher, "Google Says It Doesn't 'Sell' Your Data. Here's How the Company Shares, Monetizes, and Exploits It," Electronic Frontier Foundation, March 19, 2020.

81. Brooke Auxier et al., "Americans and Privacy."

82. Janna Anderson and Lee Rainie, "Many Tech Experts Say Digital Disruption Will Hurt Democracy," Pew Research Center, February 21, 2020.

83. Madden and Rainie, "Americans' Views."

84. Zuboff, *Surveillance Capitalism*, 61.

85. Tyler Gray, "FDA to 23andMe Founder Anne Wojcicki: Stop Marketing $99 DNA Test or Face Penalties," *Fast Company*, November 25, 2013.

86. Ashley May, "Took an Ancestry DNA Test? You Might Be a 'Genetic Informant' Unleashing Secrets About Your Relatives," *USA Today*, April 27, 2018.

87. Elizabeth Murphy, "Inside 23andMe Founder Anne Wojcicki's $99 DNA Revolution," *Fast Company*, October 14, 2013.

88. Zuboff, *Surveillance Capitalism*, 54.

89. Hodges, "Examining the Gramm-Leach-Bliley Act's Opt-Out Method."

90. Zuboff, *Surveillance Capitalism*, 235–236.

91. Information Commissioner's Office, "Principle (c): Data Minimisation."

92. Federal Trade Commission, "Fiscal Year 2019 Congressional Budget Justification," February 12, 2018.

93. Lesley Fair, "FTC's $5 Billion Facebook Settlement: Record-Breaking and History-Making," Federal Trade Commission, July 24, 2019.

94. "Feds Hit Facebook with $5B Fine—Largest Ever on Tech Company," WRAL Tech Wire, July 24, 2019.

95. Kara Swisher, "The Immunity of the Tech Giants," *New York Times*, May 1, 2020.

96. IT Governance, "GDPR Penalties."

97. Alix Pressley, "€272.5 Million in Fines Imposed by European Regulators Under GDPR," *Intelligent CIO*, January 19, 2021.

98. Mathew J. Schwartz, "Privacy Fine: Total GDPR Sanctions Reach $331 Million," BankInfo Security, January 19, 2021.

99. Privacy Shield Framework, "Privacy Shield Program Overview."

100. "EU-U.S. Privacy Shield for Data Struck Down by Court," BBC, July 16, 2020.

Toward Equal Liberty

1. "Americans' Attitudes Toward Civil Rights, Voting, Role of Government Find More Common Ground Since Pandemic," National Opinion Research Center at the University of Chicago and Carr Center for Human Rights Policy at the Harvard Kennedy School, July 20, 2021, https://carrcenter.hks.harvard.edu/reimagining-rights-responsibilities-2021-poll.

2. "National Research Finds Bipartisan Support for Expansive View of Rights," National Opinion Research Center at the University of Chicago and Carr Center for Human Rights Policy at the Harvard Kennedy School, September 15, 2020, https://carrcenter.hks.harvard.edu/reimagining-rights-responsibilities-united-states.

3. Roper Center, "Public Opinion on the Voting Rights Act," https://ropercenter.cornell.edu/blog/public-opinion-voting-rights-act

4. John Lewis, *Across That Bridge: Vision for a Change and the Future of America* (New York: Hachette Books, 2017).

INDEX

ABOUT THE AUTHORS

John Shattuck is a senior fellow at the Carr Center for Human Rights Policy at Harvard University and Professor of Practice at the Fletcher School at Tufts University. He is a former U.S. Assistant Secretary of State for Democracy, Human Rights, and Labor; former Washington director of the American Civil Liberties Union; and the author of *Freedom on Fire: Human Rights Wars and America's Response.*

Sushma Raman is the executive director of the Carr Center for Human Rights Policy at Harvard University and former program officer for the Ford Foundation and Open Society Foundation. She is the co-author (with Bill Schulz) of *The Coming Good Society: Why New Realities Demand New Rights.*

Mathias Risse is Berthold Beitz Professor in Human Rights, Global Affairs, and Philosophy and the director of the Carr Center for Human Rights Policy at Harvard University.

Date Due
